W9-CKB-092

Frommer's®
Boston

My Boston
by Marie Morris

SO YOU'RE THINKING OF VISITING BOSTON. GOOD THINKING.
You could hardly have picked a better time. The highway project that plagued downtown for the better part of the past decade (the world-famous "Big Dig") is substantially complete. Boston Harbor is cleaner than it's been in at least a generation. And even if the Red Sox haven't repeated as World Series champs by the time you read this, the 2004 title left an awful lot of people in an awfully good mood.

Some Boston destinations are so beautiful that I just have to point them out. Others are so interesting, mostly because of their historical associations, that I want you to know a little something about them. My favorites are both. They range from a family of adorable waterfowl to a legendary patriot whose first name is not "Listen, my children, and you shall hear."

I'm not a Boston native—I live here because I love it. Even after 2-plus decades, I still feel a little thrill when I see a lovely Colonial building silhouetted against a modern office tower, an ancient cobblestone street dusted with colorful autumn leaves, or a flock of sailboats dancing across the harbor and the river. In the pages that follow, I'll try to show you why.

© Rick Friedman/Corbis

"Finally!!!" said the Boston Globe. "Amen," said the Boston Herald. As every sports fan knows, the Red Sox won the World Series in 2004 for the first time in 86 years. Visiting **FENWAY PARK (left)** for the first time was already an unforgettable experience. Now—with the team and its legions of fans basking in the glow of the long-awaited title—is a great time to go.

If **BEACON HILL (above)** didn't exist, someone—probably a postcard photographer—would have to invent it. Narrow cobblestone streets, elegant Federal-style architecture, and flowering window boxes make "the Hill" the iconic Boston neighborhood. It's one of my favorite places to go walking. Just don't tackle the uneven streets in good shoes (you only make that mistake once).

Snow begins to fly, and a hush falls over the city. Step away from traffic—into a building courtyard, a college quad, or a park—and the calm is almost magical. The prettiest park in town, the **PUBLIC GARDEN (above)**, looks even better under a fresh coating of white flakes. Enjoy it while you can. Before long, the scratchy hum of snowplows will fill the air, and the spell will be broken.

The cutest thing in Boston—even cuter than all those buff college students—is **MAKE WAY FOR DUCKLINGS (right)**. The Mallard family from Robert McCloskey's beloved children's book waddles eternally across the Public Garden, heading toward the lagoon. I don't know how they'll ever get there with all those little kids climbing on them.

COPLEY SQUARE (below) is the architectural equivalent of a movie with an all-star cast—you hardly know where to look first. I like to start with Trinity Church, executed in Richardsonian Romanesque style (named for the architect, the legendary H. H. Richardson). Its blue-mirrored backdrop is I. M. Pei's distinctive John Hancock Tower.

Say hello to **PAUL REVERE (left)**, 18th-century mensch. That's the Old North Church over his shoulder. As a kid, he helped ring the church bells; as an adult, he got an important message ("one if by land, two if by sea") through lanterns in the steeple. His nearby house, where the "midnight ride" started, is one of my favorite Boston attractions: It helps visitors get to know a historic figure as a real person.

BOSTON HARBOR (above) is a perfect destination on sultry, sticky summer days when you can't remember what was so bad about winter. (Oh, right—subzero temperatures, howling winds, and waist-high snowdrifts.) The waterfront abounds with places to catch a breeze, take a break, and recharge. My favorite retreat is at the end of Long Wharf, not far from the New England Aquarium.

I've been to the **JOHN F. KENNEDY LIBRARY AND MUSEUM (left)** more times than I can count, but I always jump at the chance to accompany out-of-towners. You might think it appeals most to people who remember Camelot (which I don't), but visitors of all ages find it fascinating. The museum, in a gorgeous building designed by I. M. Pei, regularly schedules special exhibitions to complement the permanent collection.

THE MCKIM BUILDING OF THE BOSTON PUBLIC LIBRARY (below) is a showpiece of 19th-century art. The magnificent murals, sculptures, and architecture make it a fascinating place to explore, on your own or on a free guided tour. The perfect complement to this building is Trinity Church, which stands across Copley Square in all its polychrome (art lingo for "multicolored") glory.

The delightfully eccentric **ISABELLA STEWART GARDNER MUSEUM (above)** centers on a soaring courtyard filled with sculpture and changing displays of flowers and greenery. Horticulture is such an important element that the museum has its own greenhouses and even a "curator of landscape." If you harbor even a passing fondness for art or gardening, it's a wonderful refuge.

THE MINUTEMAN STATUE (right) in Concord unites two of New England's big names: sculptor Daniel Chester French and philosopher-poet Ralph Waldo Emerson. (When did people with three names stop being celebrated artists and start being assassins and serial killers?) The musket-wielding revolutionary hasn't forgotten that he's a farmer: His other hand grips a plow. The inscription on the pedestal recalls the events of April 19, 1775, in a verse that includes the lines, "Here once the embattled farmers stood / And fired the shot heard round the world."

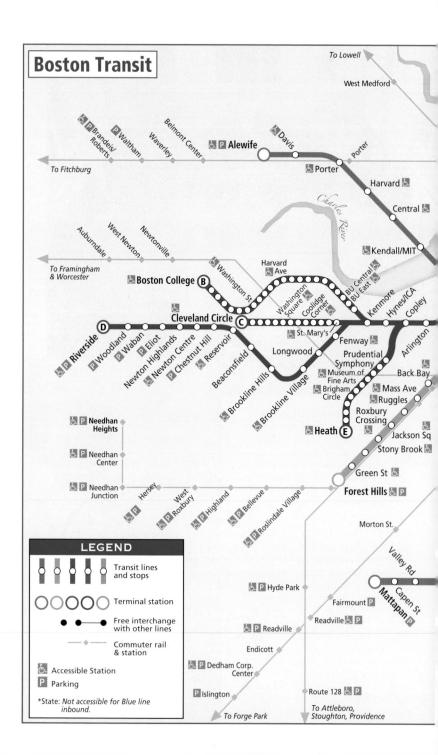

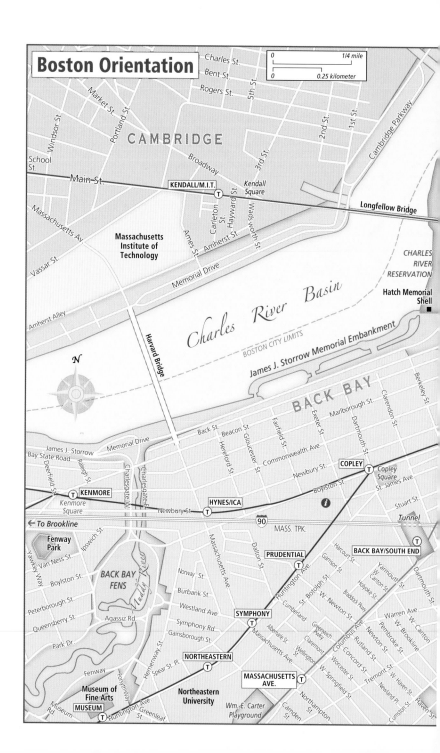

Boston Orientation

Charles St.
Bent St.
Rogers St.

0   1/4 mile
0   0.25 kilometer

Market St.
Portland St.
Windsor St.
5th St.
2nd St.
1st St.
Cambridge Parkway

CAMBRIDGE

Broadway
3rd St.

School
St.

Main St.

KENDALL/M.I.T. Ⓣ

Kendall
Square

Longfellow Bridge

Massachusetts Av.

Carleton St.
Hayward St.
Wadsworth St.

CHARLES
RIVER
RESERVATION

Massachusetts
Institute of
Technology

Ames St.
Amherst St.

Hatch Memorial
Shell ■

Vassar St.

Memorial Drive

Amherst Alley

Charles River Basin

BOSTON CITY LIMITS

James J. Storrow Memorial Embankment

N

Harvard Bridge

BACK BAY

Marlborough St.
Clarendon St.
Berkeley St.

Memorial Drive

Back St.
Beacon St.
Hereford St.
Gloucester St.
Fairfield St.
Exeter St.
Dartmouth St.

Commonwealth Ave.

James J. Storrow
Bay State Road

Raleigh St.
Deerfield St.

Charlesgate W.
Charlesgate E.

Newbury St.

COPLEY Ⓣ Copley
Square
St. James Ave.

Ⓣ KENMORE

Kenmore
Square

HYNES/ICA Ⓣ

Boylston St.

ⓘ

Stuart St.

← To Brookline

Newbury St. Ⓣ

90

MASS. TPK.

Tunnel

Fenway
Park

Ipswich St.

PRUDENTIAL Ⓣ

Harcourt St.
Garrison St.

BACK BAY/SOUTH END Ⓣ

Yawkey Way
Van Ness St.
Boylston St.

Dalton St.

Huntington Ave.
St. Botolph St.
W. Newton St.
Braddock Pky.

Yarmouth St.
Canton St.
Holyoke St.
Dartmouth St.

BACK BAY
FENS

Norway St.

Peterborough St.

Burbank St.

Warren Ave. W. Canton
Pembroke St.
W. Brookline

Queensberry St.

Westland Ave.

SYMPHONY Ⓣ

Greenwich
Pky.

Agassiz Rd.

Symphony Rd.
Gainsborough St.

Albemarle St.
Claremont
Wellington

Columbus Ave.
Rutland St.
Concord St.
W. Springfield St.
Tremont St.
W. Haven St.
Newland Pl.

Park Dr.

Muddy River

Massachusetts Ave.

Cumberland

Peterborough St.

Fenway

Hemenway St.
Spear St. Pl.

NORTHEASTERN Ⓣ

MASSACHUSETTS
AVE. Ⓣ

Northampton St.
Camden St.

Cunston St.
Haven St.

Museum of
Fine Arts

MUSEUM Ⓣ

Museum
Rd.

Huntington Ave.
Greenleaf
St.

Forsyth Way

Northeastern
University

Wm. E. Carter
Playground

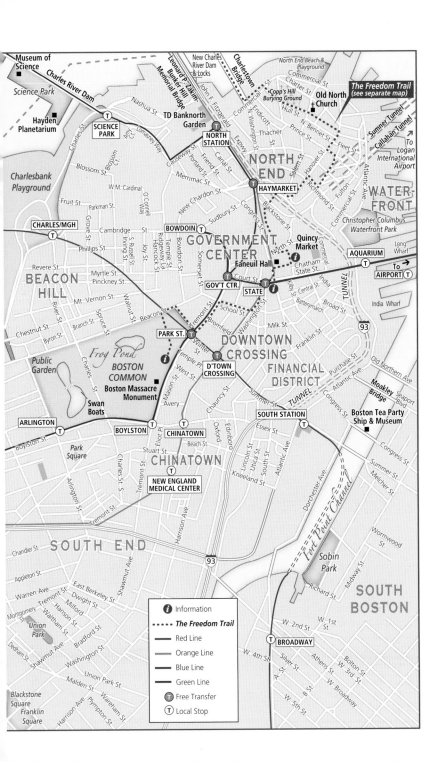

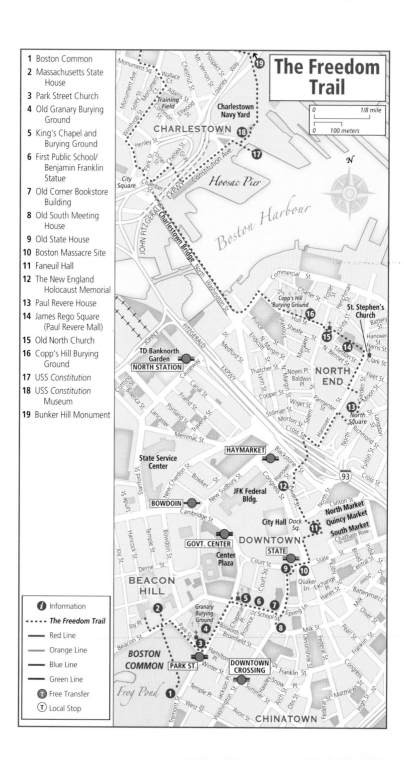

The Freedom Trail

1 Boston Common
2 Massachusetts State House
3 Park Street Church
4 Old Granary Burying Ground
5 King's Chapel and Burying Ground
6 First Public School/ Benjamin Franklin Statue
7 Old Corner Bookstore Building
8 Old South Meeting House
9 Old State House
10 Boston Massacre Site
11 Faneuil Hall
12 The New England Holocaust Memorial
13 Paul Revere House
14 James Rego Square (Paul Revere Mall)
15 Old North Church
16 Copp's Hill Burying Ground
17 USS *Constitution*
18 USS *Constitution* Museum
19 Bunker Hill Monument

0 ——————— 1/8 mile
0 ——————— 100 meters

i Information
••••• The Freedom Trail
—— Red Line
—— Orange Line
—— Blue Line
—— Green Line
Ⓣ Free Transfer
Ⓣ Local Stop

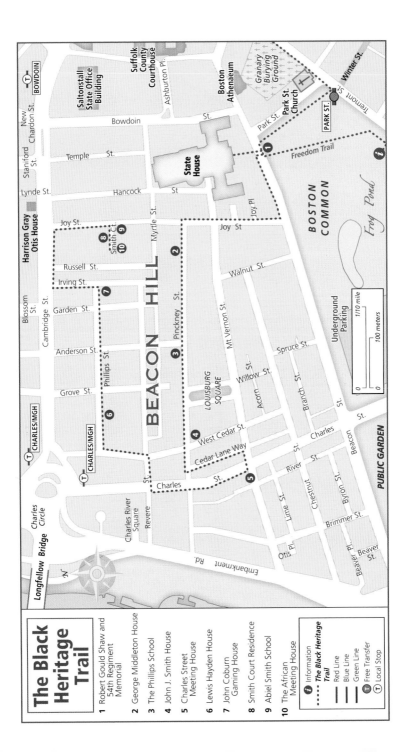

The Black Heritage Trail

1 Robert Gould Shaw and 54th Regiment Memorial
2 George Middleton House
3 The Phillips School
4 John J. Smith House
5 Charles Street Meeting House
6 Lewis Hayden House
7 John Coburn Gaming House
8 Smith Court Residence
9 Abiel Smith School
10 The African Meeting House

i Information
···· The Black Heritage Trail
Red Line
Blue Line
Green Line
Free Transfer
Ⓣ Local Stop

Saltonstall State Office Building

Suffolk County Courthouse

Boston Athenaeum

Granary Burying Ground

Ⓣ BOWDOIN

New Chardon St.

Bowdoin St.

Temple St.

Hancock St

Lynde St.

Staniford St.

Harrison Gray Otis House

State House

Joy Pl

Joy St.

Myrtle St.

Smith Ct.

Russell St.

Irving St.

Garden St.

Anderson St.

Grove St.

Blossom St.

Cambridge St.

Phillips St.

BEACON HILL

Pinckney St.

Walnut St.

Mt Vernon St.

LOUISBURG SQUARE

Willow St.

Acorn St.

Spruce St.

Branch St.

West Cedar St.

Cedar Lane Way

Charles St.

Revere St.

Charles River Square

Charles Circle

Ⓣ CHARLES/MGH

Ⓣ CHARLES/MGH

Longfellow Bridge

Embankment Rd.

Otis Pl.

Lime St.

Chestnut St.

Brimmer St.

River St.

Byron St.

Beaver Pl.

Beaver St.

Beacon St.

Charles St.

PUBLIC GARDEN

BOSTON COMMON

Frog Pond

Underground Parking

Freedom Trail

Park St. Church

PARK ST.

Winter St.

Tremont St.

Park St.

Ashburton Pl.

St.

100 meters
1/10 mile

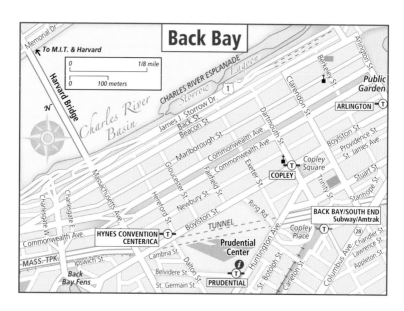

Back Bay

To M.I.T. & Harvard

Memorial Dr.

CHARLES RIVER ESPLANADE

Harvard Bridge

Lagoon

Charles River Basin

Storrow

CHARLES RIVER ESPLANADE

Storrow Dr.

James J. Storrow Dr.

Back St.

Beacon St.

Marlborough St.

Commonwealth Ave.

Commonwealth Ave.

Public Garden

Berkeley St.

Clarendon St.

Dartmouth St.

Exeter St.

ARLINGTON

COPLEY

Copley Square

Boylston St.

Providence St.

St. James Ave.

Stuart St.

Trinity St.

Stanhope St.

Massachusetts Ave.

Gloucester St.

Hereford St.

Fairfield St.

Newbury St.

Boylston St.

Ring Rd

BACK BAY/SOUTH END
Subway/Amtrak

Charlesgate W.

Charlesgate E.

Commonwealth Ave.

Ipswich St.

MASS.-TPK.

Cambria St.

TUNNEL

HYNES CONVENTION
CENTER/ICA

Prudential
Center

Copley
Place

Huntington Ave.

Columbus Ave.

Chandler St.

Lawrence St.

Appleton St.

28

Back
Bay Fens

Belvidere St.

Dalton St.

St. Germain St.

PRUDENTIAL

St. Botolph St.

Carleton St.

0   1/8 mile

0   100 meters

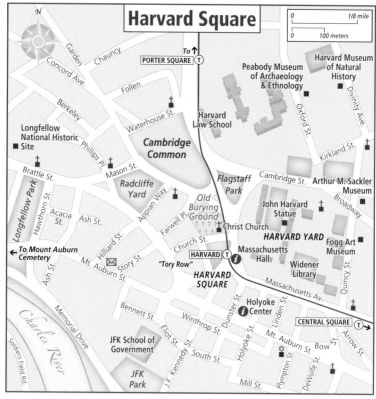

Harvard Square

N

Garden

Concord Ave.

Chauncy

To
PORTER SQUARE

Follen

Berkeley

Waterhouse St.

Harvard
Law School

Peabody Museum
of Archaeology
& Ethnology

Harvard Museum
of Natural
History

Oxford St.

Divinity Ave.

Longfellow
National Historic
Site

Phillips Pl.

Mason St.

Cambridge
Common

Kirkland St.

Brattle St.

Longfellow Park

Hawthorn St.

Acacia
St.

Ash St.

Radcliffe
Yard

Appian Way

Flagstaff
Park

Cambridge St.

Arthur M. Sackler
Museum

Broadway

John Harvard
Statue

To Mount Auburn
Cemetery

Ash St.

Hilliard St.

Story St.

Mt. Auburn St.

Farwell Pl.

Old
Burying
Ground

Church St.

Christ Church

HARVARD

"Tory Row"

HARVARD
SQUARE

Massachusetts
Hall

HARVARD YARD

Fogg Art
Museum

Widener
Library

Quincy St.

Massachusetts Ave.

Charles River

Memorial Drive

Soldiers Field Rd.

Bennett St.

Eliot St.

Winthrop St.

J.F. Kennedy St.

South St.

Dunster St.

Holyoke St.

Holyoke
Center

Linden St.

Mt. Auburn St.

Plympton St.

Bow St.

CENTRAL SQUARE

Arrow St.

DeWolfe St.

JFK School of
Government

JFK
Park

Mill St.

0   1/8 mile

0   100 meters

Frommer's®

Boston

2006

by Marie Morris

WILEY

Wiley Publishing, Inc.

About the Author

Marie Morris grew up in New York and graduated from Harvard, where she studied history. She has worked for *02138* magazine, the *Boston Herald*, *Boston* magazine, and the *New York Times*. She's the author of *Boston For Dummies* and *Frommer's Irreverent Guide to Boston*, and she covers Boston for *Frommer's New England*. She lives in Boston, not far from Paul Revere.

Published by:

Wiley Publishing, Inc.

111 River St.
Hoboken, NJ 07030-5774

ISBN-13: 978-0-7645-8890-7
ISBN-10: 0-7645-8890-7

Editor: Cate Latting
Production Editor: Melissa S. Bennett
Cartographer: Nick Trotter
Photo Editor: Richard Fox
Production by Wiley Indianapolis Composition Services

Front cover photo: Men's Crew Team at Head of the Charles Regatta
Back cover photo: Beacon Hill, Acorn Street, brick houses

For information on our other products and services or to obtain technical support, please contact our Customer Care Department within the U.S. at 800/762-2974, outside the U.S. at 317/572-3993 or fax 317/572-4002.

Wiley also publishes its books in a variety of electronic formats. Some content that appears in print may not be available in electronic formats.

Manufactured in the United States of America

5   4   3   2   1

Contents

List of Maps

Acknowledgments

Infinite thanks to Kelly Regan and Cate Latting for their encouragement and incredible patience. Tremendous gratitude to my curious and hungry research assistants, Kristin Goss, Betsy Bates, Sue Costello, Michael Dobler and Andrea Rasmussen, David Wallace and Lauren Goldberg, Bom Kim, and Dan Loss. And special thanks to my favorite readers, Emily Morris and Connor Morris.

—Marie Morris

An Invitation to the Reader

In researching this book, we discovered many wonderful places—hotels, restaurants, shops, and more. We're sure you'll find others. Please tell us about them, so we can share the information with your fellow travelers in upcoming editions. If you were disappointed with a recommendation, we'd love to know that, too. Please write to:

Frommer's Boston 2006
Wiley Publishing, Inc. • 111 River St. • Hoboken, NJ 07030-5774

An Additional Note

Please be advised that travel information is subject to change at any time—and this is especially true of prices. We therefore suggest that you write or call ahead for confirmation when making your travel plans. The authors, editors, and publisher cannot be held responsible for the experiences of readers while traveling. Your safety is important to us, however, so we encourage you to stay alert and be aware of your surroundings. Keep a close eye on cameras, purses, and wallets, all favorite targets of thieves and pickpockets.

Other Great Guides for Your Trip:

Boston For Dummies
Frommer's New England
Frommer's Cape Cod, Nantucket & Martha's Vineyard
Frommer's Portable Boston
Frommer's Best-Loved Driving Tours: New England
Frommer's Irreverent Guide to Boston
Frommer's Unofficial Guide to Campgrounds in the Northeast

Frommer's Star Ratings, Icons & Abbreviations

Every hotel, restaurant, and attraction listing in this guide has been ranked for quality, value, service, amenities, and special features using a **star-rating system.** In country, state, and regional guides, we also rate towns and regions to help you narrow down your choices and budget your time accordingly. Hotels and restaurants are rated on a scale of zero (recommended) to three stars (exceptional). Attractions, shopping, nightlife, towns, and regions are rated according to the following scale: zero stars (recommended), one star (highly recommended), two stars (very highly recommended), and three stars (must-see).

In addition to the star-rating system, we also use **seven feature icons** that point you to the great deals, in-the-know advice, and unique experiences that separate travelers from tourists. Throughout the book, look for:

Finds	Special finds—those places only insiders know about
Fun Fact	Fun facts—details that make travelers more informed and their trips more fun
Kids	Best bets for kids and advice for the whole family
Moments	Special moments—those experiences that memories are made of
Overrated	Places or experiences not worth your time or money
Tips	Insider tips—great ways to save time and money
Value	Great values—where to get the best deals

The following **abbreviations** are used for credit cards:

AE	American Express	DISC	Discover	V	Visa
DC	Diners Club	MC	MasterCard		

Frommers.com

Now that you have the guidebook to a great trip, visit our website at **www.frommers.com** for travel information on more than 3,000 destinations. With features updated regularly, we give you instant access to the most current trip-planning information available. At Frommers.com, you'll also find the best prices on airfares, accommodations, and car rentals—and you can even book travel online through our travel booking partners. At Frommers.com, you'll also find the following:

- Online updates to our most popular guidebooks
- Vacation sweepstakes and contest giveaways
- Newsletter highlighting the hottest travel trends
- Online travel message boards with featured travel discussions

What's New in Boston

Boston looks great. It has a new landmark bridge that's part of a new highway system, a sparkling-clean harbor, and a constantly evolving street pattern that shows off random sections of downtown—whether you want to see them or not. Visitors in 2006 will see the results of the massive construction job known as the **Big Dig,** which replaced the elevated highway through downtown with a tunnel. The $14.6 billion project technically wrapped up in 2005 after more than a decade and a half of widespread disruption. The parks, surface roads, and buildings that will take the place of the expressway will be in the works when you visit.

Although it's no longer new *or* news, the Boston Red Sox's 2004 **World Series** title remains one of the best conversational icebreakers ever. The team and its fans had gone 86 roller-coaster years between championships, and the celebration that ensued is still raging. Whether it concerns noisy neighbors or a visit to a relative's grave to leave a World Series banner (this actually happened—a lot), just about everyone has a story. Throw in the New England Patriots' three **Super Bowl** victories in 4 years (2002, 2004, and 2005), and the city's practically a freestanding sports bar.

The sports and entertainment arena near North Station, long known as the FleetCenter, got a new name in 2005: The **TD Banknorth Garden.** You can see it on TV during the NCAA women's basketball **Final Four** in April 2006.

Here's a look at some other developments.

GETTING TO KNOW BOSTON The MBTA (✆ **617/222-3200;** www.mbta. com) will begin phasing out the use of tokens in 2005 and 2006. The new **CharlieTicket** (paper) and **CharlieCard** (plastic) will be optional on buses and aboveground trolley routes, mandatory on the subway. The transition will proceed one line at a time; check at the station entrance to see which method of payment applies.

Also new is a bus line that links South Station and the South Boston waterfront, with plans to extend the route to Logan Airport. **Silver Line** "rapid transit service" (fancy talk for an electric bus route) also connects Downtown Crossing to the South End and Roxbury.

The popular **Night Owl** bus service, which operated into the wee hours on Friday and Saturday evenings, fell victim to budget considerations in 2005. Don't forget plenty of cab fare for your evening excursion. See chapter 5 for more information.

ACCOMMODATIONS A whopping 14 of Boston's 61 hotels have opened since 2002, with another half-dozen under construction. The latest addition is the **Bulfinch Hotel,** 107 Merrimac St. (✆ **800/4-CHOICE**), near North Station. A dramatic renovation of a century-old former warehouse, it's an ingeniously designed property near North Station.

What's really new is the nonstop upgrading of existing hotels. The most common new perk is wireless Internet access (for a fee or included in the room rate). See chapter 6.

DINING   The chic French wine bar Les Zygomates has gained a sibling, **Sorriso Trattoria,** 107 South St. (© 617/ 259-1560), a few doors down from the original. Defying the laws of genetics, the new addition to the family is Italian.

The best new hotel restaurant Boston has seen in many years is **Spire,** in the hyper-chic Nine Zero hotel, 90 Tremont St. (© 617/772-0202). It's a perfect combination of local produce and products, Mediterranean flavors and techniques, and attentive service in a gorgeous space.

Krispy Kreme Doughnuts are finally available in Boston proper, at the Shops at Prudential Center, 800 Boylston St. (© 617/262-5531).

Goofy name notwithstanding, **Picco,** 513 Tremont St. (© 617/927-0066), is a great addition to the chic South End culinary scene—a pizza joint. The "Pizza and Ice Cream Company" makes exceptionally good use of its massive wood-fired oven and house-made frozen treats.

Boston has a seemingly inexhaustible appetite for steak. The **Ruth's Chris Steak House** chain is the latest to enter the market, with a planned opening in Sept 2005 in Old City Hall, 45 School St. (© 800/544-0808). See chapter 7.

WHAT TO SEE & DO   Ambitious expansion plans call for the **Boston Tea Party Ship & Museum** (© 617/269-7150; www.bostonteapartyship.com) to double in size, gain a tearoom, and add two replicas of the ships that figured into the colonial revolt. The attraction closed after a fire in 2001; if you hope to visit, call ahead to see whether it's on schedule to reopen in 2006.

The Society for the Preservation of New England Antiquities has a new, less 19th-century-sounding name: **Historic New England.** It retains control of some of the region's most interesting historic properties, including the **Otis House Museum** (formerly the Harrison Gray Otis House) in Boston, Lincoln's **Gropius House,** and **Beauport** in Gloucester. See chapter 12.

SHOPPING   Harvard Square standby WordsWorth Books has closed, leaving behind one of the best children's bookstores in the Boston area: **Curious George Goes to WordsWorth,** 1 John F. Kennedy St., Cambridge (© 617/498-0062).

American Apparel, the California-based anti-sweatshop pioneer, has expanded its retail operation to include Boston's Back Bay. Check out the chic tees, comfy underthings, and other knitwear at 138 Newbury St. (© 617/536-4768).

Higher up the fashion food chain but just one layer of fabric above that fair-trade thong is the merchandise at **Jean Therapy,** 524 Commonwealth Ave. (© 617/266-6555). It boasts the hottest designer labels and an exceptionally helpful staff.

The **Penzeys** chain of spice stores broke into the Massachusetts market in 2005 at 1293 Mass. Ave. in Arlington (© 800/741-7787). If you don't have a car, you'll have to ride the bus, but it's absolutely worth the trip. See chapter 10.

BOSTON AFTER DARK   The turn-of-the-century wave of bank mergers has spilled over into the cultural world. The **TD Banknorth Garden** and the **Bank of America Pavilion** are the new names of the FleetCenter and the FleetBoston Pavilion, respectively.

SIDE TRIPS FROM BOSTON   The **Liberty Ride** (© 781/862-0500, ext. 702; www.libertyride.us), a bus tour that originally concentrated on Lexington, now covers Concord as well.

At press time, **Rockport** was debating the wisdom of permitting **liquor sales** in the town for the first time since shortly after the repeal of Prohibition.

The **Plymouth National Wax Museum,** one of the most beloved attractions in eastern Massachusetts, closed in 2005.

The Best of Boston

Bostonians are feeling good. They have lots of pretty things to admire, both old and new: World Series rings. Super Bowl trophies (three in 4 years). A picturesque river and a rejuvenated harbor. College campuses that incorporate buildings of all ages and styles, from colonial-era to Frank Gehry's latest brainstorm. A reconfigured interstate that passes over a landmark bridge. Acres of real estate that used to be trapped under a hideous highway.

In years to come, a footnote to the year 2004 will be the completion of the Big Dig, a highway-construction project that moved Interstate 93 into a new tunnel system and demolished the elevated expressway that used to blight downtown. It took 15 years and cost $14.6 billion, and it's a footnote? Well, yes—2004 was the year the Red Sox won the World Series for the first time since 1918.

Footnote or no, the new highway runs beneath a modern metropolis that's also a relentlessly historic destination. An ongoing building boom may overshadow the famous 18th- and 19th-century architecture, but even rampant development can't change the colonial character of the central city.

It's not perfect, of course. Nightmarish traffic, daredevil drivers, and grating accents don't help any city's reputation. Although Boston is the biggest college town in the world, it doesn't have much of a late-night scene. And far from gone is the inferiority complex epitomized by the description "like New York, but smaller." Still, as it has for over 375 years, Boston offers cosmopolitan sophistication on a comfortable scale, balancing celebration of the past with pursuit of the future.

Here's hoping your experience is memorable and delightful.

1 The Most Unforgettable Travel Experiences

- **A Sky Full of Fireworks:** Twice during Independence Day festivities and again as the New Year begins, the firmament flashes in celebration. The Fourth of July fireworks are over the Charles River; the Harborfest display (in early July) and the First Night show explode above the Inner Harbor. See "Boston Calendar of Events," in chapter 2.

- **A Ride on a Duck:** A Duck Tour, that is. Board a reconditioned amphibious World War II landing craft (on Huntington Ave., near the Prudential Center) for a sightseeing ride that includes a dip in the river—for the Duck, not you. See p. 186.

- **An Afternoon Red Sox Game:** Since 1912, baseball fans have made pilgrimages to Fenway Park, the "lyric little bandbox of a ball park" (in John Updike's words) off Kenmore Square. Since 2004, they've come to share the excitement that accompanied the team's first World Series title in 86 years. The seats are uncomfortable and expensive, but you won't care a whit as you soak up the atmosphere and bask in the sun. See p. 197.

- **A Walk Around the North End:** Boston's Little Italy (but don't call it that!) has an old-world flavor you won't want to miss. Explore the shops on Salem Street, wander the narrow side streets, enjoy some pasta, and be sure to stop for coffee and a pastry at a Hanover Street *caffè.* See "Welcome to the North End," on p. 181.

- **An Off-Season Day Trip:** Destinations that abound with out-of-towners in the summer and fall become more manageable when the weather turns cold. Don't let the CLOSED FOR THE SEASON signs put you off: Under a cloudless sky, against the indigo Atlantic, an all-but-deserted suburban town has a unique appeal. See chapter 12.

2 The Best Splurge Hotels

- **Boston Harbor Hotel,** Rowes Wharf, Waterfront (℃ 800/752-7077). Breathtaking water views and over-the-top luxury combine to make the Boston Harbor Hotel the best in downtown Boston. It's just close enough to the Financial District to allow you to walk to your meeting and just far enough away to guarantee some peace at the end of a busy day. See p. 82.

- **Charles Hotel,** 1 Bennett St., Cambridge (℃ 800/882-1818). Steps from the hubbub of Harvard Square, the Charles is a sanctuary of contemporary design and traditional pampering. Every element is elegant and tasteful, making the Charles a favorite with visiting celebrities. See p. 103.

- **Eliot Hotel,** 370 Commonwealth Ave., Back Bay (℃ 800/44-ELIOT). Everything from the location of the hotel to the layout of the suites makes the Eliot feel like a luxury apartment building. The business features and elegant traditional furnishings contribute to the atmosphere, a seamless blend of commerce and comfort. See p. 93.

- **Four Seasons Hotel,** 200 Boylston St., Back Bay (℃ 800/819-5053). The best hotel in New England has everything—and what it doesn't have on the premises, the incredible staff will track down. Superb service, plush accommodations, and lavish amenities make a stay here unforgettable. See p. 90.

3 The Best Moderately Priced Hotels

- **Charlesmark Hotel,** 655 Boylston St. (℃ 617/247-1212). The Charlesmark's thoughtful features—plush bedding, free local phone calls, friendly service, custom-designed everything—more than make up for the size of the rooms, which are on the snug side. Bonus: Units at the front of the building overlook the Boston Marathon finish line. See p. 97.

- **Doubletree Guest Suites,** 400 Soldiers Field Rd., Brighton (℃ 800/222-TREE). Prices at busy times are at the high end of the moderate range, but this hotel is still a great deal—every unit is a spacious two-room suite. The location, straddling Boston and Cambridge, is especially good if you're driving. See p. 99.

- **Harborside Inn,** 185 State St., downtown (℃ 888/723-7565). Rooms in this renovated 19th-century warehouse feel like little lofts, with hardwood floors and exposed-brick walls. A stone's throw from Faneuil Hall Marketplace and the New England Aquarium, it's also perfect if you have business in the nearby Financial District. See p. 83.

- **MidTown Hotel,** 220 Huntington Ave., Back Bay (© **800/343-1177**). A unique combination of comfortable, no-frills rooms and a handy location make this hotel the most motel-like lodging in central Boston. Best of all, the room rate includes parking for one car—a savings of as much as $35 per day. See p. 98.

- **Newbury Guest House,** 261 Newbury St., Back Bay (© **800/437-7668**). This place would be a bargain even if it weren't ideally situated in the heart of Boston's best shopping. Room prices even include continental breakfast. See p. 98.

4 The Most Unforgettable Dining Experiences

- **Durgin-Park,** 340 Faneuil Hall Marketplace (© **617/227-2038**). This Boston institution has packed 'em in since 1827. It serves classic New England fare in abundant portions at communal tables, delighting everyone from local tycoons to visiting toddlers. Well, almost everyone. The famously crotchety staff is so much a part of the legend that some people are disappointed when the waitresses are nice (as they often are). See p. 124.

- **Legal Sea Foods,** 800 Boylston St., in the Prudential Center (© **617/266-6800**) and other locations. Like the culinary equivalent of a medical specialist, Legal's does one thing and does it exceptionally well. It's a chain for a great reason: People can't get enough of the freshest seafood around. See p. 138.

- **Mr. Bartley's Burger Cottage,** 1246 Mass. Ave., Cambridge (© **617/354-6559**). Trends in food and fashion come and go, and this neighborhood sees them all. Luckily, Harvard Square has a place that puts the comfort in comfort food. Bartley's is famous for its juicy burgers, incredible onion rings, and a down-to-earth atmosphere that's increasingly rare in these parts. See p. 146.

- **Pizzeria Regina,** 11½ Thacher St. (© **617/227-0765**). My friend Matt kept looking around, insisting that a film crew had to be hiding somewhere. And with its red-and-white-checked tablecloths and fiery oven, Regina's does look like Hollywood's idea of a pizza joint. After one bite of that slightly smoky crust, you'll be sending Martin Scorsese to the back of the line. See p. 122.

- **Ye Olde Union Oyster House,** 41 Union St. (© **617/227-2750**). Wise guys sneer about all the tourists, but the Union Oyster House is a local favorite for a reason—the locals eat there, too. The unbeatable combination of historic atmosphere and traditional food has drawn crowds since 1826. After just a few minutes of gobbling fresh seafood and being hypnotized by the shuckers, you might feel sorry for the people who wound up with the pearls instead of the oysters. See p. 124.

5 The Best Free (Or Almost Free) Things to Do

- **Picnic by the Water.** Head for the harbor or river, perch on a park bench or patch of grass, put away your watch, relax, and enjoy the spectacular scene. Whether it's sailboats or ocean liners, seagulls or scullers, there's always something worth watching. My favorite spot is the end of Long Wharf, not far from Faneuil Hall Marketplace, but it's just one of thousands of pleasant spots. See chapter 7.

- **Visit a Museum:** Schedule your visit to take advantage of free or reduced admission at certain times. The **USS Constitution Museum** is free all the time; the **Children's Museum** costs just $1 after 5pm on Friday; the **Institute of Contemporary Art** is free after 5pm Wednesday; the **Harvard University Art Museums** are free before noon Saturday; and the **Harvard Natural History Museums** are free on Sunday morning year-round and from 3 to 5pm Wednesday during the academic year. The **Museum of Fine Arts** "suggests" that you pay the regular $15 admission after 4pm Wednesday, but you don't have to. See chapter 8.
- **Relish a Vicarious Thrill:** Without so much as lacing up a sneaker, you can participate in the world-famous Boston Marathon. Stretch a little.

Drink plenty of fluids. Stake out a slice of sidewalk on Commonwealth Avenue and cheer as the runners thunder past. Then put your feet up—you must be exhausted. See p. 199.

- **Prowl Newbury Street:** From the genteel Arlington Street end to the cutting-edge Mass. Avenue end, Newbury Street—Boston's legendary shopping destination—is 8 blocks of pure temptation: galleries, boutiques, jewelry and gift shops, bookstores, and more. Fortunately, window-shopping is free. See chapter 10.
- **Check Out a College Concert or Show:** Countless local student groups just want an attentive audience, and the free or minimal admission can pay off in the long run. Imagine the credit card commercial: "Ability to say you recognized the talent of [insert name of big star] in a student production? Priceless." See chapter 11.

6 The Best Outdoor Activities

- **A Ride Across the Harbor:** The ferry that connects Long Wharf and the Charlestown Navy Yard is a treasure hidden in plain sight. You might notice the boat traffic on the Inner Harbor as you make your way around downtown; for just $1.50, you can be part of it. See chapter 5.
- **An Interlude at a Cafe:** When it comes to good ideas, outdoor seating in a place with great people-watching is right up there with fire and the wheel. A passing parade of shoppers and students (on Newbury St. and in Harvard Sq.) is more interesting than suits and ties (downtown and the rest of the Back Bay), but if the breeze and the iced cappuccino are cool, what's not to like? See chapter 7.

- **A Free Concert:** The Boston area's cultural scene has no real off season. During the summer, many musicians and musical groups take their acts outside—to parks, plazas, and even a barge (behind the Boston Harbor Hotel). Plan well, and you can enjoy music alfresco almost every night. See chapter 11.
- **A Stroll (or Jog) along the River:** The bike path that hugs both shores of the Charles accommodates pedestrians, runners, and rollerbladers, as well as cyclists. The Esplanade (along one side of the Back Bay) offers an unbeatable combination of people-watching and gorgeous trees and shrubs; the Cambridge side has abundant seating and fabulous views of the Boston skyline. See chapter 8.

7 The Best Museums

- **The Concord Museum:** I think of this suburban treasure as a Goldilocks museum—it's not too big, it's not too small, it's just right. Always informative, never overwhelming, it shows and tells visitors enough about the town's history to help them make the most of a visit to this fascinating community. See p. 260.

- **The Isabella Stewart Gardner Museum:** In an extremely unscientific poll of local travel experts conducted by me, this idiosyncratic museum tied for third-most-popular thing to do. The Gardner is a magnificent repository of art and nature in a building that's as impressive as anything hanging on the walls. See p. 156.

- **The John F. Kennedy Presidential Library and Museum:** Calling a presidential library unique is both obvious and a bit of a cop-out—of course it's unique; they're all unique. This one captures the personality of its namesake as well as the spirit that continues to make the Camelot era so compelling, even 4 decades later. See p. 156.

- **The Museum of Fine Arts:** The phrase "one of the best in the world" starts to lose its meaning with overuse, which happens all the time in the Boston area. Consider the colleges, the Symphony, the drivers (just kidding), the sports teams. The MFA truly is world-class—and all over the place, you'll stumble on masterpieces so familiar that seeing them is like running into an old friend on the street. See p. 157.

8 The Best Activities for Families

- **A Visit to Faneuil Hall Marketplace:** Kids can't decide where to look first. Street performers, crowds from all over the world, an enormous food court, restaurants, bars, and shops make Faneuil Hall Marketplace (you'll also hear it called Quincy Market) Boston's most popular destination. It's conveniently located across the street from the harbor, where a stroll along the water can help your crew decompress. See p. 151.

- **An Exploration of the Museum of Science:** Children's natural curiosity takes over as they troll the displays and exhibits that cram this enormous institution. Every branch of science and field of inquiry comes into play, but always in the most accessible way imaginable. It's so much fun that your youngsters probably won't even notice it's (shh!) educational. See p. 158.

- **An Excursion to the Public Garden:** Low-tech pleasures abound in this lovely park, the perfect retreat during or after a busy day of sightseeing. Ride a Swan Boat, feed the birds, and visit with the Mallard family of *Make Way for Ducklings* fame. Marvel as the whole family starts to unwind. See p. 175.

- **A Trip to the Children's Museum:** Younger kids (under 10 or so) practically vibrate with excitement as they approach Museum Wharf. The hands-on exhibits, noisy galleries, and overall air of discovery and excitement make the Children's Museum catnip for the elementary-school set. See p. 185.

- **A Thrill "Ride":** The Mugar Omni Theater (at the Museum of Science) and the 3-D Simons IMAX Theatre (at the New England Aquarium) offer intrepid visitors hair-raising experiences in the safety of a comfortable auditorium. Most of the large-format films concentrate on the natural world. See p. 158 for the Mugar Omni Theater and p. 159 for the Simons IMAX Theatre.

2

Planning Your Trip to Boston

This chapter addresses the practical issues that arise after you select a destination. Now that you've decided to visit Boston, how do you get there? How much will it cost? When should you go? How can you learn more? You'll find answers here, along with information about the climate and the events, festivals, and parades you might want to attend.

1 Visitor Information

The **Greater Boston Convention & Visitors Bureau,** 2 Copley Place, Suite 105, Boston, MA 02116-6501 (© **888/SEE-BOSTON** or 617/536-4100, 0171/431-3434 in the U.K.; fax 617/424-7664; www.bostonusa.com), offers a comprehensive visitor information kit ($10) and a *Kids Love Boston* guide ($5). The kit includes a travel planner, a guidebook, a map, pamphlets, and coupons for shopping, dining, attraction, and nightlife discounts. Smaller guides to specific seasons or events are often available free.

For information about Cambridge, contact the **Cambridge Office for Tourism,** 4 Brattle Street, Suite 208, Cambridge, MA 02138 (© **800/862-5678** or 617/441-2884; fax 617/441-7736; www.cambridge-usa.org).

The **Massachusetts Office of Travel and Tourism,** 10 Park Plaza, Suite 4510, Boston, MA 02116 (© **800/447-MASS** or 617/973-8500; fax 617/973-8525; www.massvacation.com), distributes information about the whole state. Its free *Getaway Guide* magazine includes information about attractions and lodgings, a map, and a calendar.

For visitor center and information desk locations after you arrive, see "Visitor Information," in chapter 5.

Also see the box "Online Traveler's Toolbox," on p. 25.

2 Money

Monetary descriptions and currency exchange information for international travelers appear in chapter 3.

Like other large American cities, Boston can be an expensive destination. At the high end, it's nearly as costly as New York. At the thrifty end, an abundance of reasonably priced establishments cater to the area's large student population.

ATMs

The easiest and best way to get cash away from home is from an ATM (automated teller machine). They're widely available throughout Boston and eastern Massachusetts. Even the smallest towns usually have at least one ATM. The **Cirrus** (© **800/424-7787;** www.mastercard.com) and **PLUS** (© **800/843-7587;**

www.visa.com) networks span the globe. Another widespread system, the **NYCE** network (www.nyce.net), operates primarily in the eastern United States. Look at the back of your bank card to see which network you're on, then call or check online for ATM locations in the Boston area.

Be sure you know your personal identification number (PIN) before you leave home and be sure to find out your daily withdrawal limit before you depart. Also keep in mind that many banks impose a fee every time a card is used at a different bank's ATM. On top of this, the bank from which you withdraw cash may charge its own fee. At Massachusetts's banks, a message should appear—either on the screen or on a sticker near the terminal screen—to warn you that you're about to be charged and then offer you the chance to cancel the transaction. To compare banks' ATM fees within the U.S., use www.bankrate.com.

You can also get cash advances on your credit card at an ATM. Keep in mind that credit card companies try to protect themselves from theft by imposing withdrawal limits, so call your credit card company to check its limit before you leave home. And keep in mind that you'll pay interest from the moment of your withdrawal, even if you pay your monthly bills on time.

TRAVELER'S CHECKS

Traveler's checks are something of an anachronism from the days before the ATM made cash accessible at any time. Traveler's checks used to be the only sound alternative to traveling with large amounts of cash. They were as reliable as currency but could be replaced if lost or stolen.

These days, traveler's checks are less necessary because most cities have 24-hour ATMs that allow you to withdraw small amounts of cash as needed. However, keep in mind that you will likely pay an ATM fee if the bank is not your own, so if you're withdrawing money every day, you might be better off with traveler's checks—provided that you don't mind showing identification every time you want to cash one.

You can get traveler's checks at almost any bank. **American Express** offers denominations of $20, $50, $100, $500, and (for cardholders only) $1,000. You'll pay a service charge ranging from 1% to 4%. You can also get American Express traveler's checks over the phone by calling ℂ **800/221-7282;** Amex gold and platinum cardholders who use this number are exempt from the 1% fee.

Visa offers traveler's checks at Citibank locations nationwide, as well as at several other banks. The service charge ranges between 1.5% and 2%; checks come in denominations of $20, $50, $100, $500, and $1,000. Call ℂ **800/732-1322** for information. AAA members can obtain Visa checks without a fee at most AAA offices or by calling ℂ **866/339-3378.** **MasterCard** also offers traveler's checks. Call ℂ **800/223-9920** for a location near you.

If you carry traveler's checks, be sure to keep a record of their serial numbers *separate from your checks* in the event that they are stolen or lost. You'll get a refund faster if you know the numbers.

CREDIT CARDS

Credit cards are a safe way to carry money: They also provide a convenient record of your expenses, and they generally offer relatively good exchange rates. You can also withdraw cash advances from your credit cards at banks or ATMs, provided you know your PIN. If you've forgotten yours, or didn't even know you had one, call the number on the back of your credit card and ask the bank to send it to you. It usually takes 5 to 7 business days, though some banks will provide the number over the phone if you provide your mother's maiden name or some other personal information.

For tips and telephone numbers to call if your wallet is stolen or lost, go to "Lost or Stolen Wallet" in the "Fast Facts: Boston" section (p. 72).

3 When to Go

Boston attracts throngs of visitors year-round. Between April and November, there are hardly any slow times. Make reservations as early as possible if you plan to visit during traditionally busy periods.

The periods around college graduation (May and early June) and major citywide events (see "Boston Calendar of Events" below) are especially busy. Spring and fall are popular times for conventions. Families pour into the area in July and August, creating long lines at many attractions. Summer isn't the most expensive time to visit, though: Foliage season, from mid-September to early November, when many leaf-peepers stay in the Boston area or pass through on the way to northern New England, is a huge draw. December is less busy but still a convention time—look out for weekend bargains.

The "slow" season is January through March, when many hotels offer great deals, especially on weekends. However, this is when unpredictable weather plagues the Northeast (often affecting travel schedules) and when some suburban attractions close for the winter.

WEATHER

You've probably heard the saying about New England weather: "If you don't like it, wait 10 minutes." Variations from day to day (if not minute to minute) can be enormous. You can roast in March and freeze in June, shiver in July and sweat in November. Dressing in layers is always a good idea.

Spring and fall are the best bets for moderate temperatures, but spring (also known as mud season) is brief. It doesn't usually settle in until early May, and snow sometimes falls in April. Summers are hot, especially in July and August, and can be uncomfortably humid. Fall is when you're most likely to catch a comfortable run of dry, sunny days and cool nights. Winters are cold and usually snowy—bring a warm coat and sturdy boots.

BOSTON CALENDAR OF EVENTS

The **Greater Boston Convention & Visitors Bureau** (© 888/SEE-BOSTON or 617/536-4100; www.bostonusa.com) operates a regularly updated hot line that describes ongoing and upcoming events. The **Mayor's Office of Special Events, Tourism & Film** (© 617/635-3911; www.cityofboston.gov/calendar) can provide information about specific happenings. If you're planning at the last minute, the "Calendar" section of the Thursday *Boston Globe* and the "Edge" section of the Friday *Boston Herald* are always packed with ideas.

January

Martin Luther King, Jr., Birthday Celebration, various locations. Events include musical tributes, gospel concerts, museum displays and programs, readings, speeches, and panel discussions. Check special listings in the

Boston's Average Temperatures & Rainfall

	Jan	Feb	Mar	Apr	May	June	July	Aug	Sept	Oct	Nov	Dec
Temp. (°F)	30	31	38	49	59	68	74	72	65	55	45	34
Temp. (°C)	−1	−1	3	9	15	20	23	22	18	13	7	1
Rainfall (in.)	4.0	3.7	4.1	3.7	3.5	2.9	2.7	3.7	3.4	3.4	4.2	4.9

Fun Fact Poetry 101 (Degrees)

In Boston, you can check the weather forecast by looking up at the short column of lights on top of the old John Hancock building in the Back Bay. (The new Hancock building is the 60-story glass tower next door.) It has its own poem: *Steady blue, clear view; flashing blue, clouds due; steady red, rain ahead; flashing red, snow instead.* During the summer, flashing red means that the Red Sox game is canceled.

Thursday *Boston Globe* "Calendar" section for specifics. Third Monday in January.

Boston Cooks, various locations. Restaurants throughout the area entertain celebrity chefs and cookbook authors, who design special dinners and take turns behind the stove. Other events include classes, demonstrations, and book signings. Call the Convention & Visitors Bureau (© **888/SEE-BOSTON**) or visit www.bostoncooks.com. End of January.

Boston Wine Festival, Boston Harbor Hotel and other locations. Tastings, classes, lectures, receptions, and meals provide a lively liquid diversion throughout winter. Call the festival reservation line (© **888/660-WINE** or 617/330-9355; www.bostonwinefestival.net) for details. January to early April.

Chinese New Year, Chinatown. The dragon parade (which draws a big crowd no matter how cold it is), fireworks, and raucous festivals are part of the celebration. Special programs take place at the **Children's Museum** (© **617/426-8855;** www.bostonkids.org). Depending on the Chinese lunar calendar, the holiday falls between January 21 and February 19. In 2006, it's January 29.

February

Black History Month, various locations. Programs include special museum exhibits, children's activities, concerts, films, lectures, discussions, readings, and tours of the Black Heritage Trail led by National Park Service rangers (© **617/742-5415;** www.nps.gov/boaf). All month.

School Vacation Week, various locations. The slate of activities includes special exhibitions and programs, plays, concerts, and tours. Contact individual attractions for information on programs and extended hours. Third week of February.

March

New England Spring Flower Show, Bayside Expo Center, Dorchester. This annual harbinger of spring, presented by the **Massachusetts Horticultural Society** (© **617/933-4900;** www.masshort.org), draws huge crowds starved for a glimpse of green. Plan to take public transit. Second or third week of March.

April

NCAA Women's Basketball Final Four, TD Banknorth Garden. The event—which sold out months ago—marks the 25th anniversary of the Women's Final Four. If you're visiting for some other reason, don't expect to be able to find a reasonably priced hotel room or plane ticket. If you can, travel before or after this weekend. April 2 through 4, 2006.

Big Apple Circus (www.bigapplecircus.org), near the South Boston waterfront. The New York–based "one-ring wonder" performs in a heated tent with all seating less than 50 feet from the ring. Proceeds support the Children's Museum. Visit the museum box office or contact Ticketmaster (© 617/931-ARTS; www.ticketmaster.com). Early April to early May.

Red Sox Opening Day, Fenway Park. Even if your concierge is a magician, this is an extremely tough ticket. Check ahead (© 877/REDSOX-9; www.redsox.com) when tickets for the season go on sale in December. If you can't get tickets to Opening Day, try to see the game on **Patriots Day,** the third Monday in April. It begins at 11am so spectators can watch the Boston Marathon afterward. Early and mid-April.

Swan Boats Return to the Public Garden. Since their introduction in 1877, the Swan Boats (© 617/522-1966; www.swanboats.com) have been a symbol of Boston. Like real swans, they go away for the winter. Saturday before Patriots Day.

Patriots Day, North End, Lexington, and Concord. Festivities commemorate and reenact the events of April 18 and 19, 1775. Lanterns glow in the steeple of the **Old North Church** (© 617/523-6676; www.oldnorth. com). Participants dressed as Paul Revere and William Dawes ride from the **Paul Revere House** (© 617/523-2338; www.paulreverehouse.org) in the North End to Lexington and Concord to warn the Minutemen that "the regulars are out" (not that "the British are coming"—most colonists considered themselves British). Musket fire rings out on the town green in Lexington and then at the Old North Bridge in Concord. Contact the **Lexington Chamber of Commerce Visitor Center** (© 781/862-1450; www. lexingtonchamber.org), or the **Concord Chamber of Commerce** (© 978/369-3120; www.concord machamber.org), for information on

battle reenactments. See chapter 12 for information on visiting both towns. Third Monday of April.

Boston Marathon, Hopkinton, Massachusetts, to Boston. International stars and local amateurs join in the world's oldest and most famous marathon (www.bostonmarathon.org). The noon start means that elite runners hit Boston around 2pm; weekend warriors stagger across the Boylston Street finish line as much as 6 hours later. Third Monday of the month.

Freedom Trail Week, various locations in Boston, Cambridge, Lexington, and Concord. This is another school vacation week, with plenty of crowds and diversions. Family-friendly events include tours, concerts, talks, and other programs related to Patriots Day, the Freedom Trail, and the American Revolution. Third week of April.

May

Museum-Goers' Month, various locations. Contact individual museums for details and schedules of special exhibits, lectures, and events. See chapter 8. All month.

Boston Kite & Flight Festival, Franklin Park (© 617/635-4505). Kites of all shapes and sizes take to the air above a celebration that includes kite-making clinics, music, competitions, and other entertainment. Mid-May.

Lilac Sunday, Arnold Arboretum, Jamaica Plain. This is the only day of the year that the arboretum (© 617/524-1717; www.arboretum. harvard.edu) allows picnicking. From sunrise to sunset, wander the grounds and enjoy the sensational spring flowers, including more than 400 varieties of lilacs in bloom. Mid-May.

Street Performers Festival, Faneuil Hall Marketplace. Everyone but the pigeons gets into the act as musicians, magicians, jugglers, sword swallowers, and artists strut their stuff. Late May.

June

Boston Pride March, Back Bay to Beacon Hill (© 617/262-9405; www.bostonpride.org). The largest gay pride parade in New England is the highlight of a weeklong celebration of diversity. The parade, on the second Sunday of the month, starts at Copley Square and ends on Boston Common. Early June.

Dragon Boat Festival, Charles River near Harvard Square, Cambridge (© 617/349-4380; www.bostondragon boat.org). Teams of paddlers synchronized by a drummer propel boats with dragon heads and tails as they race 500m (1,640 ft.). The winners go to the national championships; the spectators go to a celebration of Chinese culture and food on the shore. Second or third Sunday of June.

Central Square World's Fair, Cambridge (© 617/868-3247; www.cambridgema.gov). This celebration of unity and diversity features the usual food, crafts, and kids' activities—and a twist that elevates the event far above the usual street festival: local and national musicians (rock, jazz, and blues). Early or mid-June.

Cambridge River Festival (© 617/349-4380; www.cambridgearts council.org), Memorial Drive from John F. Kennedy Street to Western Avenue. A salute to the arts, the festival incorporates live music, dancing, children's activities, crafts and art exhibits, and international food on the banks of the Charles. Mid-June.

July

Boston Harborfest, downtown, the waterfront, and the Harbor Islands. The city puts on its Sunday best for the Fourth of July, a gigantic weeklong celebration of Boston's maritime history. Events surrounding **Harborfest** (© 617/227-1528; www.boston harborfest.com) include concerts, children's activities, cruises, fireworks, the Boston Chowderfest, guided tours, talks, and USS *Constitution*'s turnaround cruise. Beginning of the month (June 28–July 4, 2006).

Boston Pops Concert and Fireworks Display, Hatch Shell, on the Esplanade. Spectators start showing up at dawn (overnight camping is not permitted) for a good spot on the lawn and spend all day waiting for the sky to get dark enough for fireworks. Others show up at the last minute—the Cambridge side of the river, near Kendall Square, and the Longfellow Bridge are good spots to watch the spectacular aerial show. The program includes the *1812 Overture,* with real cannon fire and church bells. For details, check the website (www.july4th.org). July 4.

Boston Globe **Jazz & Blues Festival,** various locations, indoors and outdoors. Big names and rising stars put on lunchtime, after-work, evening, and weekend performances, some of which are free. Venues include the Hatch Shell on the Esplanade, Newbury Street, and Copley Square. Call the festival hot line (© 617/267-4301) or pick up a copy of the paper for a schedule when you arrive in town. Some events require advance tickets. Mid-July.

Puerto Rican Festival, Franklin Park. This 5-day event, instituted in 1967, is part street fair, part cultural celebration, with plenty of live music. Late July.

August

Italian-American Feasts, North End. These weekend street fairs begin in July and end in late August with the two biggest: the Fisherman's Feast and the Feast of St. Anthony. The sublime (fresh seafood prepared while you wait, live music, dancing in the street) mingles with the ridiculous (carnival games, tacky T-shirts, fried-dough stands) to leave a lasting impression of fun and indigestion. Visit www.fisher mansfeast.com or www.saintanthonys feast.com for a preview. Weekends throughout August.

August Moon Festival, Chinatown. A celebration of the harvest and the coming of autumn, the festival (© 617/ 542-2574) includes the "dragon dance" through the crowded streets and demonstrations of crafts and martial arts. Mid-August.

September

Boston Film Festival (© 617/331-9460; www.bostonfilmfestival.org), various locations. Independent films continue on the festival circuit or make their premieres, sometimes following a lecture by an actor or filmmaker. Most screenings are open to the public without advance tickets. Mid-September.

October

Salem Haunted Happenings, various locations. Parades, parties, a special commuter-rail ride from Boston, fortune-telling, cruises, and tours lead up to a ceremony on Halloween. Contact **Destination Salem** (© 877/ SALEM-MA) or check the website (www.hauntedhappenings.org) for specifics. All month.

Ringling Brothers and Barnum & Bailey Circus, TD Banknorth Garden (© 617/624-1000 events line, 617/ 931-2000 Ticketmaster; www.tdbank northgarden.com). The Greatest Show on Earth makes its annual 2-week visit. Mid-October.

Head of the Charles Regatta, Boston and Cambridge. High school, college, and postcollegiate rowing teams and individuals—some 4,000 in all—race in front of hordes of fans along the banks of the Charles River and on the bridges spanning it. The Head of the Charles (© 617/868-6200; www. hocr.org) has an uncanny tendency to coincide with a crisp, picturesque weekend. Late October.

An Evening with Champions, Bright Athletic Center, Allston. World-class ice skaters and promising local students stage three performances to benefit the Jimmy Fund, the children's fund-raising arm of the Dana-Farber Cancer Institute. Sponsored by Harvard's **Eliot House** (© 617/493-8172; www.hcs.harvard.edu/~ewc). Late October or early November.

November

Thanksgiving Celebration, Plymouth (© 800/USA-1620; www.visit-plymouth.com). Plymouth observes the holiday with a "stroll through the ages," showcasing 17th- and 19th-century Thanksgiving preparations in historic homes. **Plimoth Plantation,** which recreates the colony's first years, serves a Victorian Thanksgiving feast. Reservations (© 800/262-9356 or 508/746-1622; www.plimoth.org) are required and are accepted beginning in August. Thanksgiving Day.

December

The Nutcracker, Opera House, Boston. Boston Ballet's annual holiday extravaganza is one of the country's biggest and best. This is *the* traditional way to expose young Bostonians (and visitors) to culture, and the spectacular sets make it practically painless. Visit the website (www.bostonballet.org) for more info. For tickets, call **Tele-charge** (© 800/447-7400 or TTY 888/ 889-8587; www.telecharge.com) as soon as you plan your trip, ask whether your hotel offers a *Nutcracker* package, or cross your fingers and visit the box office when you arrive. All month.

Boston Tea Party Reenactment, Old South Meeting House (© **617/482-6439;** www.oldsouthmeetinghouse.org) and Tea Party Ship and Museum, Congress Street Bridge (© **617/338-1773;** www.bostonteapartyship.com). Chafing under British rule, American colonists rose up on December 16, 1773, to strike a blow where it would cause real pain—in the pocketbook. A re-creation of the pre-party rally takes place at the meeting house; call ahead to see whether the ship has reopened during your visit. Mid-December.

Black Nativity, Converse Hall, Tremont Temple Baptist Church, 88 Tremont Street (© **617/723-3486;** www.blacknativity.org). Poet Langston Hughes wrote the "gospel opera," and a cast of more than 100 brings it to life. Most weekends in December.

Christmas Revels, Sanders Theatre, Cambridge. This multicultural celebration of the winter solstice features the holiday customs of a different culture each year. Recent themes have included Victorian England and Romany Gypsies. Be ready to sing along. For information, contact the **Revels** (© **617/972-8300;** www.revels.org); for tickets, call the **box office** (© **617/496-2222**). Last 2 weeks of the month.

First Night, Back Bay and the waterfront. This is the original arts-oriented, no-alcohol, citywide New Year's Eve celebration. It begins in the early afternoon and includes a parade, ice sculptures, art exhibitions, theatrical performances, and indoor and outdoor entertainment. Some attractions require tickets, but for most you just need a First Night button, available for $15 or so at visitor centers and stores around the city. The carousing wraps up at midnight with fireworks over the harbor. For details, contact **First Night** (© **617/542-1399;** www.firstnight.org) or check the newspapers when you arrive. December 31.

4 Travel Insurance

Check your existing insurance policies and credit card coverage before you buy travel insurance. You may already have coverage for lost luggage, canceled tickets, or medical expenses. The price of travel insurance varies widely, depending on the cost and length of your trip, your age and health, and the type of trip you're taking, but expect to pay between 5% and 8% of the cost of the vacation.

TRIP-CANCELLATION INSURANCE
Trip-cancellation insurance helps you get your money back if you have to back out of a trip, if you have to go home early, or if your travel supplier goes bankrupt. Allowed reasons for cancellation can range from sickness to natural disasters to the State Department declaring your destination unsafe for travel. In this unstable world, trip-cancellation insurance is a good buy if you're getting tickets well in advance—who knows what the state of the world, or of your airline, will be in 9 months? Insurance policy details vary, so read the fine print—and make sure that your airline or cruise line is on the list of carriers covered in case of bankruptcy. A good resource is **"Travel Guard Alerts,"** a list of companies considered high-risk by Travel Guard International (see website below). Protect yourself further by paying for the insurance with a credit card—by law, consumers can get their money back on goods and services not received if they report the loss within 60 days after the charge appears on their credit card statement.

Note: Many tour operators include insurance in the cost of the trip or can arrange a policy through a partnering provider, a convenient and often cost-effective way for the traveler to obtain insurance. Make sure the tour company is a reputable one, however: Some experts suggest you avoid buying insurance from the tour or cruise company you're traveling with, saying it's better to buy from a "third party" insurer than to put all your money in one place.

For more information, contact one of the following recommended insurers: **Access America** (℧ 866/807-3982; www.accessamerica.com), **Travel Guard International** (℧ 800/826-4919; www.travelguard.com), **Travel Insured International** (℧ 800/243-3174; www.travelinsured.com), and **Travelex Insurance Services** (℧ 888/457-4602; www.travelex-insurance.com).

MEDICAL INSURANCE   Most health insurance policies cover you if you get sick away from home—but check, particularly if you're insured by an HMO. If you require additional medical insurance, try **MEDEX Assistance** (℧ 410/453-6300; www.medexassist.com) or **Travel Assistance International** (℧ 800/821-2828; www.travelassistance.com; for general information on services, call the company's Worldwide Assistance Services, Inc., at ℧ **800/777-8710**).

LOST-LUGGAGE INSURANCE   On domestic flights, checked baggage is covered up to $2,500 per ticketed passenger. On international flights (including U.S. portions of international trips), baggage coverage is limited to approximately $9.07 per pound, up to approximately $635 per checked bag. If you plan to check items more valuable than the standard liability, see if your homeowner's policy covers your valuables, get baggage insurance as part of your comprehensive travel-insurance package, or buy Travel Guard's "BagTrak" product. Don't buy insurance at the airport, where it's usually overpriced. Be sure to take any valuables or irreplaceable items with you in your carry-on luggage because airline policies don't cover many valuables (including books, money, and electronics).

If your luggage is lost, immediately file a lost-luggage claim at the airport, detailing the luggage contents. For most airlines, you must report delayed, damaged, or lost baggage within 4 hours of arrival. The airlines are required to deliver luggage, once found, directly to your house or destination free of charge.

5 Health & Safety

STAYING HEALTHY

Here's hoping you won't need to evaluate Boston's reputation for excellent medical care. The greatest threat to your health is the same as in most other North American cities: overexposure to the summer sun. Be sure to pack sunscreen, sunglasses, and a hat, and don't forget to keep yourself hydrated.

WHAT TO DO IF YOU GET SICK AWAY FROM HOME

In most cases, your existing health plan will provide the coverage you need. But double-check; you may want to buy **travel medical insurance** instead. (See the section on insurance above.) Bring your insurance ID card with you when you travel. We list hospitals and emergency numbers under "Fast Facts: Boston" (p. 72).

If you suffer from a chronic illness, consult your doctor before your departure. For conditions like epilepsy, diabetes, or heart problems, wear a **Medic Alert identification tag** (℧ 888/633-4298; www.medicalert.org), which will immediately alert doctors to your condition and give them access to your records through Medic Alert's 24-hour hot line.

Pack **prescription medications** in your carry-on luggage, never in your checked baggage, and carry prescription medications in their original containers, with pharmacy labels—otherwise they won't make it through airport security. Also bring along copies of your prescriptions in case you lose your pills or run out. Don't forget an extra pair of contact lenses or prescription glasses.

If you get sick, consider asking your hotel concierge to recommend a local doctor—even his or her own. Also see "Doctors" in the "Fast Facts: Boston" section, p. 72.

STAYING SAFE

Boston and Cambridge are generally safe, especially in the areas you're likely to visit. Nevertheless, you should take the same precautions you would in any other large North American city. In general, trust your instincts—a dark, deserted street is probably deserted for a reason.

As in any city, stay out of parks (including Boston Common, the Public Garden, and the Esplanade) at night unless you're in a crowd. Specific areas to avoid at night include Boylston Street between Tremont and Washington streets, and Tremont Street from Stuart to Boylston streets. Try not to walk alone late at night in the Theater District or on the side streets around North Station. Public transportation in the areas you're likely to visit is busy and safe, but service stops between 12:30 and 1am.

6 Specialized Travel Resources

TRAVELERS WITH DISABILITIES

Boston, like all other U.S. cities, has taken the required steps to provide access for people with disabilities. Hotels must provide accessible rooms, and museums and street curbs have ramps for wheelchairs. Some smaller accommodations, including most B&Bs, have not been retrofitted. In older neighborhoods (notably Beacon Hill and the North End), you'll find many narrow streets, cobbled thoroughfares, and brick sidewalks. In the construction areas that have succeeded the Big Dig, you'll have to negotiate uneven road surfaces and pedestrian detours.

Newer stations on the Red, Blue, and Orange lines of the **subway** are wheelchair-accessible; the transit authority is currently converting the Green Line (which uses trolleys). Contact the **MBTA** (© 800/392-6100 or 617/222-3200; www.mbta.com) to see if the stations you need are accessible. All MBTA **buses** have lifts or kneelers; call © **800/LIFT-BUS** for more information. Some bus routes are wheelchair-accessible at all times, but you might have to make a reservation as much as a day in advance for others. To learn more, contact the **Office for Transportation Access,** 145 Dartmouth Street, Boston, MA 02116 (© **617/222-5438** or TTY 617/222-5854).

One taxi company with wheelchair-accessible vehicles is **Boston Cab** (© **617/536-5010**); advance notice is recommended. In addition, an **Airport Accessible Van** (© **617/561-1769**) operates within Logan Airport.

An excellent resource is **VSA Arts Massachusetts,** 2 Boylston Street, Boston, MA 02116 (© **617/350-7713,** TTY 617/350-6836; www.vsamass.org). Its comprehensive website (www.accessexpressed.net) includes general access information and specifics about more than 200 cultural facilities.

The U.S. National Park Service offers a **Golden Access Passport** that gives free lifetime entrance to all properties administered by the National Park Service—national parks, monuments, historic sites, recreation areas, and national wildlife refuges—for persons who are visually impaired or permanently disabled, regardless of age. You may pick up a Golden Access Passport at any NPS entrance fee area by showing proof of medically determined disability and eligibility for receiving benefits under federal law. For more information, go to www.nps.gov/fees_passes.htm or call ℂ **888/GO-PARKS.**

Many travel agencies offer customized tours and itineraries for travelers with disabilities. **Flying Wheels Travel** (ℂ **507/451-5005;** www.flyingwheelstravel.com) offers escorted tours and cruises that emphasize sports and private tours in minivans with lifts. **Access-Able Travel Source** (ℂ **303/232-2979;** www.access-able.com) offers extensive access information and advice for traveling around the world with disabilities. **Accessible Journeys** (ℂ **800/846-4537** or 610/521-0339; www.disabilitytravel.com) caters specifically to slow walkers and wheelchair travelers and their families and friends.

Avis Rent a Car has an "Avis Access" program that offers such services as a dedicated 24-hour toll-free number (ℂ **888/879-4273**) for customers with special travel needs; special car features such as swivel seats, spinner knobs, and hand controls; and accessible bus service.

Organizations that offer assistance to travelers with disabilities include **MossRehab** (www.mossresourcenet.org), which provides a library of accessible-travel resources online; **SATH (Society for Accessible Travel & Hospitality)** (ℂ **212/447-7284;** www.sath.org; annual membership fees: $45 adults, $30 seniors and students), which offers a wealth of resources for travelers with all types of disabilities and informed recommendations on destinations, access guides, travel agents, tour operators, vehicle rentals, and companion services; and the **American Foundation for the Blind,** or AFB (ℂ **800/232-5463;** www.afb.org), a referral resource for the blind or visually impaired that includes information on traveling with Seeing Eye dogs.

For more information specifically targeted to travelers with disabilities, the community website **iCan** (www.icanonline.net/channels/travel/index.cfm) has destination guides and several regular columns on accessible travel. Also check out the quarterly magazine **Emerging Horizons** ($14.95 per year, $19.95 outside the U.S.; www.emerginghorizons.com); and **Open World** magazine, published by SATH (see above; subscription: $13 per year, $21 outside the U.S.).

GAY & LESBIAN TRAVELERS

Overall, Boston is a gay- and lesbian-friendly destination, with a live-and-let-live attitude that long ago replaced the city's legendary Puritanism.

The **Gay, Lesbian, Bisexual and Transgender Helpline** (ℂ **888/340-4528** or 617/267-9001) offers information Monday through Friday from 6 to 11pm, and Saturday and Sunday from 5 to 10pm. *Bay Windows* (ℂ **617/266-6670;** www.baywindows.com) is a weekly newspaper that covers New England and publishes cultural listings. The weekly *Boston Phoenix* publishes cultural and nightlife listings and has a gay-interest area on its website (www.bostonphoenix.com).

An excellent guide to local gay- and lesbian-owned and gay-friendly businesses is the *Pink Pages,* 66 Charles Street #283, Boston, MA 02114 (ℂ **800/338-6550;** www.pinkweb.com). Visit the comprehensive website or order a copy for $11, including postage. You can also contact the **Boston Alliance of Gay and Lesbian Youth** (ℂ **617/227-4313;** www.bagly.org) and the **Bisexual Resource Center** (ℂ **617/424-9595;** www.biresource.org).

The **International Gay and Lesbian Travel Association** (ℂ **800/448-8550** or 954/776-2626; www.iglta.org) is the trade association for the gay and lesbian travel industry and offers an online directory of gay- and lesbian-friendly travel businesses; go to the website and click on "Members."

Many agencies offer tours and travel itineraries specifically for gay and lesbian travelers. **Above and Beyond Tours** (© 800/397-2681; www.abovebeyond tours.com) is the exclusive gay and lesbian tour operator for United Airlines. **Now, Voyager** (© 800/255-6951; www.nowvoyager.com) is a well-known San Francisco–based gay-owned and -operated travel service.

The following travel guides are available at most travel bookstores and gay and lesbian bookstores, or you can order them from **Giovanni's Room** bookstore, 1145 Pine Street, Philadelphia, PA 19107 (© 215/923-2960; www.giovannisroom. com): *Out and About* (© 800/929-2268; www.outandabout.com), which offers guidebooks and a newsletter ($20 per year; 10 issues) packed with solid information on the global gay and lesbian scene; *Spartacus International Gay Guide* (Bruno Gmünder Verlag; www.spartacusworld. com/gayguide) and *Odysseus: The International Gay Travel Planner* (Odysseus Enterprises Ltd.), are annual English-language guidebooks focused on gay men; the *Damron* guides (The Damron Company; www.damron.com), with separate annual books for gay men and lesbians; and *Gay Travel A to Z: The World of Gay & Lesbian Travel Options at Your Fingertips,* by Marianne Ferrari (Ferrari International; Box 35575, Phoenix, AZ 85069), a very good gay and lesbian guidebook series.

SENIOR TRAVEL

Mention that you're a senior citizen when you make your travel reservations. Although the major U.S. airlines (except America West) have cancelled their senior discount and coupon-book programs, many hotels still offer senior discounts. Boston-area businesses offer many discounts to seniors with identification (a driver's license, passport, or other document that shows your date of birth). The cut-off age is usually 65, sometimes 62. Restaurants, museums, and movie theaters may offer special deals. Restaurants and theaters usually offer discounts only at off-peak times, but museums and other attractions offer reduced rates at all times.

Members of **AARP,** 601 E St. NW, Washington, DC 20049 (© 888/687-2277; www.aarp.org), get discounts on hotels, airfares, and car rentals. AARP offers members a wide range of benefits, including *AARP: The Magazine* and a monthly newsletter. Anyone over 50 can join.

With the **Senior Pass,** seniors can ride the MBTA **subways** for 35¢ (a 90¢ savings) and **local buses** for 25¢ (a 65¢ savings). On zoned and express buses and on the commuter rail, the senior fare is half the regular fare. The Senior Pass is available for 50¢ on weekdays from 8:30am to 5pm at the Back Bay MBTA station, or by mail from the Office for Transportation Access, 145 Dartmouth Street, Boston, MA 02116 (© 617/222-5438 or TTY 617/222-5854). Enclose a 1×1-inch photo and 50¢.

The **U.S. National Park Service** offers a **Golden Age Passport** that gives seniors 62 years or older lifetime entrance to all properties administered by the National Park Service—national parks, monuments, historic sites, recreation areas, and national wildlife refuges—for a one-time processing fee of $10, which must be paid in person at any NPS facility that charges an entrance fee. For more information, go to www.nps.gov/fees_passes.htm or call © 888/GO-PARKS.

Many reliable agencies and organizations target the 50-plus market. **Elderhostel** (© 877/426-8056; www.elderhostel.org) arranges study programs for those 55 and over (and a spouse or companion of any age) in the U.S. and in more than 80 countries around the world. Most courses in the U.S. last 5 to 7 days, and many include airfare, accommodations in university dormitories or modest inns, meals, and tuition.

Recommended publications offering travel resources and discounts for seniors include: the quarterly magazine *Travel 50 & Beyond* (www.travel50andbeyond. com); *Travel Unlimited: Uncommon Adventures for the Mature Traveler* (Avalon); *101 Tips for Mature Travelers,* available from Grand Circle Travel (℃ **800/221-2610** or 617/350-7500; www.gct.com); and *Unbelievably Good Deals and Great Adventures That You Absolutely Can't Get Unless You're Over 50* (McGraw-Hill), by Joann Rattner Heilman.

FAMILY TRAVEL

Boston is a top-notch family destination, with tons of activities that appeal to children and relatively few that don't. Every hotel and most restaurants in the area have extensive experience meeting kids' needs.

Children (usually under 18, sometimes under 12) can stay free in their parent's hotel room when using existing bedding. Most hotels charge for cots, and some charge for cribs. Always ask whether the hotel you're considering has special offers for families. Many hotels offer family packages that include a room or a suite, breakfast, and parking, plus discount coupons for museums and restaurants. Some discount the price of a kid's room that adjoins the parent's; at others, a suite may give you as much space as—and cost less than—two standard rooms.

When you book your flight, see if your airline offers half-price tickets for children under 3 traveling in car seats.

The **Greater Boston Convention & Visitors Bureau** (℃ **888/SEE-BOSTON;** www.bostonusa.com) sells a *Kids Love Boston* guide ($5) filled with travel information for families.

Throughout this book, the "Kids" icon flags destinations that are especially welcoming and interesting to youngsters. Also consult the boxes on "Family-Friendly Hotels" (p. 95) and "Family-Friendly Restaurants" (p. 134), and the section "Especially for Kids" (p. 183).

Familyhostel (℃ **800/733-9753;** www.learn.unh.edu/familyhostel) takes the whole family, including kids ages 8 to 15, on moderately priced domestic and international learning vacations. A team of academics guides lectures, field trips, and sightseeing.

Recommended family travel Internet sites include **Family Travel Forum** (www.familytravelforum.com), a comprehensive site that offers customized trip planning; **Family Travel Network** (www.familytravelnetwork.com), an award-winning site that offers travel features, deals, and tips; and **Family Travel Files** (www.thefamilytravelfiles.com), which offers an online magazine and a directory of off-the-beaten-path tours and tour operators for families.

The Unofficial Guide to New England & New York with Kids (Wiley Publishing, Inc.), a Frommer's publication, is an excellent family resource. *How to Take Great Trips with Your Kids* (The Harvard Common Press) is full of good general advice that can apply to travel anywhere.

STUDENT TRAVEL

Students don't actually rule Boston—it just feels that way sometimes. Many museums, theaters, concert halls, and other establishments offer discounts for college and high school students with valid identification. Some restaurants near college campuses offer student discounts or other deals. Visiting students might want to check campus bulletin boards; many events are open to them. The weekly *Boston Phoenix* also lists activities for students.

STA Travel (℡ 800/781-4040; www. sta.com) is the biggest student travel agency in the world. For student discount cards, **Travel CUTS** (℡ 800/667-2887 or 416/614-2887; www.travelcuts.com) caters to both Canadian and U.S. students. Irish students should turn to **USIT** (℡ 01/602-1600; www.usitnow.ie), an Ireland-based specialist in student, youth, and independent travel.

7 Planning Your Trip Online

SURFING FOR AIRFARES

The "big three" online travel agencies, **Expedia.com, Travelocity,** and **Orbitz,** sell most of the air tickets bought on the Internet. (Canadian travelers should try Expedia.ca and Travelocity.ca; U.K. residents can go to Expedia.co.uk and Opodo.co.uk.) Each has different deals with the airlines and may offer different fares on the same flights, so it's wise to shop around. Expedia and Travelocity will also send you **e-mail notification** when a cheap fare becomes available to your favorite destination. Of the smaller travel agency websites, **SideStep** (www.sidestep.com) gets the best reviews from Frommer's authors. It's a browser add-on that purports to "search 140 sites at once," but in reality it beats competitors' fares only as often as other sites do.

Also remember to check **airline websites,** especially those for low-fare carriers such as Southwest, JetBlue, AirTran, WestJet, and Ryanair, whose fares travel agency websites often misreport or simply omit. Even with major airlines, you can often shave a few bucks from a fare by booking directly through the airline and avoiding a travel agency's transaction fee. But you'll get these discounts only by **booking online.** Most airlines offer online-only fares that even their phone agents know nothing about. For the websites of airlines that fly to and from Boston, see "Getting There," on p. 26.

Great **last-minute deals** are available through free weekly e-mail services provided directly by the airlines. Most of these are announced on Tuesday or Wednesday and must be purchased online. Most are only valid for travel that weekend, but some (such as Southwest's) can be booked weeks or months in advance. Sign up for weekly e-mail alerts at airline websites or check mega-sites that compile comprehensive lists of last-minute specials, such as **Smarter Travel.com.** For last-minute trips, **Site59.com** and **lastminutetravel.com** in the U.S. and **lastminute.com** in Europe often have better air-and-hotel package deals than the major-label sites. A website listing numerous bargain sites and airlines around the world is **www.itravelnet.com**.

If you're willing to give up some control over your flight details, use an **"opaque" fare service** like **Priceline** (www.priceline.com; www.priceline.co. uk for Europeans) or its smaller competitor **Hotwire** (www.hotwire.com). Both offer rock-bottom prices in exchange for travel on a "mystery airline" at a mysterious time of day, often with a mysterious change of planes en route. The airlines are all major, well-known carriers—and the possibility of being sent from Philadelphia to Chicago via Tampa is remote; the airlines' routing computers have gotten a lot better than they used to be. But your chances of getting a 6am or 11pm flight are pretty high. Hotwire tells you flight prices before you buy; Priceline usually has better deals than Hotwire, but you have to play the "name your price" game. If you're new at this, the helpful folks at **BiddingForTravel** (www.biddingfor travel.com) do a good job of demystifying Priceline's prices and strategies. Priceline and Hotwire are great for flights within

Frommers.com: The Complete Travel Resource

For an excellent travel-planning resource, we highly recommend Frommers.com (www.frommers.com), voted Best Travel Site by *PC Magazine*. We're a little biased, of course, but we guarantee that you'll find the travel tips, reviews, monthly vacation giveaways, bookstore, and online-booking capabilities indispensable. Among the special features are our popular **Destinations** section, where you'll get expert travel tips, hotel and dining recommendations, and advice on the sights to see for more than 3,500 destinations around the globe; the **Frommers.com Newsletter,** with the latest deals, travel trends, and money-saving secrets; our **Community** area featuring **Message Boards,** where Frommer's readers post queries and share advice (sometimes our authors show up to answer questions); and our **Photo Center,** where you can post and share vacation tips. When your research is done, the **Online Reservations System** (www.frommers.com/book_a_trip) takes you to Frommer's preferred online partners for booking your vacation at affordable prices.

North America and between the U.S. and Europe. But for flights to other parts of the world, consolidators will almost always beat their fares. *Note:* In 2004 Priceline added non-opaque service to its roster. You now have the option to pick exact flights, times, and airlines from a list of offers—or opt to bid on opaque fares as before.

For much more about airfares and savvy air-travel tips and advice, pick up a copy of *Frommer's Fly Safe, Fly Smart* (Wiley Publishing, Inc.).

SURFING FOR HOTELS

Travelers generally shop online for hotels in one of two ways: by booking through the hotel's own website or through an independent booking agency (or a fare-service agency like Priceline; see below). These Internet hotel agencies have multiplied in mind-boggling numbers of late, competing for the business of millions of consumers surfing for accommodations around the world. This competitiveness can be a boon to consumers who have the patience and time to shop and compare the online sites for good deals—but shop they must, for

prices can vary considerably from site to site. And keep in mind that hotels at the top of a site's listing may be there for no other reason than that they paid money to get the placement.

Of the "big three" sites, **Expedia** offers a long list of special deals and "virtual tours" or photos of available rooms so you can see what you're paying for (a feature that helps counter the claims that the best rooms are often held back from bargain booking websites). **Travelocity** posts unvarnished customer reviews and ranks its properties according to the AAA rating system. Also reliable are **Hotels.com** and **Quikbook.com**. An excellent free program, **TravelAxe** (www.travelaxe.net), can help you search multiple hotel sites at once, even ones you may never have heard of—and conveniently lists the total price of the room, including taxes and service charges. Another booking site, **Travelweb** (www.travelweb.com), is partly owned by the hotels it represents (including the Hilton, Hyatt, and Starwood chains) and is therefore plugged directly into the hotels' reservations systems—unlike independent online agencies, which have to fax or e-mail the hotel their reservation requests, a good portion of which get misplaced in the shuffle. More than once, travelers have arrived at the hotel, only to be told that they have no reservation. To be fair, many of the major sites are undergoing improvements in service and ease of use, and Expedia will soon be able to plug directly into the reservations systems of many hotel chains—none of which can be bad news for consumers. In the meantime, it's a good idea to **get a confirmation number** and **make a printout** of any online booking transaction.

In the opaque website category, **Priceline** and **Hotwire** are even better for hotels than for airfares; with both, you're allowed to pick the neighborhood and quality level of your hotel before offering up your money. Priceline's hotel product even covers Europe and Asia, though it's much better at getting five-star lodging for three-star prices than at finding anything at the bottom of the scale. On the down side, many hotels stick Priceline guests in their least desirable rooms. Be sure to go to the BiddingforTravel website (see above) before bidding on a hotel room on Priceline; it features a fairly up-to-date list of hotels that Priceline uses in major cities. For both Priceline and Hotwire, you pay upfront, and the fee is nonrefundable. *Note:* Some hotels do not provide loyalty program credits or points or other frequent-stay amenities when you book a room through opaque online services.

SURFING FOR RENTAL CARS

For booking rental cars online, the best deals are usually on rental-car company websites, although all the major online travel agencies also offer rental-car reservations services. Priceline and Hotwire work well for rental cars, too; the only "mystery" is which major rental company you get, and for most travelers the difference between Hertz, Avis, and Budget is negligible.

8 The 21st-Century Traveler

INTERNET ACCESS AWAY FROM HOME

Travelers have any number of ways to check their e-mail and surf the Internet on the road. Of course, using your own laptop—or a PDA or electronic organizer with a modem—gives you the most flexibility. But even if you don't have a computer, you can still gain access to your e-mail and even your office computer from the road.

WITHOUT YOUR OWN COMPUTER

It's hard nowadays to find a city that *doesn't* have a few cybercafes. Although there's no definitive directory, two places to start looking are at **www.cybercaptive. com** and **www.cybercafe.com**.

Boston is a wired city that, paradoxically, doesn't have many cybercafes. Your best bet if you're away from your hotel and just want to check e-mail is probably FedEx Kinko's (for locations, see "Internet Access" under "Fast Facts: Boston," p. 72). One business that offers access by the hour is **Tech Superpowers,** 252 Newbury Street, 3rd floor (© **617/ 267-9716;** www.newburyopen.net). In the same neighborhood, known as "upper Newbury Street," many businesses offer free wireless access.

Aside from formal cybercafes, most **public libraries** across the world offer Internet access free or for a small charge. The **Boston Public Library** (www.bpl. org) offers free computer access at all of its branches. **Hotels** that cater to business travelers usually have **in-room dataports** and **business centers,** but the charges can be exorbitant. Also, most **youth hostels** have at least one computer with Internet access.

Most major airports have **Internet kiosks** scattered throughout their gates. These kiosks, which you'll also see in shopping malls, hotel lobbies, and tourist information offices around the world, give you basic Web access for a per-minute fee that's usually higher than cybercafe prices. The kiosks' clunkiness and high price mean they should be avoided whenever possible.

To retrieve your e-mail, ask your Internet Service Provider (ISP) if it has a **Web-based interface** tied to your existing e-mail account. If your ISP doesn't have such an interface, you can use the free **Mail2web** service (www.mail2web.com) to view and reply to your home e-mail. For more flexibility, you may want to open a free Web-based e-mail account with **Yahoo! Mail** (http://mail.yahoo.com) or Microsoft's **Hotmail** (www.hotmail.com). Your home ISP may be able to forward your e-mail to the Web-based account automatically.

If you need to view files on your office computer, look into a service called **GoToMyPC** (www.gotomypc.com). The service provides a Web-based interface for you to manipulate a distant PC from anywhere—even a cybercafe—provided your "target" PC is on and has an always-on Internet connection. The service offers top-quality security, but if you're worried about hackers, use your own laptop rather than a cybercafe when tapping into this system.

WITH YOUR OWN COMPUTER

Wi-Fi (wireless fidelity) is the buzzword in computer access, and more and more hotels, cafes, and retailers are signing on as wireless "hotspots" where you can get a high-speed connection without cable wires, networking hardware, or a phone line (see below). You can get Wi-Fi connection one of several ways. Many laptops sold recently have built-in Wi-Fi capability (an 802.11b wireless Ethernet connection). Mac owners have their own networking technology, Apple AirPort. For those with older computers, an 802.11b/**Wi-Fi card** (around $50) can be plugged into your laptop. You sign up for wireless access service much as you do cellphone service, through a plan offered by one of several commercial companies that have made wireless service available in airports, hotel lobbies, and coffee shops, primarily in the U.S. (followed by the U.K. and Japan). **T-Mobile Hotspot** (www.t-mobile.com/hotspot) serves up wireless connections at more than 1,000 Starbucks coffee shops nationwide. **Boingo** (www.boingo.com) and **Wayport** (www.wayport.com) have set up networks in airports and high-class hotel lobbies. IPass providers (see below) also give you access to a few hundred wireless hotel lobby setups. Best of all, you don't need to be staying at the Four Seasons to use the hotel's network; just set yourself up on a nice couch in the lobby. The companies' pricing policies can be Byzantine, with a variety of monthly, per-connection, and per-minute plans, but in general you pay around $30 a month for limited access—and as more and more companies jump on the wireless bandwagon, prices are likely to get even more competitive.

There are places that provide **free wireless networks** in cities around the world. To locate these free hotspots, go to www.personaltelco.net/index.cgi/WirelessCommunities.

In addition, major Internet Service Providers (ISPs) have **local access numbers** around the world, allowing you to go online by simply placing a local call. Check your ISP's website or call its toll-free number and ask how you can use your current account away from home and how much it will cost.

Online Traveler's Toolbox

Veteran travelers usually carry some essential items to make their trips easier. Before I share a few of my favorite websites, here's a crucial piece of advice: Double-check information that you find on websites. If you find a description of an intriguing establishment or event, a quick phone call to ensure that the information is up-to-date can save you a lot of trouble. Following is a selection of online tools to bookmark and use:

- **Airplane Seating and Food:** Find out which seats to reserve and which to avoid (and more) on all major domestic airlines at www.seatguru.com. And check out the type of meal (with photos) you'll likely be served on airlines around the world at www.airlinemeals.com.

- **Boston.com** (www.boston.com): The *Boston Globe* operates this site, one of the most comprehensive in the region. Besides newspaper content, it offers access to a virtual forest of listings and links. The most helpful area for out-of-towners, the arts and entertainment section (www.boston.com/ae), covers dining, movies, music, and the arts.

- **Boston Online** (www.boston-online.com/glossary.html): This highly entertaining Boston-to-English dictionary both mocks and celebrates local accents.

- **Citysearch** (http://boston.citysearch.com): This site has events and nightlife listings, plus traveler-friendly info on the arts, shopping, and dining, with a significant interactive component. Before you jump at the featured entertainment options, remember that Citysearch is part of Ticketmaster.

- **Mapquest** (www.mapquest.com) and **Yahoo! Maps** (http://maps.yahoo.com): These mapping sites let you choose a specific address or destination, and in seconds they return a map and detailed directions. If you're driving in downtown Boston, check both sites *and* ask at your hotel before setting out; the changing street configuration around what's left of the Big Dig occasionally baffles even the best-maintained sites.

- **Massachusetts Bay Transportation Authority** (www.mbta.com): Look here for schedules and route maps for T subways, trolleys, buses, ferries, and commuter trains. You can also buy visitor passes online (subject to a service charge).

- **National Park Service** (www.nps.gov): This invaluable site, packed with information about hundreds of places, is especially useful in a history-rich area like eastern Massachusetts. Click on the state for site listings, which incorporate directions and loads of photos.

- **Visa ATM Locator** (www.visa.com) and **MasterCard ATM Locator** (www.mastercard.com): These sites list locations of PLUS ATMs and Cirrus ATMs worldwide, respectively.

If you're traveling outside the reach of your ISP, the **iPass** network has dial-up numbers in most of the world's countries. You'll have to sign up with an iPass provider, who will then tell you how to set up your computer for your destination(s). For a list of iPass providers, go to www.ipass.com and click on "Individual Purchase." One solid provider is **i2roam** (© **866/811-6209** or 920/235-0475; www.i2roam.com).

Wherever you go, bring a **connection kit** of the right power and phone adapters, a spare phone cord, and a spare Ethernet network cable—or find out whether your hotel supplies them to guests.

USING A CELLPHONE
ACROSS THE U.S.

Just because your cellphone works at home doesn't mean it'll work elsewhere in the country. It's a good bet that your phone will work in major cities, but check your wireless company's coverage map on its website before heading out. T-Mobile, Sprint, and Nextel are particularly weak in rural areas. If you need to stay in touch at a destination where you know your phone won't work, **rent** a phone that does from **InTouch USA** (© **800/872-7626;** www.intouchglobal. com) or a rental-car location, but be aware that you'll pay $1 a minute or more for airtime.

If you're not from the U.S., you'll be appalled at the poor reach of our **GSM (Global System for Mobiles) wireless network.** Your phone will probably work in most major U.S. cities; it definitely won't work in many rural areas. (To see where GSM phones work in the U.S., check out www.t-mobile.com/coverage/national_popup.asp). And you may or may not be able to send SMS (text messaging) home. Assume nothing—call your wireless provider and get the full scoop. In a worst-case scenario, you can always rent a phone; InTouch USA delivers to hotels.

9 Getting There

BY PLANE

The major domestic carriers that serve Boston's **Logan International Airport** (usually just called "Logan"; airport code BOS) are **AirTran** (© 800/247-8726; www.airtran.com), **American** (© 800/433-7300; www.aa.com), **America West** (© 800/235-9292; www.americawest. com), **ATA** (© 800/225-2995; www. ata.com), **Continental** (© 800/525-0280; www.continental.com), **Delta** (© 800/221-1212; www.delta.com), **JetBlue** (© 800/538-2583; www.jetblue.com), **Midwest** (© 800/452-2022; www. midwestexpress.com), **Northwest** (© 800/225-2525; www.nwa.com), **United** (© 800/241-6522; www.ual.com), and **US Airways** (© 800/428-4322; www. usairways.com). Many international carriers also fly into Boston; see chapter 3.

Logan is in East Boston at the end of the Sumner, Callahan, and Ted Williams tunnels, 3 miles across the harbor from downtown. For a preview and real-time flight arrival and departure information, visit the website (www.massport.com/logan).

At press time, Logan's new Terminal A was nearing completion after several years of construction. Its opening, scheduled for mid-2005, returned the facility to its full complement of five terminals. Each terminal has ATMs, Internet kiosks, pay phones with dataports, fax machines, and an information booth (near baggage claim). Wireless Internet access is available all over the airport for $8 a day through **Logan WiFi** (© **617/561-9434;** www.logan wifi.com). Terminals C and E have bank branches that handle currency exchange. Terminal C has a children's play space, and

Boston & Surrounding Areas

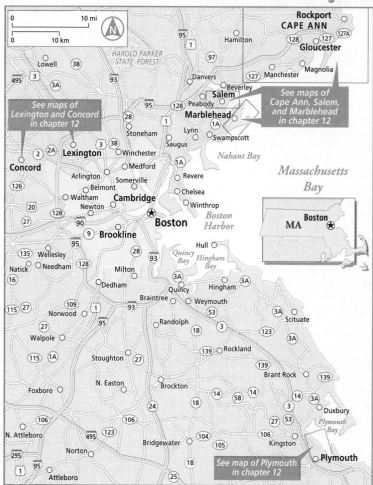

its information booth is a visitor service center where staff members have gone through concierge training and can help make hotel and restaurant reservations, plan tours, provide convention information, and buy theater and sports tickets.

See the "Let's Make a Deal" box below, for information on flying into Providence, Rhode Island, and Manchester, New Hampshire.

GETTING INTO TOWN FROM THE AIRPORT

The Massachusetts Port Authority, or **MassPort** (© **800/23-LOGAN;** www. massport.com), coordinates airport transportation. The toll-free line provides information about getting to the city and to many nearby suburbs. It's available 24 hours a day and is staffed weekdays from 8am to 7pm.

Tips Let's Make a Deal

The domestic discount airline **Southwest** (© 800/435-9792; www.southwest. com) doesn't serve Boston. But by redefining "Boston-area airport," it has helped create two magnets for budget-conscious travelers. They're not nearly as convenient as Logan (bus service into Boston can be slow), but fares to either of these airports—on Southwest and other national carriers—can be considerably cheaper than those to Logan.

T. F. Green Airport (© 888/268-7222; www.pvdairport.com; airport code PVD) is in the Providence suburb of Warwick, Rhode Island, about 60 miles south of Boston. **Bonanza** (© 888/751-8800; www.bonanzabus.com) offers bus service between the airport and Boston's South Station seven times a day; the fare is $20 one-way, $36 round-trip. Allow at least 90 minutes.

Manchester International Airport (© 603/624-6556; www.flymanchester. com; airport code MHT) is in southern New Hampshire, about 56 miles north of Boston. **Vermont Transit** (© 800/552-8737; www.vermonttransit.com) runs buses to Boston's South Station eight times a day; three continue to Logan Airport. The trip takes 60 to 90 minutes and costs $15 one-way, $25 round-trip.

The ride into town takes 10 to 45 minutes, depending on traffic, your destination, and the time of day. Except at off hours, such as early on weekend mornings, driving is the slowest way to get into central Boston. If you must travel during rush hours or on Sunday afternoon, allow plenty of extra time or plan to take the subway or water taxi (and pack accordingly).

You can get into town by subway (the T), cab, van, or boat. The **subway** is fast and cheap—Government Center is just 10 minutes away, and the fare is $1.25. Free **shuttle buses** run from each terminal to the Airport station on the Blue Line of the T from 5:30am to 1am every day, year-round. The Blue Line stops at Aquarium, State Street, and Government Center, downtown points where you can exit or transfer to the other lines.

Just getting into a **cab** at the airport costs $8.25 ($6.50 in fees plus the initial $1.75 fare). The total fare to downtown or the Back Bay runs $20 to $30. Depending on traffic, the driver might use the Ted Williams Tunnel for destinations outside downtown, such as the Back Bay. On a map, this doesn't look like the fastest route, but often it is. You can also try the **Share-A-Cab booths** at each terminal and save up to half the fare.

The Logan Airport website (www. massport.com/logan) lists numerous companies that operate **shuttle-van service** to local hotels. One-way prices start at $11 per person.

The trip to the downtown waterfront in a weather-protected **boat** takes about 7 minutes and costs $10 one-way. The free no. 66 shuttle bus connects the airport terminals to the Logan ferry dock. A commuter ferry and two on-call water-taxi services serve downtown (though the dedicated water shuttle is defunct). The ferry company, **Harbor Express** (© 617/222-6999; www.harborexpress.com), runs to Long Wharf behind the Marriott Long Wharf hotel. It operates every 20 minutes on weekdays from 7am to 8pm (Fri until 11pm), and every 30 minutes from 10am to 6pm on weekends. Hours are shorter in the winter.

The **City Water Taxi** (© 617/422-0392; www.citywatertaxi.com) connects about a dozen stops on the harbor, including the airport ferry dock. The **Rowes Wharf Water Taxi** (© 617/406-8584; www.roweswharfwatertaxi.com) serves Rowes Wharf, off Atlantic Avenue behind the Boston Harbor Hotel. Months and days of operation for water taxis are subject to change; at press time, only the Rowes Wharf taxi operates year-round. Call ahead from the dock for water taxi pickup.

Some hotels have their own **shuttles** or **limousines;** ask about them when you make your reservation. To arrange private limo service, call ahead for a reservation, especially at busy times. Your hotel can recommend a company, or try **Carey Limousine Boston** (© **800/336-4646** or 617/623-8700), **Commonwealth Limousine Service** (© **800/558-LIMO** or 617/787-1110), or **Dav-El of Boston** (© **800/343-2071** or 617/884-2600).

Unless you need it right away, seriously consider waiting to pick up your **rental car** until you're starting a day trip or other excursion. You'll avoid airport fees, tunnel tolls, hotel parking charges, and, most important, Boston traffic.

GETTING THROUGH THE AIRPORT

With the federalization of airport security, security procedures at U.S. airports are more stable and consistent than ever. Generally, you'll be fine if you arrive at the airport **1 hour** before a domestic flight and **2 hours** before an international flight; if you show up late, tell an airline employee and she'll probably whisk you to the front of the line.

Bring a **current, government-issued photo ID** such as a driver's license or passport. Keep your ID ready to show at check-in, the security checkpoint, and sometimes even the gate. (Children under 18 do not need government-issued photo IDs for domestic flights, but they do for international flights to most countries.)

The Transportation Security Administration (TSA) has phased out **gate check-in** at all U.S. airports. And **e-tickets** have made paper tickets nearly obsolete. A passenger with an e-ticket can beat the ticket-counter lines by using an airport **electronic kiosk** or even **online check-in** from his or her home computer. Online check-in involves logging on to the airline's website, viewing your reservation, and printing out your boarding pass—and the airline may even offer you bonus miles to do so! If you're using a kiosk at the airport, bring the credit card you used to book the ticket or your frequent-flier card. Print out your boarding pass from the kiosk and simply proceed to the security checkpoint with your pass and a photo ID. If you're checking bags or looking to snag an exit-row seat, you will be able to do so using most airline kiosks. Even the smaller airlines are employing the kiosk system, but always call your airline to make sure these alternatives are available. **Curbside check-in** is also a good way to avoid lines, although a few airlines still ban curbside check-in; call before you go.

Security checkpoint lines are getting shorter, but some doozies remain. If you have trouble standing for long periods, tell an airline employee; the airline will provide a wheelchair. Speed up security by **not wearing metal objects** such as big belt buckles. If you have metallic body parts, a note from your doctor can prevent a long chat with the security screeners. Keep in mind that only **ticketed passengers** are allowed past security, except for folks escorting disabled passengers or children.

Federalization has stabilized **what you can carry on** and **what you can't.** The general rule is that sharp things are out, nail clippers are okay, and food and beverages must be passed through the X-ray

Travel in the Age of Bankruptcy

Airlines go bankrupt, so protect yourself by **buying your tickets with a credit card.** The Fair Credit Billing Act guarantees that you can get your money back from the credit card company if a travel supplier goes under (and if you request the refund within 60 days of the bankruptcy). **Travel insurance** can also help, but make sure it covers "carrier default" for your specific travel provider. And be aware that if a U.S. airline goes bust midtrip, a 2001 federal law requires other carriers to take you to your destination (albeit on a space-available basis) for a fee of no more than $25, provided you rebook within 60 days of the cancellation.

machine—but that security screeners can't make you drink from your coffee cup. Bring food in your carry-on rather than checking it because explosive-detection machines used on checked luggage have been known to mistake food (especially chocolate, for some reason) for bombs. Travelers in the U.S. are allowed one carry-on bag, plus a "personal item" such as a purse, briefcase, or laptop bag. Carry-on hoarders can stuff all sorts of things into a laptop bag; as long as it has a laptop in it, it's still considered a personal item. The TSA has issued a list of restricted items; check its website (www.tsa.gov) for details.

Airport screeners may decide that your checked luggage needs to be searched by hand. You can now purchase luggage locks that allow screeners to open and re-lock a checked bag if hand-searching is necessary. Look for Travel Sentry certified locks at luggage or travel shops and Brookstone stores (you can buy them online at www.brookstone.com). Luggage inspectors can open these TSA-approved locks with a special code or key. For more information on the locks, visit www.travel sentry.org. If you use something other than TSA-approved locks, your lock will be cut off your suitcase if a TSA agent needs to hand-search your luggage.

FLYING FOR LESS: TIPS FOR GETTING THE BEST AIRFARE

Passengers sharing the same airplane cabin rarely pay the same fare. If you purchase tickets at the last minute, change

your itinerary at a moment's notice, or fly one-way, you'll likely get stuck paying the premium rate. Here are some ways to keep your airfare costs down:

- You may pay a fraction of the full fare if you book your ticket **far in advance,** can **stay over Saturday night,** or **fly midweek** or **at less busy hours.** If your schedule is flexible, say so, and ask if you can secure a cheaper fare by changing your flight plans.
- Keep an eye out in local newspapers for **promotional specials** or **fare wars,** when airlines lower prices on their most popular routes. You rarely see fare wars during peak travel times, but if you can travel in the off season, you may snag a bargain.
- Search the **Internet** for cheap fares (see "Planning Your Trip Online," earlier in this chapter).
- **Consolidators,** also known as bucket shops, are great sources for international tickets, although they usually can't beat the Internet on fares within North America. Start by looking in Sunday newspaper travel sections; U.S. travelers should focus on the *New York Times, Los Angeles Times,* and *Miami Herald.* **Beware:** Bucket shop tickets usually are nonrefundable or carry stiff cancellation penalties, often as high as 50% to 75% of the ticket price, and some put you on charter airlines, which may leave at inconvenient times and experience

delays. Several reliable consolidators are worldwide and available on the Net. **STA Travel** (© 800/781-4040; www.sta.com), the world leader in student travel, also offers good fares for travelers of all ages. **Air Tickets Direct** (© 800/778-3447; www.airticketsdirect.com) is based in Montreal and leverages the Canadian dollar for low fares; it'll also book trips to places that U.S. travel agents won't touch, such as Cuba.

• **Join frequent-flier clubs.** Accrue enough miles and you'll be rewarded with free flights and elite status. It's free, and you'll get the best choice of seats, faster response to phone inquiries, and prompter service if your luggage is stolen, your flight is canceled or delayed, or you want to change your seat. You don't need to fly to build frequent-flier miles—**frequent-flier credit cards** can provide thousands of miles for doing your everyday shopping.

• For many more tips about air travel, including a rundown of the major frequent-flier credit cards, pick up a copy of *Frommer's Fly Safe, Fly Smart* (Wiley Publishing, Inc.).

BY CAR

Driving to Boston is not difficult. (Driving *in* Boston is another story.) But parking is expensive and scarce, and downtown traffic is terrible. The **Big Dig** highway construction project is virtually complete, but widespread construction persists downtown. If you're thinking of driving to Boston only because you want to use the car to get around town, think again.

Note: The Pike's **FastLane** program is compatible with New York's EZPass; your regular transponder will work in designated lanes. If you have a prepaid device from another highway system, check before you leave home to see whether you too can zip (at the speed limit, 15 mph) through the special lanes.

If you have to drive, try to book a hotel or a special package that offers free parking (see chapter 6 for information). If you pay for parking, expect it to cost at least $25 a day downtown and build that into your budget.

Three major highways converge in Boston. **I-90,** also known as the Massachusetts Turnpike ("Mass. Pike," to the locals), is an east-west toll road that originates at Logan Airport and links up with the New York State Thruway. **I-93/U.S. 1** extends north to Canada. **I-93/Route 3,** the Southeast Expressway, connects Boston with the south, including Cape Cod. To avoid driving downtown, exit the Mass. Pike at Cambridge/Allston or at the Prudential Center in the Back Bay. **I-95** (Massachusetts Rte. 128) is a beltway about 11 miles from downtown that connects Boston to highways in Rhode Island, Connecticut, and New York to the south, and New Hampshire and Maine to the north.

The approach to Cambridge is **Storrow Drive** or **Memorial Drive,** which run along either side of the Charles River. Storrow Drive has a Harvard Square exit that leads across the Anderson Bridge to John F. Kennedy Street and into the square. Memorial Drive intersects with Kennedy Street; turn away from the bridge to reach the square.

Boston is 218 miles from New York City; driving time is about 4½ hours. The 992-mile drive from Chicago to Boston should take around 21 hours; from Washington, D.C., it takes 8 to 9 hours to cover the 468 miles.

In an emergency, you can call the **State Police** on a cellphone by dialing © *77. The **American Automobile Association** (© 800/AAA-HELP; www.aaa.com) provides members with maps, itineraries, and other travel information, and arranges free towing if you break down. At press time, the Mass. Pike was a privately operated road that arranged its own towing, but the state highway department may be taking over. If you break down there, ask the AAA operator for advice.

It's impossible to say this often enough: **When you reach your hotel, leave your car in the garage** and walk or use public transportation. Use the car for day trips, and before you set out, ask at the front desk for a route that avoids the construction area.

See p. 69 for information on renting a car in Boston.

BY TRAIN

Boston has three rail centers: **South Station,** on Atlantic Avenue at Summer Street, near the Waterfront and the Financial District; **Back Bay Station,** on Dartmouth Street between Huntington and Columbus avenues, across from the Copley Place mall; and **North Station,** on Causeway Street near the TD Banknorth Garden. **Amtrak** (© **800/USA-RAIL** or 617/482-3660; www.amtrak.com) serves all train stations, which are also linked to the MBTA **subway.** At South Station you can take the Red Line to Cambridge or to Park Street, the system's hub, where you can make connections to the Green, Blue, and Orange lines. The Orange Line connects Back Bay Station with Downtown Crossing, where there's a walkway to Park Street station and other points. North Station is a Green and Orange Line stop.

Amtrak runs to South Station from New York and points south and in between, with stops at Route 128 and Back Bay Station. Its Downeaster service (www.thedowneaster.com) connects North Station to Portland, Maine, with several stops en route. The MBTA **commuter rail** runs to Ipswich, Rockport, and Fitchburg from North Station; it also runs to points south of Boston, including Plymouth, from South Station.

Bear in mind that the train might not be cheaper than flying, especially for long

trips. As with airline ticket prices, train fares are subject to change and can fluctuate depending on the time of year, so plan as far ahead as possible to get the lowest fares. Discounts are never available Friday or Sunday afternoon. Always remember to ask for the discounted rate.

Standard service from New York takes from 4½ hours to just under 6 hours; round-trip fares at press time were $108 to $164. From Washington, D.C., count on 7½ to 8½ hours and a round-trip fare of at least $164.

High-speed **Acela Express** trains run as fast as 150 mph and are scheduled to cover the 218 miles between Boston and New York in just over 3 hours, though they often take longer. At press time, the price (from $99 one-way) was less than two-thirds of the walk-up plane fare. The trip time between Washington, D.C., and Boston is just under 6 hours, and the one-way fare is about $170. Call Amtrak or check the website for exact fares, schedules, and reservations.

BY BUS

The bus is the only way out of many small New England towns. If you're coming from almost anywhere else, consider long-distance bus travel a last resort. The exception is the **New York** route, which is so desirable that Greyhound and Peter Pan have upgraded service. It's frequent and relatively fast (4–4½ hr.), and the price is about half the regular train fare. If you can catch an express bus, which makes only one stop, it's worth the extra $5 or so.

The bus terminal, formally the **South Station Transportation Center,** is on Atlantic Avenue next to the train station. It's served by the following bus lines: **Greyhound** (© 800/231-2222 or 617/526-1800; www.greyhound.com), **American Eagle** (© 800/453-5040 or 508/993-5040), **Bonanza** (© 888/751-8800 or 617/720-4110; www.bonanza

---

Tips High- and Low-End New York Bus Options

Many travelers find standard interstate bus service inadequate; for others, it's too swanky. Both have options on the New York–Boston route.

Business-oriented **LimoLiner** (© **888/546-5469**; www.limoliner.com) service connects the Back Bay Hilton, 40 Dalton Street, to the Hilton New York, 1335 Ave. of the Americas (with an on-request stop in Framingham, Mass.). The luxury coach seats 28 and has Internet access, work tables, leather seats, and an on-board attendant. The one-way fare is $69.

At the other end of the spectrum, a number of companies run between Boston's Chinatown and New York's Chinatown. I've heard too many anecdotal accounts of unsatisfactory service to give this option an unqualified recommendation, but it's madly popular with students and other bargain-hunters. The one-way fare is about $15. The largest operator is **Fung Wah** (© **212/ 925-8889**; www.fungwahbus.com), which shuttles between Boston's South Station and Canal Street in Manhattan.

---

bus.com), **Brush Hill Tours** (© 800/ 343-1328 or 781/986-6100; fax 781/ 986-0167; www.brushhilltours.com), **Concord Trailways** (© 800/639-3317 or 617/426-8080; www.concordtrailways. com), **Peter Pan** (© 800/343-9999; www.peterpanbus.com), **Plymouth & Brockton** (© 617/773-9401 or 508/ 746-0378; www.p-b.com), and **Vermont Transit** (© 800/552-8737; www.vermont transit.com).

10 Packages for the Independent Traveler

Before you start your search for the lowest airfare, you may want to consider booking your flight as part of a travel package. Package tours are not the same thing as escorted tours. Package tours are simply a way to buy the airfare, accommodations, and other elements of your trip (such as car rentals, airport transfers, and sometimes even activities) at the same time and often at discounted prices—kind of like one-stop shopping. Tour operators buy packages in bulk and resell them to the public at a cost that usually undercuts standard rates.

One good source of package deals is the airlines themselves. Several major airlines offer air-land packages to Boston, including **American Airlines Vacations** (© 800/321-2121; www.aa.com), **Delta Vacations** (© 800/221-6666; www. deltavacations.com), **Midwest Airlines**

Vacations (© 800/444-4479; www. midwestairlinesvacations.com), **United Vacations** (© 888/854-3899; www. unitedvacations.com), and **US Airways Vacations** (© 800/422-3861; www.us airwaysvacations.com). Several big **online travel agencies**—Expedia.com, Travelocity, Orbitz, Site59, and Lastminute.com— also do a brisk business in packages. If you're unsure about the pedigree of a smaller packager, check with the Better Business Bureau in the city where the company is based or visit www.bbb.org. If a packager won't tell you where it's based, don't fly with it.

Trolley tour companies (see "Organized Tours," in chapter 8) play a prominent role in Boston tourism. The sightseeing portion of a package is often a free or discounted 1-day trolley tour.

Brush Hill Tours (© 800/343-1328 or 781/986-6100; fax 781/986-0167; www.brushhilltours.com) is Gray Line's New England incarnation. Its 3-night "Boston City Package" includes lodging, airport or train station transfers, and a tour on Beantown Trolley (which it owns). Prices start at about $300 per person, based on double occupancy. Brush Hill also offers a variety of half- and full-day escorted tours to destinations such as Plymouth, Salem, Cape Cod, and Newport, Rhode Island.

Another possibility is *Yankee* **Magazine Vacations** (© 877/481-5986; www.yankeevacations.com). The basic 3-night package includes a 1-day tour; prices start at about $200 per person and climb as you add optional side trips from the company's huge selection.

One often-overlooked option, if you live close enough to take advantage of it, is **Amtrak Vacations** (© 800/805-9114; www.amtrakvacations.com). Prices are competitive and can undercut air-land packages from many destinations. The train definitely isn't for everyone, though. Sleepers are available on long routes, but if you're paying extra for a berth, an air package might be cheaper and certainly will take less time.

Travel packages are listed in the travel section of your local Sunday newspaper. Or check ads in the national travel magazines such as *Arthur Frommer's Budget Travel Magazine*, *Travel & Leisure*, *National Geographic Traveler*, and *Condé Nast Traveler*.

Package tours can vary enormously. Some offer a better class of hotels than others. Some offer the same hotels for lower prices. Some offer flights on scheduled airlines, while others book charters. Some limit your choice of accommodations and travel days. You are often required to make a large payment up front. On the plus side, packages can save you money, offering group prices but allowing for independent travel. Some even let you add guided excursions or escorted day trips (also at prices lower than if you booked them yourself) without booking an entire escorted tour. Always shop around before booking a package—almost nothing in the travel business surprises me anymore, but the range of prices for virtually identical offerings is amazing.

Before you invest in a package tour, get some answers. Ask about the **accommodations choices** and prices for each. Then look up hotel reviews in a Frommer's guide and check their rates online for your specific dates of travel.

Finally, look for **hidden expenses.** Ask whether the total cost includes airport departure fees and taxes, for example.

11 Escorted General-Interest Tours

Escorted tours are structured group tours, with a group leader. The price usually includes everything: airfare, hotels, meals, tours, admission costs, and local transportation.

Hundreds of companies offer tours that stop in Boston, especially during foliage season, when 5- to 10-day tours of New England are wildly popular. Few spend more than 2 days in Boston, however, meaning that you'll be rushing around trying to cram maximum action into minimum time or skipping sights and activities you were looking forward to. If you plan to focus on Boston, you'll almost always be better off with a package tour (see the previous section).

If a quick stop is all you can manage, most major tour operators can accommodate you. They include **Liberty Travel** (© 888/271-1584; www.libertytravel. com), **Collette Vacations** (© 800/ 340-5158; www.collettevacations.com), **Globus and Cosmos** (© 800/851-0728;

www.globusandcosmos.com), **Maupin-tour** (℡ 800/255-4266; www.maupintour.com), and **Tauck World Discovery** (℡ 800/788-7885; www.tauck.com).

Many people derive a certain ease and security from escorted trips. Escorted tours let travelers sit back and enjoy their trip without having to spend lots of time behind the wheel or worrying about details. You know your costs up front, and there are few surprises. Escorted tours can take you to the maximum number of sights in the minimum amount of time with the least amount of hassle—you don't have to sweat over the plotting and planning of a vacation schedule. Escorted tours are particularly convenient for people with limited mobility. They can also be a great way to make new friends.

On the downside, an escorted tour often requires a big deposit up front, and lodging and dining choices are predetermined. You'll get little opportunity for serendipitous interactions with locals. The tours can be jam-packed with activities, leaving little room for individual sightseeing, whim, or adventure—and they often focus only on very touristy sites, so you miss out on the lesser-known gems.

Before you invest in an escorted tour, ask about the **cancellation policy:** Is a deposit required? Can the company cancel the trip if it doesn't get enough people? Do you get a refund if it cancels? If *you* cancel? How late can you cancel if you are unable to go? When do you pay in full? *Note:* If you choose an escorted tour, think strongly about purchasing trip-cancellation insurance, especially if the tour operator asks you to pay up front. See the section on "Travel Insurance," p. 15.

You'll also want to get a complete **schedule** of the trip to find out how much sightseeing is planned each day and whether the company allows enough time for relaxing or wandering solo.

The **size** of the group is also important to know up front. Generally, the smaller the group, the more flexible the itinerary and the less time you'll spend waiting for people to get on and off the bus. Find out the **demographics** of the group as well. What is the age range? What is the gender breakdown? Is this mostly a trip for couples or singles?

Discuss what the **price** includes. You may have to pay for transportation to and from the airport. A box lunch may be included in an excursion, but drinks might cost extra. Tips may not be included. Find out if you will be charged if you decide to opt out of certain activities or meals.

Ask about the **accommodations choices** and prices. Then look up hotel reviews in a Frommer's guide and check rates online for your specific dates of travel. You'll also want to find out what **type of room** you get. If you need a certain type of room, ask for it; don't take whatever is thrown your way. Request a nonsmoking room, a quiet room, a room with a view, or whatever you fancy.

Finally, if you plan to travel alone, you'll need to know if the company charges a **single supplement** and if it can match you up with a roommate.

12 Recommended Books & Films

A list of authors with ties to Boston could fill a book of its own and only scratch the surface. To get in the mood for Boston before visiting, let the impulse that inspired you to make the trip guide you around the bookstore or library. Here are some suggestions:

For children, *Make Way for Ducklings,* by Robert McCloskey, is a classic that tells the story of Mrs. Mallard and her babies on the loose in the Back Bay. Once your kids love this book (and they will), you can thrill them with a trip to the Public Garden, where bronze statues of the family occupy a place of honor.

Slightly older kids might know the Public Garden as the setting of part of *The Trumpet of the Swan,* by E. B. White. After reading it, a turn around the lagoon on a Swan Boat is mandatory.

An excellent historical title is *Johnny Tremain,* by Esther Forbes, a fictional boy's-eye-view account of the Revolutionary War era. The book vividly describes scenes from the American Revolution, many of which take place along the Freedom Trail.

For adults, two splendid Pulitzer Prize winners chronicle the city's history. *Paul Revere and the World He Lived In* is Forbes's look at Boston before, during, and after the Revolution. *Common Ground: A Turbulent Decade in the Lives of Three American Families,* by J. Anthony Lukas, is the definitive account of the busing crisis of the 1970s.

Architecture buffs will enjoy *Cityscapes of Boston,* by Robert Campbell and Peter Vanderwarker; *Lost Boston,* by Jane Holtz Kay; and *A.I.A. Guide to Boston,* by Susan and Michael Southworth.

The Proper Bostonians, by Cleveland Amory, and *The Friends of Eddie Coyle,* by George V. Higgins, offer looks at wildly different strata of Boston society.

"Paul Revere's Ride," Henry Wadsworth Longfellow's classic but historically inaccurate poem about the events of April 18 and 19, 1775, is collected in many anthologies. It's a must if you plan to walk the Freedom Trail or visit Lexington and Concord.

If you're venturing to Gloucester (or even if you're not), Sebastian Junger's *The Perfect Storm* makes an excellent introduction. It tells the story of a fishing boat caught in historically bad weather—and will change the way you look at fish on a menu for a long time after you finish reading—or watching. The movie version, though heavy on the special effects, was a better-than-average effort.

Television has done more than any movie to make Boston familiar to international audiences, but film is gaining fast. The Boston area is hardly Hollywood, but don't be surprised to stumble upon a crew or hear about a location shoot.

If you have time to see only one movie before your trip, make it *Good Will Hunting.* It makes Boston and Cambridge look sensational, perceptively explores the town-gown divide, and (Robin Williams's brogue notwithstanding) pulls off the nearly impossible feat of rendering local accents accurately. Coauthors and costars Ben Affleck and Matt Damon are boyhood friends from Cambridge, and Damon is a couple of semesters short of his Harvard degree.

Truth *is* stranger than fiction: The producers of *Fever Pitch,* with Jimmy Fallon and Drew Barrymore, had to reshoot the end of the movie, parts of which were filmed at Fenway Park in the fall of 2004. The story of an obsessed Red Sox fan originally concluded with yet another disappointing World Series outcome.

Good Will Hunting, The Perfect Storm, and *Mystic River* are among the best movies with Boston-area backdrops, but an awful lot of bad ones are out there. Recent releases that are worth renting for more than just the locations include *A Civil Action, The Spanish Prisoner, Next Stop Wonderland* (all Boston), *State and Main* (Manchester-by-the-Sea), and *The Love Letter* (Rockport).

Some older movies are worth setting the VCR for. They include *Blown Away* (especially the scenes when the action first shifts to Boston), *The Verdict* (Boston), *Glory* (a stylish re-creation of 19th-century Beacon Hill), *The Witches of Eastwick* (Cohasset), and the sentimental favorite, *Love Story* (Cambridge).

3

For International Visitors

Whether it's your first visit or your tenth, a trip to the United States requires careful planning. This chapter will provide you with essential information, helpful tips, and advice for the more common problems that some visitors encounter.

Be sure to consult chapter 2 for general advice, too.

1 Preparing for Your Trip

ENTRY REQUIREMENTS

Check at any U.S. embassy or consulate for current information and requirements. You can also obtain a visa application and other information online at the **U.S. State Department's** website, **www.travel.state.gov.**

VISAS The U.S. State Department has a **Visa Waiver Program** allowing citizens of certain countries to enter the United States without a visa for stays of up to 90 days. At press time these included Andorra, Australia, Austria, Belgium, Brunei, Denmark, Finland, France, Germany, Iceland, Ireland, Italy, Japan, Liechtenstein, Luxembourg, Monaco, the Netherlands, New Zealand, Norway, Portugal, San Marino, Singapore, Slovenia, Spain, Sweden, Switzerland, and the United Kingdom. Citizens of these countries need only a valid passport and a round-trip air or cruise ticket in their possession upon arrival. If they first enter the United States, they may also visit Mexico, Canada, Bermuda, and/or the Caribbean islands and return to the United States without a visa. Further information is available from any U.S. embassy or consulate. Canadian citizens may enter the United States without visas; they need only proof of residence.

Citizens of all other countries must have (1) a valid passport that expires at least 6 months later than the scheduled end of their visit to the United States, and (2) a tourist visa, which may be obtained without charge from any U.S. consulate.

To obtain a visa, the traveler must submit a completed application form (either in person or by mail) with a 1½-sq.-inch (37-sq.-mm) photo and must demonstrate binding ties to a residence abroad. Usually you can obtain a visa at once or within 24 hours, but it may take longer during the summer rush from June through August. If you cannot go in person, contact the nearest U.S. embassy or consulate for directions on applying by mail. Your travel agent or airline office may also be able to provide you with visa applications and instructions. The U.S. consulate or embassy that issues your visa will determine whether you receive a multiple- or single-entry visa and any restrictions regarding the length of your stay.

British subjects can obtain up-to-date visa information by calling the **U.S. Embassy Visa Information Line** (© 0891/200-290) or by visiting the "Consular Services" section under the "U.S. Embassy" section of the American Embassy London's website, **www.usembassy.org.uk.**

Irish citizens can obtain up-to-date visa information through the **Embassy of the USA Dublin,** 42 Elgin Rd., Dublin 4, Ireland (© **353/1-668-8777;** http://dublin.usembassy.gov), or by checking the "Consular Services" section of the website.

Australian citizens can obtain up-to-date visa information by contacting the **U.S. Embassy Canberra,** Moonah Place, Yarralumla, ACT 2600 (© **02/6214-5600**) or by checking the U.S. Diplomatic Mission's website, **http://usembassy-australia.state.gov/consular.**

Citizens of **New Zealand** can obtain up-to-date visa information by contacting the **U.S. Embassy New Zealand,** 29 Fitzherbert Terrace, Thorndon, Wellington (© **644/472-2068;** http://usembassy.org.nz), or get the information directly from the "Services to New Zealanders" section of the website.

MEDICAL REQUIREMENTS Unless you're arriving from an area known to be suffering from an epidemic (particularly cholera or yellow fever), inoculations or vaccinations are not required for entry into the United States. If you have a medical condition that requires **syringe-administered medications,** carry a valid signed prescription from your physician—the Federal Aviation Administration (FAA) no longer allows airline passengers to pack syringes in their carry-on baggage without documented proof of medical need. If you have a disease that requires treatment with **narcotics,** you should also carry documented proof with you—smuggling narcotics aboard a plane is a serious offense that carries severe penalties in the U.S.

For **HIV-positive visitors,** requirements for entering the United States are somewhat vague and change frequently. According to the latest publication of *HIV and Immigrants: A Manual for AIDS Service Providers,* the government doesn't require a medical exam for entry into the United States, but officials may stop individuals because they look sick or because they are carrying AIDS/HIV medicine.

If an HIV-positive noncitizen applies for a non-immigrant visa, the question on the application regarding communicable diseases is tricky no matter which way it's answered. If the applicant checks "no," the government may deny the visa on the grounds that the applicant committed fraud. If the applicant checks "yes" or if officials suspect the person is HIV-positive, they will deny the visa unless the applicant asks for a special waiver for visitors. This waiver is for people visiting the United States for a short time, to attend a conference, for instance, to visit close relatives, or to receive medical treatment. It can be a confusing situation. For up-to-the-minute information, contact **AIDSinfo** (© **800/448-0440** or 301/519-6616 outside the U.S.; www.aidsinfo.nih.gov) or **Gay Men's Health Crisis** (© **212/367-1000;** www.gmhc.org).

DRIVER'S LICENSES Massachusetts recognizes foreign driver's licenses, but you may want to get an international driver's license if your home license is not written in English.

PASSPORT INFORMATION

Safeguard your passport in an inconspicuous, inaccessible place like a money belt. Make a copy of the critical pages, including the passport number, and store it in a safe place, separate from the passport itself. If you lose your passport, visit the nearest consulate of your native country as soon as possible for a replacement. Passport applications are downloadable from the websites listed below.

Note: The International Civil Aviation Organization has recommended a policy requiring that *every* individual who travels by air have a passport. In response, many countries are now requiring that children traveling internationally have their own passports.

FOR RESIDENTS OF CANADA

You can pick up a passport application at one of 28 regional passport offices, most travel agencies throughout Canada, or from the central **Passport Office,** Department of Foreign Affairs and International Trade, Ottawa, ON K1A 0G3 (© **800/567-6868;** www.dfait-maeci. gc.ca/passport). Canadian children who travel must have their own passports. However, if you hold a valid Canadian passport issued before December 11, 2001, that bears the name of your child, the passport remains valid for you and your child until it expires. Passports cost C$85 for those 16 years and older (valid 5 years), C$35 for children 3 to 15 (valid 5 years), and C$20 for children under 3 (valid 3 years). Applications must be accompanied by two identical passport-sized photographs and proof of Canadian citizenship. Processing takes 5 to 10 days if you apply in person, or about 3 weeks by mail.

FOR RESIDENTS OF THE UNITED KINGDOM

To pick up an application for a standard 10-year passport (5-year passport for children under 16), visit the nearest Passport Office, major post office, or travel agency. You can also contact the **United Kingdom Passport Service** (© **0870/571-0410;** www.passport.gov.uk). Passports are £33 for adults and £19 for children under 16, with another £30 fee if you apply in person at a Passport Office. Processing takes about 2 weeks (1 week if you apply at the Passport Office).

FOR RESIDENTS OF IRELAND

You can apply for a 10-year passport, costing €57, at the **Passport Office,** Setanta Centre, Molesworth Street, Dublin 2 (© **01/671-1633;** www.irl gov.ie/iveagh). Those under age 18 and over 65 must apply for a €12 3-year passport. You can also apply at 1A South Mall, Cork (© **021/272-525**), or over the counter at most main post offices.

FOR RESIDENTS OF AUSTRALIA

You can get an application from your local post office or any branch of Passports Australia, but you must schedule an interview at the passport office to present your application materials. Call the **Australian Passport Information Service** (© **131-232**) or visit the government website, **www.passports.gov.au.** Passports for adults are A$144 and for those under 18, A$72.

FOR RESIDENTS OF NEW ZEALAND

You can pick up a passport application at any **New Zealand Passports Office** (© **0800/225-050** in New Zealand or 04/474-8100; www.passports.govt.nz) or download it from the website. Passports for adults are NZ$80 and for children under 16 NZ$40.

CUSTOMS
WHAT YOU CAN BRING IN

Every visitor over 21 years of age may bring in, free of duty, the following: (1) 1 liter of wine or hard liquor; (2) 200 cigarettes, 100 cigars (but not from Cuba), or 3 pounds of smoking tobacco; and (3) $100 worth of gifts. These exemptions are offered to travelers who spend at least 72 hours in the United States and who have not claimed them within the preceding 6 months. It is altogether forbidden to bring into the country foodstuffs (particularly fruit, cooked meats, and canned goods) and plants (vegetables, seeds, tropical plants, and the like). Foreign tourists may bring in or take out up to $10,000 in U.S. or foreign currency with no formalities; larger sums must be declared to U.S. Customs on entering or leaving, which includes filing form CM 4790. For more specific information regarding U.S. Customs and Border Protection, contact your nearest U.S. embassy or consulate, or the U.S. **Customs** office (✆ **202/927-1770;** www.customs.ustreas.gov).

WHAT YOU CAN TAKE HOME

U.K. citizens returning from a non-EU country have a customs allowance of: 200 cigarettes; 50 cigars; 250g of smoking tobacco; 2 liters of still table wine; 1 liter of spirits or strong liqueurs (over 22% volume); 2 liters of fortified wine, sparkling wine, or other liqueurs; 60cc (ml) perfume; 250cc (ml) of toilet water; and £145 worth of all other goods, including gifts and souvenirs. People under 17 cannot have the tobacco or alcohol allowance. For more information, contact HM Customs & Excise (✆ **0845/010-9000** or 020/8929-0152 from outside the U.K.; www.hmce.gov.uk).

For a clear summary of **Canadian** rules, request the booklet *I Declare,* issued by the **Canada Customs and Revenue Agency** (✆ **800/461-9999** or 204/ 983-3500; www.ccra-adrc.gc.ca). Canada allows its citizens a C$750 exemption, and you're allowed to bring back duty-free one carton of cigarettes, one can of tobacco, 40 imperial ounces of liquor, and 50 cigars. In addition, you're allowed to mail gifts to Canada valued at less than C$60 a day, provided they're unsolicited and don't contain alcohol or tobacco (write on the package "Unsolicited gift, under $60 value"). All valuables should be declared on the Y-38 form before departure from Canada, including serial numbers of valuables you already own, such as expensive foreign cameras. *Note:* The $750 exemption can be used only once a year and only after an absence of 7 days.

The duty-free allowance in **Australia** is A$400 or, for those under 18, A$200. Citizens age 18 and over can bring in 250 cigarettes or 250 grams of loose tobacco, and 1,125 milliliters of alcohol. If you're returning with valuables you already own, such as foreign-made cameras, you should file form B263. A helpful brochure available from Australian consulates or Customs offices is *Know Before You Go.* For more information, contact the **Australian Customs Service** (✆ **1300/363-263;** www.customs.gov.au).

The duty-free allowance for **New Zealand** is NZ$700. Citizens over 17 can bring in 200 cigarettes, 50 cigars, or 250 grams of tobacco (or a mixture of all three if their combined weight doesn't exceed 250g); plus 4.5 liters of wine and beer, or 1.125 liters of liquor. New Zealand currency does not carry import or export restrictions. Fill out a certificate of export, listing the valuables you are taking out of the country; that way, you can bring them back without paying duty. Most questions are answered in a free pamphlet available at New Zealand consulates and Customs offices: *New Zealand Customs Guide for Travellers, Notice no. 4.* For more information, contact **New Zealand Customs,** The Customhouse, 17–21 Whitmore Street, Box 2218, Wellington (✆ **0800/428-786** or 04/473-6099; www.customs.govt.nz).

HEALTH INSURANCE

Although it's not required of travelers, health insurance is highly recommended. Unlike many European countries, the United States does not usually offer free or low-cost medical care to its citizens or visitors. Doctors and hospitals are expensive, and in most cases will require advance payment or proof of coverage before they render their services. Policies can cover everything from the loss or theft of your baggage and trip cancellation to the guarantee of bail in case you're arrested. Good policies will also cover the costs of an accident, repatriation, or death. See "Health & Insurance" in chapter 2 for more information. European automobile clubs and travel agencies sell packages such as **Europ Assistance's**

"Worldwide Healthcare Plan" at attractive rates. **Worldwide Assistance Services, Inc.** (© 800/821-2828; www.worldwide assistance.com) is the agent for Europ Assistance in the United States.

Though lack of health insurance may prevent you from being admitted to a hospital in nonemergencies, don't worry about being left on a street corner to die: The American way is to fix you now and bill the living daylights out of you later.

INSURANCE FOR BRITISH TRAVELERS Most big travel agents offer their own insurance and will probably try to sell you a package when you book a holiday. Think before you sign. **Britain's Consumers' Association** recommends that you insist on seeing the policy and reading the fine print before buying travel insurance. **The Association of British Insurers** (© 020/7600-3333; www.abi. org.uk) gives advice by phone and publishes *Holiday Insurance,* a free guide to policy provisions and prices. You might also shop around for better deals: Try **Columbus Direct** (© 020/7375-0011; www.columbusdirect.net).

INSURANCE FOR CANADIAN TRAVELERS Canadians should check with their provincial health plan offices or call **Health Canada** (© 613/957-2991; www.hc-sc.gc.ca) to find out the extent of their coverage and what documentation and receipts they must take home in case they are treated in the United States.

MONEY

CURRENCY The U.S. monetary system is simple: The most common **bills** are the $1 (colloquially, a "buck"), $5, $10, and $20 denominations. There are also $2 bills (seldom encountered), $50 bills, and $100 bills (the last two are usually not welcome as payment for small purchases). Two designs of paper money are in circulation; the famous faces adorning the newer bills are disproportionately large. The old-style bills are still legal tender.

There are seven denominations of coins: 1¢ (1 cent, or a penny); 5¢ (5 cents, or a nickel); 10¢ (10 cents, or a dime); 25¢ (25 cents, or a quarter); 50¢ (50 cents, or a half dollar); the gold-colored Sacagawea $1 coin; and the rare, older silver dollar.

The largest banks in New England, **Bank of America** (© 800/841-4000; www.bankofamerica.com) and **Citizens Bank** (© 800/922-9999; www.citizens bank.com) operate ATMs at Logan Airport and throughout the Boston area. **Travelex** (© 800/815-1795; www. travelex.com) has an ATM in Logan's Terminal E, foreign-exchange booths in Terminals B and C, and an office at 745 Boylston Street, Back Bay (© 617/266-7560). Other reliable choices for currency exchange are **Thomas Cook Currency Services,** 160 Franklin Street (© 800/287-7362), and **Ruesch International,** 1 Boston Place (© 800/521-4685 or 617/557-4440; www.ruesch. com). Many hotels offer currency exchange; check when you make your reservation.

Note: The foreign-exchange bureaus so common in Europe are rare even at airports in the United States and nonexistent outside major cities. It's best not to change foreign money (or traveler's checks denominated in a currency other than U.S. dollars) at a small-town bank or even a branch in a big city.

For the latest market conversion rates, visit **www.oanda.com** or **www.x-rates. com**.

TRAVELER'S CHECKS Though traveler's checks are widely accepted, make sure that they're denominated in U.S. dollars because foreign-currency checks are often difficult to exchange. The three traveler's checks that are most widely recognized—and most likely to be accepted—are **Visa, American Express,** and **Thomas Cook.** Be sure to record the numbers of the checks and keep that information in a separate place in case they get lost or stolen. Most businesses are pretty good about taking traveler's checks, but you're better off cashing them in at a bank (in small amounts, of course) and paying in cash. *Remember:* You'll need identification, such as a driver's license or passport, to change a traveler's check.

CREDIT CARDS & ATMs   Credit cards are the most widely used form of payment in the United States: **Visa** (Barclaycard in Britain), **MasterCard** (Eurocard in Europe, Access in Britain, Chargex in Canada), **American Express, Diners Club,** and **Discover.** Some stores and restaurants do not take credit cards, however, so be sure to ask in advance. Most businesses display stickers near the entrance to let you know which cards they accept. (*Note:* Businesses may require a minimum purchase, usually around $10, to use a credit card.)

It is strongly recommended that you bring at least one major credit card. You must have a credit or charge card to rent a car. Hotels and airlines usually require a credit-card imprint as a deposit against expenses, and in an emergency a credit card can be priceless.

You'll find **automated teller machines (ATMs)** on just about every block—at least in almost every town—across the country. Some ATMs will allow you to draw U.S. currency against your bank and credit cards. Check with your bank before leaving home and remember that you will need your personal identification number (PIN) to do so. Most accept Visa, MasterCard, and American Express, as well as ATM cards from other U.S. banks. Expect to be charged up to $3 per transaction, however, if you're not using your own bank's ATM.

ATM cards with major credit card backing, known as "debit cards," are now a commonly acceptable form of payment in most stores and restaurants. Debit cards draw money directly from your checking account. Some stores enable you to receive "cash back" on your debit-card purchases as well.

SAFETY

GENERAL SUGGESTIONS   Although tourist areas are generally safe, U.S. urban areas tend to be less safe than those in Europe or Japan. Visitors should always stay alert, particularly in large cities such as Boston. Although the crime rate is near its lowest point in a generation, that's no consolation if you're the victim. Ask at your hotel's front desk or at a tourist office if you plan to visit an unfamiliar area and aren't sure whether it's safe.

Avoid deserted areas, especially at night. Don't go into any city park at night, even to jog or skate, unless there is an event that attracts crowds—for example, concerts and movies on Boston's Esplanade. Generally speaking, you can feel safe in areas where there are many people and many open establishments.

Avoid carrying valuables with you on the street and keep expensive cameras or electronic equipment bagged up or covered when not in use. If you're using a map, try to consult it inconspicuously—or better yet, study it before you leave your room. Hold on to your pocketbook and place your billfold in an inside pocket. In theaters, restaurants, and other public places, keep your possessions in

---

Travel Tip

Be sure to keep a copy of all your travel papers separate from your wallet or purse, and leave a copy with someone at home should you need it faxed in an emergency.

sight. And never, ever stow anything valuable in the outside pocket of a backpack.

Always lock your room door—don't assume that after you're inside the hotel you are automatically safe and no longer need to be aware of your surroundings. Hotels are open to the public, and in a large hotel, security may not be able to screen everyone who enters.

DRIVING SAFETY   Driving safety is important, too, and carjacking is not unprecedented. If you must drive—and there's no need to if you're visiting only Boston and Cambridge—the best way to protect yourself is to be aware of your surroundings. If possible, arrive and depart during daylight hours. Question your rental agency about personal safety and ask for a traveler-safety brochure when you pick up your car. Obtain written directions or a map with the route clearly marked, showing how to get to your destination. Many agencies now offer the option of renting a cellphone for the duration of your car rental; check with the rental agent when you pick up the

car. Otherwise, contact **InTouch USA** (© **800/872-7626;** www.intouchusa. com) for short-term cellphone rental.

If you drive off a highway and end up in a dodgy-looking neighborhood, leave the area as quickly as possible. If you have an accident, even on the highway, stay in your car with the doors locked until you assess the situation or until the police arrive. If you're bumped from behind on the street or are involved in a minor accident with no injuries and the situation appears to be suspicious, motion to the other driver to follow you. Never get out of your car in such situations. Go directly to the nearest police precinct, well-lit service station, or 24-hour store.

Park in well-lit and well-traveled areas whenever possible. Always keep your car doors locked, whether the vehicle is attended or unattended. Never leave any packages or valuables in sight. If someone attempts to rob you or steal your car, don't try to resist. Report the incident to the police department immediately by calling © **911.**

2 Getting to the United States

Boston is an increasingly popular direct destination, although many itineraries from overseas still go through another American or European city. Because of fluctuating demand, routes and schedules are subject to change; double-check details (especially if you're traveling in the winter) well in advance.

From Canada, **Air Canada** (© 888/ 247-2262; www.aircanada.ca) flies directly from Halifax, Montreal, Ottawa, and Toronto; **American** (© 800/223-5436; www.aa.com) from Toronto; **Delta** (© 800/241-4141; www.delta.com) from Halifax; and **United** (© 800/241-6522 in Canada, 800/538-2929 in the U.S.; www.ual.ca) from Halifax and Montreal.

From London, there's direct service from Heathrow on **American** (© 0345/

789-789 in the U.K., 800/433-7300 in the U.S.; www.aa.com), **British Airways** (© 0345/222-111 or 0845/77-333-77 in the U.K., 800/AIRWAYS in the U.S.; www.british-airways.com), **Continental** (© 01293/776-464 in the U.K., 800/ 523-3273 in the U.S.; www.continental. com); and **Virgin Atlantic** (© 01293/ 747-747 in the U.K., 800/862-8621 in the U.S.; www.virgin-atlantic.com). Some airlines also fly out of Gatwick. From Ireland, **Aer Lingus** (© 3531/ 886-8844 in Dublin, 800/IRISH-AIR in the U.S.; www.aerlingus.ie) operates frequent flights from Dublin, and **American** (© 0845/789-789 in the U.K., 01/ 602-0550 in Ireland, and 800/433-7300 in the U.S.; www.aa.com) serves Shannon daily in the summer and 5 days a week

---

Tips Prepare to Be Fingerprinted

Many international visitors traveling on visas to the United States are photographed and fingerprinted at Customs as part of a Department of Homeland Security program called **US-VISIT.** Non–U.S. citizens arriving at airports and on cruise ships must undergo an instant background check as part of the government's ongoing efforts to deter terrorism by verifying the identity of incoming and outgoing visitors. Exempt from the extra scrutiny are visitors entering by land or those from 28 countries (mostly in Europe) that don't require a visa for short-term visits. For more information, go to the Homeland Security website at **www.dhs.gov/dhspublic.**

---

the rest of the year. **Lufthansa** (© 01803/ 803-803 in Germany, 800/645-3880 in the U.S.; www.lufthansa.com) serves Boston from Frankfurt.

From France, **American** (© 0801/ 872-872 in France, 800/433-7300 in the U.S.; www.aa.com) and **Air France** (© 0820/820-820 in France, 800/237-2747 in the U.S.; www.airfrance.com) fly to Boston from Paris.

From other countries, **Northwest/ KLM** (© 474-7747 in Holland, 800/ 374-7747 in the U.S.; www.klm.com) flies from Amsterdam; **Alitalia** (© 06/ 6563-4793 in Italy, 800/223-5730 in the U.S.; www.alitalia.it) flies from Milan and seasonally (June–Oct) from Rome; **Icelandair** (© 800/223-5500 in the U.S.; www.icelandair.com) flies from Reykjavik; and **Swiss International** (© 0848/85-2000 in Switzerland, 877/ 359-7947 in the U.S.; www.swiss.com) flies from Zurich. **Qantas** (© 13-13-13 in Australia, 800/227-4500 in the U.S.; www.qantas.com.au) flies to the West Coast of the United States and can provide connecting service to Boston.

AIRLINE DISCOUNTS   The smart traveler can find numerous ways to reduce the price of a plane ticket simply by taking time to shop around. For example, overseas visitors can take advantage of the APEX (Advance Purchase Excursion) reductions offered by all major U.S. and European carriers. For more money-saving airline advice, see "Getting There," in chapter 2. For the best rates, compare fares and be flexible with the dates and times of travel.

IMMIGRATION AND CUSTOMS CLEARANCE   Visitors arriving by air, no matter what the port of entry, should cultivate patience and resignation before setting foot on U.S. soil. Getting through immigration control can take as long as 2 hours on some days, especially on summer weekends, so be sure to carry this guidebook or something else to read.

People traveling by air from Canada, Bermuda, and certain countries in the Caribbean can sometimes clear Customs and Immigration at the point of departure, which is much quicker.

3 Getting Around the United States

BY PLANE   For a list of domestic carriers that serve Boston, see p. 26.

Some large airlines (for example, Northwest and Delta) offer travelers on their transatlantic or transpacific flights special discount tickets under the name **Visit USA,** allowing mostly one-way travel from one U.S. destination to another at very low prices. These discount tickets are not on sale in the United

States and must be purchased abroad in conjunction with your international ticket. This system is the best, easiest, and fastest way to see the United States at low cost. You should obtain information well in advance from your travel agent or airline because the conditions attached to these discount tickets can be changed without notice.

BY TRAIN   International visitors can buy a **USA Rail Pass,** good for 15 or 30 days of unlimited travel on **Amtrak** (© **800/USA-RAIL;** www.amtrak.com). Passes good only in certain regions are also available.

Passes are available through many foreign travel agents. With a foreign passport, you can also buy passes at Amtrak offices in some U.S. cities, including Boston, San Francisco, Los Angeles, Chicago, New York, Miami, and Washington. Reservations are generally required, and you should make them for each part of your trip when you buy the pass (you can change them later at no cost).

Visitors should be aware of the limitations of long-distance rail travel in the United States. With a few notable exceptions—for instance, the Northeast Corridor between Boston and Washington, D.C.—service is rarely up to European standards. Delays are common, routes are limited and often infrequently served, and fares are rarely significantly lower than discount airfares.

BY CAR   Renting a car just to drive around Boston and Cambridge is not advisable. Driving is the most cost-effective, convenient, and comfortable way to see the country outside the major cities, however, especially if you have time to explore. The interstate highway system connects cities and towns all over the country; in addition to these high-speed, limited-access roadways, there's an extensive network of federal, state, and local highways and roads.

National car-rental companies with offices in Boston include **Alamo** (© 800/462-5266; www.alamo.com), **Avis** (© 800/230-4898; www.avis.com), **Budget** (© 800/527-0700; www.budget.com), **Dollar** (© 800/800-3665; www.dollar.com), **Enterprise** (© 800/726-8222; www.enterprise.com), **Hertz** (© 800/654-3131; www.hertz.com), **National** (© 800/227-7368; www.nationalcar.com), and **Thrifty** (© 800/847-4389; www.thrifty.com).

BY BUS   Although bus travel is often the most economical form of public transit for short hops between U.S. cities, it can also be slow and uncomfortable—certainly not an option for everyone (particularly when Amtrak, which is far more luxurious, generally charges similar rates). **Greyhound/Trailways** (© **800/231-2222;** www.greyhound.com), the sole nationwide bus line, offers an **International Ameripass** that must be purchased before coming to the United States or by phone through the Greyhound International Office at the Port Authority Bus Terminal in New York City (© **212/971-0492**). The pass is available from

---

Tips **Planning Pointer**

"But New York and Boston look so close on the map," says the thrifty international traveler. No matter how cheap airfare to New York is, make sure that you budget enough time and money for your connection to Boston. The transfer from airport to airport (or to the train or bus station) in the New York area can be complicated, expensive, or both.

foreign travel agents or through Greyhound's website (order at least 21 days before leaving for the U.S.) and costs less than the domestic version. Prices in 2005 ranged from $149 for 4 days to $539 for 60 days. You can get more information on the pass at the website or by calling © **402/330-8552.** In addition, special rates are available for seniors and students.

FAST FACTS: **For the International Traveler**

Also see "Fast Facts: Boston" in chapter 5 for more information.

Automobile Organizations Auto clubs will supply maps, suggested routes, guidebooks, accident and bail-bond insurance, and emergency road service. The **American Automobile Association,** or AAA (© **800/222-4357;** www.aaa. com) is the major auto club in the United States. If you belong to an auto club in your home country, inquire about AAA reciprocity before you leave. You may be able to join AAA even if you're not a member of a reciprocal club; check ahead.

Business Hours Offices are usually open weekdays from 9am to 5 or 6pm. Banks are open weekdays from 9am to 4pm or later and sometimes Saturday mornings; most offer 24-hour access to automated teller machines (ATMs). Stores typically open between 9 and 10am and close between 5 and 7pm from Monday through Saturday; most shops that open on Sunday do so around 11am or noon. Stores in shopping complexes or malls tend to stay open until about 9pm daily.

Climate See "When to Go" in chapter 2.

Currency Exchange See p. 41.

Drinking Laws The legal drinking age in Massachusetts (and the rest of the U.S) is 21; be ready to show proof of age when you buy or consume alcohol. In many bars, particularly near college campuses, you may be asked for identification if you appear to be under 30 or so. Some bars and clubs "card" (check the ID of) everyone who enters. Everyone buying alcohol at sporting events must show ID. Beer, wine, and liquor are for sale only in liquor stores and the liquor sections of supermarkets (and not until noon on Sunday in communities that allow Sunday liquor sales).

Do not carry open containers of alcohol in your car or any public area that isn't zoned for alcohol consumption. The police can—and probably will—fine you on the spot. And nothing will ruin your trip faster than getting a citation for DUI (driving under the influence), so don't even think about driving while intoxicated.

Electricity Like Canada, the United States uses 110 to 120 volts AC (60 cycles), compared with 220 to 240 volts AC (50 cycles) in most of Europe, Australia, and New Zealand. If your small appliances use 220 to 240 volts, you'll need a 110-volt transformer and a plug adapter with two flat parallel pins to operate them here. Downward converters that change 220–240 volts to 110–120 volts are difficult to find in the United States, so bring one with you.

Embassies & Consulates Embassies are in Washington, D.C.; some consulates are in Boston, and most nations have a mission to the United Nations in New York City. If your country isn't listed below, call directory assistance in Washington, D.C. (© **202/555-1212**) or visit **www.embassy.org/embassies**.

The embassy of **Australia** is at 1601 Massachusetts Ave. NW, Washington, DC 20036 (© **202/797-3000**; www.austemb.org). There is no consulate in Boston.

The embassy of **Canada** is at 501 Pennsylvania Ave. NW, Washington, DC 20001 (© **202/682-1740**; www.canadianembassy.org). The **Canadian consulate in Boston** is at 3 Copley Place, Suite 400, Boston, MA 02116 (© **617/262-3760**).

The embassy of **Ireland** is at 2234 Massachusetts Ave. NW, Washington, DC 20008 (© **202/462-3939**; www.irelandemb.org). The **Irish consulate in Boston** is at 535 Boylston Street, Boston, MA 02116 (© **617/267-9330**).

The embassy of **Japan** is at 2520 Massachusetts Ave. NW, Washington, DC 20008 (© **202/238-6700**; www.embjapan.org). The **Japanese consulate in Boston** is at Federal Reserve Plaza, 600 Atlantic Ave., 14th Floor, Boston, MA 02210 (© **617/973-9772**).

The embassy of **New Zealand** is at 37 Observatory Circle NW, Washington, DC 20008 (© **202/328-4800**; www.nzembassy.com). There is no consulate in Boston.

The embassy of the **United Kingdom** is at 3100 Massachusetts Ave. NW, Washington, DC 20008 (© **202/462-1340**; www.britainusa.com). The **Boston-area U.K. consulate** is at 1 Memorial Dr., Suite 1500, Cambridge, MA 02142 (© **617/245-4500**).

Emergencies Call © **911** to report a fire, call the police, or get an ambulance anywhere in the United States. This is a toll-free call. (No coins are required at public telephones.)

If you encounter such traveler's problems as sickness, an accident, or lost or stolen baggage, call or visit **Travelers Aid Family Services**, 17 East Street, Boston, MA 02111 (© **617/542-7286**; www.taboston.org), across Atlantic Avenue from South Station. The nationwide nonprofit social-service organization geared to helping travelers in difficult straits offers services that might include reuniting families separated while traveling, providing food and shelter to people stranded without cash, or even emotional counseling.

If you have a medical emergency that doesn't require an ambulance, you can walk into a hospital's 24-hour emergency room (usually a separate entrance). For a list of hospitals, see "Fast Facts" in chapter 5.

Gasoline (Petrol) Petrol is known as gasoline (or simply "gas") in the United States, and petrol stations are known as both gas stations and service stations. Gasoline costs less here than it does in Europe but is getting pricier (around $2 per gal. at press time), and the printed price includes taxes. One U.S. gallon equals 3.8 liters or 0.85 imperial gallons.

Holidays Banks, government offices, post offices, and some stores, restaurants, and museums close on the following legal national holidays: January 1 (New Year's Day), the third Monday in January (Martin Luther King, Jr., Day), the third Monday in February (Presidents' Day, Washington's Birthday), the last Monday in May (Memorial Day), July 4th (Independence Day), the first Monday in September (Labor Day), the second Monday in October (Columbus Day), November 11 (Veterans' Day/Armistice Day), the fourth Thursday in November (Thanksgiving Day), and December 25 (Christmas Day). Also, the Tuesday following the first Monday in November is Election Day and is a federal government holiday in presidential-election years (held every four years, next in 2008).

In Massachusetts, state offices close for **Patriots Day** on the third Monday in April, and Suffolk County offices (including Boston City Hall) close on March 17 for **Evacuation Day.**

Legal Aid If you are "pulled over"—stopped by the police—for a minor infraction such as speeding, *never* attempt to pay the fine directly to a police officer. That could be construed as attempted bribery, a much more serious charge. Pay fines by mail or directly to the clerk of the court. If you're accused of a more serious offense, say and do nothing before consulting a lawyer. Here the burden is on the state to prove a person's guilt beyond a reasonable doubt, and everyone has the right to remain silent, whether he or she is suspected of a crime or actually arrested. Under U.S. law, an arrested person is allowed one telephone call to a party of his or her choice. Call your embassy or consulate.

Mail If you aren't sure what your address will be in the United States, mail can be sent to you, in your name, c/o General Delivery at the main post office of the city or region where you expect to be. (Call ✆ **800/275-8777** for information on the nearest post office.) The addressee must pick up mail in person and must produce proof of identity (such as a driver's license or passport). Most post offices will hold your mail for up to 1 month and are open Monday to Friday from 8am to 6pm, Saturday from 9am to 2pm.

Generally found at intersections, mailboxes are blue with a red-and-white stripe and carry the inscription u.s. mail. If your mail is addressed to a U.S. destination, don't forget to add the five-digit postal code (or zip code), after the two-letter abbreviation of the state to which the mail is addressed. This is essential to prompt delivery.

At press time, domestic postage rates were 23¢ for a postcard and 37¢ for a letter. For international mail, a first-class letter of up to ½ ounce costs 80¢ (60¢ to Canada and Mexico), a first-class postcard costs 70¢ (50¢ to Canada and Mexico), and a preprinted postal aerogramme costs 70¢.

Measurements See the chart on the inside front cover of this book for details on converting metric measurements to U.S. equivalents.

Newspapers & Magazines National newspapers include the *New York Times,* *USA Today,* and the *Wall Street Journal.* National newsweeklies include *Newsweek, Time,* and *U.S. News & World Report.* The major newspapers in Boston are the *Boston Globe,* the *Boston Herald,* and the weekly *Boston Phoenix.*

Newsstands with good selections of international periodicals include **Out of Town News,** Zero Harvard Square, Cambridge (✆ **617/354-7777**); **Nini's Corner,** across the street at 1394 Massachusetts Ave. (✆ **617/547-3558**); and the newsstand on the street level of Faneuil Hall.

Radio & Television Nationally, there are six commercial over-the-air television networks—ABC, CBS, NBC, Fox, UPN, and WB—along with the Public Broadcasting System (PBS) and the cable news network CNN. Most hotels have at least basic cable, and many offer access to "premium" movie channels that show uncut theatrical releases. For the major radio and television stations in Boston, see "Fast Facts" in chapter 5.

Safety See "Safety" in the section "Preparing for Your Trip" earlier in this chapter.

Smoking Don't count on being able to light up indoors anywhere in Massachusetts. State law forbids smoking in workplaces, including restaurants, bars, and clubs.

Taxes The United States imposes no value-added tax (VAT) or other indirect national tax. Every state, county, and city may levy its own tax on purchases, including hotel bills, restaurant checks, and so on. The 5% state sales tax in Massachusetts does not apply to food, prescription drugs, newspapers, or clothing costing less than $175, but there seems to be a tax on everything else. The tax on restaurant meals and takeout food is 5%. The lodging tax in Boston and Cambridge is 12.45%.

Telephone, Telegraph, Telex & Fax The telephone system in the United States is run by private corporations, so rates, especially for long-distance service and operator-assisted calls, can vary widely. Generally, hotel surcharges on long-distance and local calls are astronomical, so you're usually better off using a **public pay telephone,** which you'll find clearly marked in most public buildings and private establishments as well as on the street. Convenience grocery stores and gas stations always have them. Many convenience groceries and packaging services sell **prepaid calling cards** in denominations up to $50; these can be the least expensive way to call home. Many public phones at airports now accept American Express, MasterCard, and Visa credit cards. **Local calls** made from public pay phones in most locales cost either 25¢ or 35¢. Pay phones do not accept pennies, and few will take anything larger than a quarter.

You may want to look into leasing a cellphone for the duration of your trip.

Most long-distance and international calls can be dialed directly from any phone. **For calls within the United States and to Canada,** dial 1 followed by the area code and the seven-digit number. **For other international calls,** dial 011 followed by the country code, city code, and the telephone number of the person you are calling.

Calls to area codes **800, 888, 877,** and **866** are toll-free. However, calls to numbers in area codes **700** and **900** (chat lines, bulletin boards, "dating" services, and so on) can be very expensive—usually a charge of 95¢ to $3 or more per minute, and they sometimes have minimum charges that can run as high as $15 or more.

For **reversed-charge or collect calls,** and for person-to-person calls, dial 0 (zero, not the letter O) followed by the area code and number you want; an operator will then come on the line, and you should specify that you are calling collect, or person-to-person, or both. If your operator-assisted call is international, ask for the overseas operator.

For **local directory assistance** ("information"), dial ✆ 411; for long-distance information, dial 1, then the appropriate area code and 555-1212.

Telegraph and telex services are provided primarily by Western Union. You can bring your telegram into the nearest Western Union office (there are hundreds across the country) or dictate it over the phone (✆ **800/325-6000**). You can also telegraph money, or have it telegraphed to you, very quickly over the Western Union system, but this service can cost as much as 15% to 20% of the amount sent.

Most hotels have **fax machines** available for guest use (be sure to ask about the charge to use it). Many hotel rooms are even wired for guests' fax machines. A less expensive way to send and receive faxes may be at stores such as the **UPS Store** (formerly Mail Boxes Etc.), a national chain of retail packing service shops. (Look in the Yellow Pages directory under "Packing Services.")

There are two kinds of telephone directories in the United States. The so-called **White Pages** list private households and business subscribers in alphabetical order. The inside front cover lists emergency numbers for police, fire, ambulance, the Coast Guard, poison-control center, crime-victims hot line, and so on. The first few pages will tell you how to make long-distance and international calls, complete with country codes and area codes. Government numbers are usually printed on blue paper within the White Pages. Printed on yellow paper, the so-called **Yellow Pages** list all local services, businesses, industries, and houses of worship according to activity with an index at the front or back. (Drugstores/pharmacies and restaurants are also listed by geographic location.) The Yellow Pages also include city plans or detailed area maps, postal zip codes, and public transportation routes.

Time The continental United States is divided into **four time zones:** Eastern Standard Time (EST), Central Standard Time (CST), Mountain Standard Time (MST), and Pacific Standard Time (PST). Alaska and Hawaii have their own zones. For example, noon in Boston (EST) is 11am in Chicago (CST), 10am in Denver (MST), 9am in Los Angeles (PST), 8am in Anchorage (AST), and 7am in Honolulu (HST).

Daylight saving time is in effect from 1am on the first Sunday in April through 1am on the last Sunday in October, except in Arizona, Hawaii, and Puerto Rico. Daylight saving time moves the clock 1 hour ahead of standard time.

Tipping Tips are a very important part of certain workers' income, and gratuities are the standard way of showing appreciation for services provided. (Tipping is certainly not compulsory if the service is poor!) In hotels, tip **bellhops** at least $1 per bag ($2–$3 if you have a lot of luggage) and tip the **chamber staff** $1 to $2 per day (more if you've left a disaster area for him or her to clean up). Tip the **doorman** or **concierge** only if he or she has provided you with some specific service (for example, calling a cab for you or obtaining difficult-to-get theater tickets). Tip the **valet-parking attendant** $1 every time you get your car.

In restaurants, bars, and nightclubs, tip **service staff** 15% to 20% of the check, tip **bartenders** 10% to 15%, tip **checkroom attendants** $1 per garment, and tip **valet-parking attendants** $1 per vehicle.

As for other service personnel, tip **cab drivers** 15% of the fare, tip **skycaps** at airports at least $1 per bag ($2–$3 if you have a lot of luggage), and tip **hairdressers** and **barbers** 15% to 20%.

Toilets Hardly any toilets are on the streets, but you can usually find one in a visitor information center, shopping center, bar, restaurant, hotel, museum, or department store—and it will probably be clean. The cleanliness of toilets at railroad and bus stations and at gasoline service stations varies widely. Some restaurants and bars, including those in Boston's tourist areas, display a sign saying that toilets are for the use of patrons only. Paying for a cup of coffee or a soft drink qualifies you as a patron. Many branches of fast-food restaurants and coffee bars have reliably clean restrooms.

Boston has freestanding, self-cleaning pay toilets in kiosks in eight high-traffic areas downtown, including City Hall Plaza (near the Government Center T stop) and Commercial Street near Snowhill Street, not far from the Freedom Trail. Admission costs 25¢. Check carefully before using these toilets—reports of drug use in the enclosed kiosks have led to increased maintenance, but you can't be too careful.

4

Suggested Boston Itineraries

Living near the Freedom Trail, I meet my beloved *Frommer's Boston* readers all the time. After I assure them that I'm not trying to pick their pockets or enlist them in a cult (why so suspicious, readers?), they usually make one of two comments. They want to know where they can find a public bathroom, or they want to praise the book's suggested itineraries.

Read on for strategies that can help you organize your time. These itineraries include sightseeing destinations, snack and meal suggestions, and shopping pointers. Two tips: **Wear comfortable shoes,** and don't ignore the built-in **breaks** that will help you feel more like a relaxed insider and less like a crazed participant in a scavenger hunt.

Unless otherwise indicated, turn to chapter 8 for descriptions of the recommended attractions and activities.

1 The Best of Boston in 1 Day

A single day affords the opportunity to sample some experiences unique to Boston. You won't have time for full immersion, but you can touch on several singular attractions and destinations. Your focus will be the downtown area, home to the city's oldest and most historic neighborhoods. *Start: Boston Common (Red or Green Line to Park Street), 15 State Street (Green or Blue Line to State), or Faneuil Hall (Green or Blue Line to Government Center).*

❶ The Freedom Trail ✿✿✿
Boston's signature attraction is a 3-mile line of red paint or brick laid out at the suggestion of a local journalist in 1958. Following the whole Freedom Trail (p. 160) can take the better part of a day, but several options that concentrate on the downtown part of the walk take 2 hours or so. Your goal is to cover—at whatever pace suits you, as carefully or as casually as you like—the first two-thirds of the trail, from **Boston Common** through **Faneuil Hall.** Start at the Boston Common Visitor Information Center with a pamphlet describing the

self-guided tour or the audio tour available for rental from the Freedom Trail Foundation. If you prefer a guided tour, check the schedule of tours with **National Park Service rangers** and **Boston By Foot.**

❷ Filene's Basement ✿✿✿
As long as you're downtown, indulge in a little discount retail therapy. The legendary store opens at 9:30am and doesn't get frantic until lunchtime on weekdays. You can fit in a visit before, after, or even (this can be our little secret) during your sightseeing. See p. 221.

Tips One Singular Sensation

On a 1-day visit, consider concentrating on just **one or two things** you're most excited about (plus a good meal or two). If what really gets you going is the Museum of Fine Arts, the Museum of Science, the Newbury Street art galleries, or even a day trip (see chapter 12), you have a good excuse for not doing more—and for a return trip to Boston!

---

3 FANEUIL HALL MARKETPLACE ★★

Giving new meaning to the term "one-stop shopping," Faneuil Hall Marketplace ((C) **617/ 523-1300**), between North, Congress, and State streets, and Atlantic Avenue, encompasses a Freedom Trail stop (the original Faneuil Hall; p. 166), retail outlets galore, numerous restaurants and bars, and tons of picnic possibilities—the main level of Quincy Market is a gigantic food court. You can eat at the marketplace, but I suggest crossing Atlantic Avenue and enjoying your snack or lunch with a glorious view. Seek out the plaza at the end of **Long Wharf** (pass the Marriott and keep going) or **Christopher Columbus Waterfront Park** (next to the Marriott, on the side opposite the New England Aquarium). If you'd rather eat indoors, head to **Durgin-Park** ★★★, 340 Faneuil Hall Marketplace ((C) **888/766-6528**; p. 124), or across the street to **Ye Olde Union Oyster House** ★, 41 Union Street ((C) **617/227-2750**; p. 124).

4 Paul Revere House ★★★

My favorite Freedom Trail stop is a little 17th-century home overlooking a picturesque cobblestone square. See p. 167.

5 The North End ★★★

The Freedom Trail continues here with another famous Paul Revere hangout, the fascinating **Old North Church** ★. But there's more to this historic neighborhood than just history. The city's "Little Italy" (but seriously, don't call it that) is a great place for wandering around. See p. 168.

6 HANOVER STREET

Coffee outlets throughout the city valiantly attempt to serve good espresso and cappuccino; the shops here always succeed—and if they don't, they don't stay in business very long. Pair your caffeine with a fresh-baked pastry, settle in at a bakery or *caffè*, and take in the scene on the North End's main drag. Top choices: 6A **Mike's Pastry**, 300 Hanover Street ((C) **617/ 742-3050**); 6B **Caffè Vittoria**, 296 Hanover Street ((C) **617/523-5063**); and 6C **Caffè dello Sport**, 308 Hanover Street ((C) **617/523-5063**). See p. 117.

7 The Waterfront

Here's where downtown Boston's small size really pays off: In almost any direction, the gorgeous harbor is a short stroll from the North End. As the day winds down, you can take a **sightseeing cruise** ★★ (p. 188) from Long Wharf or Rowes Wharf or just a **ferry** ride from Long Wharf to Charlestown and back. If a cruise doesn't appeal to you (or if it's not the season), explore the **New England Aquarium** ★ (p. 159) or the **Children's Museum** ★★ (p. 185).

Or—it's not the Waterfront, but bear with me—abandon the sightseeing after the Paul Revere House and go **shopping** on Newbury Street (see chapter 10).

Finally, head back to the hotel to wash off the grime of the day, then pick something fun from the "Suggested Evening Itineraries" box on p. 57.

Boston Suggested Itineraries

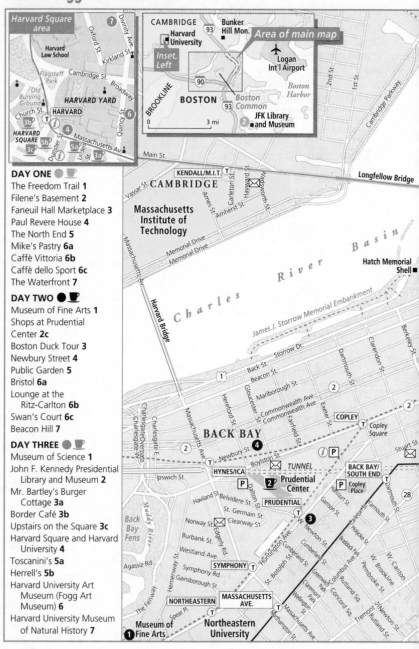

DAY ONE ● ☕

The Freedom Trail **1**
Filene's Basement **2**
Faneuil Hall Marketplace **3**
Paul Revere House **4**
The North End **5**
Mike's Pastry **6a**
Caffè Vittoria **6b**
Caffè dello Sport **6c**
The Waterfront **7**

DAY TWO ● ☕

Museum of Fine Arts **1**
Shops at Prudential
Center **2c**
Boston Duck Tour **3**
Newbury Street **4**
Public Garden **5**
Bristol **6a**
Lounge at the
Ritz-Carlton **6b**
Swan's Court **6c**
Beacon Hill **7**

DAY THREE ● ☕

Museum of Science **1**
John F. Kennedy Presidential
Library and Museum **2**
Mr. Bartley's Burger
Cottage **3a**
Border Café **3b**
Upstairs on the Square **3c**
Harvard Square and Harvard
University **4**
Toscanini's **5a**
Herrell's **5b**
Harvard University Art
Museum (Fogg Art
Museum) **6**
Harvard University Museum
of Natural History **7**

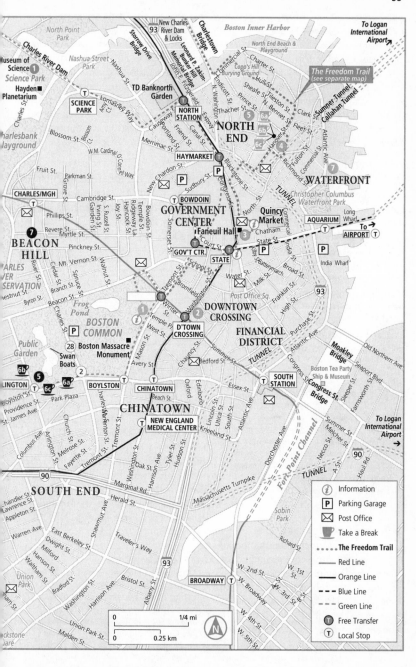

2 The Best of Boston in 2 Days

Now that you have a feel for the city, it's time to explore beyond downtown and investigate subjects other than history. The Back Bay and Beacon Hill contrast invitingly with the colonial extravaganza of Day 1, and other attractions complement the 18th-century focus of the Freedom Trail. This itinerary may require some flexibility because you probably won't have much control over when your Duck Tour starts. Aim for tickets on a tour that starts in the afternoon, when the scene on the river is liveliest. If your tour falls in the morning, the rest of this itinerary easily adjusts to accommodate it.
Start: *Museum of Fine Arts (Green Line E to Museum or Orange Line to Ruggles).*

❶ Museum of Fine Arts ★★★

Be at the museum when the doors open at 10am. The MFA can easily—and most enjoyably—take up a full day, but it doesn't have to. Check out the website before you leave home (or before you leave the hotel), so you have some sense of what you want to see. If you prefer not to explore on your own, be ready for the first guided tour of the day, which begins at 10:30am. The museum has a cafeteria, cafe, and restaurant, but I'd suggest moving along to the next stop. See p. 157.

> **☕ SHOPS AT PRUDENTIAL CENTER**
> One of my favorite branches of **Legal Sea Foods** ★★★ (p. 138) is here, on the main level off Boylston Street. If you prefer something lighter, the **food court** is nearby. To get there, you have to pass the only Boston location of **Krispy Kreme Doughnuts**, 800 Boylston Street (© 617/266-6800). See p. 131.

❸ Boston Duck Tour ★★★

This is the most entertaining motorized way to see the city. On a reconditioned World War II amphibious landing vehicle, you see the top attractions, pick up some historical background, and head for the water. Then, thrillingly, the Duck plunges into the Charles River and cruises around the basin. See p. 186.

Duck Tours don't operate from December through March (unless they're needed for a Patriots Super Bowl victory

parade, which has happened more often than not lately). An excellent alternative is a **Boston Symphony Orchestra** ★★★ or **Boston Pops** ★★★ concert at Symphony Hall (p. 235), a short walk from either the MFA or the Pru.

❹ Newbury Street

The commercial heart of the Back Bay, Newbury Street offers the best shopping in New England (see chapter 10). Familiar chains and one-of-a-kind boutiques and galleries make it a can't-miss destination for serious consumerism or just window-shopping. It's also architecturally fascinating (see "Walking Tour 1," in chapter 9).

❺ Public Garden ★★★

At the east end of Newbury Street is the most beautiful park in Boston. The Public Garden ★★ (p. 175) is lovely year-round—a visit will brighten up even the grayest off-season day—and the *Make Way for Ducklings* sculptures (p. 184) are always delightful. In warm weather, leave time for a **Swan Boat** (p. 175) ride.

> **☕ AFTERNOON TEA**
> All that walking makes a perfect excuse for a hearty meal of pastries, finger sandwiches, and, of course, tea. My favorite afternoon tea is at the ☕ **Bristol**, off the lobby of the Four Seasons. The ☕ **Lounge at the Ritz-Carlton, Boston** and ☕ **Swan's Court** at the Boston Park Plaza Hotel & Towers also put on a good show. See "Boston Tea Party, Part 2" on p. 136.

Tips **Suggested Evening Itineraries**

If you're traveling as a family, you might be getting your evening itineraries out of the TV listings. If not—or if you had the foresight to book a sitter—here are some suggestions. See chapter 7 for restaurant reviews and chapter 11 for nightlife listings.

- Dinner in the North End, and coffee and dessert at a *caffè*. Afterward, a show at the Comedy Connection at Faneuil Hall or the Improv Asylum, and a drink at the *Cheers* bar in Quincy Market.
- Dinner at Legal Sea Foods in the Prudential Center, followed (or preceded) by a visit to the 50th-floor Prudential Center Skywalk or a drink in the lounge at Top of the Hub, on the 52nd floor.
- Summer only: Assemble a picnic and head to the Hatch Shell for music or a movie, or to Boston Common for a play or concert.
- Winter only: A Boston Symphony Orchestra or Boston Ballet performance, then late supper at Brasserie Jo or dessert at Finale.
- Dinner at Sel de la Terre or the State Street Legal Sea Foods, then a stroll to the plaza at the end of Long Wharf. Hit the North End or the food court at Faneuil Hall Marketplace for dessert.
- Dinner at Bob the Chef's Jazz Cafe and music at Wally's Café or a Huntington Theatre Company performance.
- Dinner at L'Espalier, a stroll on Newbury Street, and a nightcap at the Bristol in the Four Seasons Hotel.
- Shopping at the Coop or the Harvard Book Store, then dinner at Mr. Bartley's Burger Cottage. Contemplate Harvard Yard from the Widener Library steps and finish up with ice cream at Toscanini's or Herrell's.
- Dinner at Rialto or Oleana and music at the Regattabar or Scullers Jazz Club.
- Dinner at the Green Street Grill, ice cream at Toscanini's, and music at the Middle East or T.T. the Bear's Place.
- A movie at the Kendall Square Cinema before or after dinner at the Blue Room, then music at the Cantab Lounge.
- Dinner at Redbones or Tu y Yo Mexican Fonda, and a show at Johnny D's or the Somerville Theater.

❼ Beacon Hill ★★★

The most picturesque neighborhood in town is a festival of red brick, cobblestones, and gorgeous architectural details. **Charles Street,** the main thoroughfare, is a lively shopping destination with refreshingly few chain stores. Wander on your own (see p. 213 for pointers) or seek out a guide—on summer weekdays, a **Boston By Foot** tour starts at 5:30pm.

"Suggested Evening Itineraries" (above) can help you plan the rest of your day.

3 The Best of Boston in 3 Days

You can easily expand the suggestions for the first 2 days to fill a third—for instance, your Museum of Fine Arts admission is good for another visit within 10 days, and you haven't actually completed the Freedom Trail—but you'll probably want to branch out. Today you head for Cambridge, Dorchester, or both. This itinerary may look a little skimpy, but it's packed with interesting destinations and activities. ***Start: Museum of Science (Green Line to Science Park) or Kennedy Library (Red Line to JFK/UMass, then free shuttle bus).***

---

❶ Museum of Science ★★★

❷ John F. Kennedy Presidential Library & Museum ★★

Although they're very different, both of these museums are well worth a trip and a full morning. The Museum of Science (p. 158), with its wealth of hands-on exhibits, is a great destination for families; adults and older kids who have studied American history can't get enough of the Kennedy Library (p. 156). Both museums open at 9am. Both have cafeterias, but I recommend that you wait to have lunch until you reach Cambridge at midday.

> **☕ EAT LIKE A COLLEGE KID**
> My favorite Harvard Square lunch destinations are casual places where the sightseer's uniform of jeans or shorts and sneakers fits right in. 3A **Mr. Bartley's Burger Cottage** ★★, 1246 Mass. Ave. (☎ 617/354-6559; p. 146) and the 3B **Border Café**, 32 Church Street (☎ 617/864-6100; p. 145) are prime examples; if you're feeling a bit fancier, the Monday Club Bar at 3C **Upstairs on the Square**, 91 Winthrop Street, Cambridge (☎ 617/864-1933; p. 144) is a terrific alternative.

❹ Harvard Square & Harvard University

I consider these two entities one big stop because the school couldn't exist without the neighborhood, and vice versa. Allow some time to wander around and enjoy the gentrified-boho atmosphere. Take a

tour, which begins at the university's Events & Information Center, or head out on your own (see "Walking Tour 2" in chapter 9). "The Square" is also a fun **shopping** destination (see chapter 10).

> **☕ ICE CREAM**
> Harvard Square is home to two of the best ice cream shops in this ice-cream-obsessed part of the world. I prefer 5A **Toscanini's**, 1310 Mass. Ave. (☎ 617/354-9350), to 5B **Herrell's**, 15 Dunster Street (☎ 617/497-2179)—except when I don't. If you have time, check the board in each place to see which has the more appealing daily specials. Then take your treat and wander around Harvard Yard.

❻ Harvard University Art Museums ★

❼ Harvard Museum of Natural History & Peabody Museum ★

Let your interests be your guide to the rest of the afternoon. You can make it an all-science day or mix and match. If you opt for the art museums, be sure to visit the Fogg (p. 179), with its gorgeous central courtyard; at the Museum of Natural History (p.179), the Glass Flowers are the justifiably world-famous display. All of the university museums close at 5pm.

When you've had enough, head back to the hotel. Stay in and order room service or close your eyes and point to one of the "Suggested Evening Itineraries" on p. 57.

5

Getting to Know Boston

Boston bills itself as "America's Walking City," and walking is by far the easiest way to get around. Legend has it that the street pattern originated as a network of cow paths, but the layout owes more to 17th-century London and to Boston's original shoreline. To orient yourself, it helps to look at the big picture.

This chapter provides an overview of the city's layout and neighborhoods, and lists information and resources that you might need while you're away from home. As you familiarize yourself with Boston's geography, it might help to identify neighborhoods and landmarks on the free map provided with this guide.

1 Orientation

VISITOR INFORMATION

You'll probably want to begin exploring at a **visitor information center.** The staff members are knowledgeable and helpful, and you can pick up free maps, brochures, listings of special exhibits and events, and other materials.

The **Boston National Historic Park Visitor Center,** 15 State St. (© **617/242-5642;** www.nps.gov/bost; T: Blue or Orange Line to State St.), across the street from the Old State House, is a good place to begin. National Park Service rangers staff the center, dispense information, and lead free tours of the Freedom Trail. The audiovisual show provides basic information about the 16 historic sites on the trail. The center is open daily from 9am to 5pm except January 1, Thanksgiving, and December 25.

The **Freedom Trail** (p. 160), a line of red paint or painted brick on or in the sidewalk, begins at the **Boston Common Information Center,** 147 Tremont St., on the Common. The center is open Monday through Saturday from 8:30am to 5pm, Sunday from 9am to 5pm. The **Prudential Information Center,** on the main level of the Prudential Center, 800 Boylston St., is open Monday through Friday from 8:30am to 6pm, Saturday and Sunday from 10am to 6pm. The **Greater Boston Convention & Visitors Bureau** (© **888/SEE-BOSTON** or 617/536-4100; www.bostonusa.com) operates both centers.

There's a small information booth at **Faneuil Hall Marketplace** between Quincy Market and the South Market Building. It's outdoors and staffed in the spring, summer, and fall Monday through Saturday from 10am to 6pm, Sunday from noon to 6pm.

In Cambridge, there's an information kiosk (© **800/862-5678** or 617/497-1630) in the heart of **Harvard Square,** near the T entrance at the intersection of Massachusetts Avenue, John F. Kennedy Street, and Brattle Street. It's open Monday through Saturday from 9am to 5pm, Sunday from 1 to 5pm.

PUBLICATIONS

The city's newspapers offer the most up-to-date information about events in the area. The "Calendar" section of the Thursday *Boston Globe* lists festivals, concerts, dance

Boston Orientation

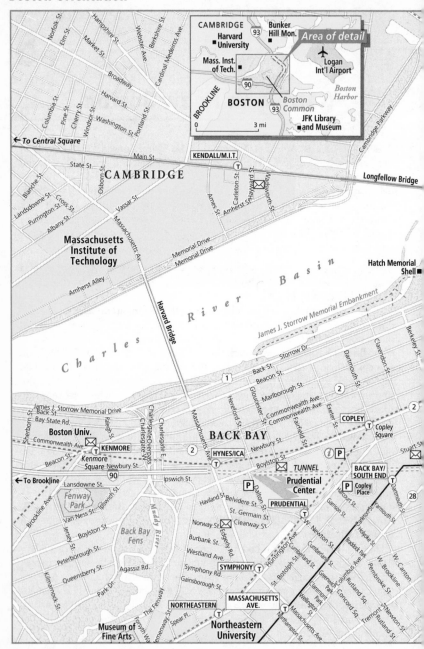

CAMBRIDGE
Bunker
Hill Mon.
Harvard
University
93
Area of detail

Mass. Inst.
of Tech.
Logan
Int'l Airport

Boston
Harbor

BROOKLINE
90

BOSTON
93
Boston
Common

JFK Library
and Museum

0   3 mi

← To Central Square

Main St.
KENDALL/M.I.T.

State St.
CAMBRIDGE
Longfellow Bridge

Massachusetts
Institute of
Technology

Charles   River   Basin

Hatch Memorial
Shell ■

Memorial Drive
Memorial Drive

Amherst Alley

Harvard Bridge

James J. Storrow Memorial Embankment

James J. Storrow Memorial Drive
Storrow Dr.

Back St.
Beacon St.
1
Back St.
Beacon St.
Marlborough St.
2
Clarendon St.
Berkeley St.

Bay State Rd.
Commonwealth Ave.
Commonwealth Ave.
2

Boston Univ.
KENMORE
BACK BAY
COPLEY
Copley
Square

Commonwealth Ave.
Newbury St.
HYNES/ICA
Kenmore
Square Newbury St.
Boylston St.
TUNNEL
BACK BAY/
SOUTH END

90
Ipswich St.
Prudential
Center
Copley
Place
28

← To Brookline
Lansdowne St.
PRUDENTIAL

Fenway
Park

Haviland St. Belvidere St.
St. Germain St.

Back Bay
Fens
Norway St. Clearway St.

Burbank St.

Westland Ave.

Symphony
Rd.
SYMPHONY

Gainsborough St.

NORTHEASTERN
MASSACHUSETTS
AVE.

Museum of
Fine Arts
Northeastern
University

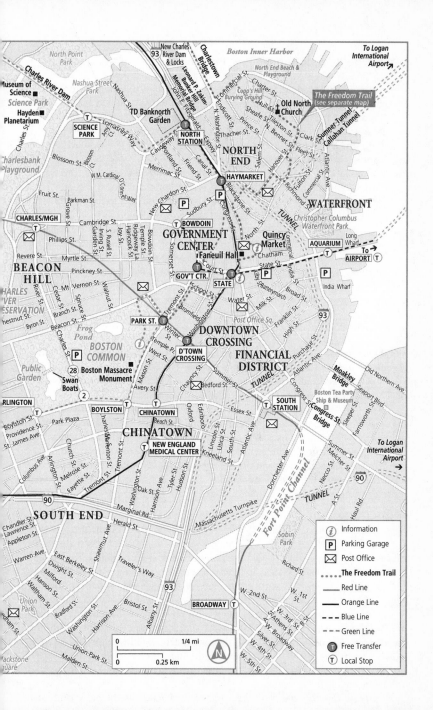

The Big Deal About the Big Dig

In a city with glorious water views, historic architecture, and gorgeous parks, the most prominent physical feature over the past decade and a half was a giant highway construction project. The $14.6 billion (yes, billion!) Central Artery/Third Harbor Tunnel project, better known as the **Big Dig,** transformed I-93 from an elevated expressway into a tunnel without closing the road through downtown Boston.

Although it's technically complete, the Big Dig just won't go away. Glitches—including copious leaking in several different tunnel sections—keep cropping up, and questions linger about who will pay to fix the problems and whether the long-term effect on traffic will be positive.

The project did leave behind a lovely landmark (the Leonard P. Zakim Bunker Hill Memorial Bridge, over the Charles River north of North Station) as well as many smaller construction sites. Parks, public spaces, and buildings are planned, but construction couldn't start until demolition of the elevated expressway was complete. To learn more, visit the website (www.mass pike.com/bigdig) or just walk around downtown.

and theater performances, club schedules, street fairs, films, and speeches. The Friday *Boston Herald* has a similar, smaller insert called "The Edge." Both papers briefly list events in their weekend editions. The free, arts-oriented *Boston Phoenix,* published on Thursday, has extensive entertainment and restaurant listings.

Where, a monthly magazine available free at most hotels throughout the city, lists information about shopping, nightlife, attractions, and current shows at museums and art galleries. Newspaper boxes dispense free copies of the weekly *Tab,* which lists neighborhood-specific event information; *Stuff@Night,* a *Phoenix* offshoot with selective listings and arts coverage; and the *Improper Bostonian,* with extensive event and restaurant listings. Available on newsstands, *Boston* magazine is a lifestyle-oriented monthly with cultural and restaurant listings.

CITY LAYOUT

When Puritan settlers established Boston in 1630, it was one-third the size it is now. Much of the city reflects the original layout, a seemingly haphazard plan that can disorient even longtime residents. Old Boston abounds with alleys, dead ends, one-way streets, streets that change names, and streets named after extinct geographical features. On the plus side, every "wrong" turn **downtown,** in the **North End,** or on **Beacon Hill** is a chance to see something interesting that you might otherwise have missed.

The most prominent feature of downtown Boston is **Boston Common.** Its borders are **Park Street,** which is 1 block long (but looms large in the geography of the T), and Beacon, Charles, Boylston, and Tremont streets. Another important street is **Massachusetts Avenue,** or "Mass. Ave.," as it's almost always called. Mass. Ave. covers 9 miles, from Roxbury through the South End, the Back Bay, Cambridge, and Arlington, ending in Lexington.

Nineteenth-century landfill projects transformed much of the city's landscape, altering the shoreline and creating the **Back Bay,** where the streets proceed in orderly parallel lines. After you've spent some frustrating time in the older part of the city, that simple plan will seem ingenious. The streets even go in alphabetical order, starting at the Public Garden with Arlington, then Berkeley, Clarendon, Dartmouth, Exeter, Fairfield, Gloucester, and Hereford (and then Mass. Ave.).

STREET MAPS

In addition to the map provided with this guide, free maps of downtown Boston and the rapid-transit lines are available at visitor information centers around the city. *Where* magazine, available free at most hotels, contains maps of central Boston and the T.

Streetwise Boston ($6.95) and *Artwise Boston* ($7.95) are sturdy, laminated maps available at most bookstores. Less detailed but more fun is MapEasy's *GuideMap to Boston* ($6.95), a hand-drawn map of the central areas and major attractions.

THE NEIGHBORHOODS IN BRIEF

These are the areas visitors are most likely to frequent. When Bostonians say **"downtown,"** they usually mean the first six neighborhoods defined here; there's no "midtown" or "uptown." The numerous neighborhoods outside central Boston include the Fenway, South Boston, Dorchester, Roxbury, West Roxbury, and Jamaica Plain. With a couple of exceptions (noted here), Boston is generally safe, but you should still take the precautions you would in any large city, especially at night.

The Waterfront This narrow area runs along the Inner Harbor, on **Atlantic Avenue** and **Commercial Street** from the Charlestown bridge (on North Washington St.) to South Station. Once filled with wharves and warehouses, today it abounds with luxury condos, marinas, restaurants, offices, and hotels. Also here are the New England Aquarium and embarkation points for harbor cruises and whale-watching expeditions.

The North End Crossing what remains of the Big Dig as you head east toward the Inner Harbor brings you to one of the city's oldest neighborhoods. Home to waves of immigrants in the course of its history, it was predominantly Italian for most of the 20th century. It's now less than half Italian American; many newcomers are young professionals who walk to work in the Financial District. Nevertheless, you'll hear Italian spoken in the streets and find a wealth of Italian restaurants, *caffès*, and shops. The main street is **Hanover Street.**

North Station Technically part of the North End but just as close to Beacon Hill, this area around **Causeway Street** is home to the **TD Banknorth Garden, North Station,** and many nightspots and restaurants. The neighborhood gets safer by the day, but wandering alone late at night (especially on the side streets away from the station) is not a good idea.

Faneuil Hall Marketplace Employees aside, Boston residents tend to be scarce at Faneuil Hall Marketplace (also called Quincy Market, after its central building). An irresistible draw

Finding an Address

There's no rhyme or reason to the street pattern, compass directions are virtually useless, and there aren't enough street signs. The best way to find an address is to call ahead and ask for directions, including landmarks, or leave extra time for wandering around. If the directions involve a T stop, be sure to ask which exit to use—most stations have more than one.

for out-of-towners and suburbanites, this cluster of restored market buildings—bounded by the Waterfront, the North End, Government Center, and **State Street**—is the city's most popular attraction. You'll find restaurants, bars, a food court, specialty shops, and Faneuil Hall itself. **Haymarket,** off I-93 on **Blackstone Street,** is home to an open-air produce market on Fridays and Saturdays.

Government Center Love it or hate it, Government Center introduced modern design to Boston's traditionally staid architecture. Flanked by Beacon Hill, Downtown Crossing, and Faneuil Hall Marketplace, it's home to state and federal offices, City Hall, and a major T stop. The redbrick wasteland of City Hall Plaza lies between **Congress** and **Cambridge streets.**

The Financial District Bounded loosely by Downtown Crossing, **Summer Street, Atlantic Avenue,** and **State Street,** the Financial District is the banking, insurance, and legal center of the city. Aside from some popular after-work spots, it's quiet at night.

Downtown Crossing The intersection that gives Downtown Crossing its name is at **Washington Street** where **Winter Street** becomes **Summer Street.** The Freedom Trail runs through this shopping and business district between Boston Common, Chinatown, the Financial District, and Government Center. Most of this neighborhood hops during the day and slows down in the evening.

Beacon Hill Narrow tree-lined streets and architectural showpieces, mostly in the Federal style, make up this residential area in the shadow of the State House. Two of the loveliest and most exclusive spots in Boston are here: Mount Vernon Street and Louisburg Square (pronounced "Lewis-burg," and

home to John Kerry). Bounded by Government Center, Boston Common, the Back Bay, and the river, it's also home to Massachusetts General Hospital. **Charles Street,** which divides the Common from the Public Garden, is the main street of Beacon Hill. Other important thoroughfares are **Beacon Street,** on the north side of the Common, and **Cambridge Street.**

Charlestown One of the oldest areas of Boston is where you'll see the Bunker Hill Monument and USS *Constitution* ("Old Ironsides"). Yuppification has brought some diversity to what was once an almost entirely white residential neighborhood, but pockets remain that have earned their reputation for insularity.

South Boston Waterfront/Seaport District Across the Fort Point Channel from the Waterfront neighborhood, this district is home to the convention center, the World Trade Center, the Seaport Hotel, the Fish Pier, a federal courthouse, Museum Wharf, and a lot of construction. **Seaport Boulevard** and **Northern Avenue** are the main drags.

Chinatown The fourth-largest Chinese community in the country is a small but growing area jammed with Asian restaurants, groceries, and gift shops. Chinatown takes up the area between Downtown Crossing and the Mass. Pike extension. The main streets are **Washington Street, Kneeland Street,** and **Beach Street.** The tiny **Theater District** extends about 1½ blocks in each direction from the intersection of Tremont and Stuart streets; be careful there at night after the crowds thin out.

The South End Cross **Stuart Street** or **Huntington Avenue** heading south from the Back Bay, and you'll find yourself in a landmark district packed with Victorian row houses and little parks. The South End has a large gay community and some of the city's best restaurants. With the gentrification of the 1980s and '90s, **Tremont Street** (particularly the end closest to downtown) gained a cachet that it hadn't known for almost a century. Long known for its ethnic, economic, and cultural diversity, the neighborhood is now thoroughly yuppified nearly all the way to Mass. Ave. *Note:* Don't confuse the South End with South Boston, a residential neighborhood on the other side of I-93.

The Back Bay Fashionable since its creation out of landfill more than a century ago, the Back Bay overflows with gorgeous architecture and chic shops. It lies between the Public Garden, the river, Kenmore Square, and either **Huntington Avenue** or **St. Botolph Street,** depending on who's describing it. Students dominate the area near **Mass Ave.** (Massachusetts Ave.) but grow scarce as property values soar near the Public Garden. This is one of the best neighborhoods in Boston for aimless walking. Major thoroughfares include **Boylston Street,** which starts at Boston Common and runs into the Fenway; largely residential **Beacon Street** and **Comm. Ave.** (Commonwealth Ave.); and boutique central, **Newbury Street.**

Huntington Avenue The honorary "Avenue of the Arts" (or, with a Boston accent, "Otts"), though not a formal neighborhood, is where you'll find the Christian Science Center, Symphony Hall (at the corner of Mass. Ave.), Northeastern University, and the Museum of Fine Arts. It begins at Copley Square and touches on the Back Bay, the Fenway, and the Longwood Medical Area before heading into the suburbs. Parts of Huntington can be a little risky, so if you're leaving the museum at night, stick to a car, a cab, or the Green Line, and travel in a group.

Kenmore Square The white-and-red CITGO sign that dominates the skyline above the intersection of **Comm. Ave.** (Commonwealth Ave.), **Beacon Street,** and **Brookline Avenue** tells you that you're approaching Kenmore Square. Its shops, bars, restaurants, and clubs attract students from adjacent Boston University. The college-town atmosphere goes out the window when the Red Sox are in town and baseball fans pour into the area on the way to historic Fenway Park, 3 blocks away.

Cambridge Boston's neighbor across the Charles River is a separate city. The areas you're likely to visit lie along the MBTA Red Line. **Harvard Square** is a magnet for students, sightseers, and well-heeled shoppers. It's an easy walk along Mass. Ave. southeast to **Central Square,** a rapidly gentrifying area dotted with ethnic restaurants and clubs. North along Mass. Ave. is **Porter Square,** a mostly residential neighborhood with some quirky shops like those that once characterized Harvard Square. Around **Kendall Square** you'll find MIT and many technology-oriented businesses.

Fun Fact **By George!**

Washington Street, the most "main" street downtown, has another distinction: As a tribute to the first president, street names (except Mass. Ave.) change when they cross Washington. For example, Bromfield becomes Franklin, Winter becomes Summer, Stuart becomes Kneeland.

2 Getting Around

ON FOOT

If you can manage a fair amount of walking, this is the way to go. You can best appreciate Boston at street level, and walking the narrow, picturesque streets takes you past many gridlocked cars.

Even more than in a typical large city, be alert. Look both ways before crossing, even on one-way streets, where many bicyclists and some drivers blithely go against the flow. The "walk" cycle of many downtown traffic signals lasts only 7 seconds, and a small but significant part of the driving population considers red lights optional anyway. Keep a close eye on the kids, especially in crosswalks. And of course you're all wearing comfortable shoes, right?

BY PUBLIC TRANSPORTATION

The **Massachusetts Bay Transportation Authority,** or MBTA (© **800/392-6100** or 617/222-3200; www.mbta.com), is known as the T, and its logo is the letter in a circle. It runs subways, trolleys, buses, and ferries in Boston and many suburbs, as well as the commuter rail, which extends as far as Providence, Rhode Island.

For information on services and discounts for seniors and travelers with disabilities, see p. 17.

BY SUBWAY & TROLLEY

Subways and trolleys take you around Boston faster than any other mode of transportation except walking. The oldest system in the country, the "T" dates to 1897, and recent and ongoing improvements have made it generally reliable. The trolleys on the ancient Green Line are the most unpredictable—leave extra time if you're on the way to a vital appointment. The system is generally safe, but always watch out for pickpockets, especially during the holiday shopping season. And remember, downtown stops are so close together that it's often faster to walk.

The subways are color-coded and are called the Red, Green, Blue, and Orange lines. The commuter rail to the suburbs is purple on system maps and is sometimes called the Purple Line. The Silver Line is a fancy name for a bus line. The local fare on the subway and trolleys is **$1.25** and can be as much as $3 for some surface-line extensions on the Green and Red lines. Transfers are free. The system is phasing in automated fare collection to replace tokens, which are worth $1.25. Route and fare information and timetables are available through the website (www.mbta.com) and at centrally located stations.

Service begins at around 5:15am and ends around 12:30am. (The exception is New Year's Eve, or First Night, when closing time is 2am and service is free after 8pm.) A sign in every station gives the time of the last train in either direction.

Tips **All's Fare on the T**

During the lifespan of this book, the MBTA plans to phase in automated fare collection one line at a time. The paper **CharlieTicket** and the plastic **CharlieCard** will replace tokens on the subway; bus and aboveground trolley passengers will still have the option to pay cash. Elaborate instructions are posted in every T station that uses the new system. For a preview, visit **www.mbta.com.**

Boston Transit

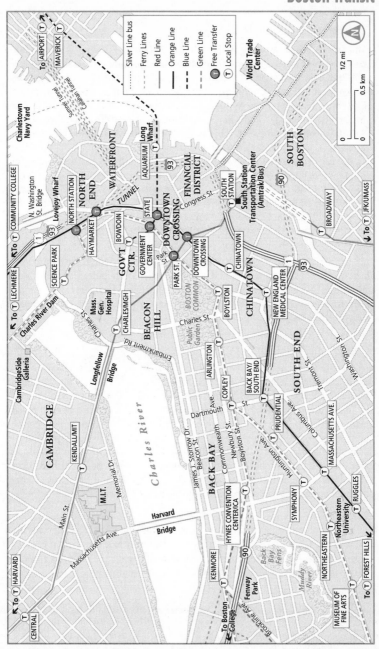

Legend:
- ········· Silver Line bus
- ──── Ferry Lines
- ──── Red Line
- ──── Orange Line
- ──── Blue Line
- ──── Green Line
- ⊤ Free Transfer
- (T) Local Stop

To AIRPORT · MAVERICK · Charlestown Navy Yard · COMMUNITY COLLEGE · N. Washington St. Bridge · Lovejoy Wharf · NORTH STATION · NORTH END · WATERFRONT · Long Wharf · AQUARIUM · FINANCIAL DISTRICT · STATE · Congress St. · SOUTH STATION · South Station Transportation Center (Amtrak/Bus) · SOUTH BOSTON · World Trade Center · BROADWAY · JFK/UMASS

SCIENCE PARK · HAYMARKET · BOWDOIN · GOV'T CTR. · GOVERNMENT CENTER · DOWNTOWN CROSSING · Park St. · PARK ST. · DOWNTOWN CROSSING · CHINATOWN · NEW ENGLAND MEDICAL CENTER · 93 · 1

To LECHMERE · Charles River Dam · CambridgeSide Galleria · Mass. Gen. Hospital · CHARLES/MGH · BEACON HILL · Charles St. · BOSTON COMMON · Public Garden · BOYLSTON · SOUTH END · Washington St.

To HARVARD · CENTRAL · CAMBRIDGE · KENDALL/MIT · M.I.T. · Main St. · Memorial Dr. · Longfellow Bridge · Embankment Rd. · Charles River · Massachusetts Ave. · Harvard Bridge · James J. Storrow Dr. · Beacon St. · Commonwealth Ave. · Newbury St. · Boylston St. · ARLINGTON · COPLEY · St. · Dartmouth Ave. · BACK BAY/SOUTH END · PRUDENTIAL · Columbus Ave. · MASSACHUSETTS AVE. · Tremont St. · SOUTH END

BACK BAY · HYNES CONVENTION CENTER/ICA · Huntington Ave. · SYMPHONY · NORTHEASTERN · Northeastern University · RUGGLES · To FOREST HILLS

KENMORE · Fenway Park · Back Bay Fens · Muddy River · MUSEUM OF FINE ARTS · To JFK/UMASS · Brookline Ave. · To Boston College

1/2 mi · 0.5 km

67

Value **Ride & Save (Maybe)**

The MBTA's **Boston Visitor Pass** (✆ **877/927-7277** or 617/222-5218; www.mbta. com) can be a great deal—but only if you plan to use public transit enough. You get unlimited travel on subway lines and local buses, in commuter rail zones 1A and 1B, and on the Inner Harbor ferry, but not on the Night Owl bus. The cost is $7.50 for 1 day (so tokens are cheaper for fewer than six trips), $18 for 3 consecutive days, and $35 for 7 consecutive days. If the timing works, the $16.50 **weekly combo pass** is a better deal. It covers subways and buses, and is good from Sunday to Saturday only.

You can order passes in advance over the phone or the Web (there's a fee for shipping), or buy them when you arrive at the Airport T stop, South Station, Back Bay Station, or North Station. They're also for sale at the Government Center and Harvard T stations; the Boston Common, Prudential Center, and Faneuil Hall Marketplace information centers; and some hotels.

At press time, budget considerations were threatening **Night Owl** bus service, which operates on Friday and Saturday until 2:30am on popular bus routes and on supplemental bus routes that parallel the subway lines. The local fare is $1.50 in coins. To see whether the service is still operating, get information, and check schedules, contact the MBTA.

BY BUS

The MBTA runs buses and "trackless trolleys" (buses with electric antennae) that provide service around town and to and around the suburbs. The local routes that you'll most likely need are **no. 1,** along Mass. Ave. from Dudley Square in Roxbury through the Back Bay and Cambridge to Harvard Square; **no. 92** and **no. 93,** which connect Haymarket and Charlestown; and **no. 77,** along Mass. Ave. north of Harvard Square to Porter Square, North Cambridge, and Arlington. The **Silver Line** (which looks like a branch of the subway on some maps but is a bus line) runs on two routes: from Temple Place, near Downtown Crossing, to the South End and Roxbury; and from South Station to the South Boston waterfront, including the convention center and the World Trade Center.

The local bus fare is **90¢;** express bus fares are $2.20 and up. Exact change is required. You can use a token, but you won't get change back.

BY FERRY

The MBTA Inner Harbor ferry connects **Long Wharf** (near the New England Aquarium) with the **Charlestown Navy Yard**—it's a good way to get back downtown from "Old Ironsides" and the Bunker Hill Monument. The fare is $1.50, or show your MBTA visitor pass. Call ✆ **617/227-4321** for more information.

BY WATER TAXI

City Water Taxi (✆ **617/422-0392;** www.citywatertaxi.com) offers on-call service in small boats that connect a dozen stops on the Inner Harbor, including the airport. It operates daily April to November from 7am to 7pm. One-way fares start at $10. The **Rowes Wharf Water Taxi** (✆ **617/406-8584;** www.roweswharfwatertaxi.com) connects the airport ferry dock, the federal courthouse in Fan Pier, the World Trade Center, and Rowes Wharf, off Atlantic Avenue behind the Boston Harbor Hotel. It runs year-round from 7am to 7pm, daily in the summer and weekdays only from October to May. The flat fare is $10 one-way.

Call ahead from the dock for pick-up.

BY TAXI

Taxis are expensive and not always easy to find—seek out a cabstand or call a dispatcher. Always ask for a receipt in case you have a complaint or lose something and need to call the company.

Cabstands are usually near hotels. There are also busy ones at Faneuil Hall Marketplace (on North St. and in front of 60 State St.), South Station, and Back Bay Station, and on either side of Mass. Ave. in Harvard Square, near the Harvard Coop bookstore and Au Bon Pain.

To call ahead for a cab, try the **Independent Taxi Operators Association,** or ITOA (© 617/426-8700); **Boston Cab** (© 617/536-5010 or 617/262-2227); **Town Taxi** (© 617/536-5000); or **Metro Cab** (© 617/242-8000). In Cambridge, call **Ambassador Brattle** (© 617/492-1100) or **Yellow Cab** (© 617/547-3000). Boston Cab will dispatch a wheelchair-accessible vehicle upon request; advance notice is recommended.

The fare structure: The first ¼ mile (when the flag drops) costs $1.75, and each additional ⅛ mile is 30¢. Wait time is extra, and the passenger pays all tolls, as well as a total of $6.50 in fees on trips leaving Logan Airport. Charging a flat rate is not allowed within the city; the police department publishes a list (available on the airport website, www.massport.com/logan) of flat rates for trips to the suburbs. If you want to report a problem or have lost something in a cab, call the police department's **Hackney Hotline** (© **617/536-8294**).

BY CAR

If you plan to visit only Boston and Cambridge, there's absolutely no reason to have a car. With its pricey parking and narrow, one-way streets, not to mention the remains of the Big Dig, Boston in particular is a motorist's nightmare. If you arrive by car, park at the hotel and use the car for day trips. Drive to Cambridge only if you're feeling flush—you'll pay to park there, too. If you're not motoring and you decide to take a day trip (see chapter 12), you'll probably want to rent a car. Here's the scoop:

RENTALS

The major car-rental firms have offices at Logan Airport and in Boston, and some have other area branches. Seriously consider waiting to pick up the car until you need it to save yourself the hassle of driving and parking. Rentals that originate in Boston carry a **$10 convention center surcharge**—you can get around it by picking up your car in Cambridge, Brookline, or another suburb.

Impressions

Boston's freeway system was insane. It was clearly designed by a person who had spent his childhood crashing toy trains. Every few hundred yards I would find my lane vanishing beneath me and other lanes merging with it from the right or left, or sometimes both. This wasn't a road system, it was mobile hysteria.

—Bill Bryson, *The Lost Continent* (1989)

If you're traveling at a busy time, especially during foliage season, reserve a car well in advance. Most companies set aside cars for nonsmokers, but you have to ask. To rent from the major national chains, you must be at least 25 years old and have a valid driver's license and credit card.

Companies with offices at the airport include **Alamo** (© 800/327-9633; www.go alamo.com), **Avis** (© 800/831-2847; www.avis.com), **Budget** (© 800/527-0700; www.budget.com), **Dollar** (© 800/800-4000; www.dollar.com), **Hertz** (© 800/654-3131; www.hertz.com), and **National** (© 800/227-7368; www.nationalcar.com). **Enterprise** (© 800/325-8007; www.enterprise.com) and **Thrifty** (© 800/367-2277; www.thrifty.com) are nearby but not on the grounds, so leave time for the shuttle bus ride.

INSURANCE

If you hold a private auto insurance policy, it probably covers you in the U.S. for loss of or damage to the rental car, and for liability in case a passenger is injured. The credit card you use to rent the car may also provide some coverage, but don't assume—check before you leave home.

Car-rental insurance typically does not cover liability if you caused the accident. Check your own auto insurance policy, the rental company policy, and your credit card coverage for the extent of coverage: Is your destination covered? Are other drivers covered? How much liability is covered if a passenger is injured? If you rely on your credit card for coverage, you may want to bring a second credit card with you because damages may be charged to your card and you may find yourself stranded with no money.

Car rental insurance costs about $20 a day.

PACKAGE DEALS

Many packages include airfare, accommodations, and a rental car with unlimited mileage. Compare these prices with the cost of booking airline tickets and renting a car separately. Don't saddle yourself with a car for a long period if you won't be using it, though. And don't forget to add the price of parking.

BOOKING ONLINE

See the "Surfing for Rental Cars" section in chapter 2 for pointers on online booking.

PARKING

It's difficult to find your way around Boston and practically impossible to find parking in some areas. Most spaces on the street are metered (and patrolled until at least 6pm Mon–Sat) and are open to nonresidents for 2 hours or less between 8am and 6pm. The penalty is a $40 ticket—even the most expensive garage is cheaper. Read the sign or meter carefully. In some areas parking is allowed only at certain hours. Rates vary in different sections of the city (usually $1/hr. downtown); bring plenty of quarters. Time limits range from 15 minutes to 2 hours.

If you blunder into a tow-away zone, retrieving the car will cost well over $100 and a lot of running around. The city tow lot (© **617/635-3900**) is at 200 Frontage Rd. in South Boston. Take a taxi, or ride the Red Line to Andrew and flag a cab.

It's best to leave the car in a garage or lot and walk, but be aware that Boston's parking is the second most expensive in the country (after Manhattan's). A full day at most garages costs no more than $25, but some downtown facilities charge as much as $35, and hourly rates can be exorbitant. Many lots charge a lower flat rate if you enter and

Tips Boston Drivers: Beware

One of the funniest intentionally-funny lines in the movie *Love Story* is, "This is Boston—everybody drives like a maniac." And that was before cellphones and SUVs. Boston drivers absolutely deserve their notoriety, and even though the truly reckless are a tiny minority, it pays to be careful. Never assume that another driver will behave as you might expect, especially when it comes to the rarely used turn signal. Watch out for cars that leave the curb and change lanes without signaling, double- and triple-park in the most inconvenient places imaginable, and travel the wrong way down one-way streets. And remember that most pedestrians and bicyclists are just drivers without their protective covering.

exit before certain times or if you park in the evening. Some restaurants offer reduced rates at nearby garages; ask when you call for reservations.

The city-run garage under **Boston Common** (✆ 617/954-2096) accepts vehicles less than 6 feet, 3 inches tall. Enter from Charles Street between Boylston and Beacon streets. The **Prudential Center** garage (✆ 617/267-1002) has entrances on Boylston Street, Huntington Avenue, and Exeter Street, and at the Sheraton Boston Hotel. Parking is discounted if you buy something at the Shops at Prudential Center and have your ticket validated. The garage at **Copley Place** (✆ 617/375-4488), off Huntington Avenue, offers a similar deal. Many businesses in Faneuil Hall Marketplace validate parking at the **75 State St. Garage** (✆ 617/742-7275).

Good-size garages downtown are at **Government Center** off Congress Street (✆ 617/227-0385), **Sudbury Street** off Congress Street (✆ 617/973-6954), the **New England Aquarium** (✆ 617/723-1731), and **Zero Post Office Square** in the Financial District (✆ 617/423-1430). In the Back Bay, there's a large facility near the Hynes Convention Center on **Dalton Street** (✆ 617/247-8006).

DRIVING RULES

When traffic permits, drivers may turn right at a red light after stopping, unless a sign is posted saying otherwise (as it often is downtown). Seat belts are mandatory for adults and children, children under 12 may not ride in the front seat, and infants and children under 5 must be strapped into car seats in the back seat. You can't be stopped just for having an unbelted adult in the car, but a youngster on the loose is reason enough to pull you over.

Be aware of two state laws, if only because drivers break them so frequently it'll take your breath away: Pedestrians in the crosswalk have the right of way (most suburbs actually enforce this one), and vehicles already in a rotary (traffic circle or roundabout) have the right of way.

BY BICYCLE

This is not a good option unless you're a real pro or plan to visit Cambridge, which has bike lanes. The streets of Boston proper, with their bloodthirsty drivers and oblivious pedestrians, are notoriously inhospitable to two-wheelers.

For information about renting a bike and about recreational biking, see "Biking" on p. 193. If you bring or rent a bike, be sure to lock it securely when leaving it unattended, even for a short time.

FAST FACTS: Boston

American Express The main office is at 1 State St. (℃ **617/723-8400**), opposite the Old State House. A nearby office is in the Financial District at 170 Federal St. (℃ **617/439-4400**). The Back Bay office is at 432 Stuart St. (℃ **617/236-1331**). All three keep the same hours: weekdays from 8:30am to 5:30pm. The Cambridge office, 39 John F. Kennedy St., Harvard Square (℃ **617/868-2600**), is open weekdays from 9am to 5:30pm, Saturday from 10am to 3pm.

Area Codes Eastern Massachusetts has eight area codes: Boston proper, **617** and **857**; immediate suburbs, **781** and **339**; northern and western suburbs, **978** and **351**; southern suburbs, **508** and **774**.

Note: To make a local call, you must dial all 10 digits.

ATM Networks **Cirrus** (℃ **800/424-7787**; www.mastercard.com), **PLUS** (℃ **800/843-7587**; www.visa.com), and **NYCE (888/456-2844**; www.nyce.net) cover most Boston-area banks.

Babysitters Many hotels maintain lists of reliable sitters; check at the front desk or with the concierge. Local agencies aren't a cost-effective option; most charge a steep annual fee on top of the daily referral charge and the sitter's hourly wage and expenses. If you're in town on business, ask whether the company you're visiting has a corporate membership in an agency.

Tip: If you already know that your visit will include a child-free evening out, make arrangements when you reserve your room.

Car Rentals See "Getting Around," earlier in this chapter.

Convention Centers Convention centers include **Bayside Expo Center,** 200 Mt. Vernon St., Dorchester (℃ **617/474-6000**; www.baysideexpo.com); **Boston Convention & Exhibition Center,** 415 Summer St., South Boston (℃ **617/867-8286**; www.advantageboston.com); **Hynes Convention Center,** 900 Boylston St. (℃ **617/954-2000** or 617/424-8585 for show info; www.jbhynes.com); and **Seaport World Trade Center,** 200 Seaport Blvd. (℃ **800/367-9822**; www.wtcb.com).

Dentists The desk staff or concierge at your hotel might be able to suggest a dentist. The **Massachusetts Dental Society** (℃ **800/342-8747** or 508/480-9797; www.massdental.org) can point you toward a member.

Doctors The desk staff or concierge at your hotel should be able to direct you to a doctor. You can also try the physician referral service at one of the area's many hospitals. Among them are Beth Israel Deaconess (℃ **800/667-5356**), Brigham and Women's (℃ **800/294-9999**), Massachusetts General (℃ **800/711-4MGH**), and Tufts–New England Medical Center (℃ **617/636-9700**).

An affiliate of Mass. General, **MGH Back Bay,** 388 Commonwealth Ave. (℃ **617/267-7171**), offers walk-in service and honors most insurance plans.

Driving Rules See "Getting Around," earlier in this chapter.

Drugstores Downtown Boston has no 24-hour pharmacy. The pharmacy at the **CVS** at 155–157 Charles St. in Boston (℃ **617/523-1028**), next to the Charles T stop, is open until midnight on weeknights, 10pm on weekends. The pharmacy at the **CVS** in the Porter Square Shopping Center, off Mass. Ave. in Cambridge

(© 617/876-5519), is open 24 hours, 7 days a week. Some emergency rooms can fill your prescription at the hospital's pharmacy.

Embassies & Consulates See "Fast Facts: For the International Traveler," in chapter 3.

Emergencies Call © 911 for fire, ambulance, or the Boston, Brookline, or Cambridge police. This is a free call from pay phones. For the state police, call © 617/523-1212, or © *77 from a cellphone.

Holidays See "Fast Facts: For the International Traveler," in chapter 3.

Hospitals **Massachusetts General Hospital,** 55 Fruit St. (© 617/726-2000), and **Tufts–New England Medical Center,** 750 Washington St. (© 617/636-5000), are closest to downtown. At the Harvard Medical Area on the Boston-Brookline border are **Beth Israel Deaconess Medical Center,** 330 Brookline Ave. (© 617/667-7000); **Brigham and Women's Hospital,** 75 Francis St. (© 617/732-5500); and **Children's Hospital,** 300 Longwood Ave. (© 617/355-6000). In Cambridge are **Mount Auburn Hospital,** 330 Mount Auburn St. (© 617/492-3500), and **Cambridge Hospital,** 1493 Cambridge St. (© 617/498-1000).

Hot Lines **AIDS Hotline** (© 800/235-2331), **Poison Control Center** (© 800/682-9211), **Rape Crisis** (© 877/627-7700 or 617/492-7273), **Samaritans Suicide Prevention** (© 617/247-0220), and **Samariteens** (© 800/252-8336 or 617/247-8050).

Information See the "Orientation" section, earlier in this chapter.

Internet Access For a tech-happy area, Boston has few cybercafes. Your hotel might have a terminal for guests' use, and many hotels offer on-premises wireless access (often for a daily fee). The ubiquitous **FedEx Kinko's** charges 10¢ to 20¢ a minute. Locations include 2 Center Plaza, Government Center (© 617/973-9000); 10 Post Office Sq., Financial District (© 617/482-4400); 187 Dartmouth St., Back Bay (© 617/262-6188); and 1 Mifflin Place, off Mount Auburn Street near Eliot Street, Harvard Square (© 617/497-0125). **Tech Superpowers,** 252 Newbury St., 3rd floor (© 617/267-9716; www.newburyopen.net), also offers access by the hour ($5/hr.; $3 minimum).

Liquor Laws The legal drinking age is 21. In many bars, particularly near college campuses, you might be asked to show identification if you appear to be under 30 or so. At sporting events, everyone buying alcohol must show ID. Liquor stores and a few supermarkets and convenience stores sell alcohol. Liquor stores and the liquor sections of other stores are open Monday though Saturday and open at noon on Sunday in communities where that's legal. Most restaurants have full liquor licenses; some serve only beer, wine, and cordials. Last call typically is 30 minutes before closing time (1am in bars, 2am in clubs).

Lost or Stolen Wallet Be sure to tell all of your credit card companies the minute you discover your wallet has been lost or stolen and file a report at the nearest police precinct. Your credit card company or insurer may require a police report number or record of the loss. Most credit card companies have an emergency toll-free number to call if your card is lost or stolen; they may be able to wire you a cash advance immediately or deliver an emergency credit card in a day or two. Visa's U.S. emergency number is © 800/847-2911 or 410/581-9994. American Express cardholders and traveler's check holders should call ✆ **800/221-7282.** MasterCard holders should call ✆ **800/307-7309** or 636/722-7111. For other credit cards, call the toll-free directory at ✆ **800/555-1212.**

Identity theft and fraud are potential complications of losing your wallet, especially if you've lost your driver's license along with your cash and credit cards. Notify the major credit-reporting bureaus immediately; placing a fraud alert on your records may protect you against liability for criminal activity. The major U.S. credit-reporting agencies are **Equifax** (✆ 800/766-0008; www. equifax.com), **Experian** (✆ 888/397-3742; www.experian.com), and **TransUnion** (✆ **800/680-7289;** www.transunion.com). Finally, if you've lost all forms of photo ID, call your airline and explain the situation; you may be able to board the plane if you have a copy of your passport or birth certificate and a copy of the police report you've filed.

Luggage Storage & Lockers The desk staff or concierge at your hotel may be able to arrange storage. Lockers at the airport are unavailable indefinitely. Ticketed Amtrak passengers can check bags (during the day only) at South Station; Back Bay Station has no luggage facilities. Some kindhearted bartenders in the North Station area may agree to watch your backpack or briefcase while you attend an event at the TD Banknorth Garden (which forbids them), but it's easier to leave the bag at the hotel.

Maps See "Orientation," earlier in this chapter.

Newspapers & Magazines The *Boston Globe* and *Boston Herald* are published daily, and the New York papers are widely available. See p. 48 for more information.

Pharmacies See "Drugstores," above.

Police Call ✆ **911** for emergencies.

Post Office The main post office, at 25 Dorchester Ave. (✆ **617/654-5302**), behind South Station, is open weekdays 6am to midnight, Saturday 8am to 7pm, Sunday and holidays noon to 7pm.

Radio AM stations include **680** (WRKO: talk, sports, Celtics games), **850** (WEEI: sports, Red Sox games), **1030** (WBZ: news, Bruins games), **1090** (WILD: urban contemporary, soul), and **1510** (WWZN: sports talk). You can catch regular traffic updates on WBZ (every 10 min.) and WRKO (every 15 min. during rush hours).

FM stations include **89.7** (WGBH: public radio, classical, jazz), **90.9** (WBUR: public radio, classical), **92.9** (WBOS: album rock), **93.7** (WQSX: dance hits), **94.5** (WJMN: dance, rap, hip-hop), **96.9** (WTKK: talk), **98.5** (WBMX: adult contemporary), **99.5** (WKLB: country), **100.7** (WZLX: classic rock), **101.7** (WFNX: progressive rock), **102.5** (WCRB: classical), **103.3** (WODS: oldies), **104.1** (WBCN: rock, Patriots games), **105.7** (WROR: '60s and '70s), and **106.7** (WMJX: pop, adult contemporary).

Restrooms The visitor center at 15 State St. has a public restroom, as do most tourist attractions, hotels, department stores, malls, and public buildings. The CambridgeSide Galleria, Copley Place, Prudential Center, and Quincy Market shopping areas and most branches of Starbucks have clean restrooms.

You'll find eight freestanding, self-cleaning **pay toilets** (25¢) around downtown. Locations include City Hall Plaza, up the steps from Congress Street, and Commercial Street at Snowhill Street, just off the Freedom Trail. Check these facilities carefully before using them; despite regular patrols, IV-drug users have been known to take advantage of the generous time limits.

Safety See p. 16

Smoking Massachusetts is an anti-tobacco stronghold. State law bans smoking in all workplaces, including restaurants, bars, and clubs.

Taxes The 5% sales tax does not apply to groceries, prescription drugs, newspapers, or clothing that costs less than $175; the tax on meals and takeout food is 5%. The lodging tax is 12.45% in Boston and Cambridge.

Taxis See "Getting Around," earlier in this chapter.

Television Stations include channels **2** (WGBH), public television; **4** (WBZ), CBS; **5** (WCVB), ABC; **7** (WHDH), NBC; **25** (WFXT), Fox; **38** (WSBK), UPN; and **56** (WLVI), WB. Cable TV is available throughout Boston and the suburbs; the regional station New England Cable News is channel 14 on Boston cable.

Time Zone See p. 50

Transit Info Call 𝄞 **617/222-3200** for the MBTA (subways, local buses, commuter rail) and 𝄞 **800/23-LOGAN** for the Massachusetts Port Authority (airport transportation).

Weather Call 𝄞 **617/936-1234.**

Where to Stay

The search for a hotel turns some travelers into the human equivalent of the dog in the "Far Side" cartoon who only hears her own name ("blah, blah, blah, *Ginger*"). Faced with a detailed description of a potential lodging, they see only what they care about: "upstairs from the meeting that starts at 6:45am," "part of a chain that lets me accumulate frequent-flyer miles," "across the street from the wedding reception."

Others shop by price alone. If that describes you, be aware that local occupancy rates have nearly returned to the lofty heights they enjoyed in the late 1990s, and the average room rate is north of $160. Nevertheless, bargains are out there, particularly at slow times.

As you go through this chapter, keep Boston's relatively small size in mind and check a map before you rule out a location. These listings use the neighborhood descriptions in chapter 5, "Getting to Know Boston." Especially downtown, the neighborhoods are so small and close together that the borders are somewhat arbitrary. The division to consider is **downtown versus the Back Bay versus Cambridge,** and not, say, the Waterfront versus the adjacent Financial District.

With enough flexibility, you probably won't have much difficulty finding a suitable place to stay in or near the city, but it's always a good idea to make a reservation. Try to book ahead if you plan on visiting between April and November, when conventions, college graduations, and vacations increase demand. Foliage season typically is the busiest and priciest time of year.

Every hotel in this area accommodates both business travelers and families. That's not to say that you'll trip over a hopscotch game in the elevator at a Hilton or a corporate takeover in the HoJo lobby, just that flexibility is the rule.

Most of the major hotel chains have a presence in the Boston area. Many of the larger establishments share a certain sameness, but even that comes with a potential bonus: Hotels with a common corporate parent may offer some flexibility. For instance, if one Starwood (Sheraton, Westin) property is overbooked, management can whisk you off to an affiliate and save you the trouble of calling around.

Besides Starwood, other chains operating in and around Boston include leisure-oriented Best Western, Holiday Inn, Howard Johnson, Radisson, and Ramada; luxury operators Fairmont, Four Seasons, Ritz-Carlton, and Sonesta; and business-traveler magnets Hilton, Hyatt, Marriott, and Wyndham (Sheraton and Westin). New players on the scene include Kimpton and the Irish chain Jurys Doyle.

The scarcest lodging option in the immediate Boston area is the moderately priced chain motel. Brands that are bargains elsewhere may be pricey here—again, especially at busy times.

Rates in this chapter are for a double room; if you're traveling alone, single rates are almost always lower. The rates given here do not include the 5.7% state hotel tax. Boston and Cambridge add a 2.75% convention center tax on top of the 4% city tax, making the total tax 12.45%. Not all suburbs impose a local tax, so some towns charge only the state tax. These listings cover Boston, Cambridge, and Brookline. If you plan to visit a suburban town and want to stay overnight, see chapter 12 for suggestions.

SAVING ON YOUR HOTEL ROOM

The **rack rate** is the maximum rate that a hotel charges for a room. Hardly anybody pays this price, however. To lower the cost of your room:

- **Ask about special rates or other discounts.** Always ask whether a price lower than the first one quoted is available or whether any special rates apply to you. You may qualify for corporate, student, military, senior, or other discounts. Mention membership in AAA, AARP, frequent-flier programs, or trade unions, which may entitle you to special deals. Find out the hotel policy on children—do kids stay free in the room or is there a special rate?
- **Dial direct.** When booking a room in a chain hotel, you'll often get a better deal from the hotel's reservation desk than from the chain's main number.
- **Book online.** Many hotels offer Internet-only discounts or supply discounted rooms to Priceline, Hotwire, or Expedia. For pointers, turn to "Surfing for Hotels," on p. 22.
- **Remember the law of supply and demand.** Business-oriented hotels are busiest during the week, so you can expect discounts over the weekend. Leisure hotels are most crowded and therefore most expensive on weekends, so discounts are usually available midweek.
- **Visit in the winter.** Boston-bound bargain hunters who don't mind cold and snow (sometimes *lots* of snow) aim for January through March, when you can find great hotel deals, especially on weekends. The Convention & Visitors Bureau's "Boston Overnight! Just for the Fun of It" winter-weekend program targets suburbanites, but out-of-towners benefit, too.
- **Look into group or long-stay discounts.** If you come as part of a large group, you should be able to negotiate a bargain rate. If you're planning a long stay (at least 5 days), you might qualify for a discount. As a rule, expect 1 night free after a 7-night stay.
- **Avoid excess charges and hidden costs.** When you book a room, ask whether the hotel charges for parking—almost every hotel in Boston and Cambridge does. Use

---

Tips Tips for Last-Minute Planners

You waited until the last minute and you can't find a room. What to do?

- Call the Hotel Hot Line (© **800/777-6001**). A service of the Greater Boston Convention & Visitors Bureau (© **888/SEE-BOSTON** or 617/536-4100; www. bostonusa.com), it can help make reservations even during the busiest times. It's staffed weekdays until 8pm, weekends until 4pm.
- If you're driving from the west, stop at the Massachusetts Turnpike's Natick rest area and try the reservation service at the visitor information center.
- If you arrive at Logan Airport without a room reservation (you daredevil), ask the staff at the **Visitor Service Center** in Terminal C for help.

(*Tips* **Where There's Smoke: Nonsmoking Rooms**

Accommodations reserved for nonsmokers have become the rule rather than the exception. However, nonsmokers should not assume that they'll get a strictly nonsmoking room without specifically requesting one. As hotels squeeze smokers into fewer and fewer rooms, the ones they use become saturated with the smell of smoke, even in lodgings that are otherwise antiseptic. To avoid this disagreeable situation, be sure that everyone who handles your reservation knows that you need a completely nonsmoking room.

---

your cellphone, prepaid phone cards, or pay phones instead of making expensive calls from hotel phones. If you know you'll be online a lot, seek out a hotel that includes high-speed or wireless access in the room rate (most newly constructed or renovated hotels do; most older properties don't). And don't be tempted by the minibar: Most hotels charge through the nose for water, soda, and snacks. Finally, ask about local taxes and service charges, which can increase the cost of a room by 15% or more.

- **Book an efficiency.** A room with a kitchenette allows you to shop for groceries and cook your own meals. This is a big money saver, especially for families on long stays.

BED & BREAKFASTS

A bed-and-breakfast can be a good alternative to a chain hotel. B&Bs are usually less expensive than hotels and often more comfortable. Most are near public transportation. Because most B&Bs are small, they fill quickly. An agency can save you a lot of calling around and can match you with a lodging that accommodates your likes and dislikes, allergies, tolerance for noise and morning chitchat, and anything else you consider important. Reserve as soon as you start planning, especially if you hope to visit during fall foliage season.

Expect to pay at least $80 a night for a double in the summer and fall, and more during special events. The room rate usually includes breakfast and parking, but be sure to ask. Many lodgings require a minimum stay of at least 2 nights, and most offer winter specials—discounts or third-night-free deals.

The following organizations can help you find your ideal B&B in Boston, Cambridge, or the greater Boston area:

- **Bed & Breakfast Agency of Boston,** 47 Commercial Wharf, Boston, MA 02110 (① **800/248-9262,** 0800/89-5128 from the U.K., or 617/720-3540; fax 617/523-5761; www.boston-bnbagency.com)
- **Host Homes of Boston,** P.O. Box 117, Waban Branch, Boston, MA 02468 (① **800/600-1308** or 617/244-1308; fax 617/244-5156; www.hosthomesof boston.com)
- **Bed & Breakfast Reservations North Shore/Greater Boston/Cape Cod** (① **800/832-2632,** 617/964-1606, or 978/281-9505; fax 978/281-9426; www.bbreserve.com)
- **Bed and Breakfast Associates Bay Colony,** P.O. Box 57166, Boston, MA 02457 (① **888/486-6018,** 0800/731-3553 from the U.K., or 617/720-0522; fax 781/455-6745; www.bnbboston.com)

1 Best Hotel Bets

- **Best Historic Hotel: The Fairmont Copley Plaza,** 138 St. James Ave. (℃ 800/ 257-7544), opened in 1912 on the original site of the Museum of Fine Arts. Designed by Henry Janeway Hardenbergh (also the architect of the Plaza in New York), it has entertained presidents and celebrities since the day its magnificent gilded lobby opened. See p. 94.
- **Best for Business Travelers: The Boston Harbor Hotel,** Rowes Wharf (℃ 800/ 752-7077), is just far enough from the Financial District to ensure some peace at the end of a busy day. And its rooms are so well-outfitted that you may not have to go out at all. See p. 82.
- **Best for a Romantic Getaway:** The intimate atmosphere and elegant furnishings make a suite at the **Eliot Hotel,** 370 Commonwealth Ave. (℃ 800/44-ELIOT), a great spot for a rendezvous. If you and your beloved need some time apart, close the French doors—you can be in separate rooms yet maintain eye contact. See p. 93.
- **Best for Families:** The **Doubletree Guest Suites,** 400 Soldiers Field Rd. (℃ 800/222-TREE), offers two rooms for the price of one, with two TVs and a refrigerator, and a nice pool. The location, straddling Boston and Cambridge, is especially good if you're driving from the west—you leave the turnpike before downtown traffic shatters the peace in the back of the minivan. See p. 99.
- **Best for Travelers with Disabilities:** The **Royal Sonesta Hotel,** 5 Cambridge Pkwy., Cambridge (℃ 800/SONESTA), trains its staff in disability awareness and offers 18 rooms (some of which adjoin standard units) equipped for the hearing, ambulatory, and vision impaired. A wheelchair ramp for use in conference rooms is available. See p. 106. Across the river, 48 fully accessible rooms at the **Westin Copley Place Boston,** 10 Huntington Ave. (℃ 800/WESTIN-1), adjoin standard units. See p. 97.
- **Best Lobby for Pretending That You're Rich:** The Edwardian wonderland that is the street level of the **Fairmont Copley Plaza Hotel** (see the earlier entry "Best Historic Hotel") is the perfect place for indulging your upper-crust fantasies. See p. 94.
- **Best for Serious Runners:** Brush up on your visualization techniques before checking into the **Charlesmark Hotel,** 655 Boylston St. (℃ 617/247-1212), which overlooks the Boston Marathon finish line. See p. 97.
- **Best Pool:** The **Sheraton Boston Hotel,** 39 Dalton St. (℃ 800/325-3535), has a great indoor-outdoor pool with a retractable dome. See p. 96.
- **Best Views:** Several hotels offer impressive views of their immediate surroundings, but for a picture-postcard panorama of Boston and Cambridge, head to the upper floors of the **Westin Copley Place Boston** (see the earlier entry "Best for Travelers with Disabilities"). See p. 97.

2 Downtown

The downtown area includes most of the **Freedom Trail** and the neighborhoods defined in chapter 5 as the **Waterfront, Faneuil Hall Marketplace,** the **Financial District,** and **Downtown Crossing.** (The North End and Government Center are in the downtown area, too, but they don't have hotels.) Accommodations in the moderate and inexpensive price categories are mostly bed-and-breakfasts; for information about B&Bs, consult the agencies listed on p. 78.

Where to Stay in Boston

Anthony's Town House **7**
Best Western Boston/The Inn
    at Longwood Medical **8**
Boston Harbor Hotel **45**
Boston Marriott Copley Place **21**
Boston Marriott Long Wharf **41**
Boston Park Plaza Hotel & Towers **28**
Brookline Courtyard by Marriott **4**
Bulfinch Hotel **37**
Chandler Inn Hotel **24**
Charlesmark Hotel **15**
Colonnade Hotel Boston **20**
Comfort Inn & Suites Boston/Airport **51**
Copley Square Hotel **17**
Doubletree Guest Suites **1**
Doubletree Hotel Boston Downtown **26**
Eliot Hotel **10**
Embassy Suites Hotel Boston
    at Logan Airport **49**
The Fairmont Copley Plaza Hotel **18**
Fifteen Beacon **35**
Four Seasons Hotel **29**
Hampton Inn Boston Logan Airport **50**
Harborside Inn **42**
Hilton Boston Back Bay **12**
Hilton Boston Logan Airport **47**
Holiday Inn Boston Brookline **6**

Holiday Inn Select Boston
    Government Center **36**
Hostelling International—Boston **11**
Hostelling International—Boston at Fenway **2**
Hotel Commonwealth **3**
Howard Johnson Inn **9**
Hyatt Harborside **48**
Hyatt Regency Boston Financial District **32**
Jurys Boston Hotel **23**
Langham Hotel Boston **43**
The Lenox Hotel **16**
Longwood Inn **5**
Marriott Residence Inn Boston Harbor **39**
The MidTown Hotel **19**
Millennium Bostonian Hotel **40**
Newbury Guest House **14**
Nine Zero **33**
Omni Parker House **34**
Onyx Hotel **38**
Radisson Hotel Boston **27**
The Ritz-Carlton, Boston **30**
The Ritz-Carlton, Boston Common **31**
Seaport Hotel **46**
Sheraton Boston Hotel **13**
The Westin Copley Place Boston **22**
Wyndham Boston **44**
YWCA Boston, Berkeley Residence **25**

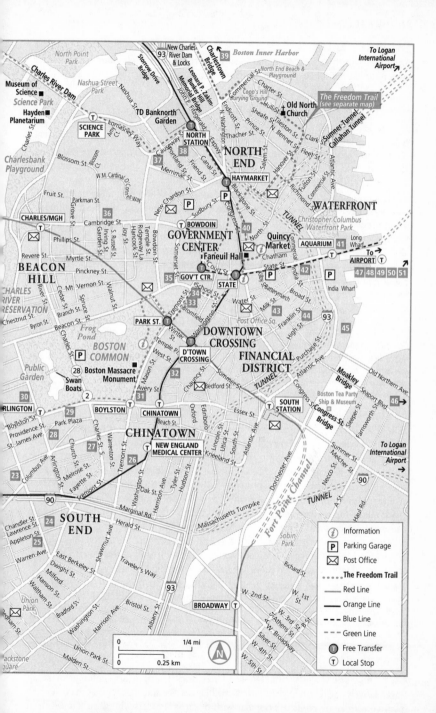

THE WATERFRONT & FANEUIL HALL MARKETPLACE

At all hotels in these neighborhoods, **ask for a room on a high floor**—the Big Dig is more or less complete, but construction continues to plague this entire area.

VERY EXPENSIVE

Boston Harbor Hotel ✿✿✿   The Boston Harbor Hotel is one of the finest hotels in town—it's in my top three or four—and certainly the prettiest, whether you approach its landmark arch by land or sea (on a water taxi or sightseeing cruise). The 16-story brick building is within walking distance of downtown and the waterfront attractions, and it prides itself on offering top-notch service and abundant amenities to travelers pursuing both business and pleasure.

The plush guest rooms (which are scheduled for renovation beginning in late 2005) look out on the harbor or the skyline. Each standard unit is a luxurious bedroom/living-room combination, with a marble bathroom and mahogany furnishings that include an armoire, a work desk, and comfortable chairs. Rooms with city views are less expensive but currently face the construction zone that has succeeded the Big Dig. The best units are suites with private terraces and dazzling water vistas. *Tip:* The grand public spaces hold a museum-quality collection of paintings, drawings, prints, and nautical charts.

Rowes Wharf (entrance on Atlantic Ave.), Boston, MA 02110. © **800/752-7077** or 617/439-7000. Fax 617/330-9450. www.bhh.com. 230 units. $295–$595 double; from $455 suite. Extra person $50. Children under 18 stay free in parent's room. Packages available. AE, DC, DISC, MC, V. Valet parking $34 weekdays, $25 weekends; self-parking $30 weekdays, $20 weekends. T: Red Line to South Station or Blue Line to Aquarium. Pets accepted. **Amenities:** Excellent restaurant (eclectic, with 15,000-bottle wine cellar); cafe; bar; 60-ft. indoor lap pool; well-appointed health club and spa; concierge; courtesy car; state-of-the-art business center with professional staff; 24-hr. room service; in-room massage; babysitting; laundry service; same-day dry cleaning. Rooms for travelers with disabilities are available. *In room:* A/C, TV w/pay movies, high-speed Internet access ($10/day), minibar, hair dryer, iron, umbrella, robes.

Boston Marriott Long Wharf ✿   The landmark Marriott's chief appeal is its location, a stone's throw from the New England Aquarium. It attracts business travelers with its proximity to the Financial District and woos families with its pool and easy access to downtown and waterfront attractions. The hotel's terraced brick exterior is one of the most recognizable sights on the harbor; inside, the seven-story atrium contributes to the airy feel of the public spaces. Rooms and bathrooms underwent extensive renovation in 2002; each large unit has either one king-size or two double beds (with pillow-top mattresses) and a table and chairs in front of the window. Rooms are quite sunny (the stand-alone building has no neighbors to block the light), decorated in earth tones with red and gold accents that complement the cherry furnishings. Rooms close to the water afford good views of the wharves and the waterfront; units closer to Atlantic Avenue have a newly peaceful post–Big Dig atmosphere.

296 State St. (at Atlantic Ave.), Boston, MA 02109. © **800/228-9290** or 617/227-0800. Fax 617/227-2867. www.marriottlongwharf.com. 400 units. Apr–Nov $249–$450 double; Dec–Mar $159–$279 double; $450–$490 suite year-round. Weekend packages available. AE, DC, DISC, MC, V. Parking $34. T: Blue Line to Aquarium. **Amenities:** Restaurant (seafood); cafe and lounge; bar and grill; indoor pool; exercise room; Jacuzzi; game room; concierge; tour desk; 24-hr. business center; room service until 2am; laundry service; same-day dry cleaning; executive-level rooms. Rooms for travelers with disabilities are available. *In room:* A/C, TV, high-speed Internet access ($10/day), fridge, coffeemaker, hair dryer, iron, safe.

Millennium Bostonian Hotel ✿✿   Three brick 19th-century buildings make up this relatively small hotel, which offers excellent service and features that make it competitive with larger rivals. It's popular with business travelers who want a break from more convention-oriented hotels, as well as with vacationers who appreciate the boutique atmosphere and access to the adjacent spa.

The traditionally appointed guest rooms vary in size and style. All boast top-of-the-line furnishings and amenities, with thoughtful extras such as heat lamps in the bathrooms. Half of the units have French doors that open onto small private balconies; the plushest rooms are good-size suites with working fireplaces or Jacuzzis. Soundproofing throughout allows views of Faneuil Hall Marketplace, Haymarket, or the construction above the Big Dig without the accompanying noise. My favorite units are on the glass-enclosed top floor.

At Faneuil Hall Marketplace, 26 North St., Boston, MA 02109. (C) **800/343-0922** or 617/523-3600. Fax 617/523-2454. www.millenniumhotels.com. 201 units. $149–$299 double; $265–$450 deluxe double; $439–$775 suite. Extra person $20. Children under 18 stay free in parent's room. Weekend, spa, family, and other packages available. AE, DC, DISC, MC, V. Valet parking $35. T: Green or Blue Line to Government Center, or Orange Line to Haymarket. **Amenities:** Restaurant (contemporary American); lobby lounge (the Atrium, p. 248); small fitness room; access to nearby health club ($10); in-room exercise equipment delivery on request; concierge; tour desk; car-rental desk; business center; salon; 24-hr. room service; massage; babysitting; laundry service; same-day dry cleaning; executive-level rooms. Rooms for travelers with disabilities are available. *In room:* A/C, TV w/pay movies, high-speed Internet access ($10/day), minibar, hair dryer, iron, safe, umbrella, robes.

MODERATE

Harborside Inn ★★ *Value* Under the same management as the Newbury Guest House (p. 98) in the Back Bay, the Harborside Inn offers a similar combination of location and (for this neighborhood) value. The renovated 1858 warehouse is across the street from Faneuil Hall Marketplace and the harbor, and a short walk from the Financial District. The nicely appointed guest rooms have queen-size beds, hardwood floors, Oriental rugs, and Victorian-style furniture. The rooms surround a skylit atrium; those with city views are more expensive but can be noisier (though that's less of a problem now that so much traffic is underground). Still, they're preferable to the interior rooms, whose windows open only to the atrium. Rooms on the top floors of the eight-story building have lower ceilings but better views.

185 State St. (between Atlantic Ave. and the Custom House Tower), Boston, MA 02109. (C) **888/723-7565** or 617/723-7500. Fax 617/670-6015. www.harborsideinnboston.com. 54 units. $120–$210 double; $235–$310 suite. Extra person $15. Packages and long-term rates available. Rates may be higher during special events. AE, DC, DISC, MC, V. Off-site parking $20; reservation required. T: Blue Line to Aquarium or Orange Line to State. **Amenities:** Restaurant (international bistro); access to nearby health club ($15); concierge; room service until 10pm; laundry service; dry cleaning. Rooms for travelers with disabilities are available. *In room:* A/C, TV, wireless Internet access ($10/day), hair dryer, iron.

FINANCIAL DISTRICT & DOWNTOWN CROSSING

Besides being great for business travelers, the hotels in this area are closer than their Waterfront competitors to the major shopping areas and the start of the Freedom Trail. All offer sensational weekend packages, especially in the winter.

VERY EXPENSIVE

Hyatt Regency Boston Financial District ★ *Value* This centrally located 22-story hotel lives two lives: It's a busy convention and business destination during the week, and its excellent weekend packages make it a magnet for sightseers. The building's plain exterior contrasts with the elegant European style and luxurious appointments that take over in the second-floor lobby. Guest rooms cluster around four atriums and have semiprivate lobbies, creating the effect of several small hotels in one. Rooms are decorated in soft earth tones, with lots of cushy upholstery and luxe linens on the king-size or European twin-size beds. They have flat-screen TVs and are large enough to hold sitting areas, desks, and settees. The property is in excellent condition: Hyatt took over the former Swissôtel Boston in 2003 and completed $10.5 million in guest-room renovations in early 2005. Ask for a room on a high floor—this neighborhood was ugly even before construction began all along adjacent Washington Street.

1 Ave. de Lafayette (off Washington St.), Boston, MA 02111. ℂ **800/233-1234** or 617/912-1234. Fax 617/451-0054. www.hyattregencyboston.com. 500 units. $189–$375 double; $300–$450 suite. Extra person $25. Children under 12 stay free in parent's room. AE, DC, DISC, MC, V. Valet parking $34; self-parking $26. T: Red Line to Downtown Crossing, or Green Line to Park St. or Boylston. **Amenities:** Restaurant (American/Continental); bar; 52-ft. indoor pool; health club; steam room; sauna; concierge; business center; 24-hr. room service; massage; babysitting; laundry service; same-day dry cleaning; executive-level rooms. Rooms for travelers with disabilities are available. *In room:* A/C, TV/VCR w/pay movies, high-speed Internet access ($10/day), minibar, coffeemaker, hair dryer, iron.

Langham Hotel Boston 🐱🐱 This is one of the best business hotels in the city, with the most central location if your destination is the Financial District. Vacationing visitors, who take advantage of the excellent weekend rates, are near the waterfront and downtown attractions but are not all that close to public transit.

Elegantly decorated and large enough to hold a generous work area, the guest rooms have 153 configurations, including loft suites with two bathrooms. A glass mansard roof surrounds the top three stories, where a number of rooms have large sloped windows and excellent views. Buildings envelop the hotel on three sides; the most desirable rooms are on the side that faces the park in Post Office Square. The imposing nine-story building, designed by R. Clipston Sturgis in 1922 in the style of a 16th-century Roman palace, originally housed the Federal Reserve Bank. Langham, a Hong Kong–based chain of luxury hotels with properties in England and the Pacific, acquired its first North American property, the former Le Meridien Boston, in 2004.

250 Franklin St. (at Post Office Sq.), Boston, MA 02110. ℂ **800/543-4300** or 617/451-1900. Fax 617/423-2844. www.langhamhotels.com. 326 units. $295–$515 double; $485–$1,330 suite. Extra person $30. Weekend rates from $159 per night. AE, DC, DISC, MC, V. Valet parking $39 Sun–Thurs, $25 Fri–Sat; self-parking $28 Sun–Thurs, $8 Fri–Sat. T: Red Line to Downtown Crossing or South Station, or Blue or Orange Line to State. Pets accepted. **Amenities:** Restaurant (French); cafe with Sun jazz brunch and Sat "Chocolate Bar Buffet" (Sept–May); bar with live piano most nights; 40-ft. indoor pool; well-equipped health club; concierge; weekend courtesy car to Newbury St.; staffed business center with library; 24-hr. room service; in-room massage; laundry service; same-day dry cleaning. Rooms for travelers with disabilities are available. *In room:* A/C, TV, fax, dataport, minibar, coffeemaker, hair dryer, iron, safe.

Nine Zero 🐱 This is anything but a traditional Boston hotel. Sleek and sophisticated, it feels almost like a transplant from New York or L.A.—and that's a good thing. The contemporary atmosphere distinguishes Nine Zero from the traditional establishments that dominate this market, but the service is in the old-school customer-is-always-right mold. The decent-sized guest rooms and oversize bathrooms contain opulent features, including luxurious linens and toiletries, down comforters, cordless two-line phones, and extensive business amenities. The 19-story hotel (new construction, not a rehab) opened in 2002. This neighborhood is convenient for both business and leisure travelers: It's within easy walking distance of most downtown destinations and 2 blocks from the subway to Cambridge.

90 Tremont St. (near Bromfield St.), Boston, MA 02108. ℂ **866/NINE-ZERO** or 617/772-5800. Fax 617/772-5810. www.ninezerohotel.com. 189 units. $289–$500 double; $500–$5,000 suite. Packages available. AE, DC, DISC, MC, V. Valet parking $35. T: Red or Green Line to Park St. Pets accepted. **Amenities:** Restaurant (Spire, p. 127); bar; exercise room; access to nearby health club ($10); concierge; tour desk; business center; 24-hr. room service; in-room massage;

babysitting; laundry service; same-day dry cleaning. Rooms for travelers with disabilities are available. *In room:* A/C, TV w/pay movies, high-speed and wireless Internet access, minibar, coffeemaker, hair dryer, iron, safe.

Wyndham Boston ★★ This luxury hotel is contemporary yet conservative—21st-century technology in an Art Deco package. The meticulously designed hotel (a complete rehab of the 1928 Batterymarch Building) opened in 1999. Like other downtown lodgings, it draws business travelers during the week and leisure travelers on weekends. The 14-story building is near Faneuil Hall Marketplace and the waterfront, but not all that close (by downtown standards) to the T. The spacious guest rooms have 9½-foot ceilings and cordless two-line phones. The best units, on the upper floors, afford great views of the harbor and downtown. Soundproofing throughout makes the whole building—even the halls—exceptionally quiet. The Wyndham's closest competitor, literally and figuratively, is the Langham, which is less convenient to public transit but has a swimming pool.

89 Broad St., Boston, MA 02110. © **800/WYNDHAM** or 617/556-0006. Fax 617/556-0053. www.wyndham.com. 362 units. $149–$399 double weekdays; $129–$249 double weekends; $224–$474 suite weekdays, $204–$324 suite weekends. Children under 13 stay free in parent's room. Weekend, holiday, family, and other packages available. AE, DC, DISC, MC, V. Valet parking $32. T: Blue or Orange Line to State, or Red Line to South Station. **Amenities:** Restaurant (California-Italian); bar; 24-hr. exercise room; sauna; concierge; staffed business center; 24-hr. room service; laundry service; same-day dry cleaning. Rooms for travelers with disabilities are available. *In room:* A/C, TV w/pay movies, high-speed Internet access ($10/day), minibar, coffeemaker, hair dryer, iron, umbrella, robes.

EXPENSIVE

Omni Parker House ★★ The Parker House has operated continuously longer than any other hotel in America (since 1855!), but it's hardly stuck in the 19th century. Room rates include high-speed Internet access, and regular renovation (most recently, a $3 million update completed in early 2005) keeps the property in excellent shape. Guest rooms, a patchwork of more than 50 configurations, aren't huge, but they are thoughtfully laid out and nicely appointed. Many overlook Old City Hall or Government Center. The hotel is popular with business travelers, who can book a unit with an expanded work area, as well as sightseers, who can economize by taking advantage of a weekend deal, especially in the winter, or by booking an "economy petite single." The pattern on the bedspreads, so gaudy that it's elegant, is a reproduction of the original, and the lobby of the 14-story hotel boasts its original American oak paneling.

60 School St., Boston, MA 02108. © **800/THE-OMNI** or 617/227-8600. Fax 617/742-5729. www.omnihotels.com. 551 units (some with shower only). $149–$229 double; $179–$249 deluxe double; $229–$339 executive double; $199–$349 suite. Children under 18 stay free in parent's room. Weekend packages and AARP discount available. AE,

---

(*Fun Fact* **Food for Thought**

Yes, this is the Parker House of Parker House roll fame. The rolls were invented (if food is "invented") here, as was Boston cream pie.

That's not the hotel's only claim to fame. Malcolm X and Ho Chi Minh both worked there, and the room that's now Parker's Bar played host to a well-known group: Henry Wadsworth Longfellow, Oliver Wendell Holmes, Ralph Waldo Emerson, Nathaniel Hawthorne, and sometimes Charles Dickens, who made up a literary salon called the Saturday Club.

DC, DISC, MC, V. Valet parking $36. T: Green or Blue Line to Government Center, or Red Line to Park St. Pets accepted; deposit required. **Amenities:** 2 restaurants (New England); bar; 24-hr. exercise room; access to nearby health club ($20); concierge; tour desk; airport shuttle; business center; 24-hr. room service; laundry service; same-day dry cleaning; executive-level rooms. Rooms for travelers with disabilities are available. *In room:* A/C, TV w/pay movies and Nintendo, high-speed Internet access, minibar, coffeemaker, hair dryer, iron, robes.

3 Beacon Hill/North Station

Less expensive lodgings in this neighborhood are mostly B&Bs. Save time by checking with the agencies listed on p. 78.

VERY EXPENSIVE

Fifteen Beacon ★★   Nonstop pampering, high-tech appointments, and outrageously luxurious rooms make this boutique hotel *the* name to drop with the expense-be-hanged set. The 10-story hotel has attracted demanding travelers, especially businesspeople, since it opened in 2000. Management bends over backward to keep them returning, with attentive service and lavish perks—for instance, at check-in, guests receive business cards listing the personal phone and fax numbers that they'll have during their stay. The guest rooms, individually decorated in austere but plush style that's more SoHo than Beacon Hill, contain queen-size canopy beds with Italian linens (300 thread count, of course), surround-sound stereo systems, gas fireplaces, and 4-inch TVs in the bathroom. "Studio" units have a sitting area. The lobby restaurant, though overpriced and a bit cramped, is one of the best places in the city to see (or be) movers and shakers, especially at breakfast.

15 Beacon St., Boston, MA 02108. ℂ 877/XV-BEACON or 617/670-1500. Fax 617/670-2525. www.xvbeacon.com. 60 units (some with shower only). From $395 double; from $1,200 suite. Valet parking $34. T: Red or Green Line to Park St., or Blue Line to Government Center. Pets under 20 lb. accepted. **Amenities:** Restaurant (French); bar; fitness room; access to nearby health club ($15); concierge; courtesy car; 24-hr. room service; in-room massage; babysitting; laundry service; same-day dry cleaning. Rooms for travelers with disabilities are available. *In room:* A/C, TV w/pay movies, fax/copier/printer, high-speed Internet access, minibar, hair dryer, iron, safe, umbrella, robes.

EXPENSIVE

Onyx Hotel ★ *Kids*   This plush boutique hotel opened in 2004 on a side street near North Station, within easy walking distance of downtown and Beacon Hill. It's a stone's throw from the commuter rail, but so comfortable that you might not want to commute too far. The 10-story hotel is contemporary in style, decorated in soothing jewel tones with sleek lines and high ceilings that make the decent-size rooms feel even bigger. Each room holds a large work desk and has a well-appointed bathroom. The best units are the top-floor suites, but any room with a floor-to-ceiling window feels like a mini-palace. This neighborhood is somewhat run-down, but it's improving more quickly than any other part of town, thanks to the end of the Big Dig and the demolition of the elevated Green Line. The Onyx is the second hotel that the kid-friendly Kimpton chain has opened in the Boston area (Hotel Marlowe was the first; see "Cambridge," later in this chapter).

155 Portland St., Boston, MA 02114. ℂ 866/660-6699, 800/KIMPTON, or 617/557-9955. Fax 617/557-0005. www.onyxhotel.com. 112 units. $209–$329 double. Extra person $25. Rates include evening cocktail reception. Children under 18 stay free in parent's room. Weekend, family, and other packages, AARP and AAA discounts available. AE, DC, DISC, MC, V. Valet parking $32. T: Green or Orange Line to North Station. Pets accepted. **Amenities:** Lounge; exercise room; access to nearby health club ($15); weekday courtesy car to Financial District; 24-hr. room service; massage; same-day dry cleaning. Rooms for travelers with disabilities are available. *In room:* A/C, TV w/pay movies, high-speed and wireless Internet access, minibar, coffeemaker, hair dryer, iron, safe, umbrella, robes.

MODERATE

Bulfinch Hotel ⚡ One block from North Station, the Bulfinch is as appealing for its design as for its convenient location and relatively reasonable rates. Every room in the 1904 building is different, with architectural details that enhance the "budget boutique" feel. Rooms are on the small side, but custom furnishings—so deftly executed that they almost feel built in—create the illusion of more space. Plush fabrics in cool neutrals and earth tones (including suede headboards), flat-screen TVs, and marble bathrooms set off the contemporary, uncluttered design. The hotel, which opened in 2004, offers business features such as work desks, cordless phones, and high-speed Internet access (included in the room rate). The best units are junior suites—oversized doubles—known as "nose rooms" because they're in the pointed end of the triangular building; each has windows on three sides of the king-sized bed. All rooms in the nine-story building (which gained three floors in its renovation into a hotel) are nonsmoking.

107 Merrimac St., Boston, MA 02114. ⓒ **800/4-CHOICE** or 617/624-0202. Fax 617/624-0211. www.bulfinchhotel. com. 80 units (most with shower only). $169–$219 double; $199–$259 jr. suite. Children under 18 stay free in parent's room. Packages and AAA, AARP, and military discounts available. AE, DC, DISC, MC, V. Parking $25 in nearby garage. T: Green or Orange Line to North Station. Pets under 40 lb. accepted; $50 fee. **Amenities:** Restaurant (steakhouse); exercise room; concierge; room service; same-day dry cleaning. Rooms for travelers with disabilities are available. *In room:* A/C, TV, high-speed Internet access, coffeemaker, hair dryer, iron.

Holiday Inn Select Boston Government Center ⚡ At the base of Beacon Hill, near Massachusetts General Hospital, this 15-story hotel is one of the chain's leaders in the battle for the business traveler. It also attracts guests with business at the hospital, and the staff is sensitive to the needs of patients and relatives. The location is convenient to downtown, within walking distance of the Back Bay, and not far from East Cambridge. The good-size guest rooms have contemporary furnishings and plenty of business amenities, such as wireless Internet access (included in the room rate). Each unit has a picture-window view of the city, the State House, or the parking structure; ask for a room on a high floor, facing Blossom Street if possible. The building is part of a small retail complex with a supermarket and shops, which should have reopened after extensive renovations by the time you visit.

5 Blossom St., Boston, MA 02114. ⓒ **800/HOLIDAY** or 617/742-7630. Fax 617/742-4192. www.hiselect.com/ bos-government. 303 units (some with shower only). $130–$259 double; $451 suite. Extra person $20. Rollaway $20. Children under 18 stay free in parent's room. Weekend and corporate packages and 10% AARP discount available. AE, DC, DISC, MC, V. Parking $36. T: Red Line to Charles/MGH. **Amenities:** Restaurant (American); lounge; outdoor heated pool; small exercise room; access to nearby health club ($10); concierge; tour desk; car-rental desk; room service until 10pm; coin laundry; laundry service; executive-level rooms. Rooms for travelers with disabilities are available. *In room:* A/C, TV w/pay movies, wireless Internet access, coffeemaker, hair dryer, iron.

4 Charlestown

EXPENSIVE

Marriott Residence Inn Boston Harbor ⚡⚡ *Value* Combining the familiar suburban brand and a prime urban location, the Residence Inn opened in 2003. It's the only chain hotel in Charlestown, and easy access to water transportation (especially in warm weather, when the water taxi stops at the hotel dock) makes it competitive with far more expensive downtown properties. Adjacent to the Charlestown Navy Yard, the hotel consists of studio and one- and two-bedroom suites with full kitchens; many have harbor views. Even the smallest units, the studio suites, are generous in size. The lobby pool and fitness room adjoin the hotel dock and offer water views. Most rooms in the eight-story building afford impressive views of the harbor or the Charles River and the Zakim–Bunker Hill Bridge. Patrons tend to be business travelers on weeknights (many are here on extended stays) and families on weekends, especially in the summer. Prices listed here are for 1 to 4 nights; longer stays mean ever-greater discounts.

34–44 Charles River Ave., Charlestown, MA 02129. © **866/296-2297**, 800/331-3131 (Marriott), or 617/242-9000. Fax 617/242-5554. www.marriott.com/bostw. 168 units. $179–$209 double May–Dec; $169–$199 double Jan–Apr. Rates include full breakfast. Children stay free in parent's room. Weekend, family, and other packages from $129/night. AAA, government, and long-term discounts available. AE, DC, DISC, MC, V. Valet parking $25. T: Green Line to North Station; shuttle-bus ride or 10-min. walk. Or Blue Line to Aquarium and ferry from Long Wharf to Navy Yard; 5-min. walk. Or Orange Line to Community College; 10-min. walk. Pets accepted; $150 fee. **Amenities:** Cafe (New England) with seasonal outdoor seating; indoor lap pool; exercise room; access to nearby YMCA with pool ($8); Jacuzzi; shuttle to North Station; business center; room service until 9:30pm; coin laundry; laundry service; dry cleaning. Rooms for travelers with disabilities are available. *In room:* A/C, TV w/pay movies, high-speed and wireless Internet access, kitchen, fridge, coffeemaker, hair dryer, iron.

5 South Boston Waterfront (Seaport District)

EXPENSIVE

Seaport Hotel ★★ *Kids* The independent Seaport Hotel was a pioneer on the South Boston waterfront, and a neighborhood is slowing developing around it. The hotel, which opened in 1998, was designed and built (by Fidelity Investments) with every feature the pampered, techno-savvy business travelers might dream of. This is the closest hotel to the convention center (which won't have its own until late 2006). It's across the street from and affiliated with the World Trade Center, and about 10 minutes by cab from the airport or the Financial District. If you plan to take public transit, leave time for the trip from South Station or for a long walk through and around construction.

The decent-size rooms have all the usual perks plus extras such as Logan Airport flight information on the TV and fog-free mirrors in the well-appointed bathrooms. The views (of the city or the harbor) are excellent, especially from the higher floors. The kid-conscious staff, pool, great weekend packages, and proximity to the Children's Museum make this a good choice for families, too.

1 Seaport Lane, Boston, MA 02210. © **877/SEAPORT** or 617/385-4000. Fax 617/385-4001. www.seaportboston. com. 426 units. $189–$299 double; $450–$1,700 suite. Service charge $3 per room per night. Children under 17 stay free in parent's room. Weekend and family packages available. AE, DC, DISC, MC, V. Valet parking $33; self-parking $25. T: Red Line to South Station, then hotel shuttle or Silver Line bus, or walk 20 min. Or water taxi to World Trade Center. Pets under 50 lb. accepted. **Amenities:** Well-regarded restaurant (contemporary American); cafe; lounge; 50-ft. indoor pool; well-equipped health club; spa; bike rental; concierge; car-rental desk; shuttle to South Station, North Station, and State Street; 24-hr. business center with professional staff (7am–8pm); 24-hr. room service; massage; laundry service; same-day dry cleaning. *In room:* A/C, TV w/pay movies, high-speed and wireless Internet access, minibar, coffeemaker, hair dryer, iron, safe, robes.

6 Chinatown/Theater District

VERY EXPENSIVE

The Ritz-Carlton, Boston Common ★ This plush, ultramodern hotel is at the heart of an enormous complex that incorporates offices, condos, a 19-screen movie theater, and the state-of-the-art Sports Club/LA. Challenging the Four Seasons's claim to the hottest visiting celebrities, the "new Ritz" opened in 2001. It has the cachet and top-notch service of the original, traditional Ritz (p. 92), without a ruffle in sight. The good-size guest rooms contain the latest in indulgent amenities, including luxury linens and feather duvets, and the large bathrooms have phones and a separate tub and shower room. Guest rooms contain Bose radio/CD players, and suites have Bang + Olufsen CD stereos. Rooms occupy the top four floors of the 12-story building, with the public spaces at street level. You'll pay more for a room with a view of the Common. This neighborhood is the urban-planning equivalent of a self-fulfilling prophecy: The area is not the greatest, but the presence of the hotel automatically improves it—and as the other phases of the development open, it's sure to improve even more.

10 Avery St. (between Tremont and Washington sts.), Boston, MA 02111. © **800/241-3333** or 617/574-7100. Fax 617/574-7200. www.ritzcarlton.com. 193 units. $295–$525 double; from $395 Club Level or suite. Weekend and other packages available. AE, DC, DISC, MC, V. Valet parking $37. T: Green Line to Boylston. Pets accepted. **Amenities:** Restaurant (contemporary American); bar; lounge; access ($20/day) to adjoining Sports Club/LA, 100,000-sq.-ft. facility with lap pool, complete spa services, salon, regulation basketball court, 10,000-sq.-ft. weight room, steam rooms, saunas, 5 exercise studios, and 4 squash courts; concierge; courtesy car; airport shuttle; business center; 24-hr. room service; in-room massage; babysitting; laundry service; same-day dry cleaning; club-level rooms. Rooms for travelers with disabilities are available. *In room:* A/C, TV w/pay movies, high-speed Internet access ($10/day), minibar, hair dryer, iron, safe.

EXPENSIVE

Radisson Hotel Boston ★
Popular with business travelers, tour groups, and vacationers alike, the Radisson is an attractive hotel in a less-than-attractive neighborhood. Though not very scenic, the Theater District is convenient to both the Back Bay and downtown, and this would be a prime property anywhere. The guest rooms are among the largest in the city, and each has a private balcony with great views from the higher floors. Each has a king or two queen beds and enough room to hold a sitting area. The hotel underwent a complete renovation in 1997 and an upgrade in 2003. The best units are the executive-level rooms on the top five floors of the 24-story building. The **Stuart Street Playhouse** (© **617/426-4499**), a small theater in the hotel, often stages one-person shows. The hotel also has a seasonal **golf school** and practice facility (© **617/457-2699**).

200 Stuart St. (at Charles St. S.), Boston, MA 02116. © **800/333-3333** or 617/482-1800. Fax 617/451-2750. www.radisson.com/bostonma. 356 units (some with shower only). $159–$359 double. Extra person $20. Cot $20. Cribs free. Children under 18 stay free in parent's room. Weekend, theater, and other packages available. AE, DC, DISC, MC, V. Valet parking $30; self-parking $28. T: Green Line to Boylston, or Orange Line to New England Medical Center. **Amenities:** Cafe; indoor pool; exercise room; concierge; business center; room service until 11pm; in-room massage; babysitting; laundry service; same-day dry cleaning; executive-level rooms. Rooms for travelers with disabilities are available. *In room:* A/C, TV w/pay movies, high-speed Internet access, coffeemaker, hair dryer, iron.

MODERATE

Doubletree Hotel Boston Downtown ★ *Value*
The Doubletree is conveniently located in Chinatown, within easy walking distance of both downtown and the Back Bay, and is a much better deal than most competitors in either of those neighborhoods. The six-story building is a former high school with high ceilings and compact, well-designed rooms. Ask for a unit that faces away from busy Washington Street, and your view will be of a cityscape rather than the hospital across the street (Tufts–New England Medical Center). Nice details include Asian touches in the contemporary decor and features such as a fish tank in the lobby, installed in accordance with the principles of feng shui. Don't confuse this hotel with its all-suite corporate sibling near

Cambridge (p. 99). This Doubletree adjoins the Wang YMCA of Chinatown, and room rates include access to its extensive facilities.

821 Washington St., Boston, MA 02111. © **800/222-TREE** or 617/956-7900. Fax 617/956-7901. doubletree.hilton. com. 267 units (some with shower only). $129–$299 double; $189–$359 suite. Extra person $10. Children under 17 stay free in parent's room. Weekend and other packages, AAA, AARP, and military discounts available. AE, DC, DISC, MC, V. Valet parking $30. T: Orange Line to New England Medical Center. **Amenities:** Restaurant and lounge (American/Asian); cafe; access to adjoining YMCA with Olympic-size pool; concierge; business center; room service until 11:30pm; same-day dry cleaning; executive-level rooms. Rooms for travelers with disabilities are available. *In room:* A/C, TV w/pay movies, wireless Internet access ($10/day), minibar, coffeemaker, hair dryer, iron, safe.

7 The South End

Berkeley Street runs from the Back Bay across the Mass. Pike to the most convenient corner of the sprawling South End, where you'll find these two lodgings.

MODERATE

Chandler Inn Hotel ⭐ *Value* The comfortable, unpretentious Chandler Inn is a bargain for its location, just 2 blocks from the Back Bay. The guest rooms and bathrooms are small, but each unit has individual climate control and tasteful contemporary-style furniture, including desks, small wardrobes, and TV armoires. Each holds a queen or double bed or two twin beds, without enough room to squeeze in a cot. The staff is welcoming and helpful. The eight-story building gained two new elevators in 2004, eliminating my only serious caveat about this property. It's a gay-friendly hotel (Fritz, the bar next to the lobby, is a neighborhood hangout) and often books up early. Plan ahead.

26 Chandler St. (at Berkeley St.), Boston, MA 02116. © **800/842-3450** or 617/482-3450. Fax 617/542-3428. www. chandlerinn.com. 56 units. Apr–Dec $139–$169 double; Jan–Mar $129–$139 double. Children under 12 stay free in parent's room. AE, DC, DISC, MC, V. No parking available. T: Orange Line to Back Bay. Pets under 25 lb. accepted with prior approval. **Amenities:** Lounge; access to nearby health club ($10). *In room:* A/C, TV, dataport, hair dryer.

INEXPENSIVE

YWCA Boston, Berkeley Residence This pleasant, convenient women-only hotel and residence offers a dining room, patio garden, piano, and library. The well-kept public areas also include a TV lounge. The dorm-style guest rooms are basic, containing little more than beds, but they're well maintained and comfortable—not plush, but not cells either. That description might not seem to justify the prices, but check around a little before you turn up your nose.

40 Berkeley St., Boston, MA 02116. © **617/375-2524.** Fax 617/375-2525. www.ywcaboston.org. 200 units, none with bathroom. $60 single; $86 double; $99 triple. Rates include full breakfast. Long-term rates available (5-week minimum). MC, V. No parking available. T: Orange Line to Back Bay or Green Line to Arlington. No children accepted. **Amenities:** Cafeteria; computer with Internet access; coin-op laundry. Rooms for travelers with disabilities are available. *In room:* No phone.

8 The Back Bay

BOSTON COMMON/PUBLIC GARDEN

VERY EXPENSIVE

Four Seasons Hotel ⭐⭐⭐ Many hotels offer exquisite service, a beautiful location, elegant guest rooms and public areas, a terrific health club, and wonderful restaurants. But no other hotel in Boston—indeed, in New England—combines every

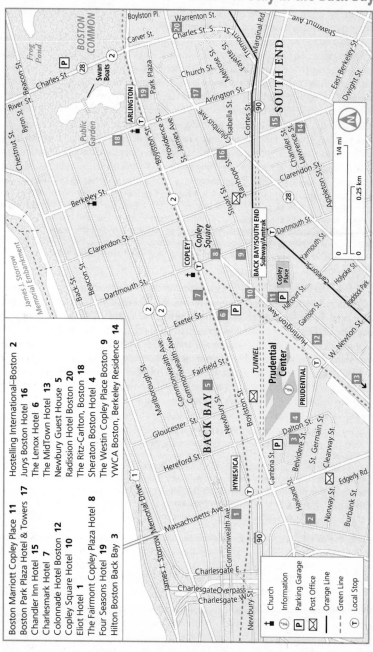

BOSTON COMMON

Boylston Pl.
Warrenton St.
Carver St.
Charles St. S.
Boylston St.
River St.
Beacon St.
Byron St.
Charles St.
Chestnut St.
Frog Pond
Public Garden
Swan Boats
ARLINGTON
Park Plaza
Church St.
Arlington St.
St. James Ave.
Providence Ave.
Columbus Ave.
Isabella St.
Cortes St.
Marginal Rd.
Tremont St.
Fayette St.
Melrose St.
Shawmut Ave.
East Berkeley St.
Dwight St.
SOUTH END
Berkeley St.
Clarendon St.
Back St.
Beacon St.
Dartmouth St.
Stanhope St.
Chandler St.
Lawrence St.
Appleton St.
Clarendon St.
Dartmouth St.
Yarmouth St.
Holyoke St.
Braddock Park
BACK BAY/SOUTH END Subway/Amtrak
Copley Square
COPLEY
Copley Place
Harcourt St.
Garrison St.
W. Newton St.
Huntington Ave.
Clearway St.
St. Germain St.
Dalton St.
Belvidere St.
Prudential Center
PRUDENTIAL
TUNNEL
Exeter St.
Marlborough St.
Commonwealth Ave.
Fairfield St.
Gloucester St.
Hereford St.
Newbury St.
Boylston St.
BACK BAY
HYNES/ICA
Massachusetts Ave.
Commonwealth Ave.
Haviland St.
Cambria St.
Norway St.
Edgerly Rd.
Burbank St.
Charlesgate E.
CharlesgateOverpass
Charlesgate W.
Newbury St.
James J. Storrow Memorial Drive
James J. Storrow Memorial Embankment

1/4 mi
0.25 km

N

Boston Marriott Copley Place **11**
Boston Park Plaza Hotel & Towers **17**
Chandler Inn Hotel **15**
Charlesmark Hotel **7**
Colonnade Hotel Boston **12**
Copley Square Hotel **10**
Eliot Hotel **1**
The Fairmont Copley Plaza Hotel **8**
Four Seasons Hotel **19**
Hilton Boston Back Bay **3**

Hostelling International–Boston **2**
Jurys Boston Hotel **16**
The Lenox Hotel **6**
The MidTown Hotel **13**
Newbury Guest House **5**
Radisson Hotel Boston **20**
The Ritz-Carlton, Boston **18**
Sheraton Boston Hotel **4**
The Westin Copley Place Boston **9**
YWCA Boston, Berkeley Residence **14**

Church
Information
Parking Garage
Post Office
Orange Line
Green Line
Local Stop

element of a luxury hotel as seamlessly as the Four Seasons. If I were traveling with someone else's credit cards, I'd head straight here.

Overlooking the Public Garden, this 16-story brick-and-glass building (the hotel occupies eight floors) incorporates the traditional and the contemporary. The spacious accommodations feel more like stylish apartments than hotel rooms, with lots of plush fabrics (including dramatic window coverings), elaborate moldings, and marble bathrooms. The best units overlook the Public Garden; city views from the back of the hotel aren't as desirable but can be engaging, especially from the higher floors. The staff caters to children with bedtime snacks and toys, and you can ask at the concierge desk for duck food to take to the Public Garden. Small pets even enjoy a special menu and amenities. Larger accommodations range from executive suites with parlor areas to luxurious deluxe suites with sweeping views.

200 Boylston St., Boston, MA 02116. © **800/819-5053** or 617/338-4400. Fax 617/423-0154. www.fourseasons. com/boston. 272 units. $425–$650 double; from $695 1-bedroom suite; from $2,200 2-bedroom suite. Weekend and family packages available. AE, DC, DISC, MC, V. Valet parking $37. T: Green Line to Arlington. Pets under 15 lb. accepted. **Amenities:** Restaurant (Aujourd'hui, p. 136); bar (Bristol Lounge, p. 136); 44-ft. pool and Jacuzzi overlooking the Public Garden; newly renovated health club and spa; concierge; tour desk; limo to downtown; business center; 24-hr. room service; in-room massage; babysitting; laundry service; same-day dry cleaning. Rooms for travelers with disabilities are available. *In room:* A/C, TV w/pay movies, high-speed Internet access ($10/day), minibar, hair dryer, iron, safe, robes.

The Ritz-Carlton, Boston ★   This legendary hotel overlooking the Public Garden has attracted both the "proper Bostonian" and the celebrated visitor since 1927. A top-to-bottom $60 million restoration completed in 2002 upgraded the building throughout. One of the most traditional lodgings in town, it offers fewer amenities than its sister property in the Theater District and the archrival Four Seasons, but the original Ritz maintains the cachet accumulated during nearly 8 decades of doing everything in style.

The elegantly appointed guest rooms have plush linens, feather duvets, crystal chandeliers, three phones (one in the bathroom), and windows that open. You'll pay more for a room with a view. The best units are the suites, which have wood-burning fireplaces; the "fireplace butler" can help you choose the right wood.

15 Arlington St., Boston, MA 02116. © **800/241-3333** or 617/536-5700. Fax 617/536-1335. www.ritzcarlton.com. 273 units. $295–$495 double; from $395 suite. Extra person $20. Weekend, family, and other packages available. AE, DC, DISC, MC, V. Valet parking $37. T: Green Line to Arlington. Pets accepted. **Amenities:** 2 restaurants; bar; lounge; exercise room; access to Sports Club/LA ($20; see Ritz-Carlton, Boston Common listing, above); concierge; courtesy car; airport shuttle; business center; 24-hr. room service; in-room massage; babysitting; laundry service; same-day dry cleaning; club-level rooms. Rooms for travelers with disabilities are available. *In room:* A/C, TV w/pay movies, high-speed Internet access ($10/day), minibar, hair dryer, iron, safe.

EXPENSIVE

Boston Park Plaza Hotel & Towers ★   A Boston mainstay—it was built as the Statler Hilton in 1927—the Park Plaza does a hopping convention and function business. It's the antithesis of generic, with an old-fashioned atmosphere and a cavernous, ornate lobby, yet it offers modern comforts. A $60 million renovation completed in 2001 updated the hotel throughout, with new furniture, accessories, carpets, and bathtubs in the guest rooms. The least expensive units are quite small; if you're not a crash-and-dash traveler, the extra space might be worth the extra money. Don't expect personalized service in a hotel this large—the typical guest is busy with convention activities or meetings. The lobby of the 15-story building is a little commercial hub, with a travel agency, pharmacy, currency exchange, and Amtrak and airline ticket offices.

Tips **Planning Pointer**

If your trip involves a cultural event—for example, a big museum show—look into a hotel package that includes tickets. Usually offered on weekends, these deals always save time and can save money.

---

64 Arlington St., Boston, MA 02116. ℂ **800/225-2008** or 617/426-2000. Fax 617/423-1708. www.bostonparkplaza. com. 950 units (some with shower only). $139–$299 double; $375–$2,000 suite. Extra person $25. Children under 18 stay free in parent's room. Senior discount and weekend and family packages available. AE, DC, DISC, MC, V. Parking $34. T: Green Line to Arlington. **Amenities:** 3 restaurants; bar (Whiskey Park, p. 248); exercise room; concierge; business center; salon; room service until midnight. Rooms for travelers with disabilities are available. *In room:* A/C, TV w/pay movies, high-speed Internet access ($10/day), coffeemaker, hair dryer, iron.

COPLEY SQUARE/HYNES CONVENTION CENTER
VERY EXPENSIVE

Colonnade Hotel Boston ★★ *Kids*   The seasonal "rooftop resort" and swimming pool are probably this hotel's best-known features, with excellent service a close runner-up. Adjacent to Copley Place and the Prudential Center, the independently owned Colonnade is a slice of Europe in the all-American shopping paradise of the Back Bay. It caters to working travelers, to visitors engaging in retail therapy, and to children of all ages with the "VIKids" program and a rubber ducky in every bathroom. You might hear a dozen languages spoken by the guests and the friendly, professional staff of the 11-story concrete-and-glass hotel.

The elegance of the quiet, high-ceilinged public spaces carries over to the large guest rooms. All have contemporary oak or mahogany furnishings and marble bathrooms (each with its own phone). Units on the Huntington Avenue side overlook the bustling Prudential Center complex, while rooms at the back survey the pleasant patchwork of the South End. Suites have dining rooms and sitting areas, and the "author's suite" contains autographed copies of the work of celebrated (or at least published) literary guests.

120 Huntington Ave., Boston, MA 02116. ℂ **800/962-3030** or 617/424-7000. Fax 617/424-1717. www.colonnade hotel.com. 285 units. $175–$425 double; $575–$1,750 suite. Children under 12 stay free in parent's room. Weekend, family, and other packages available. AE, DC, DISC, MC, V. Parking $34. T: Green Line E to Prudential. Pets accepted. **Amenities:** Restaurant (Brasserie Jo, p. 139); bar; heated outdoor rooftop pool; state-of-the-art fitness center; concierge; 24-hr. business center; 24-hr. room service; in-room massage; babysitting; laundry service; same-day dry cleaning. Rooms for travelers with disabilities are available. *In room:* A/C, TV w/pay movies, wireless Internet access ($10/day), minibar, hair dryer, iron, safe.

Eliot Hotel ★★   This exquisite hotel combines the flavor of Yankee Boston with European-style service and abundant amenities. On tree-lined Commonwealth Avenue, it feels more like a classy apartment building than a hotel, with a romantic atmosphere and top-notch business features. Every unit is a spacious suite with antique furnishings, down comforters, and authentic botanical prints. French doors separate the living rooms and bedrooms, and bathrooms are outfitted in Italian marble. Many suites have a pantry with a microwave. The 1925 building is near Boston University and MIT (across the river), and the location contrasts pleasantly with the bustle of Newbury Street, a block away.

370 Commonwealth Ave. (at Mass. Ave.), Boston, MA 02215. ℂ **800/44-ELIOT** or 617/267-1607. Fax 617/536-9114. www.eliothotel.com. 95 units (some with shower only). $255–$415 1-bedroom suite for 2; $470–$750 2-bedroom

suite. Extra person $20. Children under 18 stay free in parent's room. Packages available. AE, DC, MC, V. Valet parking $34. T: Green Line B, C, or D to Hynes/ICA. Pets accepted. **Amenities:** Restaurant (eclectic); sashimi bar; free access to nearby health club; concierge; business center; 24-hr. room service; in-room massage; babysitting; laundry service; same-day dry cleaning. Rooms for travelers with disabilities are available. *In room:* A/C, TV w/pay movies, high-speed Internet access ($10/day), minibar, hair dryer, iron, umbrella, robes.

The Fairmont Copley Plaza ★★   The "grande dame of Boston" is a classic "grand hotel," an old-fashioned lodging that recalls the days when an out-of-town trip (by train, of course) was an event, not an ordeal. Built in 1912, the six-story Renaissance-revival building faces Copley Square, with Trinity Church and the Boston Public Library on either side. In 2004, the hotel completed a $34 million renovation and redecoration intended to give the spacious guest rooms more of a residential feel. It was a rousing success, especially if your residence is a mansion. The posh draperies and upholstery and the custom-made furnishings, which include oversize desks and pillow-top mattresses, reflect the elegance of the opulent public spaces. Rooms that face the lovely square or Clarendon Street afford better views than those that overlook busy Dartmouth Street. Known for superb service, the Copley Plaza boasts countless little details (courtesy-car service in a London taxi, a resident black Lab whom guests can book for a walk or run, a weekend romance package that includes the price of a diamond engagement ring) that go well past "the customer is always right" to "the customer is spoiled rotten"—and isn't that what you look for in this price category?

138 St. James Ave., Boston, MA 02116. © 800/257-7544 or 617/267-5300. Fax 617/267-7668. www.fairmont.com/copleyplaza. 383 units. From $249 double; from $429 suite. Extra person $30. Weekend and other packages available. AE, DC, MC, V. Valet parking $32. T: Green Line to Copley, or Orange Line to Back Bay. Pets accepted; $25/day. **Amenities:** Restaurant (steakhouse); lounge (Oak Bar, p. 249); exercise room; access to nearby health club ($15); concierge; tour desk; courtesy car; business center; 24-hr. room service; laundry service; same-day dry cleaning; concierge-level rooms. Rooms for travelers with disabilities are available. *In room:* A/C, TV w/pay movies, high-speed Internet access ($14/day), minibar, hair dryer, iron, safe, umbrella, robes.

The Lenox Hotel ★★   The Lenox was the latest thing when it opened in 1900, and in its second century, it echoes that *fin de siècle* splendor everywhere, from the ornate lobby to the spacious, luxurious rooms. The central location makes the hotel popular with business travelers, and its relatively small size and accommodating staff make it a welcome alternative to the huge convention hotels that dominate this neighborhood. The high-ceilinged guest rooms are large enough to contain sitting areas, and custom-designed wood furnishings and marble bathrooms add to the anything-but-generic vibe. The best accommodations are the 12 corner units with wood-burning fireplaces; rooms on the top two floors of the 11-story hotel have excellent views.

61 Exeter St. (at Boylston St.), Boston, MA 02116. © 800/225-7676 or 617/536-5300. Fax 617/236-0351. www.lenoxhotel.com. 212 units (some with shower only). $179–$329 double; $495 junior suite; $695 one-bedroom fireplace suite. Extra person $40. Children under 17 stay free in parent's room. Corporate, weekend, and family packages available. AE, DC, DISC, MC, V. Valet parking $36. T: Green Line to Copley. **Amenities:** Well-regarded restaurant (contemporary American); bar; pub; small exercise room; bike rental; concierge; tour desk; car-rental desk; airport shuttle; business center; room service until 11pm; babysitting; laundry service; same-day dry cleaning. Rooms for travelers with disabilities and wheelchair lift to the lobby are available. *In room:* A/C, TV w/pay movies, wireless Internet access, hair dryer, iron.

EXPENSIVE
Boston Marriott Copley Place ★   This 38-story tower offers something for everyone—complete business facilities, a good-size pool, and direct access to Boston's shopping wonderland. It's extremely popular with convention and meeting planners

Kids Family-Friendly Hotels

Almost every hotel in the Boston area regularly plays host to children, and many offer special family packages. Moderately priced chains have the most experience with youngsters—you can't go wrong at a **Howard Johnson** or **Holiday Inn**—but their higher-end competitors put on a good show.

Units at the **Doubletree Guest Suites** (p. 99) are a great deal—they have two rooms in which to spread out, and they cost far less than adjoining rooms at any other hotel this nice. You can use the in-room coffeemaker and refrigerator to prepare breakfast, then splurge on lunch and dinner.

In the Back Bay, the **Colonnade Hotel Boston** (p. 93) offers a family weekend package that includes parking, breakfast for two adults, up to four passes (for 2 adults and 2 children) to an attraction of your choice, and a fanny pack for younger guests that holds sunglasses, a pad and pen, a yo-yo, and a toy duck.

The **Seaport Hotel** (p. 88), near Museum Wharf, offers excellent weekend deals, splendid views of the harbor and airport, underwater music piped into the swimming pool, and even a grandparent-grandchild package.

In Cambridge, the **Royal Sonesta Hotel** (p. 106) is around the corner from the Museum of Science and has a large indoor/outdoor pool. It fills the vacation months with Summerfest, which includes free use of bicycles, ice cream, and boat rides along the Charles River. On off-season weekends, the Family Fun package includes four passes to the Museum of Science or the New England Aquarium.

Across the street, **Hotel Marlowe** (p. 106) boasts an excellent location, the welcoming atmosphere that family travelers have come to expect from the Kimpton chain, and special weekend packages. The **Onyx Hotel** (p. 86), another Kimpton property, shares the company's accommodating, light-hearted philosophy but is in a more congested urban neighborhood.

The riverfront **Hyatt Regency Cambridge** (p. 103) courts families with its pool, bicycle rentals, easy access to the banks of the Charles, and discounted rates (subject to availability) on a separate room for the kids.

and is the hotel component of countless package deals. The guest rooms, which were refurbished in 2002, have Queen Anne–style mahogany furniture and are large enough to hold a desk, a table, and either two armchairs or an armchair and an ottoman. As at the Back Bay's other high-rise lodgings, ask for the highest possible floor and you'll enjoy excellent views. Besides booking hordes of vacationers, this Marriott and the Sheraton Boston (see below) are New England's biggest convention hotels; the Sheraton has a better pool, but both have upgraded their accommodations and service to the point where you can't go wrong by letting price and frequent-traveler points distinguish between them. And if you're planning at the last minute, a hotel this large offers pretty good odds of finding a room.

110 Huntington Ave., Boston, MA 02116. ✆ **800/228-9290** or 617/236-5800. Fax 617/236-5885. www.copley marriott.com. 1,147 units. $159–$329 double; $500–$1,200 suite. Children stay free in parent's room. Weekend and

other packages available. AE, DC, DISC, MC, V. Valet parking $35; self-parking $28. T: Orange Line to Back Bay, Green Line to Copley, or Green Line E to Prudential. **Amenities:** Restaurant (American); heated indoor pool; well-equipped health club; Jacuzzi; sauna; game room; concierge; tour desk; car-rental desk; airport shuttle; full-service business center; 24-hr. room service; massage; laundry service; same-day dry cleaning; concierge-level rooms. Rooms for travelers with disabilities are available. *In room:* A/C, TV w/pay movies, high-speed Internet access ($10/day), fridge, coffeemaker, hair dryer, iron, safe.

Hilton Boston Back Bay ☆ Across the street from the Prudential Center complex, the Hilton is primarily a top-notch business hotel, but vacationing families also find it convenient and comfortable. Guest rooms are large, soundproofed, and furnished in modern style, with oversize work desks. Units on higher floors of the 26-story tower enjoy excellent views. The weekend packages, especially during the winter, can be a great deal. The Sheraton, across the street, is three times the Hilton's size (which generally means less personalized service), has a better pool, and books more vacation and function business.

40 Dalton St., Boston, MA 02115. © **800/874-0663,** 800/HILTONS, or 617/236-1100. Fax 617/867-6104. www.bostonbackbay.hilton.com. 385 units (some with shower only). $179–$295 double; from $450 suite. Extra person $20. Rollaway $20. Children under 18 stay free in parent's room. Packages and AAA discount available. AE, DC, DISC, MC, V. Valet parking $36; self-parking $20. T: Green Line B, C, or D to Hynes/ICA. Pets accepted. **Amenities:** Restaurant (American/Continental); bar; indoor pool; well-equipped fitness center; concierge; courtesy car; 24-hr. business center; 24-hr. room service; laundry service; same-day dry cleaning; executive-level rooms. Rooms for travelers with disabilities are available. *In room:* A/C, TV w/pay movies, high-speed Internet access ($13/stay), minibar, coffeemaker, hair dryer, iron.

Jurys Boston Hotel ☆☆ Jurys Doyle, a well-known Irish chain, isn't all that familiar in Boston, but this building is: It used to be police headquarters. These days the welcome is considerably warmer and the business and leisure clientele a lot more satisfied than the former guests. One wing and the top two floors of the 1925 building are new construction, and the limestone-and-brick structure looks great, with dramatic public areas. Decorated in peaceful, muted colors, the luxurious guest rooms have nice touches such as a work area with an ergonomic chair, down comforters, good-size bathrooms (not a sure thing in a renovation project), and windows that open but also do a good job of muffling street noise. Still, light sleepers will want to face away from busy Berkeley Street and perhaps request a room on the second floor, where windows are smaller than elsewhere.

350 Stuart St. (at Berkeley St.), Boston, MA 02116. © **866/JD-HOTELS** or 617/266-7200. Fax 617/266-7203. www.jurysdoyle.com. 225 units (some with shower only). $155–$435 double; $275–$575 1-bedroom suite; from $1,150 2-bedroom suite. Children under 16 stay free in parent's room. Extra person $20. Weekend, family, and other packages from $155 per night. AE, DC, DISC, MC, V. Valet parking $36. T: Orange Line to Back Bay or Green Line to Arlington or Copley. **Amenities:** Restaurant (American); Irish bar; coffee and wine bar; exercise room; business center; 24-hr. room service; laundry service; same-day dry cleaning. Rooms for travelers with disabilities are available. *In room:* A/C, TV w/pay movies, wireless Internet access, fridge, hair dryer, iron, safe, umbrella, robes.

Sheraton Boston Hotel ☆ Its central location, range of accommodations, extensive convention and function facilities, and huge pool make this 29-story hotel one of the most popular in the city. If you're on a budget, though, you'll likely be able to get a better deal elsewhere by shopping around. The Sheraton attracts both business and leisure travelers with direct access to the Hynes Convention Center and the Prudential Center complex. Because it's so big, it often has available rooms when smaller properties are full. A $110 million overhaul completed in 2001 upgraded the entire property, including the lobby and meeting facilities. The fairly large guest rooms are decorated in sleek contemporary style and contain the chain's signature sleigh beds. Units on the highest floors are club-level suites, but even standard accommodations on higher floors afford gorgeous views.

39 Dalton St., Boston, MA 02199. ✆ **800/325-3535** or 617/236-2000. Fax 617/236-1702. www.sheraton.com/boston. 1,215 units. $129–$409 double; $309–$1,800 suite. Children under 17 stay free in parent's room. Weekend packages available. 25% discount for students, faculty, and retired persons with ID, depending on availability. AE, DC, DISC, MC, V. Valet parking $35; self-parking $33. T: Green Line E to Prudential, or B, C, or D to Hynes/ICA. Dogs under 40 lb. accepted with prior approval. **Amenities:** Restaurant (New England); lounge; heated indoor/outdoor pool; well-equipped health club; Jacuzzi; sauna; concierge; airport shuttle; business center; room service until 11pm; laundry service; same-day dry cleaning; executive-level rooms. Rooms for travelers with disabilities are available. *In room:* A/C, TV w/pay movies, high-speed Internet access ($10/day), coffeemaker, hair dryer, iron.

The Westin Copley Place Boston 🏛🏛 Towering 36 stories above Copley Square, the Westin attracts business travelers, convention-goers, sightseers, and dedicated shoppers. Sky bridges link the hotel to Copley Place and the Prudential Center complex, and Copley Square is across the street from the pedestrian entrance. The spacious guest rooms—all on the eighth floor or higher—have traditional oak and mahogany furniture, with Westin's beloved pillow-top mattresses. All rooms underwent refurbishment in 2000 and 2001. You might not notice any of that at first because you'll be captivated by the best views in town. Any qualms that you might have had about choosing a huge chain hotel will fade as you survey downtown Boston, the airport and harbor, and the Charles River and Cambridge.

10 Huntington Ave., Boston, MA 02116. ✆ **800/WESTIN-1** or 617/262-9600. Fax 617/424-7483. www.westin.com/copleyplace. 803 units. $199–$459 double; $899–$3,300 suite. Extra person $25–$50. Weekend packages available. AE, DC, DISC, MC, V. Valet parking $36. T: Green Line to Copley, or Orange Line to Back Bay. Dogs under 20 lb. accepted. **Amenities:** 3 restaurants (a branch of New York's famous Palm steakhouse, Turner Fisheries, breakfast cafe); bar; indoor pool; health club and spa; children's programs; concierge; car-rental desk; airport shuttle; well-equipped business center; shopping arcade; salon; 24-hr. room service; in-room massage; laundry service; executive-level rooms. 48 guest units for travelers with disabilities adjoin standard units. *In room:* A/C, TV/VCR w/pay movies, high-speed Internet access ($11/day), minibar, coffeemaker, hair dryer, iron, safe, robes.

MODERATE

Charlesmark Hotel 🏛🏛 *Value* In an excellent location overlooking the Boston Marathon finish line, the Charlesmark has a boutique feel and great prices. It's both luxurious and—literally, not figuratively—no frills. The sleek, contemporary design evokes a yacht, using custom furnishings (and pillow-top mattresses) to pack plenty of comfort into the compact spaces of the 1886 building. The rooms are small, but with enough space to hold a comfortable chair. The amenities don't challenge the perks of the large hotels in this neighborhood, but they're more than sufficient for most business or leisure travelers. The second-floor lobby holds a computer and printer for guests' use. Rates include breakfast and light refreshments such as bottled water and fruit, part of management's policy not to pile a lot of incidentals onto your bill (also the rationale for free local phone calls). The only real drawback is that the building has just one elevator—and if that's your biggest problem, you're doing pretty well.

655 Boylston St. (between Dartmouth and Exeter sts.), Boston, MA 02116. ✆ **617/247-1212.** Fax 617/247-1224. www.thecharlesmark.com. 33 units (most with shower only). $99–$249 double. Rates include continental breakfast. Children stay free in parent's room. AE, DC, DISC, MC, V. Self-parking $32 in nearby garage. T: Green Line to Copley. Pets accepted with prior approval. **Amenities:** Access to nearby health club ($10); laundry service. Rooms for travelers with disabilities are available. *In room:* A/C, TV, high-speed Internet access, mini-fridge, hair dryer.

Copley Square Hotel ✦   The Copley Square Hotel offers a great location and the pluses and minuses of its relatively small size. Built in 1891, the seven-story hotel extends attentive service that's hard to find at the nearby megahotels, without those giants' abundant amenities—though room rates do include wireless Internet access. If you don't need to engineer a corporate takeover from your room, it's a fine choice, but larger (albeit more expensive) competitors generally offer more features. Each unit has a queen- or king-size bed or two double beds; some are on the small side. Rooms are decorated in an elaborate style that suits the Edwardian-era building, with richly patterned (though not too frilly-floral) fabrics and heavy carved furniture.

47 Huntington Ave., Boston, MA 02116. ✆ 800/225-7062 or 617/536-9000. Fax 617/267-3547. www.copley squarehotel.com. 143 units (some with shower only). $139–$295 double; $405 family suite. Rates include afternoon tea. Children under 17 stay free in parent's room. Packages and senior discounts available. AE, DC, DISC, MC, V. Parking in adjacent garage $34. T: Green Line to Copley, or Orange Line to Back Bay. **Amenities:** 2 restaurants (American, Asian/Mediterranean); nightclub; access to exercise room at nearby Lenox Hotel (see review above); bike rental; concierge; tour desk; car-rental desk; airport shuttle; business center; room service until 11pm; babysitting; laundry service; same-day dry cleaning. Rooms for travelers with disabilities are available. *In room:* A/C, TV w/pay movies, wireless Internet access, coffeemaker, hair dryer, iron.

The MidTown Hotel ✦ *Value*   Even without free parking and an outdoor pool, this centrally located two-story hotel would be a good deal for families and budget-conscious businesspeople. It also books a lot of tour groups. The boxy white building is on a busy street within walking distance of Symphony Hall and the Museum of Fine Arts. The well-maintained rooms are large, bright, and attractively outfitted in no-frills contemporary style, although bathrooms are on the small side. Some units have connecting doors that allow families to spread out. The best rooms are at the back of the building, away from Huntington Avenue. Many rooms have two-line phones and high-speed Internet access; photocopying and fax services are available at the front desk.

220 Huntington Ave., Boston, MA 02445. ✆ 800/343-1177 or 617/262-1000. Fax 617/262-8739. www.midtown hotel.com. 159 units. $119–$259 double; $139–$279 suite. Extra person $15. Children under 18 stay free in parent's room. Packages and AAA, AARP, and government employees' discounts available, subject to availability. AE, DC, DISC, MC, V. Free parking (1 car per room). T: Green Line E to Prudential, or Orange Line to Mass. Ave. Pets accepted. **Amenities:** Restaurant (Italian); heated outdoor pool; access to nearby health club ($5–$10); concierge; airport shuttle; laundry service; same-day dry cleaning. Rooms for travelers with disabilities are available. *In room:* A/C, TV w/pay movies, wireless Internet access ($11/day), coffeemaker, hair dryer, iron.

Newbury Guest House ✦ *Value*   After just a little shopping in the Back Bay, you'll appreciate what a find this cozy inn is: a bargain on Newbury Street. It's a pair of brick town houses built in the 1880s and combined into a refined guesthouse. It offers comfortable furnishings, a pleasant staff, nifty architectural details, and a buffet breakfast served in the ground-level dining room, which adjoins a brick patio. Rooms are modest in size but nicely appointed (with high-speed Internet access, included in the room rate) and well maintained. The largest and most expensive are the bay-window units, which overlook the lively street. The B&B opened in 1991, and it operates near capacity year-round, drawing business travelers during the week and sightseers on weekends. At these prices in this location, there's only one caveat: Reserve early.

261 Newbury St. (between Fairfield and Gloucester sts.), Boston, MA 02116. ✆ 800/437-7668 or 617/437-7666. Fax 617/670-6100. www.newburyguesthouse.com. 32 units (some with shower only). $140–$195 double. Winter discounts and packages available. Extra person $15. Rates include continental breakfast. Rates may be higher during special events. Minimum 2 nights on weekends. AE, DC, DISC, MC, V. Parking $15 (reservation required). T: Green Line B, C, or D to Hynes/ICA. **Amenities:** Access to nearby health club ($25). Rooms for travelers with disabilities are available. *In room:* A/C, TV, wireless Internet access, hair dryer, iron.

INEXPENSIVE

Hostelling International–Boston   This hostel near the Berklee College of Music and Symphony Hall caters to students, youth groups, and other travelers in search of comfortable, no-frills lodging. Accommodations are dorm-style, with six beds per room. There are also a couple of private rooms. The air-conditioned hostel has two full dine-in kitchens, 29 bathrooms, a large common room, and meeting and workshop space. It provides linens, or you can bring your own; sleeping bags are not permitted. The enthusiastic staff organizes free and inexpensive cultural, educational, and recreational programs on the premises and throughout the Boston area. Hostelling International also operates a summer-only hostel just outside Kenmore Square (p. 102).

12 Hemenway St., Boston, MA 02115. ℂ **888/999-4678** or 617/536-9455. Fax 617/424-6558. www.bostonhostel. org. 205 beds. Members of Hostelling International–American Youth Hostels $32 per bed; nonmembers $35 per bed. Members $87 per private unit; nonmembers $93 per private unit. Children 3–12 half-price; children under 3 free. Rates include continental breakfast. MC, V. T: Green Line B, C, or D to Hynes/ICA. **Amenities:** Access to nearby health club ($6); shuttle; coin laundry; Internet access (fee). 1st-floor units and bathrooms are wheelchair accessible; wheelchair lift at building entrance. *In room:* A/C, lockers, no phone.

9 Outskirts & Brookline

What Bostonians consider "outskirts" would be centrally located in many larger cities. Brookline starts about 3 blocks beyond Boston's Kenmore Square. Staying in this area means essentially becoming a commuter to downtown Boston (unless you're in town only to visit Fenway Park or the Longwood Medical Area). It's not a great choice if your destination is Cambridge because of the unwieldy public transit connections.

VERY EXPENSIVE

Hotel Commonwealth ★★   Like a Hollywood starlet strolling the red carpet in vintage Chanel, this boutique hotel is a hot young thing with a traditional, elegant look. Opened in 2003 in a brand-new six-story building in the heart of Kenmore Square, it boasts extensive business features as well as luxurious amenities such as Frette linens and large marble bathrooms. Formerly quite scruffy, Kenmore Square has undergone a face-lift—helped immeasurably by the construction of the hotel, which draws a lot of business from nearby Boston University and from local cultural institutions. My favorite guest rooms are the huge Commonwealth units; each has a king bed and a heavy curtain that draws across the center of the room, separating the sleeping area and the "parlor." These rooms overlook the bustling street, outdoor restaurant seating, and a new bus station. You might prefer a Fenway room—they're smaller, but they face the legendary ballpark (directly across the Mass. Turnpike).

500 Commonwealth Ave., Boston, MA 02215. ℂ **866/784-4000** or 617/933-5000. Fax 617/266-6888. www.hotel commonwealth.com. 150 units. $209–$349 standard double; $229–$389 mini-suite or parlor room. Extra person $20. Children under 18 stay free in parent's room. Packages and AAA discount available. AE, DC, DISC, MC, V. Valet parking $34. T: Green Line B, C, or D to Kenmore. Pets accepted; $25 deposit. **Amenities:** 2 restaurants (seafood, bistro); lounge; exercise room; concierge; business center; room service; babysitting; laundry service; same-day dry cleaning. Rooms for travelers with disabilities are available. *In room:* A/C, TV/DVD w/pay movies, wireless Internet access, minibar, hair dryer, iron, safe, umbrella, robes.

EXPENSIVE

Doubletree Guest Suites ★★ *(Kids)* *(Value)*   This hotel is one of the best deals in town—every unit is a two-room suite with a living room, bedroom, and bathroom. Business travelers can entertain in their rooms, and families can spread out, making this a good choice for both. Overlooking the Charles River at the Allston/Cambridge exit of the Mass. Pike, the hotel is near Cambridge and the riverfront bike-and-jogging path, but not in an actual neighborhood. Shuttle service to local destinations makes the location easier to handle.

The suites, which were renovated in 2002, surround a 15-story atrium. Rooms are large and attractively furnished, and most bedrooms have a king-size bed (some have two oversize twins) and a writing desk. Each living room contains a full-size sofa bed, a dining table, and a good-size refrigerator. The Hyatt Regency Cambridge, the hotel's nearest rival, is more convenient but generally more expensive.

400 Soldiers Field Rd., Boston, MA 02134. © **800/222-TREE** or 617/783-0090. Fax 617/783-0897. www.doubletree. com. 308 units. $129–$309 double. Extra person $20. Children under 18 stay free in parent's room. Packages available. AARP and AAA discounts available. AE, DC, DISC, MC, V. Valet parking $27; self-parking $20. Pets accepted with prior approval. **Amenities:** Restaurant (American); lounge; excellent Scullers Jazz Club (p. 244); indoor pool; exercise room; free access to nearby health club; Jacuzzi; sauna; concierge; shuttle service to Cambridge and downtown Boston; 24-hr. business center; room service until 3am; coin-op laundry; laundry service; same-day dry cleaning. Suites for travelers with disabilities are available. *In room:* A/C, TV w/pay movies, wireless Internet access ($10/day), fridge, coffeemaker, hair dryer, iron.

MODERATE

The 188-room **Brookline Courtyard by Marriott,** 40 Webster St., Brookline (© **866/ 296-2296,** 800/321-2211, or 617/734-1393; fax 617/734-1392; www.brookline courtyard.com), is off Beacon Street in Coolidge Corner. The eight-story hotel has a breakfast cafe, an indoor pool, an exercise room, and shuttle service to the nearby Longwood Medical Area. Prices for a double start at $159, which includes high-speed Internet access.

Best Western Boston/The Inn at Longwood Medical ☆ Next to Children's Hospital in the Longwood Medical Area, this eight-story hotel is a good base for those with business at the hospitals. Beth Israel Deaconess and Brigham and Women's hospitals, the Dana-Farber Cancer Institute, and the Joslin Diabetes Center are within walking distance. Near museums, colleges, and Fenway Park, the hotel is about 20 minutes from downtown Boston by T.

Guest rooms are quite large and furnished in contemporary style, and rates include local phone calls and wireless Internet access. Try to stay on the highest floor possible, not just because the views are better but because the busy intersection of Longwood and Brookline avenues is less than scenic. Suites have kitchen facilities that make them a good choice for long-term guests. The hotel adjoins the Longwood Galleria business complex, which has a food court and shops, including a drugstore.

342 Longwood Ave., Boston, MA 02115. © **800/GOT-BEST** or 617/731-4700, TTY 617/731-9088. Fax 617/731-4870. www.innatlongwood.com. 161 units (18 with kitchenette). $139–$209 double; $219–$259 suite. Extra person $15. Children under 18 stay free in parent's room. Family packages and long-term discounts available. AE, DC, DISC, MC, V. Parking $17. T: Green Line D or E to Longwood. **Amenities:** Restaurant (international); lounge; access to nearby health club ($8); concierge; room service until 12:30am; coin laundry; laundry service; same-day dry cleaning. Rooms for travelers with disabilities are available. *In room:* A/C, TV w/pay movies, high-speed Internet access, coffeemaker, hair dryer, iron.

Holiday Inn Boston Brookline ☆☆ *(Kids)* Just 15 minutes from downtown Boston on the subway, this six-story hotel is more than just another Holiday Inn. In a mostly residential area not far from the Longwood Medical Area, it offers up-to-date accommodations at lower prices than more centrally located hotels. Many guests are visiting

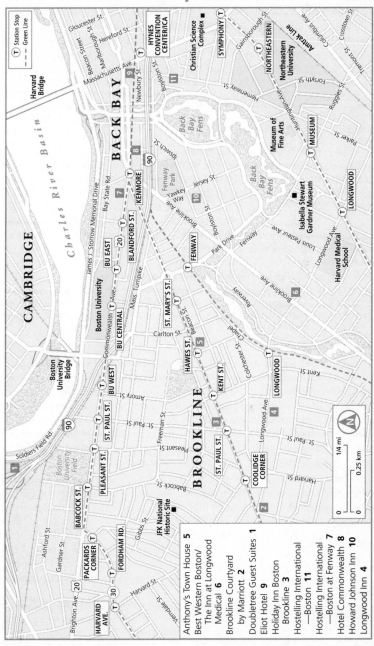

Where to Stay from Mass. Ave. to Brookline

- Station Stop ⓣ
- Green Line ---

Harvard Bridge

Gloucester St.
Marlborough St.
Hereford St.
Beacon Street
Massachusetts Ave.
Newbury St.

HYNES CONVENTION CENTER/ICA

Christian Science Complex ■

SYMPHONY ⓣ

BACK BAY

Gainsborough St.
Columbus Ave.
Tremont St.
Crosstown St.

NORTHEASTERN ⓣ
Northeastern University
Forsyth St.
Ruggles St.

Amtrak Line

Boylston St.

CAMBRIDGE

Charles River Basin

James J. Storrow Memorial Drive

Back Bay Fens

Ipswich St.

Museum of Fine Arts

MUSEUM ⓣ

Parker St.

LONGWOOD ⓣ

Isabella Stewart Gardner Museum ■

Harvard Medical School

Louis Pasteur Ave.

Longwood Ave.

Bay State Rd.
KENMORE ⓣ
BU EAST ⓣ
BLANDFORD ST. ⓣ

Fenway Park

Yawkey Way
Jersey St.
Boylston St.

Back Bay Fens

Park Drive
Fenway

FENWAY ⓣ

Boston University
BU CENTRAL ⓣ
Commonwealth Ave.
Mass. Turnpike

ST. MARY'S ST. ⓣ
Beacon St.
Carlton St.
Chapel

Brookline Ave.

Riverway

Brookline Ave.

Boston University Bridge

BU WEST ⓣ
Amory St.
ST. PAUL ST. ⓣ
St. Paul St.
Freeman St.
Pleasant St.

HAWES ST. ⓣ
KENT ST. ⓣ

LONGWOOD ⓣ

Colchester St.

Kent St.

Longwood Ave.

Boston University Field

PLEASANT ST. ⓣ

BROOKLINE

ST. PAUL ST. ⓣ
Babcock St.

COOLIDGE CORNER ⓣ

St. Paul St.

Harvard St.

BABCOCK ST. ⓣ

JFK National Historic Site ■

Gibbs St.

FORDHAM RD. ⓣ

PACKARDS CORNER ⓣ

Ashford St.
Gardner St.

Brighton Ave.
HARVARD AVE. ⓣ

Vendome St.
Harvard St.

Soldiers Field Rd.

N

1/4 mi
0.25 km
0

Anthony's Town House **5**
Best Western Boston/
The Inn at Longwood
Medical **6**
Brookline Courtyard
by Marriott **2**
Doubletree Guest Suites **1**
Eliot Hotel **9**
Holiday Inn Boston
Brookline **3**
Hostelling International
—Boston **11**
Hostelling International
—Boston at Fenway **7**
Hotel Commonwealth **8**
Howard Johnson Inn **10**
Longwood Inn **4**

101

the nearby hospitals and Boston University. The well-maintained rooms are large and well appointed, with oversize work desks. Units at the front of the building have more interesting views, though they may be slightly noisier because of the busy trolley route below. The bustling Coolidge Corner neighborhood is a 10-minute walk away.

1200 Beacon St., Brookline, MA 02446. © **800/HOLIDAY** or 617/277-1200. www.bos-brookline.holiday-inn.com. 225 units (some with shower only). $139–$239 double; $209–$309 suite. Extra person $10. Children under 18 stay free in parent's room. AE, MC, V. Parking $15. T: Green Line C to St. Paul St. Pets accepted; $15 charge. **Amenities:** Restaurant (American); lounge; coffee shop; small indoor pool; exercise room; Jacuzzi; shuttle to hospitals; laundry service; same-day dry cleaning. Rooms for travelers with disabilities are available. *In room:* A/C, TV, dataport, coffee-maker, hair dryer, iron.

Howard Johnson Inn *(Kids)*   This motel is as close to Fenway Park as you can get without buying a ticket. The outdoor pool makes it particularly attractive to vacationing families. Some of the decent-sized rooms have microwaves and refrigerators (convenient if you plan to eat some meals in). The location, a busy street in a commercial-residential neighborhood, is convenient to the Back Bay, the Museum of Fine Arts, and the Isabella Stewart Gardner Museum, but not all that close to public transit—a consideration when you're hauling kids through the summer heat. During baseball season, guests contend with crowded sidewalks and the raucous Red Sox fans who flood the area.

1271 Boylston St., Boston, MA 02215. © **800/446-4656** or 617/267-8300. Fax 617/864-0242. www.hojo.com. 94 units. $125–$195 double. Extra person $10. Children under 18 stay free in parent's room. Family packages and senior and AAA discounts available. AE, DC, DISC, MC, V. Parking $10. T: Green Line B, C, or D to Kenmore; 10-min. walk. Pets accepted. **Amenities:** Restaurant (Chinese); lounge; outdoor pool; babysitting; laundry service; dry cleaning. *In room:* A/C, TV, dataport, fridge in some rooms, coffeemaker.

INEXPENSIVE

A summer-only hostel occupies a former Howard Johnson hotel just outside Kenmore Square: **Hostelling International—Boston at Fenway,** 575 Commonwealth Ave. (© **617/267-8599;** fax 617/424-6558; www.hifenway.org; T: Green Line B, C, or D to Kenmore). The 485-bed hostel offers well-equipped accommodations in a building that doubles as a Boston University dorm during the school year. Rates are $35 per bed for members of Hostelling International–American Youth Hostels, $38 for nonmembers.

Anthony's Town House   The Anthony family has operated this four-story brownstone guesthouse since 1944, and a stay here is very much like spending the night at Grandma's. Many patrons are Europeans accustomed to guesthouse accommodations with shared bathrooms, and budget-minded Americans won't be disappointed. Each floor has three high-ceilinged rooms furnished in rather ornate Queen Anne or Victorian style and one bathroom with an enclosed shower. Smaller rooms (one per floor) have twin beds; the large front rooms have bay windows. Guests have the use of two refrigerators. The guesthouse is 1 mile from Boston's Kenmore Square, about 15 minutes from downtown by T, and 2 blocks from a busy commercial strip. The late-19th-century building is on the National Register of Historic Places, and there's no smoking on the premises.

1085 Beacon St., Brookline, MA 02446. © **617/566-3972.** Fax 617/232-1085. www.anthonystownhouse.com. 10 units, none with private bathroom. $68–$98 double. Extra person $10. Weekly rates and winter discounts available. No credit cards. Limited free parking. T: Green Line C to Hawes St. *In room:* A/C, TV, no phone.

Longwood Inn   In a residential area 3 blocks from the Boston-Brookline border, this well-maintained three-story Victorian guesthouse offers comfortable accommodations at modest rates. Like the neighborhood, the interior style is homey, with accents that suit the building's architecture. Guests have the use of a fully equipped kitchen and common dining room. There's one apartment with a private bathroom, kitchen, and balcony. Tennis courts, a running track, and a playground at the school next door are open to the public. Public transportation is easily accessible, and the Longwood Medical Area and busy Coolidge Corner neighborhood are within walking distance.

123 Longwood Ave., Brookline, MA 02446. © **617/566-8615.** Fax 617/738-1070. www.longwood-inn.com. 22 units, 17 with private bathroom (4 with shower only). Apr–Nov $89–$109 double; Dec–Mar $69–$89 double. 1-bedroom apt. (sleeps 4-plus) $99–$119. Weekly rates available. AE, DISC, MC, V. Free parking. T: Green Line D to Longwood, or C to Coolidge Corner. *In room:* A/C, TV.

10 Cambridge

Across the Charles River from Boston, Cambridge has its own attractions and excellent hotels. Graduation season (May and early June) is especially busy, but campus events can cause high demand at unexpected times, so plan ahead.

VERY EXPENSIVE

The Charles Hotel ★★★   This nine-story brick hotel, located a block away from Harvard Square, has been *the* place for business and leisure travelers to Cambridge since it opened in 1985. Much of its fame derives from its excellent restaurants, jazz bar, and day spa; the service is equally impeccable. In the recently refurbished guest rooms, the style is contemporary country, with custom adaptations of early American Shaker furniture. The austere design contrasts with the swanky amenities, which include down quilts and Bose Wave radios; bathrooms contain telephones and TVs. And it wouldn't be Cambridge if your intellectual needs went unfulfilled—there's a library in the lobby.

1 Bennett St., Cambridge, MA 02138. © **800/882-1818** or 617/864-1200. Fax 617/864-5715. www.charleshotel. com. 293 units. $229–$599 double; $279–$4,000 suite. Extra person $20. Weekend packages available. AE, DC, MC, V. Valet or self-parking $28. T: Red Line to Harvard. Pets under 25 lb. accepted; $50 fee. **Amenities:** 2 restaurants (Rialto, one of Boston's best [p. 144], and Henrietta's Table, with a lavish Sun brunch); bar; Regattabar jazz club (p. 244); free access to adjacent health club with glass-enclosed pool, Jacuzzi, and exercise room; adjacent spa and salon; concierge; car-rental desk; business center; 24-hr. room service; in-room massage; babysitting; laundry service; same-day dry cleaning. Rooms for travelers with disabilities are available. *In room:* A/C, TV/DVD, high-speed Internet access ($11/day), minibar, hair dryer, iron, safe.

The Hyatt Regency Cambridge ★★ *Kids*   Location is the Hyatt Regency's main drawback but also part of its considerable appeal. Across the street from the Charles River and not far from the Allston/Brighton exit of the turnpike, the hotel is convenient to Kendall and Harvard squares and Boston University. Shuttle service and luxurious appointments help make up for the not-exactly-taxing distance from downtown Boston (about 10 min. by car). The dramatic brick building encloses a 16-story atrium with glass elevators, fountains, trees, and balconies. The best of the spacious guest rooms afford breathtaking views of Boston and the river. A business destination during the week, the hotel also courts families (see "Family-Friendly Hotels," on p. 95) with special two-room rates, subject to availability. If you plan to rely on public transit, allow plenty of time for bus rides and acquaint yourself with the hotel shuttle schedule. The closest competitor is the Doubletree, which is even less centrally located but consists of all suites.

575 Memorial Dr., Cambridge, MA 02139. © **800/233-1234** or 617/492-1234. Fax 617/491-6906. www.cambridge. hyatt.com. 469 units (some with shower only). $245–$465 double weekday; $129–$309 double weekend;

Where to Stay in Cambridge

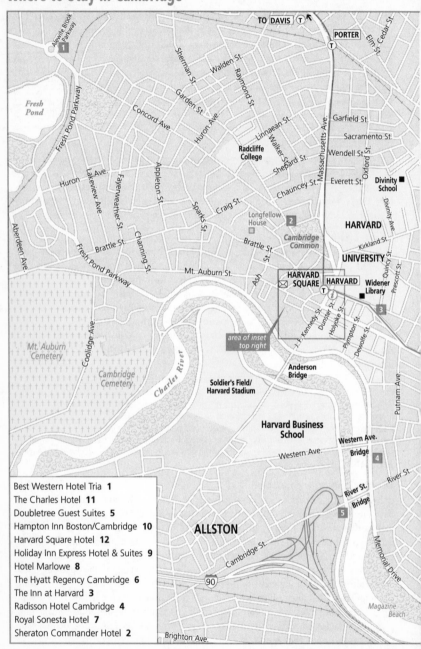

Best Western Hotel Tria **1**
The Charles Hotel **11**
Doubletree Guest Suites **5**
Hampton Inn Boston/Cambridge **10**
Harvard Square Hotel **12**
Holiday Inn Express Hotel & Suites **9**
Hotel Marlowe **8**
The Hyatt Regency Cambridge **6**
The Inn at Harvard **3**
Radisson Hotel Cambridge **4**
Royal Sonesta Hotel **7**
Sheraton Commander Hotel **2**

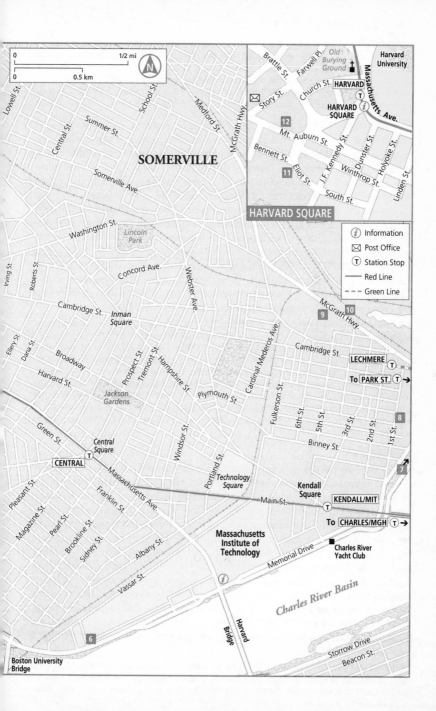

HARVARD SQUARE

SOMERVILLE

Somerville Ave.

Lincoln Park

Concord Ave.

Washington St.

Cambridge St.

Inman Square

Broadway

Harvard St.

Jackson Gardens

Green St.

Central Square

CENTRAL (T)

Massachusetts Ave.

Technology Square

Kendall Square

KENDALL/MIT (T)

Main St.

To **CHARLES/MGH** (T) →

Massachusetts Institute of Technology

Memorial Drive

Charles River Yacht Club

Charles River Basin

Storrow Drive

Beacon St.

Boston University Bridge

Harvard Bridge

Binney St.

Cambridge St.

LECHMERE (T)

To **PARK ST.** (T) →

McGrath Hwy.

Brattle St.

Farwell Pl.

Old Burying Ground

Harvard University

Story St.

Church St.

HARVARD (T)

HARVARD SQUARE

Massachusetts Ave.

Mt. Auburn St.

Bennett St.

Eliot St.

J.F. Kennedy St.

Dunster St.

Winthrop St.

Holyoke St.

Linden St.

South St.

12

11

(i) Information

⊠ Post Office

(T) Station Stop

— Red Line

- - - Green Line

0   1/2 mi

0   0.5 km

N

Lowell St.

Central St.

Summer St.

School St.

Medford St.

McGrath Hwy.

Irving St.

Roberts St.

Ellery St.

Dana St.

Webster Ave.

Prospect St.

Tremont St.

Hampshire St.

Windsor St.

Plymouth St.

Portland St.

Fulkerson St.

6th St.

5th St.

3rd St.

2nd St.

1st St.

Cardinal Medeiros Ave.

Pleasant St.

Magazine St.

Pearl St.

Brookline St.

Sidney St.

Franklin St.

Albany St.

Vassar St.

9

10

8

7

6

$450–$750 suite. Extra person $25. Children under 18 stay free in parent's room. Weekend packages available. AE, DC, DISC, MC, V. Valet parking $22; self-parking $20. **Amenities:** Revolving rooftop restaurant and lounge (Italian); lobby restaurant and lounge (international); 75-ft. indoor lap pool; rooftop health club; Jacuzzi; sauna; bike rental; concierge; shuttle to Cambridge and Boston destinations; business center; room service until late evening; in-room massage; laundry service; dry cleaning; ATM and currency exchange. Rooms for travelers with disabilities are available. *In room:* A/C, TV, fax, high-speed Internet access, coffeemaker, hair dryer, iron.

Royal Sonesta Hotel ★★ *Kids*   This luxurious hotel is in a curious location—it's close to only a few things but convenient to everything, making it a good choice for both business travelers (who can take advantage of wireless Internet access throughout the building) and families (see "Family-Friendly Hotels," on p. 95). The Cambridge-Side Galleria mall is across the street, the Museum of Science is around the corner, and downtown Boston is closer than Harvard Square. In the other direction, MIT and Kendall Square are 10 minutes away on foot. Even in the midst of all this activity, the hotel achieves a serene atmosphere, thanks in part to the helpful staff. Most of the spacious rooms in the 10-story building have lovely views of the river or the city (higher prices are for better views). Everything is custom-designed in modern, comfortable style and is regularly refurbished. Original contemporary artwork, including pieces by Andy Warhol and Frank Stella, hangs throughout the public spaces and guest rooms. The closest competition is Hotel Marlowe (see below), across the street, which offers less extensive fitness options (there's no pool) and fewer river views.

5 Cambridge Pkwy., Cambridge, MA 02142. ✆ 800/SONESTA or 617/806-4200. Fax 617/806-4232. www.sonesta. com/boston. 400 units (some with shower only). $239–$279 standard double; $259–$299 superior double; $279–$319 deluxe double; $339–$1,000 suite. Extra person $25. Children under 18 stay free in parent's room. Weekend, family, and other packages available. AE, DC, DISC, MC, V. Valet or self-parking $19. T: Green Line to Lechmere; 10-min. walk. Pets accepted with prior approval. **Amenities:** Restaurant (a branch of Davio's, p. 138); cafe with seasonal outdoor seating; heated indoor/outdoor pool with retractable roof; well-equipped health club and spa; bike rental (seasonal); concierge; courtesy van; business center; room service until 1am; massage; laundry service; dry cleaning. Rooms for travelers with disabilities are available; staff is trained in disability awareness. *In room:* A/C, TV w/pay movies and Sony PlayStation, high-speed wireless Internet access ($10/day), minibar, coffeemaker, hair dryer, iron, safe.

EXPENSIVE

Hotel Marlowe ★★ *Kids*   Hotel Marlowe reminds me of Cambridge as a whole— it's fun and funky, but serious when it needs to be. The hotel opened in 2003 in a new eight-story building adjacent to the CambridgeSide Galleria mall, around the corner from the Museum of Science—a great location for families. It offers abundant amenities for both business and leisure travelers. The good-size guest rooms are elegantly decorated, with quirky-boutique-hotel touches like leopard-print carpeting and a faux-fur throw across the foot of the bed. They're big enough to hold a work desk and an armchair. Rooms have down comforters, three phones (one in the bathroom), and high-speed Internet access (included in the room rates). They overlook the river (across the busy boulevard), a small canal, or the landscaped courtyard/driveway that shields the lobby from the street. The hotel is part of the detail-oriented Kimpton chain, best known for the beloved Hotel Monaco brand. The closest competitor is the Royal Sonesta Hotel (see above), across the street, which is more expensive but has a pool and health club.

25 Edwin H. Land Blvd., Cambridge, MA 02141. ✆ 800/825-7040, 800/KIMPTON, or 617/868-8000. Fax 617/868-8001. www.hotelmarlowe.com. 236 units (some with shower only). $189–$349 double; from $389 suite. Extra person $25. Rates include morning coffee and tea, evening cocktail reception, and use of bikes. Children under 18 stay

free in parent's room. Weekend, family, and other packages available. AARP and AAA discounts available. AE, DC, DISC, MC, V. Valet parking $28; self-parking $20. T: Green Line to Lechmere or Red Line to Kendall. Pets accepted. **Amenities:** Restaurant (American brasserie); bar; exercise room; concierge; business center; 24-hr. room service; laundry service; same-day dry cleaning. Rooms for travelers with disabilities are available. *In room:* A/C, TV w/pay movies, high-speed Internet access, minibar, coffeemaker, hair dryer, iron, safe, umbrella, robes.

The Inn at Harvard ★★   The redbrick Inn at Harvard looks like just another college building—it's adjacent to Harvard Yard, and its Georgian-style architecture would fit nicely on campus. Inside, however, there's no mistaking it for anything other than an elegant hotel, popular with business travelers and university visitors. The elegant guest rooms, which were redecorated in 2002, contain pillow-top beds, either a lounge chair or two armchairs around a table, a work area, and an original painting from the Fogg Art Museum. Some units have dormer windows and window seats. The four-story skylit atrium holds the "living room," a huge, well-appointed guest lounge that's suitable for meeting with a visitor if you don't want to conduct business in your room.

1201 Mass. Ave. (at Quincy St.), Cambridge, MA 02138. © 800/458-5886 or 617/491-2222. Fax 617/520-3711. www.theinnatharvard.com. 113 units (some with shower only). $129–$259 double; $1,200 presidential suite. AAA and AARP discounts available. AE, DC, DISC, MC, V. Valet parking $30. T: Red Line to Harvard. **Amenities:** Restaurant (New England); dining privileges at the nearby Harvard Faculty Club; free access to nearby health club; room service until 10:30pm; laundry service; same-day dry cleaning. Rooms for travelers with disabilities are available. *In room:* A/C, TV, wireless Internet access ($10/day), coffeemaker, hair dryer, iron, umbrella, robes.

Sheraton Commander Hotel ★   This six-story hotel in the heart of Cambridge's historic district opened in 1927, and it's exactly what you'd expect of a traditional hostelry within sight of the Harvard campus. The colonial-style decor begins in the elegant lobby and extends to the decent-size guest rooms, which are attractively furnished and well maintained. Ask the pleasant front-desk staff for a room facing Cambridge Common; even if you aren't on a (relatively) high floor, you'll have a decent view. Suites have two TVs, and some have wet bars, refrigerators, and whirlpools. The Sheraton Commander doesn't have the Charles Hotel's cachet and amenities, but it doesn't have the Charles's prices, either. Plan far ahead if you're visiting during a Harvard event.

16 Garden St., Cambridge, MA 02138. © 800/325-3535 or 617/547-4800. Fax 617/234-1396. www.sheraton commander.com. 175 units (some with shower only). $109–$385 double; $295–$750 suite. Extra person $20. Children under 18 stay free in parent's room. Weekend packages and AAA and AARP discounts available. AE, DC, DISC, MC, V. Valet parking $18. T: Red Line to Harvard. **Amenities:** Restaurant (American); lounge; exercise room; concierge; business center; room service until 11pm; laundry service; dry cleaning; executive-level rooms. Rooms for travelers with disabilities are available. *In room:* A/C, TV w/pay movies, high-speed Internet access, coffeemaker, hair dryer, iron.

MODERATE

The **Hampton Inn Boston/Cambridge,** 191 Msgr. O'Brien Hwy., Cambridge (© **800/HAMPTON** or 617/494-5300; www.bostoncambridge.hamptoninn.com), is a 5-minute walk from the Green Line Lechmere stop. Rates at the 114-room hotel start at $109 for a double and include parking, continental breakfast, and high-speed Internet access. The Hampton Inn is 1 block closer to the T than the Holiday Inn Express (see listing below), but on the opposite side of the very busy street from the station.

Best Western Hotel Tria ★   This four-story establishment underwent a $3 million renovation in 2003. It offers a sophisticated blend of chain-motel convenience and boutique-hotel features—such as a "soap menu." Guest rooms are spacious, with sleek but comfy contemporary furnishings, and are at least one floor up from the busy street. Room rates include 30 free minutes of local phone calls. The commercial neighborhood is nothing to write home about, but the pool and free parking and breakfast help make up for the less-than-scenic location. A 2½-mile jogging trail circles Fresh Pond, across the street. A restaurant is next door, and a shopping center with a 10-screen movie theater is nearby. Boston lies about a 15-minute drive or a 30-minute T ride away; Lexington and Concord are less than a half-hour away by car.

220 Alewife Brook Pkwy., Cambridge, MA 02138. ✆ 866/333-8742 or 617/491-8000. Fax 617/491-4932. www. hoteltria.com. 69 units. Mid-Mar to Oct $129–$299 double; Nov to mid-Mar $109–$159 double. Extra person $10. Rates include continental breakfast. Rates may be higher during special events. Children under 17 stay free in parent's room. AE, DC, MC, V. Parking $10. T: Red Line to Alewife, 10-min. walk. Pets accepted; reservation required; $25 fee; $100 deposit. **Amenities:** Indoor pool; access to nearby health club ($10); Jacuzzi; tour desk; shuttle service; same-day dry cleaning. *In room:* A/C, TV, wireless Internet access, coffeemaker, hair dryer, iron, robes.

Harvard Square Hotel   Smack in the middle of "the Square," this six-story brick hotel is a favorite with visiting parents and budget-conscious business travelers. The lobby and the unpretentious guest rooms were renovated in 2003 and 2004. The rooms are relatively small but comfortable and neatly decorated in contemporary style; some overlook Harvard Square. The front desk handles faxing and copying.

110 Mount Auburn St., Cambridge, MA 02138. ✆ 800/458-5886 or 617/864-5200. Fax 617/492-4896. www. harvardsquarehotel.com. 73 units (some with shower only). $99–$189 double. Extra person $10. Children under 17 stay free in parent's room. Corporate rates and AAA and AARP discounts available. AE, DC, DISC, MC, V. Parking $27. T: Red Line to Harvard. **Amenities:** Dining privileges at the Harvard Faculty Club; free access to nearby health club; car-rental desk; laundry service; dry cleaning. Rooms for travelers with disabilities are available. *In room:* A/C, TV, wireless Internet access ($10/day), fridge, coffeemaker, hair dryer, iron, umbrella.

Holiday Inn Express Hotel & Suites *Value*   A limited-services lodging on a busy street, the Holiday Inn Express is a great deal. It's comfortable and convenient—just a 5-minute walk from the Green Line—for businesspeople on tight budgets as well as vacationers. Each decent-size room has a fridge and microwave, making this a good choice if you plan to eat some meals in. The eight-story building sits slightly back from the street, but you'll still want to be as high up as possible to get away from traffic noise. If you're willing to do without a restaurant, business center, or exercise facility, you'll probably find that the reasonable rates, which include local phone calls and parking—a big plus in Cambridge—more than make up for the lack of extras.

250 Msgr. O'Brien Hwy., Cambridge, MA 02141. ✆ 888/887-7690 or 617/577-7600. Fax 617/354-1313. www. hiexpress.com/boscambridgema. 112 units. From $104 double; from $125 suite. Rates include continental breakfast. Discounts for hospital patients and families available, subject to availability. AE, DC, DISC, MC, V. Free parking. T: Green Line to Lechmere. **Amenities:** Access to nearby health club ($10); laundry service; same-day dry cleaning. Rooms for travelers with disabilities are available; some units adjoin standard units. *In room:* A/C, TV w/pay movies, high-speed Internet access, fridge, coffeemaker, hair dryer, iron.

Radisson Hotel Cambridge ✇   An attractive, modern 16-story tower across the street from the Charles River, the Radisson is convenient to both Cambridge and Boston and has an indoor swimming pool. Each decent-sized unit has a picture window, and some have private balconies. The rooms underwent a $500,000 spruce-up in early 2005. Prices vary with the size of the unit, the floor, and the view; the panorama of the Boston skyline from higher floors on the river side of the building is worth the extra money. Wireless Internet access (included in the room rate) is available throughout the building. The hotel, a onetime Howard Johnson, is near the major college campuses and the Mass. Pike. It's 10 minutes by car from downtown Boston but not near public transit—leave time for the hotel shuttle.

777 Memorial Dr., Cambridge, MA 02139. (*C*) **800/333-3333** or 617/492-7777. Fax 617/492-6038. www.radisson. com/cambridgema. 204 units. $109–$269 double. Extra person $10. Rollaway $20. Cribs free. Children under 18 stay free in parent's room. Packages and AARP and AAA discounts available. AE, DC, DISC, MC, V. Parking $15. **Amenities:** 2 restaurants (Japanese, Greek); indoor pool; concierge; shuttle to Cambridge T stops; business center; room service until 10pm; laundry service; same-day dry cleaning. Rooms for travelers with disabilities are available. *In room:* A/C, TV w/pay movies, wireless Internet access, coffeemaker, hair dryer, iron.

11 At & Near the Airport

EXPENSIVE

The **Embassy Suites Hotel Boston at Logan Airport,** 207 Porter St., E. Boston, MA 02128 ((*C*) **800/EMBASSY** or 617/567-5000; www.embassysuites.com), is a 273-unit hotel with an indoor pool. Each suite in the 10-story hotel has a living room with a pullout couch. Room rates, which start at $159, include breakfast, high-speed Internet access, and shuttle service to the airport and the Airport T stop.

Hilton Boston Logan Airport ⟨★★⟩   Smack in the middle of the airport, the Hilton draws most of its guests from meetings, conventions, and canceled flights. It's convenient and well equipped for business travelers, and it's an excellent fallback for vacationers in search of a deal who don't mind a short commute to downtown. Guest rooms are large and tastefully furnished, with plenty of business features, including two-line speakerphones. The best units, on the higher floors of the 10-story building (which opened in 1999), afford sensational views of the airport and harbor. The big concern with a hotel this close to the runways is noise, but the picture-window views of approaching aircraft look like TV with the sound off. A shuttle bus connects the hotel to all airport locations; walkways also link the building to Terminals A (nearby) and E (a long walk). The Hyatt Harborside (see below) is the closest competition— it's at the edge of the airport, which means less commotion outside but less convenient access to the T.

85 Terminal Rd., Logan International Airport, Boston, MA 02128. (*C*) **800/HILTONS** or 617/568-6700. Fax 617/568-6800. www.hiltonbostonloganairport.com. 599 units. $99–$299 double; from $500 suite. Children under 18 stay free in parent's room. Weekend and other packages available. AE, DC, DISC, MC, V. Valet parking $26; self-parking $22. T: Blue Line to Airport, then take shuttle bus. Pets accepted. **Amenities:** Restaurant (American); Irish pub; coffee counter; indoor lap pool; health club; concierge; 24-hr. shuttle bus service to airport destinations, including car-rental offices and ferry dock, with on-bus electronic check-in; well-equipped business center; 24-hr. room service; laundry service; same-day dry cleaning; executive-level rooms. *In room:* A/C, TV, high-speed Internet access ($13/stay), minibar, coffeemaker, hair dryer, iron.

Hyatt Harborside ⟨★⟩   This striking 14-story waterfront hotel offers unobstructed views of the harbor and city skyline. It caters to the convention and business trade. Sightseers whose budget for transportation doesn't include a fair amount of time (on the shuttle bus and subway) or money (on parking, cabs, or water taxis, which serve the adjacent dock) will be better off closer to downtown.

The good-size guest rooms, which were renovated in 2000, afford dramatic views from the higher floors. They have all the features you'd expect at a deluxe hotel, including oversize work desks. The surprises here are in the public areas; the lobby is a work of art, with a map inlaid in the floor and the "sky" on the rotunda ceiling. And the building's tower is a lighthouse—the airport control tower manages the beacon so that it doesn't interfere with runway lights.

101 Harborside Dr., Boston, MA 02128. © **800/233-1234** or 617/568-1234. Fax 617/567-8856. www.harborside. hyatt.com. 270 units (some with shower only). From $169 double. Children under 12 stay free in parent's room. AE, DC, DISC, MC, V. Parking $20. T: Blue Line to Airport, then take shuttle bus. By car, follow signs to Logan Airport and take Harborside Dr. past car-rental area and tunnel entrance. **Amenities:** Restaurant (New England); lounge; 40-ft. indoor pool; exercise room; Jacuzzi; sauna; concierge; 24-hr. airport shuttle service; business center; room service until midnight; laundry service; same-day dry cleaning; executive-level rooms. Rooms for travelers with disabilities are available. *In room:* A/C, TV w/pay movies, high-speed Internet access, coffeemaker, hair dryer, iron.

MODERATE

If you can't get a room at the Comfort Inn, consider the **Hampton Inn Boston Logan Airport,** 2300 Lee Burbank Hwy., Revere (© **800/426-7866** or 781/286-5665; www. hamptoninn.com), on an ugly commercial-industrial strip about 3 miles north of the airport. A free shuttle bus serves the 227-room hotel, which has a pool; rates start at about $129 for a double and include continental breakfast.

Comfort Inn & Suites Boston/Airport ★ *Value*   Although it loses points for the misleading name—the airport is about 3½ miles south—the well-equipped Comfort Inn ranks high. The eight-story hotel, which opened in 2001, sits on a hill set back from the street near a busy traffic circle. It offers a good range of amenities for business and leisure travelers, an attentive staff, and an indoor pool. And it's a deal—room rates include high-speed Internet access, local phone calls, and continental breakfast. Suites are oversize rooms that contain sofa beds, and king suites have refrigerators as well. The somewhat inconvenient location translates to reasonable rates, and the North Shore is easily accessible if you plan to take a day trip. Revere Beach is about 2 minutes away by car.

85 American Legion Hwy. (Route 60), Revere, MA 02151. © **877/485-3600** or 781/485-3600. Fax 781/485-3601. www.comfortinnboston.com. 208 units. $79–$169 double; $119–$199 suite. Rates include continental breakfast. Senior and AAA discounts available. AE, DC, DISC, MC, V. Free parking. T: Blue Line to Airport, then take shuttle bus. Pets accepted; $10/stay. **Amenities:** Restaurant (Italian/American); lounge; indoor pool; exercise room; shuttle to subway and airport; business center; room service (4–10pm); coin-op laundry; same-day dry cleaning. Rooms for travelers with disabilities are available. *In room:* A/C, TV w/pay movies, high-speed Internet access, coffeemaker, hair dryer, iron.

Where to Dine

Friends tell me I'm too tough, that a so-so meal at a particular restaurant shouldn't automatically exclude it from this chapter.

I think that isn't tough enough, and here's why: I live here. I can try that disappointing restaurant again. You're here for just a few days, and you probably don't have the time—or the inclination or the budget—to be throwing around second chances.

That's not to say that every restaurant in this chapter gets high marks for every aspect of every meal. If the space isn't the loveliest, the service isn't the greatest, or (rarely) the food is less impressive than some other element of the experience, I'll point that out.

The days when restaurant snobs sniffed that they had to go to New York to get a decent meal are long gone. Especially in warm weather, when excellent local produce appears on menus in every price range, the Boston area holds its own with any other market in the country. Celebrity chefs and rising stars spice up a dynamic restaurant scene, and traditional favorites occupy an important niche. The huge student population seeks out value, which it often finds at ethnic restaurants.

The guiding thought for this chapter, without regard to price, was, "If this were your only meal in Boston, would you be delighted with it?" At all the restaurants we list, the answer, for one reason or another, is yes.

THE FOOD

Seafood is a specialty in Boston, and you'll find it on the menu at almost every restaurant—trendy or classic, expensive or cheap, American (whatever that is) or ethnic. Some pointers: **Scrod** or **schrod** is a generic term for fresh white-fleshed fish, usually served in filets. **Local shellfish** includes Ipswich and Essex clams, Atlantic lobsters, Wellfleet oysters, scallops, mussels, and shrimp.

Lobster was once so abundant that the Indians showed the Pilgrims how to use the ugly crustaceans as fertilizer, and prisoners rioted when it turned up on the menu too often. Order lobster boiled or steamed and you'll get a plastic bib, drawn butter (for dipping), a nutcracker (for the claws and tail), and a pick (for the legs). Restaurants price lobsters by the pound; the ones in this chapter typically charge at least $15 to $20 for a "chicken" (1- to 1¼-lb.) lobster, and more for the bigger specimens. If you want someone else to do the work, lobster is available in a "pie" (casserole), in a "roll" (sandwich), stuffed and baked or broiled, in or over pasta, in salad, and in bisque.

Well-made **New England clam chowder** is studded with fresh clams and thickened with cream. Recipes vary, but they never, ever include tomatoes. (Tomatoes go in Manhattan clam chowder.) If you want clams but not soup, many places serve **steamers,** or soft-shell clams cooked in the shell, as an appetizer or main dish. More common are hard-shell clams—**littlenecks** (small) or **cherrystones** (medium-size)—served raw, like oysters.

Note: The axiom that you should order **oysters** only in months with an "R" in them originates in biology. Summer is

---

Tips **Time Is Money**

Lunch is an excellent, economical way to check out a fancy restaurant without breaking the bank. At restaurants that take reservations, it's always a good idea to make them, particularly for dinner. To make reservations online, visit **www.opentable.com**, which handles many local restaurants. Boston-area restaurants are far less busy early in the week than they are Friday through Sunday. If you're flexible about when you indulge in fine cuisine and when you go for pizza and a movie, choose the low-budget option on the weekend and pamper yourself on a weeknight.

---

breeding season, when the energy that usually goes into bulking up (and making lots of juicy meat) gets diverted to reproduction. To experience the best the oyster has to offer, wait till the weather turns colder.

Traditional **Boston baked beans,** which date from colonial days, when cooking on the Sabbath was forbidden, earned Boston the nickname "Beantown." House-made baked beans can be hard to find (Durgin-Park does an excellent rendition), but where you do, you'll probably also find good cornbread and **brown bread**—more like a steamed pudding of whole wheat and rye flour, cornmeal, molasses, buttermilk, and usually raisins.

Finally, **Boston cream pie** is golden layer cake sandwiched around custard and topped with chocolate glaze—no cream, no pie.

1 Best Restaurant Bets

- **Best Investment (of time and money):** Dinner at **L'Espalier,** 30 Gloucester St. (© **617/262-3023**), is an event. For your event, whatever the occasion, the grand cuisine and solicitous service will make it unforgettable. See p. 134.
- **Best Seafood: Legal Sea Foods,** 800 Boylston St., in the Prudential Center (© **617/266-6800**) and other locations, does one thing and does it exceptionally well. It's a chain for a great reason: People can't get enough of the freshest seafood around. See p. 138.
- **Best Place for a Classic Boston Experience: Durgin-Park,** 340 Faneuil Hall Marketplace (© **617/227-2038**), has packed 'em in since 1827. From tycoon to out-of-towner, everyone is happy here except the famously crotchety waitresses. It's a classic, not a relic. See p. 124.
- **Best Spot for Romance:** Soaring ceilings, colorful decor, and (seasonally) a roaring fire make the atmosphere in the Monday Club Bar at **Upstairs on the Square,** 91 Winthrop St., Cambridge (© **617/864-1933**), perfect for a rendezvous. See p. 144.
- **Best Spot for a Celebration:** Cool your heels at the bar at **Dalí,** 415 Washington St., Somerville (© **617/661-3254**), and toast your good news with sangria while you wait for a table. (Finally, a restaurant that makes you glad it doesn't take reservations.) The dishes on the *tapas* menu are perfect for sharing, and the atmosphere is lively and festive. See p. 147.
- **Best Spot for a Business Lunch:** Plenty of deals go down at private clubs and formal restaurants, but that can take hours. Leave an impression with your

no-nonsense approach and a quick but delicious meal at **Cosí Sandwich Bar,** 53 State St. (© **617/723-4447**), 14 Milk St. (© **617/426-7565**), or 133 Federal St. (© **617/292-2674**). See p 125.

- **Best Wine List:** Organized by characteristics (from light to rich) rather than by vintage or provenance, the excellent offerings at the **Blue Room,** 1 Kendall Sq., Cambridge (© **617/494-9034**), are arranged in the most user-friendly way imaginable. See p. 146.
- **Best Value:** At the **Midwest Grill,** 1124 Cambridge St., Cambridge (© **617/354-7536**), the hits just keep on coming. The sword-wielding waiters bring succulent grilled meats until you ask (or beg) them to stop. Arrive hungry and you'll definitely get your money's worth. See p. 149.
- **Best for Kids:** The wood-fired brick ovens of the **Bertucci's** chain are magnets for little eyes, and the pizza that comes out of them is equally enthralling. Picky parents will be happy here, too. Try the locations at Faneuil Hall Marketplace (© **617/227-7889**); 43 Stanhope St., Back Bay (© **617/247-6161**); 533 Commonwealth Ave., Kenmore Square (© **617/236-1030**); 21 Brattle St., Harvard Square, Cambridge (© **617/864-4748**); and 799 Main St., Cambridge (© **617/661-8356**). See p. 134.
- **Best Raw Bar:** The raw bar at **Ye Olde Union Oyster House,** 41 Union St. (© **617/227-2750**), is a tasty blend of new and old: The shellfish is ultrafresh, and the restaurant has been a Boston institution for the better part of 2 centuries. See p. 124.
- **Best American Cuisine:** Maybe it's not "cuisine," but what's more American than a burger? **Mr. Bartley's Burger Cottage,** 1246 Mass. Ave., Cambridge (© **617/354-6559**), is famous for its burgers, its onion rings, and a down-to-earth atmosphere that's increasingly rare in Harvard Square. See p. 146.
- **Best French Cuisine: Sel de la Terre,** 255 State St. (© **617/720-1300**). Technically, it's Provençal. Not so technically, it's delicious. Fresh New England ingredients go into the thoroughly French end product. Try as many different breads as you can without ruining your meal. See p. 116.
- **Best Italian Cuisine:** By far the best restaurant in the North End, **Mamma Maria,** 3 North Sq. (© **617/523-0077**), is one of the best in town. In a lovely setting, it offers remarkable regional Italian fare in a spaghetti-and-meatballs neighborhood. See p. 117.
- **Best Brunch:** The insane displays at many top hotels are well worth the monetary and caloric compromises. If you're looking for a delicious meal that won't destroy your budget and waistline, join the throng at the **S&S Restaurant,** 1334 Cambridge St., Cambridge (© **617/354-0777**). See p. 150.

2 Restaurants by Cuisine

AFGHAN

The Helmand ✿ (Cambridge, $$, p. 148)

AMERICAN

The Bristol ✿✿ (Back Bay, $$$, p. 136)

Grill 23 & Bar ✿ (Back Bay, $$$$, p. 133)

Hamersley's Bistro ✿ (South End, $$$$, p. 131)

Jacob Wirth Company (Theater District, $$, p. 130)

Key to Abbreviations: $$$$ = Very Expensive $$$ = Expensive $$ = Moderate $ = Inexpensive

Milk Street Café kiosk (Financial District, $, p. 137)

Mr. Bartley's Burger Cottage ★★ (Cambridge, $, p. 146)

Troquet ★★ (Theater District, $$$$, p. 128)

Zaftigs Delicatessen (Kenmore Square to Brookline, $, p. 140)

ASIAN

Billy Tse Restaurant (North End, $$, p. 120)

BARBECUE

East Coast Grill & Raw Bar ★★ (Cambridge, $$$, p. 147)

Redbones ★ (Somerville, $$, p. 149)

BRAZILIAN

Midwest Grill ★ (Cambridge, $$, p. 149)

CAJUN

Bob the Chef's Jazz Cafe ★ (South End, $$, p. 132)

Border Café (Cambridge, $$, p. 145)

CAMBODIAN

The Elephant Walk ★ (Kenmore Square to Brookline, $$$, p. 140)

CANTONESE

East Ocean City (Chinatown, $$, p. 130)

Grand Chau Chow ★ (Chinatown, $$, p. 130)

CARIBBEAN

Green Street Grill ★ (Cambridge, $$, p. 148)

CHINESE

Billy Tse Restaurant (North End, $$, p. 120)

East Ocean City (Chinatown, $$, p. 130)

Grand Chau Chow ★ (Chinatown, $$, p. 130)

CONTINENTAL

Locke-Ober ★ (Downtown Crossing, $$$$, p. 125)

DELI

S&S Restaurant ★★ (Cambridge, $, p. 150)

Zaftigs Delicatessen (Kenmore Square to Brookline, $, p. 140)

ECLECTIC

The Blue Room ★★★ (Cambridge, $$$, p. 146)

Icarus ★★ (South End, $$$$, p. 131)

Olives ★★ (Charlestown, $$$$, p. 127)

Upstairs on the Square ★★ (Cambridge, $$$$, p. 144)

FRENCH

Brasserie Jo ★ (Back Bay, $$, p. 139)

The Elephant Walk ★ (Kenmore Square to Brookline, $$$, p. 140)

Garden of Eden (South End, $$, p. 132)

Hamersley's Bistro ★ (South End, $$$$, p. 131)

L'Espalier ★★★ (Back Bay, $$$$, p. 134)

Les Zygomates ★★ (Financial District, $$$, p. 123)

No. 9 Park ★ (Beacon Hill, $$$$, p. 126)

Sel de la Terre ★★ (Waterfront, $$$, p. 116)

GERMAN

Jacob Wirth Company (Theater District, $$, p. 130)

INDIAN

Bombay Club (Cambridge, $$, p. 145)

ITALIAN

Artú (North End, $$, p. 117)

Cosí Sandwich Bar ★ (Financial District, $, p. 125)

Daily Catch ★ (North End, $$, p. 120)

Davio's ★★ (Back Bay, $$$, p. 138)

Galleria Umberto Rosticceria (North End, $, p. 122)

Giacomo's Ristorante ★★ (North End, $$, p. 120)

La Groceria Ristorante Italiano (Cambridge, $$, p. 149)

La Summa ⚑ (North End, $$, p. 121)

Mamma Maria ⚑⚑⚑ (North End, $$$$, p. 117)

No. 9 Park ⚑ (Beacon Hill, $$$$, p. 126)

Piccola Venezia (North End, $$, p. 122)

JAPANESE

Ginza Japanese Restaurant ⚑ (Chinatown, $$$, p. 128)

MEDITERRANEAN

Casablanca ⚑ (Cambridge, $$$, p. 145)

La Groceria Ristorante Italiano (Cambridge, $$, p. 149)

Oleana ⚑⚑ (Cambridge, $$$, p. 148)

Rialto ⚑⚑ (Cambridge, $$$$, p. 144)

Spire ⚑⚑ (Beacon Hill, $$$$, p. 127)

MEXICAN

Casa Romero ⚑ (Back Bay, $$$, p. 137)

Tu y Yo Mexican Fonda (Cambridge, $$, p. 150)

MIDDLE EASTERN

Café Jaffa (Back Bay, $, p. 140)

NEW ENGLAND

Durgin-Park ⚑⚑⚑ (Faneuil Hall, $$, p. 124)

L'Espalier ⚑⚑⚑ (Back Bay, $$$$, p. 134)

Spire ⚑⚑ (Beacon Hill, $$$$, p. 127)

Ye Olde Union Oyster House ⚑ (Faneuil Hall, $$$, p. 124)

PIZZA

Picco (South End, $, p. 133)

Pizzeria Regina ⚑⚑ (North End, $, p. 122)

SANDWICHES

Cosí Sandwich Bar ⚑ (Financial District, $, p. 125)

Garden of Eden (South End, $$, p. 132)

Nashoba Brook Bakery ⚑ (South End, $, p. 133)

SEAFOOD

Daily Catch ⚑ (North End, $$, p. 120)

East Coast Grill & Raw Bar ⚑⚑ (Cambridge, $$$, p. 147)

East Ocean City (Chinatown, $$, p. 130)

Giacomo's Ristorante ⚑⚑ (North End, $$, p. 120)

Green Street Grill ⚑ (Cambridge, $$, p. 148)

Jasper White's Summer Shack ⚑ (Cambridge, $$$, p. 147)

Jimmy's Harborside Restaurant (Waterfront, $$$, p. 116)

Legal Sea Foods ⚑⚑⚑ (Back Bay, $$$, p. 138)

Ye Olde Union Oyster House ⚑ (Faneuil Hall, $$$, p. 124)

SOUTHERN

Bob the Chef's Jazz Cafe ⚑ (South End, $$, p. 132)

SPANISH

Dalí ⚑⚑ (Cambridge, $$$, p. 147)

Tapéo (Back Bay, $$$, p. 136)

SUSHI

Billy Tse Restaurant (North End, $$, p. 120)

Ginza Japanese Restaurant ⚑ (Chinatown, $$$, p. 128)

TEX-MEX

Border Café (Cambridge, $$, p. 145)

Fajitas & 'Ritas (Downtown Crossing, $, p. 126)

THAI

Bangkok City ⚑ (Back Bay, $$, p. 139)

VEGETARIAN/VIETNAMESE

Buddha's Delight ⚑ (Chinatown, $, p. 130)

⌐Tips **The Experts Dine Out and Weigh In**

In preparing the 2005 edition of *Frommer's Boston*, I asked local travel insiders—hoteliers, restaurateurs, publicity managers, merchants, and other hospitality experts—to name their two favorite attractions and activities. A Boston Duck Tour was the most popular of the 160 responses.

For this edition, I asked for the names of two restaurants: a place to take out-of-towners looking to eat where the locals do and a special-occasion destination. The experts came up with a whopping 228 choices; they named 146 local places (114 of which got one vote each) and 82 fancy ones (including 65 one-shot deals). The overwhelming winner was **Legal Sea Foods,** with 12 votes as a local favorite and 6 as a special-occasion spot. Next most popular was **Upstairs on the Square,** with 12 votes (5 and 7). Third-place **No. 9 Park** got 10 votes, all in the special-occasion category; 4 of those were from other restaurant owners and managers (a higher proportion than for any other place).

The responses were literally and figuratively all over the map: I can't stand a couple of them, hadn't even heard of a couple (in the distant suburbs), and laughed out loud at the choice of Hooters for a special occasion—but really, aren't *all* Hooters occasions special?

WINE BARS

Les Zygomates ⭐⭐ (Financial District, $$$, p. 123)

Troquet ⭐⭐ (Theater District, $$$$, p. 128)

3 The Waterfront

EXPENSIVE

Legal Sea Foods (p. 138) has a branch at 255 State St. (© **617/227-3115;** www.legal seafoods.com), opposite the Aquarium.

Jimmy's Harborside Restaurant SEAFOOD   This Boston landmark—the sign out front reads HOME OF THE CHOWDER KING—offers tasty seafood and fine views of the harbor to businesspeople at lunch and tourists at dinner. In the summer, seating extends outside onto the harbor-front deck. You might start with the "King's" fish chowder, with generous chunks of whitefish, or excellent Maine crab cakes. Entrees include simple but flavorful seafood preparations (grilled, broiled, blackened, or fried) and more ambitious specialties—for instance, bouillabaisse and Jimmy's famous finnan haddie (smoked haddock in cream sauce), which is famous for good reason. If you don't like fish, wait until Friday or Saturday night and come for prime rib.

242 Northern Ave. © **617/423-1000.** www.jimmysharborside.com. Reservations recommended at dinner. Main courses $9–$34 at lunch, $18–$39 at dinner. AE, DC, DISC, MC, V. Mon–Thurs noon–9:30pm; Fri–Sat noon–10pm (lunch until 4pm); Sun 4–9pm. Closed Dec 25. Valet parking available. T: Red Line to South Station, then Silver Line bus or 25-min. walk.

Sel de la Terre ⭐⭐ FRENCH   A stone's throw from Boston Harbor, Sel de la Terre is a peaceful slice of southern France. Executive chef Geoff Gardner (a partner with

L'Espalier owners Frank and Catherine McClelland) uses fresh local ingredients in his subtly flavorful food: scallops handled so gently that they're still sweet, roasted chicken almost as juicy as a good peach, luscious salmon with truffled cauliflower purée. Banquettes, earth tones, and professional service attract a go-go business-lunch crowd (dinner is calmer). The unusual pricing structure—the same amount for every dish—feels like a deal when you're tucking into a generous portion of steak frites with Black Angus rib-eye, less of a bargain if you're eating ravioli. The sly sense of humor that's apparent in the restaurant's name ("salt of the earth") crops up on the children's menu, which includes *tartine au fromage fondu* ("grilled cheese sandwich" to non-Francophones). Whatever your age, try a side of sublime *pommes frites* (french fries). The *boulangerie* (bakery) at the entrance sells out-of-this-world breads, and there's seasonal outdoor seating.

255 State St. ✆ 617/720-1300. www.seldelaterre.com. Reservations recommended. Main courses $14 at lunch, $24 at dinner; sandwiches (lunch only) $8.50. Children's menu $7. AE, DC, DISC, MC, V. Mon–Fri 11:30am–2:30pm, Sat–Sun 11am–3:30pm; daily 5–10pm. Valet and validated parking available at dinner. T: Blue Line to Aquarium.

4 The North End

Boston's Italian-American enclave has dozens of restaurants; many are tiny and don't serve dessert and coffee. Hit the *caffès* for an espresso or cappuccino and fresh pastry in an atmosphere where lingering is welcome. My favorite dessert destinations are **Caffè dello Sport,** 308 Hanover St. (✆ **617/523-5063**), and **Caffè Vittoria,** 296 Hanover St. (✆ **617/227-7606**). There's also table service at **Mike's Pastry,** 300 Hanover St. (✆ **617/742-3050**), a bakery that's famous for its bustling takeout business and its cannoli. If you plan to eat in, find what you want in the cases first, then take a seat and order from the server.

VERY EXPENSIVE

Mamma Maria ★★★ NORTHERN ITALIAN   In a town house overlooking North Square and the Paul Revere House, the best restaurant in the North End offers innovative cuisine and a level of sophistication far removed from the neighborhood's familiar "hello, dear" service. The menu changes seasonally. Start with excellent soup, risotto, or a pasta special; I'd go for any of those over the less exciting cured-meat sampler. The superb entrees are unlike anything else in this neighborhood, except in size—portions are more than generous. Fork-tender *osso buco,* a limited-quantity nightly special, is almost enough for two, but you'll want it all for yourself. You can't go wrong with main-course pastas, either, and the fresh seafood specials (say, handmade lobster tortelli with grilled asparagus and oyster mushrooms) are uniformly marvelous. The pasta, bread, and desserts are homemade, the wine list excellent, and the atmosphere oh-so-romantic.

3 North Sq. ✆ 617/523-0077. www.mammamaria.com. Reservations recommended. Main courses $24–$35. AE, DC, DISC, MC, V. Sun–Thurs 5–9:30pm; Fri–Sat 5–10:30pm. Valet parking available. T: Green or Orange Line to Haymarket.

MODERATE

Artú ITALIAN   Plates of roasted vegetables draw your eye to the front window, and the accompanying aromas will reel in the rest of you. Don't resist—this is a neighborhood favorite for a reason and a good stop for Freedom Trail walkers. The best appetizer is a sampler of those gorgeous veggies. Move on to superb roasted meats or

Where to Dine in Boston

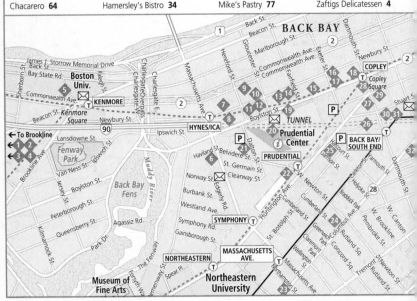

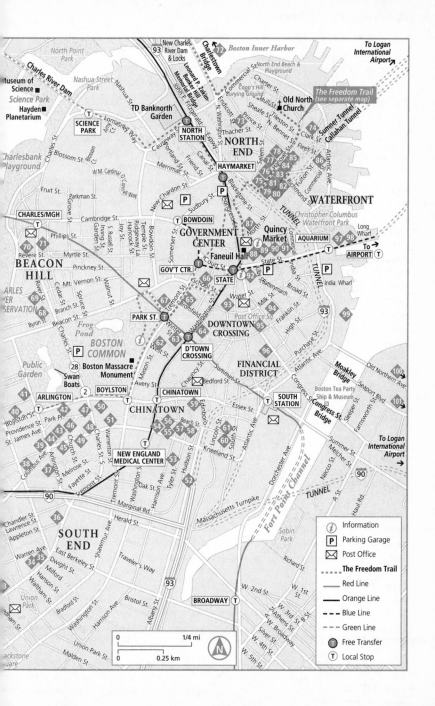

119

bounteous home-style pasta dishes. Roast lamb, ziti with sausage and broccoli rabe, and chicken stuffed with ham and cheese are all terrific. *Panini* (sandwiches) are big in size and flavor—the prosciutto, mozzarella, and tomato is sublime, and chicken parmigiana is tender and filling. This isn't a great place for quiet conversation, especially during dinner in the noisy main room, but do you really want to talk with your mouth full?

There's another Artú on **Beacon Hill** at 89 Charles St. (© 617/227-9023). It keeps the same hours, except that it opens at 4pm on Sunday and Monday.

6 Prince St. © 617/742-4336. Reservations recommended at dinner, not accepted Sat. Main courses $9.50–$18; sandwiches $4.75–$7. AE, MC, V. Daily 11am–11pm. T: Green or Orange Line to Haymarket.

Billy Tse Restaurant CHINESE/PAN-ASIAN/SUSHI   A pan-Asian restaurant on the edge of the Italian North End might seem incongruous, but this casual spot is no ordinary Chinese restaurant. It serves excellent renditions of the usual dishes, and the kitchen also has a flair for fresh seafood. The pan-Asian selections and sushi are just as enjoyable as the Chinese classics. Start with wonderful soup, sinfully good crab Rangoon, or fried calamari with garlic and pepper. Main dishes range from nine kinds of fried rice to scallops with garlic sauce to the signature "Ocean Three Treasures," shrimp, calamari, and scallops in a scrumptious sake sauce.

Be sure to ask about the daily specials—bitter Chinese broccoli, when it's available, is deftly prepared. Lunch specials, served until 4pm, include vegetable fried rice or vegetable lo mein. You can eat in the comfortable main dining room or near the bar, which has French doors that open to the street. Although it's opposite a trolley stop, Billy Tse doesn't have an especially touristy clientele—the neighborhood patrons obviously welcome a break from pizza and pasta.

240 Commercial St. © 617/227-9990. Reservations recommended at dinner on weekends. Main courses $7–$33 (most items less than $17); lunch specials $6–$8; sushi from $3.75. AE, DC, DISC, MC, V. Mon–Thurs 11:30am–11:30pm; Fri–Sat 11:30am–midnight; Sun 11:30am–11pm. Closed 1 week in Feb. T: Green or Orange Line to Haymarket, or Blue Line to Aquarium.

Daily Catch ✸ SOUTHERN ITALIAN/SEAFOOD   This storefront restaurant is about the size of a large kitchen (it seats just 20), but it packs a wallop—of garlic. A North End favorite for over 30 years, it offers excellent food, chummy service, and very little elbow room. The surprisingly varied menu includes calamari stuffed with bread crumbs, parsley, and garlic; fresh clams; squid-ink pasta *puttanesca;* and a variety of broiled, fried, and sautéed fish and shellfish. Squid meatballs *(polpetti)* freak some people out, but they're delicious. Fried calamari makes an excellent appetizer, monkfish Marsala a terrific main course. All food is prepared to order, and some dishes arrive at the table still in the frying pan.

This is the original Daily Catch. Two others accept credit cards (AE, MC, V): The **Brookline** location, at 441 Harvard St. (© 617/734-5696), opens at 5pm nightly; the branch at the Moakley Federal Courthouse, 2 Northern Ave., in the **Seaport District** (© 617/772-4400), serves lunch and dinner in the summer, lunch only in winter.

323 Hanover St. © 617/523-8567. www.dailycatch.com. Reservations not accepted. Main courses $12–$19. No credit cards. Sun–Thurs 11:30am–10pm; Fri–Sat 11:30am–11pm. T: Green or Orange Line to Haymarket.

Giacomo's Ristorante ✸✸ ITALIAN/SEAFOOD   Fans of Giacomo's seem to have adopted the U.S. Postal Service's motto: They brave snow, sleet, rain, and gloom of night. The line forms early and grows long, especially on weekends. No reservations,

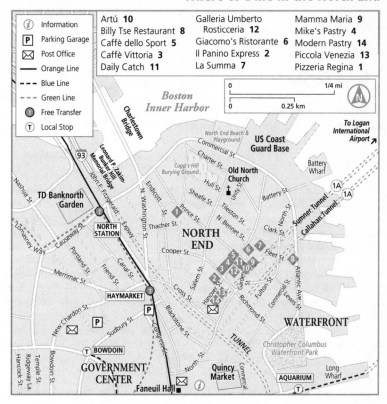

ⓘ Information	Artú **10**
Ⓟ Parking Garage	Billy Tse Restaurant **8**
⊠ Post Office	Caffè dello Sport **5**
— Orange Line	Caffè Vittoria **3**
--- Blue Line	Daily Catch **11**
--- Green Line	
① Free Transfer	
Ⓣ Local Stop	

Galleria Umberto
  Rosticceria **12**
Giacomo's Ristorante **6**
Il Panino Express **2**
La Summa **7**

Mamma Maria **9**
Mike's Pastry **4**
Modern Pastry **14**
Piccola Venezia **13**
Pizzeria Regina **1**

cash only, a tiny dining room with an open kitchen—what's the attraction? The food is terrific, there's plenty of it, and the we're-all-in-this-together atmosphere certainly helps. My dad is a New York ethnic-dining snob, and this is his favorite Boston restaurant.

The fried calamari appetizer, served with marinara sauce, is ultralight and crisp. You can take the chef's advice or put together your own main dish from the list of ingredients on a board on the wall. The best suggestion is salmon and sun-dried tomatoes in tomato cream sauce over fettuccine; any dish with shrimp is delectable, too. Non-seafood offerings such as butternut squash ravioli in mascarpone cheese sauce are equally memorable. Service is friendly but incredibly swift, and lingering is not encouraged—but unless you have a heart of stone, you won't want to take up a table when people are standing outside waiting for your seat in (no kidding) 90°F (32°C) heat or an ice storm.

355 Hanover St. ☎ **617/523-9026.** Reservations not accepted. Main courses $11–$18. No credit cards. Mon–Thurs 5–10pm; Fri–Sat 5–10:30pm; Sun 4–10pm. T: Green or Orange Line to Haymarket.

La Summa ✿ SOUTHERN ITALIAN Because La Summa isn't on the restaurant rows of Hanover and Salem streets, it maintains a cozy neighborhood atmosphere. Unlike some neighborhood places, it's friendly to outsiders—you'll feel welcome even if your server doesn't greet you by name. La Summa is worth seeking out just for the wonderful homemade pasta and desserts, and the more elaborate entrees are scrumptious, too. You might start with ravioli or superb soup (our waitress one night didn't know exactly what was in the butternut squash soup because, and I quote, "My mother made it"). Or stick to the salad that comes with each meal and save room for sweets.

Try any seafood special, *pappardelle e melanzane* (strips of eggplant tossed with ethereal fresh pasta in a light marinara sauce), shrimp in light marinara sauce over linguini, or the house special—veal, chicken, sausage, shrimp, artichokes, *pepperoncini* (pickled hot peppers), olives, and mushrooms in white-wine sauce. Desserts, especially tiramisu, are terrific.

30 Fleet St. ⓒ **617/523-9503.** Reservations recommended on weekends. Main courses $11–$24. AE, DC, DISC, MC, V. Sun–Fri 4:30–10:30pm; Sat 4:30–11pm. T: Green or Orange Line to Haymarket.

Piccola Venezia ITALIAN The glass front wall of Piccola Venezia ("little Venice") shows off the exposed-brick dining room, decorated with photos and posters and filled with happy locals and out-of-towners. Portions are large, and the homey food tends to be heavy on red sauce, although more sophisticated dishes are available. The delicious sautéed mushroom appetizer is solidly in the latter category; a more traditional starter is tasty *pasta e fagioli* (bean and pasta soup). Then dig into spaghetti and meatballs, chicken parmigiana, eggplant *rolatini,* or grilled pork chops with vinegar peppers. This is a good place to try traditional Italian-American favorites such as polenta (home-style, not the yuppie croutons available at so many other places) and *baccala* (reconstituted salt cod).

263 Hanover St. ⓒ **617/523-3888.** Reservations recommended at dinner. Main courses $12–$21; lunch specialties $5–$10. AE, DISC, MC, V. Sun–Thurs 11:30am–9:30pm, Fri–Sat 11:30am–10:30pm (lunch Mon–Sat until 3pm). Validated parking available. T: Green or Orange Line to Haymarket.

INEXPENSIVE

Galleria Umberto Rosticceria *(Value* ITALIAN The long, fast-moving line of businesspeople and visitors tips you off to the fact that this cafeteria-style spot just off the Freedom Trail is a bargain. The food is good, too. You can fill up on a couple of slices of pizza, but if you're feeling adventurous, try *arancini* (a deep-fried rice ball filled with ground beef, peas, and cheese). Calzones—ham and cheese; spinach; spinach and cheese; or spinach, sausage, and cheese—and potato croquettes (*panzarotti*) are also tasty. Study the cases while you wait and be ready to order at once when you reach the head of the line. Have a quick lunch and get on with your sightseeing.

289 Hanover St. ⓒ **617/227-5709.** All items $3.50 or less. No credit cards. Mon–Sat 10:45am–2:30pm. Closed July. T: Green or Orange Line to Haymarket.

Pizzeria Regina *★★* PIZZA Regina's looks almost like a movie set, but look a little closer—this local legend is the place the movie sets are trying to re-create. Busy

---

Finds Go Straight to the Source

The tiramisu at many North End restaurants comes from **Modern Pastry,** 257 Hanover St. (ⓒ **617/523-3783**). The surreally good concoction ($3.50 a slice at the shop) makes an excellent picnic dessert in the summer—head 4 blocks down Richmond Street to eat in Christopher Columbus Waterfront Park, off Atlantic Avenue.

Breakfast & Sunday Brunch

Several top hotels serve Sunday brunch buffets of monstrous proportions—outrageous spreads that are outrageously expensive. They're worth the investment for a special occasion, but you can have a less incapacitating experience for considerably less money.

My top choice is in Cambridge: the **S&S Restaurant** (p. 150). Across the river, **Charlie's Sandwich Shoppe,** 429 Columbus Ave. (© **617/536-7669**), is a longtime South End favorite not far from the Back Bay—just the right distance to walk off some blueberry-waffle calories. The **Paramount,** 44 Charles St., Beacon Hill (© **617/720-1152**), is a classic destination for eggs and a glimpse of the real community behind the neighborhood's redbrick facade. In Jamaica Plain, locals tough out long weekend waits for the delicious specials and strong coffee at the **Centre Street Café,** 669 Centre St. (© **617/524-9217**).

If you have your heart set on a fancy brunch at a hotel, make reservations (especially on holidays) but do *not* make elaborate dinner plans. **Aujour-d'hui** (p. 136), in the Four Seasons Hotel, 200 Boylston St. (© **617/451-2071**) charges $58 for adults, $28 children; at **Café Fleuri,** in the Langham Hotel Boston, 250 Franklin St. (© **617/451-1900**), adults pay $39 to $49, children $17; at **Meritage,** in the Boston Harbor Hotel (© **617/439-3995**), brunch costs $45 for adults, $20 for children.

waitresses who might call you "dear" weave through the boisterous dining room delivering peerless pizza steaming hot from the brick oven. (You can also drop in for a slice, weekdays at lunch only.) Let it cool a little before you dig in. Nouveau ingredients such as sun-dried tomatoes appear on the list of toppings, but that's not authentic. House-made sausage, maybe some pepperoni, and a couple of beers—now, *that's* authentic.

11½ Thacher St. © **617/227-0765.** www.pizzeriaregina.com. Reservations not accepted. Pizza $10–$17. No credit cards. Mon–Thurs 11am–11:30pm; Fri–Sat 11am–midnight; Sun noon–11pm. T: Green or Orange Line to Haymarket.

5 Faneuil Hall Marketplace & the Financial District

EXPENSIVE

The national chain **McCormick & Schmick's Seafood Restaurant** has a branch at Faneuil Hall Marketplace in the North Market Building (© **617/720-5522**).

Les Zygomates ★★ FRENCH/WINE BAR   Tucked away near South Station, this delightful bistro and wine bar is worth seeking out. Bostonians have done so for a decade, despite the construction that dominated this neighborhood for most of that time. The bar in the high-ceilinged, brick-walled space serves a great selection of wine, available by the bottle, the glass, and the 2-ounce "taste." The efficient staff will guide you to a good accompaniment for chef-owner Ian Just's delicious food. Salads are excellent, lightly dressed and garden-fresh, and main courses are hearty and filling but not heavy. Roasted salmon with arugula, shaved fennel, pear tomatoes, and roasted

---

Tips **It's Nothing Personal**

State law requires the scary disclaimer that appears on menus to alert you to the potential danger of eating raw or undercooked meat (such as rare burgers), seafood (such as raw oysters), poultry, or eggs.

---

almonds is toothsome, and meat-lovers will savor beef short ribs with creamy polenta. For dessert, try not to fight over warm chocolate cake. A popular business-lunch destination, Les Zygomates has a chic, romantic atmosphere at night, when live jazz (in its own dining room) helps set the mood.

Up the street and under the same management, **Sorriso Trattoria** (© **617/259-1560;** www.sorrisoboston.com), 107 South St., serves sophisticated country Italian cuisine, including brick-oven pizza. It's open for lunch weekdays and dinner Monday through Saturday. And the name is a clever tribute to the original restaurant: *Les zygomates* is French for the muscles that make you smile; *sorriso* is Italian for "smile."

129 South St. © **617/542-5108.** www.winebar.com. Reservations recommended. Main courses $9–$14 at lunch, $18–$26 at dinner; *prix fixe* $15 at lunch, $29 at dinner. AE, DC, DISC, MC, V. Mon–Fri 11:30am–1am (lunch until 2pm, dinner until 10:30pm); Sat 6pm–1am (dinner until 11:30pm). Valet parking available at dinner. T: Red Line to South Station.

Ye Olde Union Oyster House ★ NEW ENGLAND/SEAFOOD   America's oldest restaurant in continuous service, the Union Oyster House opened in 1826, and the booths and oyster bar haven't moved since. The food is tasty, traditional New England fare, popular with visitors walking on the adjacent Freedom Trail and savvy locals. They're not looking for anything fancy, and you shouldn't, either—the best bets are simple, classic preparations. At the crescent-shaped bar on the lower level of the cramped, low-ceilinged building (a National Historic Landmark "where Daniel Webster drank many a toddy in his day"), try oyster stew or the cold seafood sampler of oysters, clams, and shrimp to start. Follow with a broiled or grilled dish such as scrod or salmon, or perhaps fried seafood or grilled pork loin. A "shore dinner" of chowder, steamers or mussels, lobster, corn, potatoes, and dessert is an excellent introduction to local favorites. For dessert, try gingerbread with whipped cream. *Tip:* A plaque marks John F. Kennedy's favorite booth (no. 18), where he often sat to read the Sunday papers.

41 Union St. (between North and Hanover sts.). © **617/227-2750.** www.unionoysterhouse.com. Reservations recommended. Main courses $10–$21 at lunch, $17–$30 at dinner. Children's menu $5–$11. AE, DC, DISC, MC, V. Sun–Thurs 11am–9:30pm (lunch menu until 5pm); Fri–Sat 11am–10pm (lunch until 6pm). Union Bar daily 11am–midnight (lunch until 3pm, late supper until 11pm). Validated and valet parking available. T: Green or Orange Line to Haymarket.

MODERATE

Durgin-Park ★★★ *Kids* NEW ENGLAND   For huge portions of delicious food, a rowdy atmosphere where CEOs share tables with students, and run-ins with the famously cranky waitresses, people have poured into Durgin-Park since 1827. It's everything it's cracked up to be—a tourist magnet that attracts many locals, where everyone's disappointed when the waitresses are nice, as they often are. Approximately 2,000 people a day join the line that stretches down a flight of stairs to the first floor of Faneuil Hall Marketplace's North Market building. The queue moves quickly, and you'll probably wind up seated at a long table with other people (though smaller tables are available).

The food is wonderful, and there's plenty of it—prime rib the size of a hubcap, lamb chops, fried seafood, and juicy roast turkey are sure bets. The cooks broil steaks and chops on an open fire over wood charcoal. Fresh seafood arrives twice daily, and fish dinners are broiled to order. Boston baked beans are a signature dish, and this is the best place to try them. For dessert, strawberry shortcake is justly celebrated, and Indian pudding (molasses and cornmeal baked for hours and served with ice cream) is a New England classic.

340 Faneuil Hall Marketplace. ℂ 617/227-2038. www.durgin-park.com. Reservations accepted only for parties of 15 or more. Main courses $7–$11 at lunch, $10–$25 at dinner; specials $19–$40. Children's menu $8–$9. AE, DC, DISC, MC, V. Mon–Sat 11:30am–10pm; Sun 11:30am–0pm. Validated parking available. T: Green or Blue Line to Government Center, Orange Line to Haymarket, or Blue Line to Aquarium.

INEXPENSIVE

Cosí Sandwich Bar ⚜ SANDWICHES/ITALIAN   Flavorful fillings on delectable bread make Cosí (pronounced "cozy," for some reason) a downtown lunch hot spot. This location, right on the Freedom Trail, makes a delicious refueling stop. Italian flatbread baked fresh all day—so tasty that it's even good plain—gets split open and filled with your choice of meat, fish, vegetables, cheese, and spreads. The more fillings you choose, the more you pay; the total can really climb, so don't go wild if you're on a budget. Tandoori chicken with caramelized onions is sensational, as is smoked salmon with spinach-artichoke spread. For dessert, order s'mores, and a staffer will bring you a contraption that holds an actual fire.

Other branches are at 14 Milk St. (ℂ 617/426-7565), near Downtown Crossing, and 133 Federal St. (ℂ 617/292-2674), which has patio seating in warm weather.

53 State St. (at Congress St.). ℂ 617/723-4447. www.getcosi.com. Sandwiches $6–$10; soups and salads $4–$7. AE, DC, MC, V. Mon–Thurs 7am–6pm; Fri 7am–5pm. T: Orange or Blue Line to State.

6 Downtown Crossing

VERY EXPENSIVE

Locke-Ober ⚜ CONTINENTAL   "Locke's" is *the* traditional Boston restaurant, a power-broker favorite since 1875. It changed hands and underwent a refurbishment in 2001, but that was just cosmetic—even with some physical upgrades and a new owner (famed Boston restaurateur Lydia Shire), it feels like a time machine. In an alley off the Winter Street pedestrian mall, the wood-paneled restaurant entertainingly

---

⌒ Tips Boston Restaurant Week

The third week of August is the annual Boston Restaurant Week, when dozens of terrific spots serve a three-course *prix-fixe* lunch for the decimal equivalent of the year—in 2006, $20.06—and many offer dinner for just $10 more. The Convention & Visitors Bureau (ℂ 888/SEE-BOSTON; www.bostonusa.com) lists names of participating restaurants and individual numbers to call for reservations. Ask whether the menu is set yet and seek out restaurants that really get into the spirit by offering more than just one or two choices for each course. Popular places book up quickly, so plan accordingly.

Finds **The Lunch Line**

Every weekday without fail, a line forms in front of a takeout window on the Franklin Street side of Filene's. Downtown diners can't get enough of the scrumptious Chilean sandwiches at **Chacarero,** 426 Washington St. (ⓒ **617/542-0392;** www.chacarero.com). At the first window, on the right, order chicken, beef, or vegetarian "with everything"—tomatoes, cheese, avocado, hot sauce, and (unexpected but delicious) green beans. Take your receipt to the end of the fast-moving line at the pickup window, seek out a seat, and pat yourself on the back. For less than $7, you're a savvy Bostonian.

---

evokes a Waspy men's club. The long, mirrored downstairs bar dates from 1880, and the service is 19th-century-style courtly.

The food is unapologetically old-fashioned, with contemporary touches: Traditional fish cakes come with new-fangled jasmine rice, salmon is brushed with *mirin* and soy sauce, and delectable scalloped potatoes accompany the signature roast beef hash. Other traditions, including excellent steaks and chops, Wiener schnitzel a la Holstein, and broiled scrod with brown bread, endure. So does Locke-Ober, an "only in Boston" experience if ever there was one.

3 Winter Place. ⓒ **617/542-1340.** www.lockeober.com. Reservations recommended. Jacket suggested for men; no shorts or sneakers. Main courses $11–$32 at lunch; $28–$49 at dinner. AE, DISC, MC, V. Mon–Fri 11:30am–2:30pm; Mon–Thurs 5:30–10pm, Fri–Sat 5:30–11pm. Valet parking available after 5:30pm. T: Red or Orange Line to Downtown Crossing or Green Line to Park St.

INEXPENSIVE

There's a **Cosí Sandwich Bar** (see above) at 14 Milk St. (ⓒ **617/426-7565**).

Fajitas & 'Ritas TEX-MEX This entertaining restaurant is one of the most fun places around. It serves nachos, quesadillas, burritos, and—oh, yeah, fajitas. There's nothing exotic, just the usual beef, chicken, shrimp, beans, and so forth. You can also try barbecue items, such as smoked brisket or pulled pork, or tequila-marinated chicken wings. Mark your selections on a checklist, and a member of the somewhat harried staff quickly returns with big portions of fresh food—this place is too busy for anything to be sitting around for very long. As the name indicates, 'ritas (margaritas) are a house specialty. Primarily a casual business destination at lunch, it's livelier at dinner—probably thanks to all those margaritas—and a perfect stop before or after a movie at the nearby Loews Boston Common theater.

25 West St. (between Washington and Tremont sts.). ⓒ **617/426-1222.** www.fajitasandritas.com. Reservations accepted only for parties of 8 or more. Main dishes $5–$8 at lunch, $5–$12 at dinner. AE, DC, DISC, MC, V. Mon–Tues 11:30am–9pm; Wed–Thurs 11:30am–10pm; Fri–Sat 11:30am–11pm; Sun 2–8pm. T: Red or Green Line to Park St., or Orange Line to Downtown Crossing.

7 Beacon Hill

VERY EXPENSIVE

No. 9 Park ★ FRENCH COUNTRY/ITALIAN One of Boston's most acclaimed restaurants sits in the shadow of the State House, an area better known for politicians' pubs than for fine dining. Legislators must make room for foodies here, thanks to chef-owner Barbara Lynch's flair for strong flavors and superb pasta. To start, try beet salad—an upright cylinder of shredded vegetables atop blue cheese, surrounded by greens (always on the menu because the regulars mutiny when it isn't)—or oysters on the half shell with unusually tasty mignonette sauce. Move on to veal porterhouse served with mushroom fricassee, Casco Bay cod with *brandade* ravioli, or a sampler of those famous pastas. For dessert, the hot chocolate trio is worth every calorie. My only complaint is that the austere but comfortable space can get quite loud. The cafe area near the front door is even noisier, but the smaller plates of more casual food are equally appetizing.

9 Park St. ✆ 617/742-9991. www.no9park.com. Reservations recommended in restaurant, not accepted in cafe. Main courses $17–$25 at lunch, $29–$43 at dinner, $15–$25 in cafe; chef's tasting menu $85 for 7 courses, $110 for 9 courses. AE, DC, MC, V. Mon–Fri 11:30am–2:30pm; Mon–Sat 5:30–10pm (cafe until 11pm). Valet parking available at dinner. T: Green or Red Line to Park St.

Spire ★★ MEDITERRANEAN/NEW ENGLAND International flavors, a stylish dining room, superb local ingredients, and an unfailingly inventive kitchen make Spire a prime destination for business meals and special occasions. I've been recommending it all over town—it's sophisticated but comfortable, sleek but romantic, something of a scene (especially in the bar) but exceptionally welcoming. I'd come here just for the incredible soups, from corn chowder at the height of its summer sweetness to rich pumpkin in the dead of winter. Main courses include creative sandwiches and salads at lunch, hearty portions of traditional yet unusual dishes (roasted duck breast with faro, pomegranate, spiced pecans, and chestnut-flower honey; spice-crusted skate wing with cucumber and mango) at dinner. Flowing fabrics and cushy upholstery soften the lines of the rather stark second-floor space, which overlooks the Old Granary Burying Ground. And the service is just the right combination of friendly, efficient, and unobtrusive.

In the Nine Zero hotel, 90 Tremont St. ✆ 617/772-0202. www.spirerestaurant.com. Reservations recommended. Main courses $11–$18 at lunch, $23–$39 at dinner; bar food $5–$18. AE, DC, DISC, MC, V. Mon–Fri 6:30–10:30am, 11:30am–2pm; Sat–Sun 8am–2pm (brunch); Mon–Sat 5:30–10pm, Sun 5:30–9pm. Bar Mon–Sat noon–1:30am (food served until 10:30pm); Sun noon–midnight (food served until 9:30pm). Valet parking available. T: Green or Red Line to Park St.

MODERATE
Artú (p. 117) has a branch at 89 Charles St. (✆ 617/227-9023). It's open Sunday and Monday from 4 to 11pm, Tuesday through Saturday from 11am to 11pm.

8 Charlestown
VERY EXPENSIVE
Olives ★★ ECLECTIC Olives has lost a bit of its mystique. Celebrity chef-owner Todd English, busy with other ventures around the country, is seldom on hand. The bistro cuisine that was cutting-edge a decade ago is no longer a great adventure. Even accepting reservations—a new policy after years of complaints—compromised the aura that surrounds a red-hot dining destination.

Then why is it still so busy? Because English, however overexposed, is a culinary genius, and his hot property has cooled into a classic. In the glass-walled dining room, you'll find the noise level high (thanks partly to the open kitchen), the service uneven, and the customers festive. The regularly changing menu always includes the delicious

Olives tart (olives, caramelized onions, and anchovies) and juicy spit-roasted chicken flavored with herbs and garlic. Be sure to check out the seafood specials—perhaps crisp-skin black sea bass with horseradish mashed potatoes and string beans, or any grilled-tuna dish. When you order your entree, the server will ask if you want falling chocolate cake for dessert. Say yes.

10 City Sq. ℃ 617/242-1999. www.toddenglish.com/Restaurants/Olives.html. Reservations recommended. Main courses $19–$33. AE, DC, MC, V. Mon–Fri 5:30–10pm; Sat 5–10:30pm. Valet parking available. T: Orange or Green Line to North Station; 10-min. walk.

9 Chinatown/Theater District

The most entertaining and delicious introduction to Chinatown's cuisine is **dim sum** (see "Yum, Yum, Dim Sum," below). If you're eating dinner, you should know that many restaurants have a second menu for Chinese patrons (often written in Chinese). You can ask for it or tell your waiter that you want your meal Chinese-style.

If you're serious about sweets, consider ending—or even beginning—your meal at **Finale,** 1 Columbus Ave. (p. 239).

The area around Park Square (Columbus Ave. and South Charles St., between the Theater District and the Public Garden) is a hotbed of upscale national chain restaurants. None of these places offers a unique or even unusual experience, but they're all reliable destinations if you're feeling homesick or unadventurous. They include **Fleming's Prime Steakhouse & Wine Bar,** 217 Stuart St. (℃ 617/292-0808); **Maggiano's Little Italy,** 4 Columbus Ave. (℃ 617/542-3456); **McCormick & Schmick's Seafood Restaurant,** 34 Columbus Ave., in the Boston Park Plaza Hotel (℃ 617/482-3999); and **P.F. Chang's China Bistro,** 8 Park Plaza (℃ 617/573-0821).

VERY EXPENSIVE

Troquet ★★ NEW AMERICAN/WINE BAR   Troquet is French slang for "small wine cafe," and it's a good name for this sophisticated two-level restaurant. The second-floor dining room overlooks Boston Common, and the ground floor is a lounge that serves "creative cocktails" and small plates. Troquet offers 40-plus wines by the 2- or 4-ounce glass and hundreds more by the bottle. Because the markup is lower than usual, sampling several selections is surprisingly affordable. The menu recommends pairings, and you'll want just the right thing to complement the exceptional cuisine, which emphasizes seasonal ingredients and never overwhelms the wine. The word that keeps coming back to me is *subtle*—a salad of marinated beets and baby greens was flavorful but not overpowering; braised shirt-rib cannelloni with smoked bacon was rich and earthy; *panko*-crusted cod seemed perfumed rather than punched up with red curry and kafir lime. Best of all, whether you're a novice or a pro, the staff offers as much wine advice as you need. I'll offer some dessert advice: chocolate fondant cake.

140 Boylston St. ℃ 617/695-9463. www.troquetboston.com. Reservations recommended. Main courses $26–$38; lounge menu $9–$22. AE, DC, DISC, MC, V. Dining room Tues–Sat 5–10:30pm; lounge daily 5pm–1am (food served until midnight). T: Green Line to Boylston.

EXPENSIVE

There's a branch of **Legal Sea Foods** (p. 138) at 36 Park Sq., between Columbus Avenue and Stuart Street (℃ 617/426-4444; www.legalseafoods.com).

Ginza Japanese Restaurant ★ JAPANESE/SUSHI   On a side street in Chinatown, you'll find one of the city's best Japanese restaurants. Track down the nondescript

Yum, Yum, Dim Sum

Many Chinatown restaurants offer **dim sum,** the traditional midday meal featuring appetizer-style dishes. You'll see steamed buns *(bao)* filled with pork or bean paste; meat, shrimp, and vegetable dumplings; spareribs; shrimp-stuffed eggplant; sticky rice dotted with sausage and vegetables; spring rolls; sweets such as sesame balls and coconut gelatin; and more. Waitresses wheel carts laden with tempting dishes to your table, and you order by pointing (unless you know Chinese). The waitress then stamps your check with the symbol of the dish, adding about $1 to $3 to your tab for each selection. Unless you're ravenous or you order a la carte items from the regular menu, the total usually won't be more than about $10 to $12 per person.

Dim sum varies from restaurant to restaurant, chef to chef, and even day to day; if something looks familiar, don't be surprised if it's different from what you're accustomed to and equally good. This is a great group activity, especially on weekends. The selection is wider than on weekdays, and you'll see three generations of families sharing large tables. Even picky children can usually find something they enjoy. If you don't eat pork and shrimp, be aware that many, but not all, dishes include one or the other; calorie counters should know that many dishes (again, not all) are fried.

Empire Garden Restaurant ★★, 690–698 Washington St., 2nd floor (✆ **617/482-8898**), serves a dazzling variety of dishes in a cavernous, ornate former theater balcony. Also known as Emperor's Garden, it narrowly gets my vote over **China Pearl** ★, 9 Tyler St., 2nd floor (✆ **617/426-4338**), and **Chau Chow City,** 83 Essex St. (✆ **617/338-8158**). All three are excellent.

---

entrance up the street from the Chinatown arch, settle into one of the two rooms (in a booth, if you're lucky), and watch as kimono-clad waitresses glide past, bearing sushi boats the size of small children. Ginza is a magnet for Japanese expatriates, sushi-lovers, and, in the wee hours, club-hoppers. It's not the only place in town where expert chefs work wonders with ocean-fresh ingredients, but it serves some of the most creative creations (including "spider *maki,*" a soft-shelled crab fried and tucked into a seaweed wrapper with avocado, cucumber, and flying-fish roe). An excellent starter is *edamame*—addictive boiled and salted soybeans served in the pod (you pull the beans out with your teeth). Then let your imagination run wild, or trust the chefs to assemble something dazzling. Green-tea ice cream makes an unusually satisfying dessert, but nobody will blame you for finishing with another round of California *maki.*

Ginza has a branch in **Brookline,** at 1002 Beacon St. (✆ **617/566-9688**). It serves a similar menu, but not to night-crawlers—the late nights are Friday and Saturday, when closing time is 10:30pm.

14 Hudson St. ✆ **617/338-2261.** Reservations accepted only for parties of 6 or more. Sushi from $3.50; main courses $11–$20. AE, DC, MC, V. Mon–Fri 11:30am–2:30pm; Sat–Sun 11:30am–4pm; Sun–Mon 5pm–2am; Tues–Sat 5pm–4am. T: Orange Line to New England Medical Center.

MODERATE

East Ocean City CANTONESE/CHINESE/SEAFOOD Don't get too attached to the inhabitants of the fish tanks here—they might turn up on your plate. Tanks make up one wall of the high-ceilinged space, decorated with lots of glass and other hard surfaces that make it rather noisy. The comprehensive menu offers a huge range of dishes, but, as the name indicates, seafood is the focus. It's fresh, delicious, and carefully prepared. One specialty is clams in black-bean sauce, a spicy rendering of a messy, delectable dish. Just about anything that swims can be ordered steamed with ginger and scallions; for variety, check out the tasty noodle dishes.

25–29 Beach St. ✆ 617/542-2504. Reservations accepted only for parties of 6 or more. Main courses $5–$26; lunch specials (Mon–Fri until 3pm) $5. AE, MC, V. Sun–Thurs 11am–3am; Fri–Sat 11am–4am. Validated parking available weeknights and weekends. T: Orange Line to Chinatown.

Grand Chau Chow ✿ CANTONESE/CHINESE This is one of the best and busiest restaurants in Chinatown. It offers niceties that the smaller restaurants don't, such as tablecloths and tuxedoed waiters, as well as a nearly encyclopedic menu. Clams with black-bean sauce is a signature dish, as is gray sole with fried fins and bones. If you have the heart, you can watch your dinner swimming around in the large fish tanks, both salt- and freshwater. Stick to seafood and you can't go wrong. Lunch specials are a great deal, but skip the *chow fun,* which quickly turns gelatinous. If you're in town during Chinese New Year celebrations, phone ahead and request a multi-course banquet for your group (about $25 a person).

45 Beach St. ✆ 617/292-5166. Reservations accepted only for parties of 10 or more. Main courses $6–$24. AE, DC, DISC, MC, V. Sun–Thurs 10am–3am; Fri–Sat 10am–4am. T: Orange Line to Chinatown.

Jacob Wirth Company GERMAN/AMERICAN In the heart of the Theater District, "Jake's" has been serving Bostonians since 1868—even before there were theaters here. The wood floor and brass accents give the room the feeling of a saloon, and the menu incorporates traditional pub grub and more contemporary fare. The hearty German specialties include Wiener schnitzel, mixed grills, bratwurst, knockwurst, and potato pancakes. Daily specials, a large selection of sandwiches and brews on tap, and a variety of salads round out the menu. Service at lunchtime is snappy, but if you want to be on time for the theater, be ready to remind your server.

31–37 Stuart St. ✆ 617/338-8586. www.jacobwirth.com. Reservations recommended at dinner. Main courses $7–$27; most less than $20. AE, DC, DISC, MC, V. Tues–Thurs 11:30am–11pm; Fri–Sat 11:30am–midnight; Sun 11:30am–8pm. Validated parking available. T: Green Line to Boylston, or Orange Line to New England Medical Center.

INEXPENSIVE

Buddha's Delight ✿ *Value* VEGETARIAN/VIETNAMESE Fresh and healthy intersect with cheap and filling at this busy restaurant. The menu lists "chicken," "shrimp," "pork," and even "lobster"—in quotes because the kitchen doesn't use meat, poultry, fish, or dairy (some beverages have condensed milk). The chefs fry and barbecue tofu and gluten into more-than-reasonable facsimiles using techniques owner Cuong Van Tran learned from Buddhist monks in a temple outside Los Angeles. Between trying to figure out how they do it and savoring Vietnamese cuisine's strong, clear flavors, you might not miss your usual protein. To start, try fried "pork" dumplings or a delectable salad. Move on to "shrimp" with rice noodles, any of the house specialties, or excellent *chow fun.*

5 Beach St. ✆ 617/451-2395. Main courses $5.50–$13; lunch specials $6.50. MC, V. Sun–Thurs 11am–9:30pm; Fri–Sat 11am–10:30pm. T: Orange Line to Chinatown.

Moments **Hey There, Sugar**

Do what you will with this information: Boston's only branch of **Krispy Kreme Doughnuts** is in the food court on the main level of the Shops at Prudential Center, 800 Boylston St. (© **617/262-5531;** www.krispykreme.com; T: Green Line E to Prudential or B, C, or D to Hynes/ICA). Make sure the HOT light is lit before you satisfy your craving for an original glazed.

10 The South End

VERY EXPENSIVE

Hamersley's Bistro ☆ FRENCH/AMERICAN   This is the place that put the South End on Boston's culinary map, a pioneering restaurant (it opened in 1987) that's both classic and contemporary. It's one of the most beloved special-occasion restaurants in the Boston area. The husband-and-wife team of Gordon and Fiona Hamersley presides over a long dining room with lots of soft surfaces that absorb sound, so you can see but not quite hear what's going on at the tables around you. That means you'll have to quiz one of the courteous servers about the dish that just passed by—perhaps a starter of smoked salmon on a potato cake or sesame-crusted tuna with spicy bok choy.

The menu changes seasonally and offers about a dozen carefully considered entrees noted for their emphasis on local ingredients and classic preparations. I find the famed roast chicken with garlic, lemon, and parsley a bit tame, but cassoulet with pork, duck confit, and garlic sausage is a gorgeously executed combination of flavors and textures. This kitchen also has a way with seafood—perhaps tiger shrimp and spicy peppers with coconut-and-lime sauce over jasmine rice. The wine list is excellent, and there's seasonal outdoor seating.

553 Tremont St. © 617/423-2700. www.hamersleysbistro.com. Reservations recommended. Main courses $24–$39; tasting menu varies. AE, DISC, MC, V. Mon–Fri 6–10pm; Sat 5:30–10:30pm; Sun 5:30–9:30pm. Closed Jan 1–10. Valet parking available. T: Orange Line to Back Bay.

Icarus ☆☆ ECLECTIC   This shamelessly romantic subterranean restaurant is perfect for everything from helping a friend heal a broken heart to celebrating a milestone anniversary. Marble accents and dark-wood trim lend an elegant air to the two-level dining room, and the service is efficient but not formal. Chef and co-owner Chris Douglass uses choice local seafood, poultry, meats, and produce to create his imaginative dishes. The menu changes regularly. You might start with braised exotic mushrooms atop polenta, succulent avocado soup, or the daily "pasta whim" (but make sure the server quotes the price, which can be extravagant). Move on to pine-nut-and-lemon-crusted lamb chops served with lamb *osso buco* or a scrumptious seafood special like seared striped bass with garlic *crostini*, white anchovies, and *romesco* sauce. Finally, save room for dessert: The trio of seasonal fruit sorbets is one of the best nonchocolate desserts I've ever tasted.

3 Appleton St. © 617/426-1790. www.icarusrestaurant.com. Reservations recommended. Main courses $27–$34. AE, DC, DISC, MC, V. Mon–Thurs 6–10pm; Fri 6–10:30pm; Sat 5:30–10:30pm; Sun 5:30–10pm. Valet parking available. T: Green Line to Arlington or Orange Line to Back Bay.

MODERATE

Bob the Chef's Jazz Cafe ✈ SOUTHERN/CAJUN   Bob the Chef's resembles a yuppie fern bar, but it serves generous portions of delicious Southern specialties against a backdrop of jazz. The music is live Thursday through Saturday beginning at 7:30pm and at the Sunday buffet brunch. You'll find dishes such as fried chicken, served alone or with barbecued ribs; meatloaf; "soul fish" (in cornmeal batter); and Creole specialties such as jambalaya and shrimp étouffée. Dinners come with a corn muffin and your choice of two side dishes—including black-eyed peas, creamy macaroni and cheese, collard greens, and candied yams. The kitchen fries in vegetable oil, not the customary lard, and uses smoked turkey everywhere you'd expect bacon for flavoring. Vegetarians even have several options. For dessert, try the amazing sweet-potato pie, which makes pumpkin pie taste like vanilla pudding.

604 Columbus Ave. ✆ 617/536-6204. www.bobthechefs.com. Reservations recommended on weekends; accepted only for parties of 4 or more. Main courses $9–$15; brunch $19 adult, $14 child. AE, DISC, MC, V. Mon–Thurs 5am–2am (food served until 10pm); Fri–Sat 11:30am–2am (food served until midnight); Sun 10am–10pm (brunch until 2:30pm). T: Orange Line to Mass. Ave.

Garden of Eden SANDWICHES/FRENCH   Almost as well known for its people-watching as for its cuisine, Garden of Eden sits on a busy corner on the South End's main drag. It's a good place to go for neighborhood gossip as well as tasty food served at communal tables (and on the patio in good weather). You can order everything from breakfast to cappuccino with a delectable pastry to a full meal. The unusual sandwiches on fresh-baked bread are especially popular—chicken breast and Swiss cheese with cucumbers and Dijon vinaigrette on whole-wheat raisin-pecan sounds like too much, but it's just right; the namesake sandwich of mesclun, red onion, blue cheese, and (of course) apples on a baguette is equally satisfying. Dinner entrees are French country comfort food—coq au vin, yummy macaroni and cheese, chicken pot-pie, and the like.

571 Tremont St. ✆ 617/247-8377. www.goeboston.com. Sandwiches and salads $5–$9.50; main courses $5.50–$15. AE, DC, DISC, MC, V. Mon–Fri 7am–11pm; Sat–Sun 7:30am–11pm. T: Orange Line to Back Bay.

Tips Where's the Beef?

Say "Boston," think "seafood," right? Apparently not. Branches of most of the national steakhouse chains dot the city, and they're all at the top of their game—a rising tide lifts all boats, as the seafood folks say.

At press time, **Ruth's Chris Steak House** (✆ 800/544-0808; www.ruthschris. com) was slated to open in Sept 2005 in Old City Hall, 45 School St. It's up against not only the local favorites—**Grill 23 & Bar** (p. 133); the **Oak Room,** in the Fairmont Copley Plaza Hotel, 138 St. James Ave. (✆ 617/267-5300); and **Abe & Louie's,** 793 Boylston St. (✆ 617/536-6300)—but also the **Palm,** in the Westin Copley Place Boston, 200 Dartmouth St. (✆ 617/867-9292); the **Capital Grille,** 359 Newbury St. (✆ 617/262-8900); **Smith & Wollensky,** 101 Arlington St. (✆ 617/432-1112); **Fleming's Prime Steakhouse & Wine Bar,** 217 Stuart St. (✆ 617/292-0808); and **Morton's of Chicago,** 1 Exeter Plaza, Boylston Street at Exeter Street (✆ 617/266-5858).

INEXPENSIVE

Nashoba Brook Bakery ✿ SANDWICHES   This little neighborhood cafe serves baked goods so scrumptious you'll wish the South End were your neighborhood. The soups, salads, breads, and pastries make a commute every day from the original location in suburban Concord (p. 264). Everything is fresh and delicious, especially the sandwiches—like ham and cheese with the tasty addition of apple slices—on incredible artisan breads. You can sit toward the front, where you'll have a view of the street, or closer to the counter, where you can ponder what to order for a snack to eat later.

288 Columbus Ave. ⓒ 617/236-0777. www.slowrise.com. Most items less than $6. MC, V. Mon–Fri 7am–6pm; Sat 8am–5pm; Sun 8am–4pm. T: Orange Line to Back Bay.

Picco PIZZA   The cutesy name—short for "Pizza and Ice Cream Company"—may seem like a red flag. Ignore it. Picco serves traditional and yuppified pizza and phenomenal ice cream in an airy space up the street from the Boston Center for the Arts. The pizza menu ranges from traditional Margherita (tomato, basil, and cheese) to the "Alsatian variation," topped with a lip-smacking combo of caramelized onions, bacon, sour cream, roasted garlic, and Gruyère. The crust—a little smoky from the wood-fired oven, blistered in spots, thin but not crackery—is as good as the toppings. If you're not in a pizza mood, the menu includes a selection of calzones, soups, salads, and sandwiches. Somewhat unexpectedly, Picco also has a fantastic wine list. And what about the "IC" part of the name? The ice cream sandwich didn't do it for me because the cookies weren't nearly as good as the filling, but all of the other desserts—including a huge brownie sundae, chocolate soufflé (a daily special), and even a dish of plain old vanilla—were scrumptious.

513 Tremont St. ⓒ 617/927-0066. Pizza $10 and up; sandwiches and salads $5–$10. MC, V. Daily 11am–11pm. T: Orange Line to Back Bay.

11 The Back Bay

VERY EXPENSIVE

Grill 23 & Bar ✿ AMERICAN   This is the best steakhouse in town, a wood-paneled, glass-walled place with a businesslike air. Actually, it's more than just a steakhouse. A briefcase-toting crowd fills the two levels to chow down on traditional slabs of beef and chops as well as more-creative options. Steak au poivre and lamb chops are perfectly grilled, crusty, juicy, and tender. The inventively updated meatloaf incorporates sirloin and chorizo, and pork shank comes with toasted pasta and dandelion and onion greens. Fish dishes aren't quite as memorable as the meat offerings, but hey, it's a steakhouse. The bountiful a la carte side dishes include creamed spinach and out-of-this-world garlic mashed potatoes. Desserts are toothsome but (this is *not* your father's steakhouse) don't always include cheesecake. The service is exactly right for the setting, helpful but not familiar.

Caveats: The excellent wine list is quite pricey, and the noise level rises as the evening progresses. Still, you probably won't realize that you're shouting until you're outside yelling about what a good meal you had.

161 Berkeley St. ⓒ 617/542-2255. www.grill23.com. Reservations recommended. Main courses $24–$44; Kobe beef from $39. AE, DC, DISC, MC, V. Mon–Thurs 5:30–10:30pm; Fri–Sat 5:30–11pm; Sun 5:30–10pm. Valet parking available. T: Green Line to Arlington.

Kids Family-Friendly Restaurants

Like chocolate and champagne, well-behaved children are welcome almost everywhere. Most Boston-area restaurants can accommodate families, and many youngsters can be stunned into tranquility if a place is fancy enough. If your kids can't or won't sign a good-conduct pledge, here are some suggestions.

The nonstop activity and smart-mouthed service at **Durgin-Park** (p. 124) will entrance any child, and parents of picky eaters appreciate the straightforward New England fare. Other good non-chain choices are **Redbones** (p. 149), **Jasper White's Summer Shack** (p. 147), and **La Groceria Ristorante Italiano** (p. 149).

The **Bertucci's** chain of pizzerias (www.bertuccis.com) appeals to children and adults equally, with wood-fired brick ovens that are visible from many tables, great rolls made from pizza dough, and pizzas and pastas that range from basic to sophisticated. There are convenient branches at Faneuil Hall Marketplace (© **617/227-7889**), on Merchants Row off State Street; in the Back Bay at 43 Stanhope St. (© **617/247-6161**), around the corner from the Hard Rock Cafe; at 533 Commonwealth Avenue, Kenmore Square (© **617/236-1030**); and in Cambridge at 21 Brattle St., Harvard Square (© **617/864-4748**), and 799 Main St. (© **617/661-8356**), a short walk from Central Square.

The **Hard Rock Cafe,** 131 Clarendon St., Back Bay (© **617/424-ROCK**), serves music with its food—and your kids will think you're so cool.

The **California Pizza Kitchen** chain has two Boston locations, at 137 Stuart St., in the Theater District (© **617/720-0999**), and the Prudential Center, near the Huntington Avenue entrance (© **617/247-0888**), and a branch at the CambridgeSide Galleria mall (© **617/225-2772**).

L'Espalier ★★★ NEW ENGLAND/FRENCH   Dinner at L'Espalier is a unique experience, very much like spending the evening at the home of a dear friend who has only your pleasure in mind—and a dozen helpers in the kitchen. Owners Catherine and Frank McClelland (he's the chef) preside over one of Boston's favorite special-occasion destinations, which consists of three dining rooms on the second floor of an 1886 town house. The space is formal yet inviting, the service excellent, the food magnificent. The imaginative kitchen uses classic techniques to turn the freshest and most interesting ingredients available—many from small New England purveyors of everything from seafood to game to organic produce—into unforgettable dishes. The regularly changing menu might include arctic char with Wellfleet clams, apple chutney, and coconut-lemongrass sauce; Amish chicken with lobster; or roasted venison loin with root vegetable purée, trumpet royale mushrooms, and escargot. The breads, sorbets, ice creams, and alarmingly good desserts (many adapted from the family's heirloom cookbooks) are made in-house. Even if you order one of the superb soufflés, ask to see the beautiful desserts. Or finish with the celebrated cheese tray, which always includes two local selections.

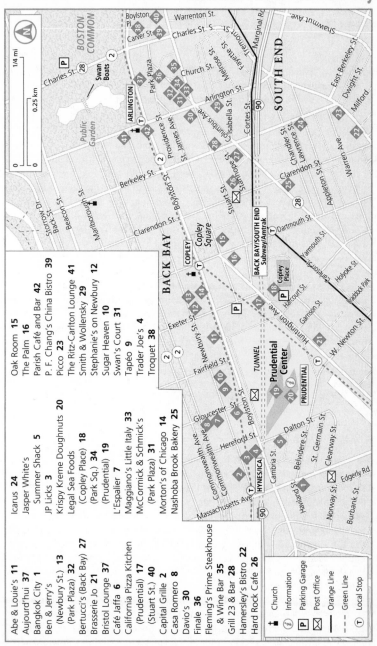

Abe & Louie's **11**
Aujourd'hui **37**
Bangkok City **1**
Ben & Jerry's
  Summer Shack **5**
JP Licks **3**
Krispy Kreme Doughnuts **20**
Legal Sea Foods
  (Copley Place) **18**
  (Park Sq.) **34**
  (Prudential) **19**
L'Espalier **7**
Maggiano's Little Italy **33**
McCormick & Schmick's
  (Park Plaza) **31**
Morton's of Chicago **14**
Nashoba Brook Bakery **25**

Bertucci's (Back Bay) **27**
Brasserie Jo **21**
Bristol Lounge **37**
Café Jaffa **6**
California Pizza Kitchen
  (Prudential) **17**
  (Stuart St.) **40**
Capital Grille **2**
Casa Romero **8**
Davio's **30**
Finale **36**
Fleming's Prime Steakhouse
  & Wine Bar **35**
Grill 23 & Bar **28**
Hamersley's Bistro **22**
Hard Rock Cafe **26**

Icarus **24**
Jasper White's
  Summer Shack **5**

Oak Room **15**
The Palm **16**
Parish Café and Bar **42**
P. F. Chang's China Bistro **39**
Picco **23**
The Ritz-Carlton Lounge **41**
Smith & Wollensky **29**
Stephanie's on Newbury **12**
Sugar Heaven **10**
Swan's Court **31**
Tapéo **9**
Trader Joe's **4**
Troquet **38**

Church
Information
P Parking Garage
⊠ Post Office
–––– Orange Line
| Green Line
Ⓣ Local Stop

BOSTON COMMON

Public Garden

Swan Boats

Charles St.

ARLINGTON

BACK BAY

Copley Square

COPLEY

BACK BAY/SOUTH END
Subway/Amtrak

Copley Place

SOUTH END

PRUDENTIAL

Prudential Center

HYNES/ICA

TUNNEL

Warrenton St.
Boylston Pl.
Carver St.
Charles St. S.
Tremont St.
Melrose St.
Fayette St.
Church St.
Park Plaza
Arlington St.
Columbus Ave.
Isabella St.
Cortes St.
St. James Ave.
Providence St.
Berkeley St.
Back St.
Beacon St.
Marlborough St.
Commonwealth Ave.
Commonwealth Ave.
Newbury St.
Boylston St.
Clarendon St.
Dartmouth St.
Exeter St.
Fairfield St.
Gloucester St.
Hereford St.
Massachusetts Ave.
Cambria St.
Belvidere St.
St. Germain St.
Dalton St.
Clearway St.
Haviland St.
Norway St.
Burbank St.
Edgerly Rd.
Huntington Ave.
Stuart St.
Stanhope St.
Harcourt St.
Garrison St.
W. Newton St.
Yarmouth St.
Cahners Pl.
Holyoke St.
Braddock Park
Chandler St.
Lawrence St.
Appleton St.
Clarendon St.
Warren Ave.
East Berkeley St.
Dwight St.
Milford
Shawmut Ave.
Marginal Rd.
Storrow Dr.

1/4 mi
0.25 km

135

30 Gloucester St. ℂ 617/262-3023. www.lespalier.com. Reservations recommended. *Prix fixe* (3 courses) $80; degustation menu (7 courses) $88. AE, DC, DISC, MC, V. Mon–Sat 5:30–10pm. Valet parking available. T: Green Line B, C, or D to Hynes/ICA.

EXPENSIVE

Tapéo, 266 Newbury St. (ℂ **617/267-4799**), has the same owners and menu as **Dalí** (p. 147). **Jasper White's Summer Shack** (p. 147) has a branch at 50 Dalton St. (ℂ **617/867-9955**), in the Kings bowling complex, across the street from the Sheraton Boston Hotel.

The Bristol ★★ AMERICAN   The Bristol is to a regular restaurant as the Four Seasons is to a regular hotel: It looks about the same, but everything is just *better.* Columns and cushy banquettes break up a large space with floor-to-ceiling windows, red-leather accents, and plenty of wood paneling; there's seating in the lively bar and the stylish dining area. The all-day menu extends from pricey breakfast items to tasty bar bites to sophisticated versions of classic dishes. The juicy burgers are famous, the soups and salads depend on what's fresh and seasonal, and the main courses are top-of-the-line comfort food (seared cod, roasted chicken, creamy lobster risotto). Desserts are inventive versions of apple pie, fudge cake, cheesecake, and other traditional favorites. In keeping with the quality of every other element of the experience, the service is fantastic.

The hotel's fine-dining restaurant, **Aujourd'hui** (ℂ **617/351-2037**) is one of Boston's top special-occasion and expense-account destinations. In a gorgeous second-floor space overlooking the Public Garden, it serves modern French cuisine (main courses $26–$42) daily from 5:30 to 10:30pm and a bountiful New England Sunday brunch buffet ($58 adults, $28 children) from 11am to 3pm. Reservations are strongly recommended.

In the Four Seasons Hotel, 200 Boylston St. ℂ 617/351-2037. www.fourseasons.com/boston. Reservations recommended. Main courses $14–$28 at lunch, $16–$33 at dinner; bar menu $8–$27. AE, DC, DISC, MC, V. Mon–Thurs 6:30am–11:30pm; Fri–Sat 6:30am–12:30am; Sun 10am–12:30am. Valet parking available. T: Green Line to Arlington.

Finds Boston Tea Party, Part 2

In Boston, the only city that has a tea party named after it, the tradition of afternoon tea at a posh hotel is alive and well. The best afternoon tea in town is at the **Bristol** in the Four Seasons Hotel, 200 Boylston St. (ℂ **617/351-2037**). The gorgeous room, lovely view, and courtly ritual elevate scones, pastries, tea sandwiches, and nut bread from delicious to unforgettable. The Bristol serves tea ($24) every day from 3 to 4:30pm; reservations are essential. The Ritz-Carlton, Boston, 15 Arlington St. (ℂ **617/536-5700**), serves tea in the celebrated **Lounge** Wednesday through Sunday at 2:30 and 4pm. Prices range from $16 for the children's tea to $38 for a luxurious spread of pastries and sandwiches with a glass of champagne. You'll need reservations. **Swan's Court** in the Boston Park Plaza Hotel & Towers, 64 Arlington St. (ℂ **617/426-2000**), serves finger sandwiches, tea breads, petits fours, and chocolate-covered strawberries daily from 3 to 5pm. The price is $21. Less formal but still delicious is the a la carte service at **Intrigue** (ℂ **617/856-7744**), in the Boston Harbor Hotel, Rowes Wharf, which serves tea daily.

Quick Bites & Picnic Provisions

Takeout food particularly appeals to two kinds of out-of-towners: eat-and-run sightseers and picnickers looking to take advantage of the acres of waterfront property in Boston and Cambridge. Some suggestions:

If you're walking the Freedom Trail, pick up food at **Faneuil Hall Marketplace** and cross Atlantic Avenue or buy a tasty sandwich in the North End at **Il Panino Express,** 266 Hanover St. (© 617/720-5720), and stroll down Richmond Street toward the harbor. From either direction, walk past the Marriott to the end of Long Wharf and eat on the plaza as you watch the boats and planes, or stay to the left of the hotel and eat in Christopher Columbus Waterfront Park, overlooking the marina.

In the **Financial District,** the **Milk Street Café** operates a kiosk (© 617/350-7275) in the park at Zero Post Office Square. Its kosher offerings include salads, sandwiches (on bread and rolled up in a pita), fish dishes, fruit, and pastries. Eat in the park or head to the harbor.

Two neighborhoods abut the Charles River Esplanade, a great destination for a picnic, concert, or movie. In the **Back Bay,** stop at **Trader Joe's,** 899 Boylston St. (© 617/262-6505), for prepared food. At the foot of **Beacon Hill,** pick up all you need for a do-it-yourself feast at **Savenor's Market,** 160 Charles St. (© 617/723-6328). Or call ahead to **Figs,** 42 Charles St. (© 617/742-3447), a minuscule pizzeria that's an offshoot of the celebrated Olives. The upscale fare isn't cheap, but avoiding the long line is worth the price—as is the delectable pizza.

On the Cambridge side of the river, **Harvard Square** is close enough to the water to allow a riverside repast. **Formaggio's,** in the Garage Mall, 81 Mount Auburn St. (© 617/547-4795), serves excellent gourmet sandwiches and salads. Take yours to John F. Kennedy Park, on Memorial Drive and Kennedy Street, or right to the riverbank.

Casa Romero ★ *Finds* MEXICAN   There's something about restaurants in alleys. They feel like secret clubs, and stumbling upon one can make a hungry diner feel like a daring explorer. Casa Romero is just such a place. The tiled floor, wood furnishings, dim lighting, and clay pots lend an authentic feel—you're definitely not at the local Tex-Mex counter. The food is excellent, with generous portions of spicy-hot and milder dishes; the friendly staff will help you negotiate the menu. If the soup of the day is garlic, don't miss it. Main-dish specialties include several kinds of enchiladas, an unusual combination of chicken stuffed with cactus and cheese and served with mole poblano sauce (a spicy concoction with a hint of chocolate), and the restaurant's signature dish, succulent pork tenderloin marinated with oranges and chipotle peppers. The walled garden is the "find" here; on a summer evening, it's a peaceful retreat.

30 Gloucester St., side entrance. © 617/536-4341. www.casaromero.com. Reservations recommended. Main courses $14–$27. DISC, MC, V. Mon–Thurs 5–10pm; Fri–Sat 5–11pm; Sun 11am–9pm (brunch until 2:30pm). Validated parking available. T: Green Line B, C, or D to Hynes/ICA.

Tips **Beat the Rush**

If you plan to dine in a neighborhood that's near a performing arts or sports venue, try to arrive after the performance or game begins so you don't get caught in the frenzy. This is especially true in the Symphony Hall area and the Theater District, as well as Harvard Square, the North End (when there's an event at the TD Banknorth Garden), and Kenmore Square (during baseball season).

Davio's ★★ CREATIVE NORTHERN ITALIAN   A cavernous space with a surprisingly comfortable vibe, Davio's offers robust cuisine that contrasts delightfully with the chic setting. It's stylish but not trendy: Owner-chef Steve DiFillippo built the restaurant's excellent reputation on its top-notch kitchen and dedicated staff. All of the traditional dishes—homemade sausage, savory soups, out-of-this-world pasta and risotto—shine. A la carte grilled meats are worthy of a top-notch steakhouse, but I prefer main courses such as roasted salmon with spinach risotto and crabmeat herb butter, or double-cut pork chop with creamy potatoes, apple-onion jam, and crispy *guanciale* (a bacon-like pork product). The excellent breads and desserts are made in-house. Davio's also has an exceptional wine list, including some rare and expensive Italian vintages. Despite the open kitchen, the bar in the middle of the room, and the lively lounge area, the noise level allows for conversation, even at busy times.

The Davio's in **Cambridge,** at the Royal Sonesta Hotel, 5 Cambridge Pkwy. (© **617/661-4810**), keeps the same hours and offers outdoor seating in good weather.

75 Arlington St. © **617/357-4810.** www.davios.com. Reservations recommended. Main courses $8–$25 at lunch, $15–$41 at dinner; Kobe beef $49. AE, DC, DISC, MC, V. Mon–Fri 11:30am–3pm; daily 5–11pm. Lounge menu Sun–Thurs 3–11pm; Fri–Sat 3pm–midnight. Validated and valet parking available. T: Green Line to Arlington.

Legal Sea Foods ★★★ SEAFOOD   Out-of-towners sometimes react suspiciously when I recommend Legal's—they're expecting a secret insider tip, and I'm suggesting a place they've already heard of. Just remember that this family-owned business enjoys an international reputation for serving only the freshest, best-quality fish and shellfish, which it processes at its own state-of-the-art plant. The menu includes regular selections (scrod, haddock, bluefish, salmon, shrimp, calamari, and lobster, among others) plus whatever was at the market that morning, prepared in every imaginable way, and it's all splendid. The clam chowder is great, the fish chowder lighter but equally good. Entrees run the gamut from grilled fish served plain or with Cajun spices (try the arctic char) to seafood *fra'diavolo* on fresh linguine to salmon baked in parchment with vegetables and white wine. Or go the luxurious route and order a mammoth lobster. The classic dessert is ice cream bonbons, but the Boston cream pie is so good that you might come back just for that. And the wide-ranging, reasonably priced wine list is exceptional.

I suggest the Prudential Center branch because it takes reservations (at lunch only), a deviation from a long tradition. Another tradition that's mercifully fading is the policy of serving each dish when it's ready—these days, you'll probably get your food at the same time as the rest of your party.

Legal's has other locations at 255 State St., on the waterfront (© **617/227-3115;** T: Blue Line to Aquarium); at 36 Park Sq., between Columbus Avenue and Stuart Street (© **617/426-4444;** T: Green Line to Arlington); and at Copley Place, 2nd level

(© 617/266-7775; T: Orange Line to Back Bay or Green Line to Copley). In Cambridge, branches are in the courtyard of the Charles Hotel, 20 University Rd. (© 617/491-9400; T: Red Line to Harvard), and at 5 Cambridge Center (© 617/864-3400; T: Red Line to Kendall/MIT).

In the Prudential Center, 800 Boylston St. © 617/266-6800. www.legalseafoods.com. Reservations recommended at lunch, not accepted at dinner. Main courses $8–$17 at lunch, $12–$35 at dinner. AE, DC, DISC, MC, V. Mon–Thurs 11am–10:30pm; Fri–Sat 11am–11:30pm; Sun noon–10pm. T: Green Line B, C, or D to Hynes/ICA or E to Prudential.

MODERATE

Bangkok City ✦ THAI   In a neighborhood overflowing with Thai restaurants, this is my top choice. In the large dining room, the cordial staff and tempting aromas greet you as you check out the exotic decor and lengthy menu. Appetizers are the usual dumplings and satays, plus unique items like "Boston triangles" (tasty fried pork-and-shrimp patties). Entrees range from mild pad Thai to blow-your-hair-back curries, with many vegetarian options. The mix-and-match selection of proteins and sauces is larger than at many other Thai restaurants, so you can let your palate's imagination run wild. The friend who steered me to this place comes here just for the zesty salt-and-pepper squid. He also passed along this tip: Ask for the Thai menu. It's just a photocopied sheet, with many of the same dishes as the regular menu, but it's a great help in narrowing down your choices.

167 Mass. Ave. © 617/266-8884. www.bkkcity.net. Reservations recommended before Symphony and Pops performances. Main courses $7–$10 at lunch; $8–$17 at dinner. AE, DC, DISC, MC, V. Mon–Sat 11:30am–3pm; Mon–Thurs 5–10pm; Fri 5–10:30pm; Sat 5–11pm; Sun 3–10pm. T: Green Line B, C, or D to Hynes/ICA.

Brasserie Jo ✦ REGIONAL FRENCH   One of the most discriminating diners I know lit up like a marquee upon hearing that Boston has a branch of this Chicago favorite. The food is classic—house-made pâtés, fresh baguettes, superb shellfish, salade Niçoise, Alsatian onion tart, *choucroute*, coq au vin—but never boring. The house beer, an Alsace-style draft, is a good accompaniment. The casual, all-day French brasserie and bar fits well in this neighborhood, where shoppers can always use a break but might not want a full meal. It's also a good bet before or after a Symphony or Pops performance, and it's popular for business lunches. The noise level can be high when the spacious room is full—have your tête-à-tête at a table near the bar.

In the Colonnade Hotel, 120 Huntington Ave. © 617/425-3240. www.brasseriejoboston.com. Reservations recommended at dinner. Main courses $6–$15 at lunch, $15–$27 at dinner; *plats du jour* $18–$32. AE, DC, DISC, MC, V. Mon–Fri 6:30am–11pm; Sat 7am–11pm; Sun 7am–10pm; late-night menu daily until 1am. Valet and garage parking available. T: Green Line E to Prudential.

INEXPENSIVE

The Boston Public Library, 700 Boylston St. (© 617/536-5400; www.bpl.org), is home to a restaurant, **Novel,** that serves lunch and afternoon tea on weekdays only

---

⌐Finds How Sweet It Is

What a world! The low-carb craze just won't go away, but a place with the delightfully unsubtle name **Sugar Heaven** is thriving. The self-serve calorie castle at 218 Newbury St. (© 617/266-6969) carries hundreds of confections, makes its own cotton candy, and stays open till midnight daily. That sound you hear is your dentist whimpering.

and the less expensive **Sebastian's Map Room Café,** which serves meals and snacks Monday through Saturday from 9am to 5pm.

Café Jaffa MIDDLE EASTERN   A long, narrow brick room with a glass front, Café Jaffa looks more like a snazzy pizza place than the excellent Middle Eastern restaurant it is. The reasonable prices, high quality, and large portions draw hordes of students and other thrifty diners for traditional Middle Eastern offerings such as falafel, baba ghanouj, and hummus, as well as burgers and steak tips. Lamb, beef, and chicken kabobs come with Greek salad, rice pilaf, and pita bread. For dessert, try the baklava if it's fresh (give it a pass if not). There is a short list of beer and wine, and many fancy coffee offerings.

48 Gloucester St. ℭ **617/536-0230.** Main courses $5–$16. AE, DC, DISC, MC, V. Mon–Thurs 11am–10:30pm; Fri–Sat 11am–11pm; Sun noon–10pm. T: Green Line B, C, or D to Hynes/ICA.

12 Kenmore Square to Brookline

EXPENSIVE

Ginza Japanese Restaurant (p. 128) has a second location at 1002 Beacon St., Brookline (ℭ **617/566-9688**). Unlike the Boston location, the Brookline branch doesn't cater to an after-hours crowd; its late nights are Friday and Saturday, when closing time is 10:30pm.

The Elephant Walk ⭐ FRENCH/CAMBODIAN   France meets Cambodia on the menu at this madly popular spot, 4 blocks from Kenmore Square and decorated with lots of pachyderms. The menu is French on one side and Cambodian on the other, but the boundary is quite porous. Many Cambodian dishes have part-French names, such as *poulet dhomrei* (chicken with Asian basil, bamboo shoots, fresh pineapple, and lemongrass) and *curry de crevettes* (shrimp curry with picture-perfect vegetables). My mouth is still burning from *loc lac,* fork-tender beef cubes in addictively spicy sauce. On the French side, you'll find pork tenderloin with mushroom-soy sauce and brown jasmine rice, and pan-seared tuna with three-peppercorn crust. Many dishes are available with tofu substituted for animal protein. The pleasant staff members will help if you need guidance. Ask to be seated in the plant-filled front room, which is less noisy than the main dining room and has a view of the street.

900 Beacon St., Boston. ℭ **617/247-1500.** www.elephantwalk.com. Reservations recommended at dinner Sun–Thurs, not accepted Fri–Sat. Main courses $7–$26 at lunch (most items under $11); $11–$27 at dinner. AE, DC, DISC, MC, V. Mon–Fri 11:30am–2:30pm; Sun–Thurs 5–10pm; Fri–Sat 5–11pm. Valet parking available at dinner. T: Green Line C to St. Mary's St.

MODERATE

There's a branch of the **Daily Catch** (p. 120) at 441 Harvard St., Brookline (ℭ **617/ 734-5696;** www.dailycatch.com).

INEXPENSIVE

Zaftigs Delicatessen DELI/AMERICAN   The magical phrase "breakfast served all day" might be enough to lure you to this bustling restaurant, but even breakfast haters (yes, there is such an animal) will be happy at Zaftigs. The name, Yiddish for "pleasingly plump," is no joke—everything is good, and portions are more than generous. Try fluffy pancakes, challah French toast, or a terrific omelet. They share the menu with wonderful overstuffed deli sandwiches as well as entrees that seem basic

The Great Outdoors: Alfresco Dining

Cambridge is a better destination for outdoor dining than Boston, but both cities offer agreeable spots to lounge under the sun or stars.

Across the street from the Charles River near Kendall Square, the **Sail Loft,** 1 Memorial Dr. (© 617/225-2222), opens onto a leafy plaza that usually picks up a breeze from the water. Both restaurant patios at the **Royal Sonesta Hotel,** 5 Cambridge Pkwy. (© 617/491-3600), have great views. The hotel's **Gallery Café** is casual; its **Davio's** (p. 138) is a bit fancier. On one of Harvard Square's main drags, **Shay's Pub & Wine Bar,** 58 John F. Kennedy St. (© 617/864-9161), has a small, lively seating area. More peaceful are the patios at the **Blue Room** (p. 146) and **Oleana** (p. 148).

On the other side of the river, try the airy terrace at **Intrigue** (© 617/856-7744), in the Boston Harbor Hotel, Rowes Wharf, which overlooks the harbor and the airport. Most bars and restaurants in **Faneuil Hall Marketplace** offer outdoor seating and great people-watching. In the Back Bay, Newbury Street is similarly diverting; a good vantage point is **Stephanie's on Newbury,** 190 Newbury St. (© 617/236-0990). A popular shopping stop and after-work hangout is the **Parish Café and Bar,** 361 Boylston St. (© 617/247-4777), where the sandwich menu is a "greatest hits" roster of top local chefs' creations. A laid-back alternative in this area is the hideaway garden at **Casa Romero** (p. 137).

but demonstrate a certain flair. Roasted chicken is juicy and flavorful, meatloaf and gravy equally enjoyable. The knock on Boston-area deli food is that (well, duh) it's not New York, but the hard-core deli items here are more than acceptable. The gefilte fish is light, citrus twinkles in the blintz filling, and the chicken soup is excellent.

335 Harvard St., Brookline. © 617/975-0075. www.zaftigs.com. Reservations recommended at dinner; limited number accepted. Main courses $8–$17; breakfast items $3.50–$11. AE, DISC, MC, V. Daily 8am–10pm. T: Green Line C to Coolidge Corner.

13 Cambridge

The dining scene in Cambridge, as in Boston, offers something for everyone, from penny-pinching students to the tycoons that many of them aspire to become. The Red Line runs from Boston to Harvard Square, and many of the restaurants listed here are within walking distance of the square; others (including a couple of real finds over the Somerville border) are under the heading "Outside Harvard Square."

To locate the restaurants reviewed in this section, see the "Where to Dine in Cambridge" map on p. 142.

HARVARD SQUARE & VICINITY

A brilliant idea cooked up by a pair of Harvard Business School students, **Finale** (p. 239), 30 Dunster St. (© 617/441-9797), specializes in dessert.

Where to Dine in Cambridge

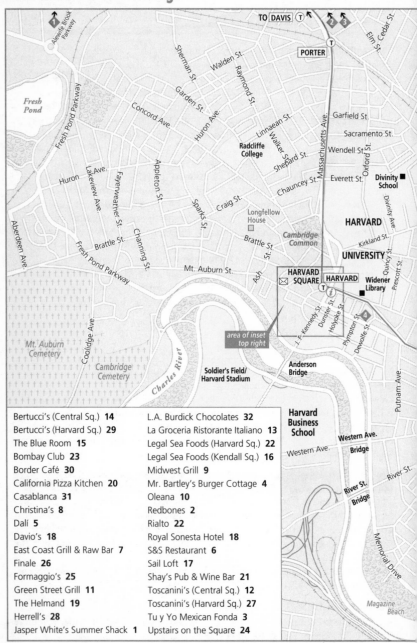

Bertucci's (Central Sq.) **14**
Bertucci's (Harvard Sq.) **29**
The Blue Room **15**
Bombay Club **23**
Border Café **30**
California Pizza Kitchen **20**
Casablanca **31**
Christina's **8**
Dalí **5**
Davio's **18**
East Coast Grill & Raw Bar **7**
Finale **26**
Formaggio's **25**
Green Street Grill **11**
The Helmand **19**
Herrell's **28**
Jasper White's Summer Shack **1**

L.A. Burdick Chocolates **32**
La Groceria Ristorante Italiano **13**
Legal Sea Foods (Harvard Sq.) **22**
Legal Sea Foods (Kendall Sq.) **16**
Midwest Grill **9**
Mr. Bartley's Burger Cottage **4**
Oleana **10**
Redbones **2**
Rialto **22**
Royal Sonesta Hotel **18**
S&S Restaurant **6**
Sail Loft **17**
Shay's Pub & Wine Bar **21**
Toscanini's (Central Sq.) **12**
Toscanini's (Harvard Sq.) **27**
Tu y Yo Mexican Fonda **3**
Upstairs on the Square **24**

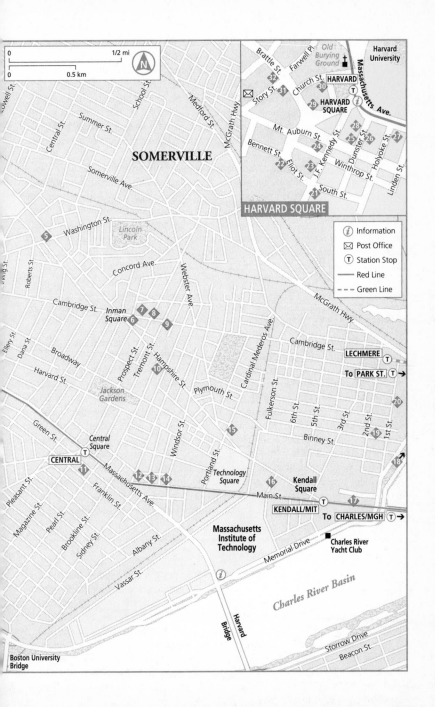

VERY EXPENSIVE

Rialto ⭐⭐ MEDITERRANEAN   Rialto is one of the Boston area's favorite special-occasion restaurants. Every element is carefully thought out, from the architecture to chef Jody Adams's extraordinary food. It's a dramatic but comfortable room, with floor-to-ceiling windows overlooking Harvard Square, cushy banquettes, and standing lamps that cast a golden glow. It attracts a chic crowd, but it's not such a scene that out-of-towners will feel left behind. I find the service a bit standoffish, but the legions of friends who wouldn't think of celebrating birthdays and anniversaries anywhere else heartily disagree.

The menu changes regularly. You might start with grilled Wellfleet clams with garlic bread, or Provençal fisherman's soup with rouille, Gruyère, and basil oil—the very essence of seafood. Main courses are so good that you might as well close your eyes and point. Tuscan-style steak with portobella-and-arugula salad is wonderful, and any seafood dish is a guaranteed winner—say, seared tuna with preserved-lemon vinaigrette, wheat berries, and slow-cooked tomatoes. A plate of creamy potato slices and mushrooms is so rich and juicy that it's almost like eating meat. For dessert, seasonal sorbets are a great choice, alone or in a combination with another dessert choice, such as lemon pound cake with Meyer lemon sorbet.

In the Charles Hotel, 1 Bennett St. © 617/661-5050. www.rialto-restaurant.com. Reservations recommended. Main courses $22–$37. AE, DC, MC, V. Mon–Fri 5:30–10pm, Sat 5:30–11pm, Sun 5:30–9pm. Bar Sun–Thurs 5pm–midnight, Fri–Sat 5pm–1am. Valet and validated parking available. T: Red Line to Harvard.

Upstairs on the Square ⭐⭐ ECLECTIC   Upstairs on the Square is the reincarnation of a longtime Harvard Square favorite, Upstairs at the Pudding. It opened in its new location in 2002 and immediately reestablished itself as the kind of restaurant that puts the "special" in "special occasion." In my casual poll of local travel experts (p. 116), only world-famous Legal Sea Foods got more votes. Upstairs on the Square consists of two distinct spaces; I prefer the more casual one to its fancier counterpart, but both are delightful. The second-floor Monday Club Bar dining room is a relaxed yet romantic space where firelight flickers on jewel-toned walls. The food—unusual salads and sandwiches (including a daily grilled-cheese option at lunch), pizza, fried chicken, steak with baked potato and onion rings—is homey and satisfying, and the bar is a tweedy Cambridge scene. The Soiree Room, atop the four-story building, is the place for that big anniversary dinner: It's a jewel box of pinks and golds under a low, mirrored ceiling. The menu is enjoyably old-fashioned, with straightforward main courses (a slab of

---

Kids **The Scoop on Ice Cream**

No less an expert than Ben Cohen of Ben & Jerry's has described Boston as "a great place for ice cream." That goes for Cambridge, too—residents of both cities famously defy even the most frigid weather to get their fix. I like Cambridge better: Try **Christina's,** 1255 Cambridge St., Inman Square (© 617/492-7021); **Herrell's,** 15 Dunster St., Harvard Square (© 617/497-2179); or **Toscanini's,** 1310 Mass. Ave., Harvard Square (© 617/354-9350), and 899 Main St., Central Square (© 617/491-5877). Favorite Boston destinations include **Ben & Jerry's,** 174 Newbury St. (© 617/536-5456) and 20 Park Plaza (© 617/426-0890); **JP Licks,** 352 Newbury St. (© 617/236-1666); and **Steve's,** Quincy Market, Faneuil Hall Marketplace (© 617/367-0569).

swordfish, luscious ribeye steak) that contrast with bolder starters—delectable Jerusalem artichoke or watercress soup, simple but superb endive and watercress salad. In both rooms, you'll find outstanding wine selections and desserts.

91 Winthrop St. ⓒ 617/864-1933. www.upstairsonthesquare.com. Reservations recommended. Main courses $11–$26 downstairs, $24–$42 upstairs. AE, DC, DISC, MC, V. Downstairs Mon–Fri 11:30am–2:30pm; Sun brunch 11am–2pm; daily 5pm–1am. Upstairs Mon–Sat 5:30–10pm; Sun brunch 11am–2pm. Validated and valet parking available. T: Red Line to Harvard.

EXPENSIVE

There's a **Legal Sea Foods** (p. 138) in the Charles Hotel courtyard, 20 University Rd. (ⓒ 617/491-9400).

Casablanca ★ MEDITERRANEAN This old-time Harvard Square favorite has long been better known for its hopping bar scene than for its food, but these days the dining room is the place where you're sure to get lucky. Service is erratic (it's better at lunch than at dinner), and there's plenty to look at while you wait. The walls of the long, sky-lit dining room and crowded, noisy bar sport murals of scenes from the movie. Humphrey Bogart looks as though he might lean down to ask for a taste of grilled squid and shrimp with black chick peas and roasted-tomato vinaigrette, or juicy grilled lamb steak with cannellini beans and escarole. The appetizers are so good that you might want to assemble them into a meal. Just be sure to leave room for dessert. Pistachio baklava is a good choice, as is butterscotch pie.

40 Brattle St. ⓒ 617/876-0999. www.casablanca-restaurant.com. Reservations recommended at dinner. Main courses $8–$12 at lunch, $19–$24 at dinner. AE, DC, MC, V. Mon–Sat 11:30am–2:30pm; Sun–Thurs 5:30–10pm; Fri–Sat 5:30–11pm. Validated parking available. T: Red Line to Harvard.

MODERATE

Bombay Club _Value_ INDIAN This third-floor spot overlooking Harvard Square gained fame through its lunch buffet, a generous assortment of some of the best items on the menu. The buffet's reasonable price and the lively scene make midday the best time to dine here. At all times, the food—a selection of typical dishes from across the subcontinent—is flavorful and fresh, with yogurt and cheese made in-house daily. The breads, baked to perfection in a traditional charcoal-fired clay oven, and the lamb offerings are especially tasty. The "chef's recommendations," platters of assorted meat or vegetarian dishes, make good samplers if you're new to the cuisine or can't make up your mind. If grazing isn't your thing, tandoori kabobs, _rogan josh_ (lamb in garlicky tomato sauce), and fiery chicken vindaloo merit ordering full portions.

57 John F. Kennedy St. ⓒ 617/661-8100. www.bombayclub.com. Lunch buffet $8 Mon–Fri, $12 Sat–Sun; main courses $5–$9 at lunch, $11–$18 at dinner. AE, DC, MC, V. Daily 11:30am–11pm (lunch until 3pm). Discounted parking available. T: Red Line to Harvard.

Border Café TEX-MEX/CAJUN When you see this restaurant, your thoughts might turn to, of all people, baseball Hall of Famer Yogi Berra. He supposedly said, "Nobody goes there anymore; it's too crowded." He was talking about a New York club, but people have been saying the same thing about this Harvard Square hangout for nearly 20 years. Patrons loiter at the bar for hours, enhancing the festival atmosphere. Many are waiting to be seated for generous portions of tasty (if not completely authentic) food. The menu features Tex-Mex, Cajun, and some Caribbean specialties, and the beleaguered staff keeps the chips and salsa coming. When you shout your order over the roar of the crowd, try the excellent chorizo appetizer, enchiladas

---

Tips **Sweet-Tooth Alert**

As a rule, nonfranchise businesses that carve out a niche in Harvard Square do one thing and do it extremely well. Case in point: **L.A. Burdick Chocolates,** 52 Brattle St., Cambridge (© **617/491-4340;** www.burdickchocolate.com; T: Red Line to Harvard). The amazing confections include sublime hot chocolate to stay or go.

(seafood is particularly delectable), any kind of tacos, or popcorn shrimp. Fajitas for one or two, sizzling noisily, are also a popular choice. Set aside a couple of hours, get into a party mood, and ask to be seated downstairs if you want to be able to hear your companions.

32 Church St. © **617/864-6100.** Reservations not accepted. Main courses $7–$15. AE, MC, V. Daily 11am–11pm. T: Red Line to Harvard.

INEXPENSIVE

Mr. Bartley's Burger Cottage ★★ AMERICAN   Great burgers and the best onion rings in the world make Bartley's a perennial favorite with a cross section of Cambridge, from Harvard students to regular folks. The 40-plus-year-old family business isn't a cottage, but a high-ceilinged, crowded room plastered with signs and posters (there's also a small outdoor seating area). Burgers bear the names of local and national celebrities, notably political figures; the names change, but the ingredients stay the same.

Anything you can think of to put on ground beef is available, from American cheese to grilled pineapple. Good dishes that don't involve meat include veggie burgers and creamy, garlicky hummus. And Bartley's is one of the only places in the area where you can still get a real raspberry lime rickey (raspberry syrup, lime juice, lime wedges, and club soda—the taste of summer even in the winter).

1246 Mass. Ave. © **617/354-6559.** www.mrbartleys.com. Burgers $8–$13; main courses, salads, and sandwiches $5–$9. No credit cards. Mon–Sat 11am–9pm. Closed Dec 25–Jan 1. T: Red Line to Harvard.

OUTSIDE HARVARD SQUARE
EXPENSIVE

There's a **Legal Sea Foods** (p. 138) at 5 Cambridge Center, Kendall Square (© **617/864-3400**). **Davio's** (p. 138) has a branch at the Royal Sonesta Hotel, 5 Cambridge Pkwy (© **617/661-4810**), that's open daily from 11:30am to 10pm.

The Blue Room ★★★ ECLECTIC   The Blue Room sits below plaza level in an office-retail complex, a slice of foodie paradise in high-tech heaven. Its out-of-the-way location means that it doesn't get as much publicity as it deserves, but it's one of the best restaurants in the Boston area. The cuisine is a rousing combination of top-notch ingredients and layers of aggressive flavors, the service is excellent, and the crowded dining room is not as noisy as you might fear when you first spy the open kitchen through the glass front wall. Upholstery and carpeting help soften the din, but this is still not a place for cooing lovers—it's a place for food lovers, who savor the regularly changing menu.

Appetizers range from imaginative salads to roasted-garlic soup to delectable pizza. Entrees tend to be roasted, grilled, or braised, with at least one well-conceived vegetarian choice. Roast chicken is the most boring choice on most restaurant menus, but this version, served with garlic mashed potatoes, is world-class. Seafood is always a wise choice (braised cod with littlenecks—yum!), and braised lamb shank will make you forget the pangs of beef withdrawal you suffered after the latest mad cow scare. In warm weather, there's seating on the brick patio.

1 Kendall Sq. © 617/494-9034. www.theblueroom.net. Reservations recommended. Main courses $18–$24. AE, DC, DISC, MC, V. Sun–Thurs 5:30–10pm; Fri–Sat 5:30–11pm; Sun brunch 11am–2:30pm. Validated parking available. T: Red Line to Kendall/MIT; 10-min. walk.

Dalí ★★ SPANISH   This festive restaurant casts an irresistible spell—it doesn't take reservations, it's noisy and inconvenient, and it still fills with people cheerfully waiting an hour or more for a table. The bar offers plenty to look at while you wait, including gorgeous tiles, carved wood, and eclectic artwork. The payoff is authentic Spanish food, notably *tapas*—little plates of hot or cold creations that burst with flavor.

Entrees include excellent paella, but most people come with friends and explore the three dozen or more *tapas* offerings, all perfect for sharing. They include *patatas alioli* (garlic potatoes), *albóndigas de salmón* (salmon balls with not-too-salty caper sauce), *setas al ajillo* (sautéed mushrooms), and *lomito al cabrales* (pork tenderloin with blue goat cheese and mushrooms). The helpful staff sometimes seems rushed but never fails to supply bread for sopping up juices and sangria for washing it all down. Finish with excellent flan or luscious *tarta de chocolates*.

The owners of Dalí also run **Tapéo** at 266 Newbury St. (© 617/267-4799), between Fairfield and Dartmouth streets in Boston's **Back Bay.** It offers the same menu and similarly wacky decor in a more sedate two-level setting.

415 Washington St., Somerville. © 617/661-3254. www.dalirestaurant.com. Reservations not accepted. *Tapas* $4.50–$9.50; main courses $23–$25. AE, DC, MC, V. Daily summer 6–11pm; winter 5:30–11pm. T: Red Line to Harvard; follow Kirkland St. to intersection of Washington and Beacon sts. (20 min. walk or $5 cab ride).

East Coast Grill & Raw Bar ★★ SEAFOOD/BARBECUE   Huge portions, a dizzying menu, and funky decor have made the East Coast Grill madly popular for over 20 years. The kitchen handles fresh seafood (an encyclopedic variety), barbecue, and grilled fish and meats with equal authority. The influence of founder Chris Schlesinger, a national expert on grilling and spicy food, is apparent in the exuberant menu descriptions ("super fresh catch o' the moment," "West Indies party beef from hell!"). To start, check out the raw-bar offerings or try the sublime fried oysters. The seafood entrees are exceptional—always check the specials board because you may luck into something like plantain-crusted cod, my new favorite. Barbecue comes on abundant platters in three styles: Texas beef, Memphis spareribs, and North Carolina pork. Desserts are just decent, but there's a great ice-cream store (Christina's) up the street. *A note to parents:* Because there's no children's menu, I don't feel comfortable adding a "Kids" icon, but the menu includes plenty of options for less adventuresome palates, and during a recent meal (anonymous, as always) with two well-behaved but active little boys, the staff couldn't have been nicer.

1271 Cambridge St., Inman Sq. © 617/491-6568. www.eastcoastgrill.net. Reservations accepted only for parties of 5 or more, Sun–Thurs. Main courses $14–$30; sandwich plates $8–$9. AE, MC, V. Sun–Thurs 5:30–10pm; Fri–Sat 5:30–10:30pm; Sun brunch 11am–2:30pm. Validated parking available. T: Red Line to Harvard, then no. 69 (Harvard-Lechmere) bus to Inman Sq.; or Red Line to Central, 10-min. walk on Prospect St.

Jasper White's Summer Shack ★ *Kids* SEAFOOD   An enormous space with a lobster tank in the middle of the floor, the Summer Shack feels like an overgrown seaside clam shack—but one that's been to cooking school. All the basics are here: raw bar, excellent french fries, and even a clambake (a lobster, clams, mussels, potatoes, sausage, and corn on the cob). But check the name again—Jasper White is nationally renowned for seafood, and his pan-roasted lobster, on the aptly named "big bucks lobster" section of the menu, has been a local foodie favorite for 2 decades (since his days at the fine-dining restaurant Jasper's). Yes, the contrast is incongruous, but it works. You might find yourself sitting at a picnic table between a kid chowing down on a corn dog and a suburban couple savoring wok-seared lobster with ginger and scallions or steamed mussels in wine-and-herb broth—and they'll all be equally happy. You'll be able to hear them exclaiming, too: When it's full, this is one of the loudest restaurants in the Boston area. Arrive early, ask to sit on the second level (just a few steps up, but much quieter), and you might be able to have a conversation.

There's another Summer Shack in Boston's **Back Bay,** at 50 Dalton St. (✆ **617/ 867-9955**), in the upscale Kings bowling complex. It's open 11am to 11pm Sunday through Wednesday, until 1am Thursday through Saturday.

149 Alewife Brook Pkwy. ✆ **617/520-9500.** www.summershackrestaurant.com. Reservations accepted only for parties of 8 or more. Main courses $12–$23; sandwiches $5–$15; lobster and specials market price. AE, DISC, MC, V. Mon–Fri 11:30am–2:30pm; Sun–Thurs 5–10pm; Fri–Sat 5–11pm. Free parking. T: Red Line to Alewife.

Oleana ★★ MEDITERRANEAN   Both casual neighborhood place and culinary travelogue, Oleana occupies a cozy space outside Inman Square. The wonderful food and welcoming atmosphere make it one of the best restaurants in the Boston area. The seasonal menu, which features cuisine typical of and inspired by the Mediterranean, relies on fresh ingredients and chef and co-owner Ana (short for Oleana) Sortun's signature unusual flavors. Fava bean moussaka accompanies juicy grilled lamb steak with Turkish spices. Tempting aromas signal the arrival of roasted cod with black-truffle rice pilaf and egg-lemon sauce. Even better is spicy tuna, in a peppery sauce that trades intense heat for intense flavor, a perfect match for the meaty fish. Service is polished, portions are generous, and the dessert menu is heavy on house-made ice cream. In warm weather, there's seating on the peaceful patio.

134 Hampshire St., Inman Sq. ✆ **617/661-0505.** www.oleanarestaurant.com. Reservations recommended. Main courses $15–$24; vegetarian tasting menu $38. AE, MC, V. Sun–Thurs 5:30–10pm; Fri–Sat 5:30–11pm. Free parking. T: Red Line to Central; 10-min. walk.

MODERATE

Green Street Grill ★ CARIBBEAN/SEAFOOD   Visitors ask conspiratorially, "Where do people who live here *really* go to eat?" This is one good answer. The Green Street Grill is a splash of the tropics on a colorless side street. Formerly a divey bar, the artsy two-level space attracts a lively local crowd with generous portions of exotic, flavorful cuisine. The food isn't the go-on-I-dare-you Caribbean pepperfest that put this kitchen on the map, but you can still try curried goat. Less challenging dishes include a bounteous bowl of spicy Caribbean seafood and vegetable stew, and short ribs so tender you don't even need a knife. There's a short dessert menu and a lengthy menu of martinis and tropical drinks. Stick around for the live music (see p. 246 for the bar listing).

280 Green St., Central Sq. ✆ **617/876-1655.** Reservations accepted only for parties of 6 or more. Main courses $13–$20. AE, DC, MC, V. Sun–Wed 5:30–10pm, Thurs–Sat 5:30–10:30pm; Sun brunch 11am–2:30pm. (Bar closes at 1am Sun–Wed, 2am Thurs–Sat.) T: Red Line to Central Sq.

The Helmand ★ AFGHAN   Never exactly a secret, the Helmand enjoyed a burst of publicity when Afghanistan moved into the headlines, and it's hardly had a slow night since—make a reservation. The elegant setting belies the reasonable prices at this spacious spot near the CambridgeSide Galleria mall. The delectable flavors and textures evoke Middle Eastern, Indian, and Pakistani cuisine. Many dishes are vegetarian, and meat is often one element of a dish rather than the centerpiece. Every meal comes with delectable bread made fresh in a wood-fired brick oven near the entrance.

To start, you might try slightly sweet baked pumpkin topped with spicy ground meat sauce—a great contrast of flavors and textures—or *aushak,* pasta pockets filled with leeks or potatoes and buried under a sauce of split peas and carrots. *Aushak,* also available as a main course, also come with meat sauce. In several dishes, grilling brings out the flavor of lamb and chicken. Other entrees include several versions of what Americans would call stew, including *deygee kabob,* an excellent mélange of lamb, yellow split peas, onion, and red peppers. For dessert, don't miss the Afghan version of baklava.

143 First St. ✆ **617/492-4646.** Reservations recommended. Main courses $12–$20. AE, MC, V. Sun–Thurs 5–10pm; Fri–Sat 5–11pm. T: Green Line to Lechmere.

La Groceria Ristorante Italiano *Kids* ITALIAN/MEDITERRANEAN   The Mastromauro family has dished up large portions of delicious food at this colorful, welcoming restaurant since 1971. You'll see business meetings at lunch, family outings at dinner, and students at all times. Cheery voices bounce off the stucco walls and tile floors, but it seldom gets terribly noisy, probably because everyone's mouth is full. You might start with the house garlic bread, lavished with chopped tomato, red onion, fennel seed, and olive oil. The antipasto platter overflows with the chef's choice of meats, cheeses, and roasted vegetables. Main dishes include Italian specialties such as lasagna, chicken Marsala, and homemade pasta from the machine that you'll see as you enter—the daily specials are always good bets—and Mediterranean selections like bouillabaisse.

853 Main St., Central Sq. ✆ **617/497-4214.** www.lagroceriarestaurant.com. Reservations recommended at dinner. Main courses $7–$15 at lunch, $14–$19 at dinner. Children's menu $9. AE, DC, DISC, MC, V. Mon–Fri 11:30am–10pm (lunch until 4pm); Sat 2:30–10pm; Sun 2–9pm. Free parking. T: Red Line to Central Sq.

Midwest Grill ✦ *Value* BRAZILIAN   As soon as you open the door of the Midwest Grill, the aroma of garlic and meat starts your mouth watering. Distractions abound: personable waiters, lively music, the salad bar–like selection of side dishes (superb potatoes, black-bean stew, salads, olives, and rice). But you can't ignore the scent of meat juices dripping onto an open fire. Finally, here come the waiters, bearing the long, swordlike skewers of meat that make up *rodizio,* or Brazilian barbecue. They slice off portions of perfectly grilled pork, lamb, or beef, as you help with salad tongs. They return with sausage, chicken, and even chicken hearts. Take a break and check out the gregarious families, voracious students, and other carnivores (there's also a vegetarian plate), then flag down a circulating waiter and dig in again.

1124 Cambridge St., Inman Sq. ✆ **617/354-7536.** Reservations recommended Mon–Thurs; accepted only for parties of 8 or more Fri–Sun. *Rodizio* $17 at lunch, $22 at dinner; main courses $11–$16. AE, DISC, MC, V. Daily 11:30am–11:30pm. T: Red Line to Harvard, then no. 69 (Harvard-Lechmere) bus just past Inman Sq.; or Red Line to Central, 10-min. walk on Prospect St.

Redbones ✦ *Kids* BARBECUE   Geographically, this raucous restaurant is in Somerville, but in spirit it's on a Southern back road—where the sun is hot, the beer is cold, and a slab of meat is done to a turn. Barbecued ribs (Memphis-, Texas-, and Arkansas-style), smoked beef brisket, fried Louisiana catfish, and grilled chicken come with appropriate side dishes such as coleslaw and beans. The chummy staff can help you choose sweet, hot, mild, or vinegar sauce. The best non-barbecue dish is a starter or dinner of succulent buffalo shrimp, swimming in hot sauce. Portions are large, so pace yourself. You'll want to try the appetizers and sides—catfish "catfingers," succotash, corn pudding—and desserts, especially pecan pie and the "white trash sundae" (ice-cream sandwiches sliced up and festooned with fudge sauce and whipped cream—not as gross as it sounds). The only less-than-tasty dish I've had here was watery broccoli, but that's what I get for ordering a vegetable other than coleslaw. There's a huge selection of beers and valet parking for your bike in warm weather. Given a choice, sit upstairs—Underbones, downstairs, is a noisy bar.

55 Chester St. (off Elm St.), Somerville. © 617/628-2200. www.redbones.com. Reservations recommended; accepted Sun–Thurs. Main courses $6–$19; children's menu $5. No credit cards. Mon–Sat 11:30am–10:30pm; Sun noon–10:30pm; daily lunch until 4pm, late-night menu until 12:30am. T: Red Line to Davis.

Tu y Yo Mexican Fonda REGIONAL MEXICAN A large, colorful storefront near the Tufts University campus, Tu y Yo specializes in authentic Mexican food in a style that dates to the 16th century. Settlers lived and ate at *fondas,* or boarding houses, that served home-style cooking. They ate well, too—I've never had a disappointing meal here. The menu looks short, but many dishes are available with a choice of beef, chicken, pork, sausage, shrimp, or fish, and in vegetarian versions. Weekly specials expand your options further. To start, try *sopes* (fried disks of *masa,* or corn flour) topped with beans, cheese, and onions or stuffed tortillas known as *gringas.* Many main-course descriptions include the dish's date and place of origin (owner Epi Guzman's family figures prominently), but even the options that have no pedigree are delicious. I especially like spinach a la Carlos (with potatoes in a garlic sauce) and *pollo Chiapas* (chicken breast marinated in orange and annatto sauce). For the full experience, try one of the three versions of sangria and finish with cinnamon-infused coffee and unbelievable flan.

858 Broadway, Powderhouse Sq., Somerville. © 617/623-5411. www.tuyyomexicanfonda.com. Reservations recommended; accepted Sun–Wed. Main courses $10–$16. MC, V. Mon–Thurs 5–10pm; Fri–Sat 4–11pm; Sun 4–9pm. T: Red Line to Davis, 10-min. walk (follow College Ave. to the traffic circle and take sharp left).

INEXPENSIVE

S&S Restaurant ★★ DELI *Es* is Yiddish for "eat," and this Cambridge classic is as straightforward as its name ("eat and eat"). Founded in 1919 by the great-grandmother of the current owners, the wildly popular brunch spot draws what seems to be half of Cambridge at busy times on weekends. It's northeast of Harvard Square and west of MIT, and worth a visit during the week, too. With huge windows and lots of light wood and plants, it looks contemporary, but the brunch offerings are traditional dishes such as pancakes, waffles, fruit salad, and fantastic omelets and cinnamon rolls. The bagels are among the best in the area; you'll also find traditional deli items (corned beef, pastrami, tongue, potato pancakes, and blintzes), and breakfast anytime. Be early for brunch, or plan to spend a good chunk of your Saturday or Sunday standing around people-watching and getting hungry. Or dine on a weekday and soak up the neighborhood atmosphere.

1334 Cambridge St., Inman Sq. © 617/354-0777. www.sandsrestaurant.com. Main courses $4–$14. AE, MC, V. Mon–Wed 7am–11pm; Thurs–Fri 7am–midnight; Sat 8am–midnight; Sun 8am–10pm; brunch Sat–Sun until 4pm. T: Red Line to Harvard, then no. 69 (Harvard-Lechmere) bus to Inman Sq.; or Red Line to Central, 10-min. walk on Prospect St.

8

What to See & Do in Boston

Whether you want to immerse yourself in the colonial era or just cruise around the harbor, Boston offers something for everyone, and plenty of it. Throw out your preconceptions of the city as some sort of open-air history museum—although that's certainly one of the guises it can assume—and allow your interests to dictate where you go.

It's possible but not advisable to take in most of the major attractions in 2 or 3 days if you don't linger anywhere too long. For a more enjoyable, less rushed visit, plan fewer activities and spend more time on them. For descriptions of suggested itineraries, see p. 52.

Mergers and budget cuts have slashed corporate and government contributions to many cultural organizations. Admissions fees and hours in this chapter are current at press time, but establishments that rely heavily on outside aid may cost a bit more or be keeping shorter hours by the time you visit. If you're on a tight budget or schedule, call ahead.

Increased security has led some attractions to require that adult patrons show ID before entering. Double-check that you have your license or passport before you leave the hotel.

The **Boston Tea Party Ship & Museum** (© **617/269-7150;** www.bostonteapartyship.com) closed after a fire in 2001; at press time, it was scheduled to reopen in 2006. Plans called for the construction of two more ships, doubling the size of the museum, and adding a tearoom. If you hope to visit, call ahead to see whether it's open.

1 The Top Attractions

The attractions in this section are easily accessible by **public transportation;** given the difficulty and expense of parking, it's preferable to take the T everywhere. Even the Kennedy Library, which has a large free parking lot, operates a free shuttle bus that connects it to the Red Line. To maximize your enjoyment, try to visit these attractions during relatively slow times. If possible, especially in the summer, sightsee on weekdays; if you're traveling without children, aim for times when school is in session. And if you're in town on a July or August weekend, relax and try to convince yourself that you love crowds.

Faneuil Hall Marketplace ★★ Kids   Since Boston's most popular attraction opened in 1976, cities all over the country have imitated the "festival market" concept. Each complex of shops, food counters, restaurants, bars, and public spaces reflects its city, and Faneuil Hall Marketplace is no exception. Its popularity with visitors and suburbanites is so great that you might understandably think the only Bostonians in the crowd are employees.

The marketplace includes five buildings—the central three-building complex is on the National Register of Historic Places—set on brick and stone plazas that teem with

Boston Attractions

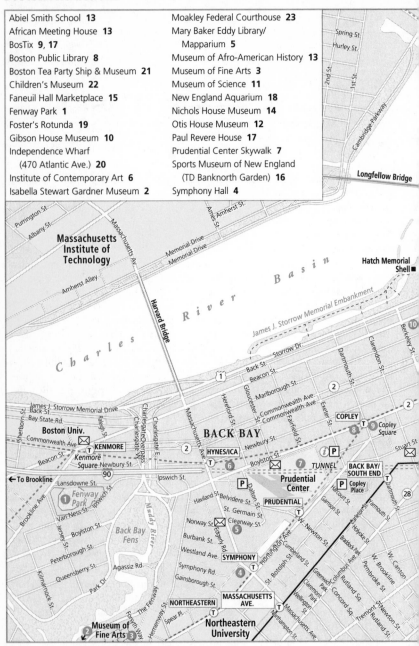

Abiel Smith School **13**
African Meeting House **13**
BosTix **9, 17**
Boston Public Library **8**
Boston Tea Party Ship & Museum **21**
Children's Museum **22**
Faneuil Hall Marketplace **15**
Fenway Park **1**
Foster's Rotunda **19**
Gibson House Museum **10**
Independence Wharf
    (470 Atlantic Ave.) **20**
Institute of Contemporary Art **6**
Isabella Stewart Gardner Museum **2**

Moakley Federal Courthouse **23**
Mary Baker Eddy Library/
    Mapparium **5**
Museum of Afro-American History **13**
Museum of Fine Arts **3**
Museum of Science **11**
New England Aquarium **18**
Nichols House Museum **14**
Otis House Museum **12**
Paul Revere House **17**
Prudential Center Skywalk **7**
Sports Museum of New England
    (TD Banknorth Garden) **16**
Symphony Hall **4**

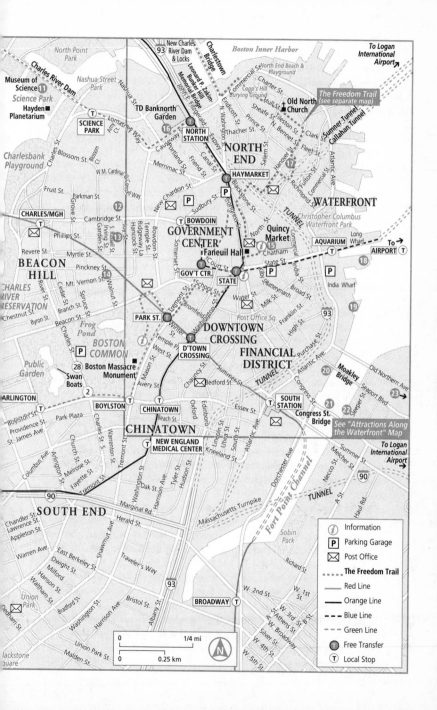

crowds shopping, eating, performing, watching performers, and just people-watching. In warm weather, it's busy from just after dawn until well past dark. **Quincy Market** (you'll also hear the whole complex called by that name) is the central three-level Greek revival–style building. It reopened after extensive renovations on August 26, 1976, 150 years after Mayor Josiah Quincy opened the original market. The **South Market building** reopened on August 26, 1977, the **North Market building** on August 26, 1978.

The central corridor of Quincy Market is the food court, where you can find anything from a fish taco to a full Greek dinner, a slice of pizza to an ice cream sundae. On either side, under glass canopies, are full-service restaurants as well as pushcarts that sell everything from crafts created by New England artisans to hokey souvenirs. Here you'll find a bar that exactly replicates the set of the TV show *Cheers.* In the plaza between the **South Canopy** and the South Market building is an **information kiosk,** and throughout the complex you'll find a mix of predictable chain stores and unique shops (see chapter 10). On warm evenings, the tables that spill outdoors from

Value **Let's Make a Deal**

As you plan your sightseeing, consider these money-saving options:

If you concentrate on the included attractions, a **CityPass** offers great savings. It's a booklet of tickets (so you can go straight to the entrance) to the Harvard Museum of Natural History, the Kennedy Library, the New England Aquarium, the Museum of Fine Arts, the Museum of Science, and the Prudential Center Skywalk. If you visit all five, the price gives adults a 50% savings. It feels like an even better deal on a steamy day when the line at the aquarium is long. At press time, the cost was $37 for adults, $26 for youths 3 to 17, subject to change as admission prices rise. The passes, good for 9 days from the date of purchase (except in the winter, when they're good for up to 3½ months), are on sale at participating attractions, through the Greater Boston Convention & Visitors Bureau (② 800/SEE-BOSTON; www.bostonusa.com), through some hotel concierge desks and travel agents, and from www.citypass.com.

The **Go Boston Card** (② 617/742-5950; www.gobostoncard.com) includes admission to more than 30 Boston-area museums and attractions, plus dining and shopping discounts, a guidebook, and a 2-day Beantown Trolley ticket. You'll want to do some careful planning before you invest in this card—it costs $45 for 1 day, $75 for 2 days, $95 for 3 days, and $115 for 5 days, with discounts for children and winter travelers—but if you strategize wisely, it's a great value. The Go Boston Card is available through the website; at the Boston Common and Prudential Center visitor information centers; from the Gray Line office at the Transportation Building, 16 Charles St. S.; at many concierge desks; and as part of numerous hotel packages.

The MBTA's **Boston Visitor Pass** (② 877/927-7277 or 617/222-5218; www.mbta.com) can be a good deal—but only if you plan to use public transit often. See p. 68.

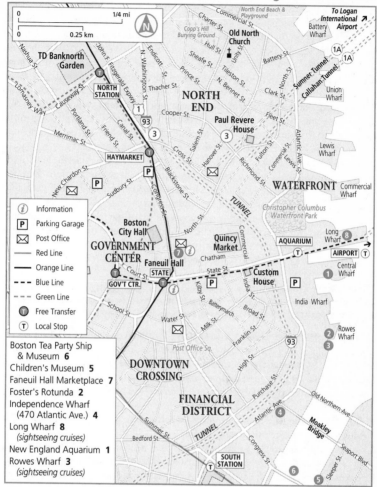

Boston Tea Party Ship
& Museum **6**
Children's Museum **5**
Faneuil Hall Marketplace **7**
Foster's Rotunda **2**
Independence Wharf
(470 Atlantic Ave.) **4**
Long Wharf **8**
(*sightseeing cruises*)
New England Aquarium **1**
Rowes Wharf **3**
(*sightseeing cruises*)

the restaurants and bars fill with people. One constant since the year after the market—the *original* market—opened is **Durgin-Park** ★★★ (p. 124), a traditional New England restaurant with traditionally crabby waitresses.

The original **Faneuil Hall** ★ sometimes gets overlooked, but it's well worth a visit. Known as the "Cradle of Liberty" for its role as a center of inspirational (some might say inflammatory) speech in the years leading to the Revolutionary War, the building opened in 1742 and was expanded using a Charles Bulfinch design in 1805. National Park Service rangers give **free 20-minute talks** every half-hour from 9am to 5pm in the second-floor auditorium.

Between North, Congress, and State sts. and Atlantic Ave. ⓒ 617/523-1300. www.faneuilhallmarketplace.com. Marketplace Mon–Sat 10am–9pm, Sun noon–6pm. Food court opens earlier; some restaurants close later. T: Green Line to Government Center, Orange Line to Haymarket or State, or Blue Line to Aquarium or State.

Isabella Stewart Gardner Museum ★★ Isabella Stewart Gardner (1840–1924) was an incorrigible individualist long before strong-willed behavior was acceptable for women in polite Boston society, and her iconoclasm paid off for art lovers. "Mrs. Jack" designed her exquisite home in the style of a 15th-century Venetian palace and filled it with European, American, and Asian painting and sculpture, much of it chosen with the help of her friend and protégé Bernard Berenson. You'll see works by Titian, Botticelli, Raphael, Rembrandt, Matisse, and Mrs. Gardner's friends James McNeill Whistler and John Singer Sargent. Titian's magnificent *Europa,* which many scholars consider his finest work, is one of the most important Renaissance paintings in the United States. I took a casual poll of local travel experts while writing the 2005 edition of this book, and the Gardner was the most popular museum.

The building, which opened to the public after Mrs. Gardner's death, holds a glorious hodgepodge of furniture and architectural details imported from European churches and palaces. The *pièce de résistance* is the magnificent skylit courtyard, filled year-round with fresh flowers from the museum greenhouse. Although the terms of Mrs. Gardner's will forbid changing the arrangement of the museum's content, there has been some evolution: A special exhibition gallery features two or three changing shows a year, often by contemporary artists in residence.

See p. 237 for a description of the **concert series** ★ (© **617/734-1359**). The cafe serves lunch and desserts, and there's an excellent gift shop.

280 The Fenway. © 617/566-1401. www.gardnermuseum.org. Admission adults $11 weekends, $10 weekdays; $7 seniors; $5 college students with ID; free for children under 18 and adults named Isabella with ID. Tues–Sun (and some Mon holidays) 11am–5pm. Closed Thanksgiving, Dec 25, and Dec 31. T: Green Line E to Museum.

John F. Kennedy Presidential Library and Museum ★★ *Kids* The Kennedy era springs to life at this dramatic library, museum, and educational research complex overlooking Dorchester Bay. It captures the 35th president's accomplishments and legacy in video and sound recordings and fascinating displays of memorabilia and photos. Far from being a static experience, it changes regularly, with temporary shows and reinterpreted displays that highlight and complement the permanent installations. *JFK in World War II,* an exhibit scheduled to run through April 2006, explores Lt. Kennedy's experiences in the Pacific theater.

Your visit begins with a 17-minute film narrated by John F. Kennedy—a detail that seems eerie for a moment, then perfectly natural. Through skillfully edited audio clips, he discusses his childhood, education, war experience, and early political career. Then you enter the museum to spend as much time as you like on each exhibit. Starting with the 1960 presidential campaign, the displays immerse you in the era. The galleries hold campaign souvenirs, a film of Kennedy debating Richard Nixon and delivering his inaugural address, a replica of the Oval Office, gifts from foreign dignitaries, letters, documents, and keepsakes. There's a film about the Cuban Missile Crisis and displays on Attorney General Robert F. Kennedy, First Lady Jacqueline Bouvier Kennedy, the civil rights movement, the Peace Corps, the space program, and the Kennedy family. As the tour winds down, you pass through a darkened chamber where news reports of John Kennedy's assassination and funeral play. The final room, the soaring glass-enclosed

More JFK

For details about visiting President Kennedy's birthplace in suburban Brookline, see p. 173.

---

pavilion that is the heart of the I. M. Pei design, affords a glorious view of the water and the Boston skyline.

Columbia Point. (*C*) 866/JFK-1960 or 617/514-1600. www.jfklibrary.org. Admission $10 adults; $8 seniors, students with ID, and youths 13–17; free for children under 13. Surcharges may apply for special exhibitions. Daily 9am–5pm (last film begins at 3:55pm). Closed Jan 1, Thanksgiving, and Dec 25. T: Red Line to JFK/UMass, then take free shuttle bus, which runs every 20 min. By car, take Southeast Expressway (I-93/Rte. 3) south to Exit 15 (Morrissey Blvd./JFK Library), turn left onto Columbia Rd., and follow signs to free parking lot.

Museum of Fine Arts ✯✯✯ *Kids*   One of the world's great art museums, the MFA works nonstop to become even more accessible and interesting. Every installation reflects a curatorial attitude that makes even those who go in with a feeling of obligation leave with a sense of discovery and wonder. That includes children, who can launch a scavenger hunt, admire the mummies, or participate in family-friendly programs scheduled year-round (and extra offerings during school vacations).

Among the numerous highlights of the magnificent collections are the **Impressionist** ✯✯✯ paintings (including one of the largest collections of Monets outside of Paris), Asian and Old Kingdom Egyptian collections, classical art, Buddhist temple, and medieval sculpture and tapestries.

The works that you might find most familiar are paintings and sculpture by Americans and Europeans. Some favorites: Renoir's *Dance at Bougival,* Childe Hassam's *Boston Common at Twilight,* Gilbert Stuart's 1796 portrait of George Washington, John Singleton Copley's 1768 portrait of Paul Revere (which looks suspiciously like the Samuel Adams beer logo), a bronze casting of Edgar Degas's sculpture *Little Dancer,* John Singer Sargent's *The Daughters of Edward Darley Boit,* Gauguin's *Where Do We Come From? What Are We? Where Are We Going?,* and Fitz Hugh Lane's Luminist masterpieces. There are also outstanding holdings of prints, photographs, furnishings, and decorative arts, including the finest collection of Paul Revere silver in the world.

None of this comes cheap: The MFA's adult admission fee (which covers two visits within 10 days) is among the highest in the country. A Boston CityPass or Go Boston card (see the "Let's Make a Deal" box on p. 154) is a bargain if you plan to visit enough of the other included attractions.

To begin, pick up a floor plan at the information desk or take a free guided tour (weekdays except Mon holidays 10:30am–3pm, Wed at 6:15pm, and Sat–Sun 11am–3pm). The I. M. Pei–designed West Wing (1981) contains the main entrance, an auditorium, and an atrium with a tree-lined "sidewalk" cafe. There are also a restaurant and a cafeteria. The excellent Museum Shop carries abundant souvenirs and a huge book selection.

An ambitious expansion project began in 2005. While construction proceeds, the museum is rearranging some collections and closing some exhibition spaces. Check ahead before visiting if you have your heart set on seeing a particular piece of art.

(*Kids*) **On Top of the World**

The **Prudential Center Skywalk** ★★, 800 Boylston St. (✆ **617/859-0648**), offers a 360-degree view of Boston and far beyond. From the enclosed observation deck on the 50th floor of the Prudential Tower, you can see for miles, even (when it's clear) as far as the mountains of southern New Hampshire to the north and the beaches of Cape Cod to the south. Away from the windows, interactive audiovisual exhibits chronicle the city's history. The admission price includes a narrated audio tour. Call before visiting because the space sometimes closes for private events. Hours are 10am to 10pm daily. Admission is $9.50 for adults, $7 for seniors, and $6.50 for children under 12; adults must show a photo ID to enter the Prudential Tower. T: Green Line E to Prudential, or B, C, or D to Hynes/ICA.

Special exhibitions during the lifespan of this book include *Ansel Adams* (Aug 21–Dec 31, 2005), which includes some 175 photographs; *West African Gold: Akan Regalia from the Glassell Collection* (Nov 2, 2005–March 26, 2006); *Cubism* (Dec 7, 2005–Apr 16, 2006); and *David Hockney Portraits* (Feb 26–May 14, 2006).

465 Huntington Ave. ✆ 617/267-9300. www.mfa.org. Admission $15 adults, $13 students and seniors when entire museum is open; or $13 and $11, respectively, when only West Wing is open. Children under 18 $6.50 on school days before 3pm, otherwise free. Admission good for 2 visits within 10 days. Voluntary contribution ($15 suggested) Wed 4–9:45pm. Surcharges may apply for special exhibitions. No admission fee for Museum Shop, library, restaurants, or auditoriums. Entire museum Sat–Tues 10am–4:45pm, Wed 10am–9:45pm, Thurs–Fri 10am–5pm; West Wing only, Thurs–Fri 5–9:45pm. Closed Jan 1, Patriots Day, July 4, Thanksgiving, and Dec 25. T: Green Line E to Museum, or Orange Line to Ruggles.

Museum of Science ★★★ (*Kids*) For the ultimate pain-free educational experience, head to the Museum of Science. The demonstrations, experiments, and interactive displays introduce facts and concepts so effortlessly that everyone winds up learning something. Take a couple of hours or a whole day to explore the permanent and temporary exhibits, most of them hands-on and all of them great fun.

Among the 500-plus exhibits, you might meet a dinosaur or a live butterfly, find out how much you'd weigh on the moon, battle urban traffic (in a computer model), or climb into a space module. Activity centers and exhibits focus on fields of interest—natural history (with live animals), computers, the human body—while others take an interdisciplinary approach. **Investigate!** teaches visitors to think like scientists, formulating questions, finding evidence, and drawing conclusions through activities such as strapping on a skin sensor to measure reactions to stimuli or sifting through an archaeological site. In the **Seeing Is Deceiving** section, auditory and visual illusions challenge your belief in what is "real." The **Science in the Park** exhibit introduces the concepts of Newtonian physics through familiar recreational tools such as playground equipment and skateboards.

The separate-admission **theaters** are worth planning for. Even if you're skipping the exhibits, try to see a show. If you're making a day of it, buy all your tickets at once—shows sometimes sell out. Tickets are for sale in person and, subject to a service charge, over the phone and on the Web. The **Mugar Omni Theater** ★★★, which shows

IMAX movies, is an intense experience, bombarding you with images on a five-story domed screen and digital sound. The engulfing sensations and steep pitch of the seating area will have you hanging on for dear life, whether the film is about Bengal tigers, the Nile, or volcanoes, earthquakes, and tornados. Features change every 4 to 6 months. The **Charles Hayden Planetarium** 👾👾 takes visitors into space with daily star shows and shows on special topics that change several times a year. On weekends, rock-music laser shows take over. At the entrance is a hands-on astronomy exhibit called **Welcome to the Universe.**

The museum has a terrific gift shop, with toys and games that promote learning without lecturing. The ground-floor Galaxy Cafés have spectacular views of the skyline and river. There's a parking garage on the premises, but it's on a busy street, and entering and exiting can be harrowing; take the T.

Science Park, off O'Brien Hwy. on bridge between Boston and Cambridge. 📞 **617/723-2500**. www.mos.org. Admission to exhibit halls $14 adults, $12 seniors, $11 children 3–11, free for children under 3. Admission to Mugar Omni Theater, Hayden Planetarium, or laser shows $8.50 adults, $7.50 seniors, $6.50 children 3–11, free for children under 3. July 5 to Labor Day Sat–Thurs 9am–7pm, Fri 9am–9pm; day after Labor Day to July 4th Sat–Thurs 9am–5pm, Fri 9am–9pm. Closed Thanksgiving and Dec 25. T: Green Line to Science Park.

New England Aquarium 👾 *Kids*   This complex is home to more than 15,000 fish and aquatic mammals, and at busy times, it seems to contain at least that many people—in July and August, try to make this your first stop of the morning, especially on weekends. You'll want to spend at least half a day here, and huge afternoon crowds can make getting around painfully slow. Also consider investing in a Boston CityPass (see the "Let's Make a Deal" box on p. 154); it allows you to skip the ticket line, which can be uncomfortably long, and may represent a savings on the steep admission charge. The **Simons IMAX Theatre** 👾👾👾, which has its own building, hours, and admission fees, is worth planning for, too. Its 85-foot-by-65-foot screen shows 3-D films with digital sound that concentrate on the natural world. It's a dizzying experience.

The focal point of the main building is the four-story, 200,000-gallon **Giant Ocean Tank.** A four-story spiral ramp encircles the tank, which contains a replica of a Caribbean coral reef and an assortment of sea creatures that seem to coexist amazingly well. Part of the reason for the peace might be that scuba divers feed the sharks twice a day. The two-floor **Amazing Jellies** exhibit is home to hundreds of eye-catching jellyfish. At the **Edge of the Sea** exhibit, visitors can touch the sea stars, sea urchins, and horseshoe crabs in the tide pool. The **Aquarium Medical Center** is especially involving—it's a working veterinary hospital. Other exhibits show off tropical sea creatures (including clownfish—you know, Nemo), freshwater specimens, denizens of the Amazon, marine life in the Gulf of Maine, and the ecology of Boston Harbor.

Finds Gone Fishing

Many fascinating interactive exhibits from the defunct Computer Museum now delight patrons of the Museum of Science. The most popular is the **Virtual Fish-Tank** 👾👾👾, which uses 3-D computer graphics and character-animation software that allows visitors to design their own virtual fish. You can even "build" fish on your home computer (visit www.virtualfishtank.com) and launch them at the museum.

Tips   A Note on Online Ticketing

Many museums and other attractions sell tickets online, subject to a service charge, through their websites or by linking to an agency. This can be handy, but it can also cost you some flexibility and perhaps some money. If there's even a small chance that your plans will change, make sure you **understand the refund policy** before you enter your credit card info—you may not be able to return or exchange prepaid tickets.

Discounts are available when you combine a visit to the aquarium with an IMAX film or a whale watch (p. 190).

Central Wharf (off State St. and Atlantic Ave.). ✆ 617/973-5200. www.newenglandaquarium.org. Admission $16 adults, $14 seniors, $9 children 3–11. Free for children under 3 and for those visiting only the outdoor exhibits, cafe, and gift shop. July to Labor Day Mon–Thurs 9am–6pm, Fri–Sun and holidays 9am–7pm; day after Labor Day to June Mon–Fri 9am–5pm, Sat–Sun and holidays 9am–6pm. Simons IMAX Theatre: ✆ 866/815-4629 or 617/973-5206. Tickets $9 adults, $7 seniors and children 3–11. Thurs–Sat 10am–8pm; Sun–Mon 10am–6pm. Closed Dec 25 and until noon Jan 1. T: Blue Line to Aquarium.

2 The Freedom Trail

A line of red paint or red brick on the sidewalk, the 3-mile **Freedom Trail** ★★★ links 16 historic sights, many of them associated with the Revolution and the early days of the United States. The route cuts across downtown, passing through the busy shopping area around Downtown Crossing, the Financial District, and the North End, on the way to Charlestown. Markers identify the stops, and plaques point the way from one to the next.

The nonprofit **Freedom Trail Foundation** (✆ 617/357-8300; www.thefreedom trail.org) is an excellent resource as you plan your visit. Call for a guide or, even better, check out the interactive website. It lists a plethora of tours, talks, and other activities, and if you're interested, it offers the only legal way to rub gravestones.

This section lists the stops on the trail in the customary order, from Boston Common to the Bunker Hill Monument. It's important to remember that this is the *suggested* route, and nobody's checking up on you. You don't have to visit every stop or even go in order—you can skip around, start in Charlestown and work backward, visit different sights on different days, or even (horrors!) omit some sights. Here's a suggestion: If you find yourself sighing and saying "should" a lot, take a break.

A hard-core history fiend who peers at every artifact and reads every plaque can easily spend 4 hours along the trail. A family with restless children will probably appreciate the enforced efficiency of a free 90-minute ranger-led tour. The excursions, from the **Boston National Historic Park Visitor Center,** 15 State St. (✆ 617/242-5642; www.nps.gov/bost), cover the "heart" of the trail, from the Old South Meeting House to the Old North Church. At press time, tours were offered daily from mid-April to November. You don't need a reservation, but call for schedules and to check whether off-season tours are available.

The best time to start on the trail is in the morning. During the summer and fall, aim for a weekday if possible. Try not to set out later than midafternoon because attractions will be closing and you'll run into the evening rush hour.

The Freedom Trail

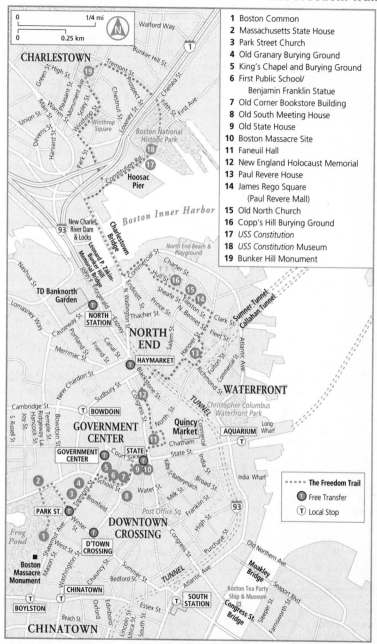

1 Boston Common
2 Massachusetts State House
3 Park Street Church
4 Old Granary Burying Ground
5 King's Chapel and Burying Ground
6 First Public School/
   Benjamin Franklin Statue
7 Old Corner Bookstore Building
8 Old South Meeting House
9 Old State House
10 Boston Massacre Site
11 Faneuil Hall
12 New England Holocaust Memorial
13 Paul Revere House
14 James Rego Square
   (Paul Revere Mall)
15 Old North Church
16 Copp's Hill Burying Ground
17 USS Constitution
18 USS Constitution Museum
19 Bunker Hill Monument

Moments A Pep Talk: Get Lost!

Almost nothing is as stereotypical or as distressing as sightseers shuffling along in lockstep, looking only at what's described in their travel guides and going only where the Freedom Trail takes them. This is a _guide_book, not the boot-camp curriculum, and getting really lost in downtown Boston is nearly impossible—it's just too small. If time allows, wander away from the trail and look around on your own. I promise you won't be sorry.

Boston Common In 1634, when their settlement was just 4 years old, the town fathers paid the Rev. William Blackstone £30 for this property. In 1640 it was set aside as common land. The 45 or so acres of the country's oldest public park have served as a cow pasture, a military camp, and the site of hangings, protest marches, and visits by dignitaries. Today the Common is a bit run-down, especially compared with the adjacent Public Garden, but it buzzes with activity all day. You might see a demonstration, a musical performance, a picnic lunch, or a game of tag—almost anything but a cow. Cows have been banned since 1830, which seems to be one of the few events related to the Common that isn't commemorated with a plaque.

One of the loveliest markers is on this route; head up the hill from the train station inside the fence. At Beacon Street is a **memorial** _★★★_ designed by Augustus Saint-Gaudens to celebrate the deeds (indeed, the very existence) of Col. Robert Gould Shaw and the Union Army's **54th Massachusetts Colored Regiment,** who fought in the Civil War. You might remember the story of the first American army unit made up of free black soldiers from the movie _Glory._

To continue on the Freedom Trail: Cross Beacon Street.

Between Beacon, Park, Tremont, Boylston, and Charles sts. Visitor information center: 146 Tremont St. ℂ **888/SEE-BOSTON** or 617/536-4100. www.bostonusa.com. Mon–Sat 8:30am–5pm; Sun 9am–5pm. T: Green or Red Line to Park St.

Massachusetts State House Boston is one of the only American cities where a building whose cornerstone was laid in 1795 (by Gov. Samuel Adams) would be called the "new" anything. Nevertheless, this is the new State House, as opposed to the Old State House (see below). The great Federal-era architect Charles Bulfinch designed the central building of the state capitol, and in 1802 copper sheathing manufactured by Paul Revere replaced the shingles on the landmark dome. Gold leaf now covers the dome; during World War II blackouts, it was painted black. The state legislature, or Massachusetts General Court, meets here. The House of Representatives congregates under a wooden fish, the **Sacred Cod.** John Rowe, known as "Merchant" Rowe (Rowes Wharf bears his name), donated the carving in 1784 as a reminder of the importance of fishing to the local economy. Take a self-guided tour or call ahead to schedule a conducted tour.

Whether or not you go inside, be sure to study some of the many statues outside. Subjects range from **Mary Dyer,** a Quaker hanged on the Common in 1660 for refusing to abandon her religious beliefs, to Pres. **John F. Kennedy.** The 60-foot monument at the rear (off Bowdoin St.) illustrates Beacon Hill's original height, before the top was shorn off to use in 19th-century landfill projects.

To continue on the Freedom Trail: Walk down Park Street (which Bulfinch laid out in 1804) to Tremont Street.

Beacon St. at Park St. © 617/727-3676. www.mass.gov/statehouse. Mon–Fri 9am–5pm. Free tours Mon–Fri 10am–3:30pm. T: Green or Red Line to Park St., or Blue Line to Bowdoin (weekdays only).

Park Street Church   Henry James described this 1809 structure with a 217-foot steeple as "the most interesting mass of bricks and mortar in America." The church has accumulated an impressive number of firsts: The first missionaries to Hawaii left from here in 1819; the prominent abolitionist William Lloyd Garrison gave his first antislavery speech here on July 4, 1829; and "America" (commonly known as "My Country 'Tis of Thee") was first sung here on July 4, 1831. You're standing on **"Brimstone Corner,"** named either for the passion of the Congregational ministers who declaimed from the pulpit or for the fact that gunpowder (made from brimstone) was stored in the basement during the War of 1812. This was part of the site of a huge granary that became a public building after the Revolutionary War. In the 1790s, the sails for USS *Constitution* ("Old Ironsides") were manufactured in that building.

   To continue on the Freedom Trail: Walk away from the Common on Tremont Street.

1 Park St. © 617/523-3383. www.parkstreet.org. Tours July–Aug Tues–Sat 9:30am–3:30pm. Sun services year-round 8:30 and 11am, 4 and 6pm. T: Green or Red Line to Park St.

Old Granary Burying Ground ✪   This cemetery, established in 1660, was once part of Boston Common. You'll see the graves of patriots **Samuel Adams, Paul Revere, John Hancock,** and **James Otis;** merchant **Peter Faneuil** (spelled "Funal"); and Benjamin Franklin's parents. Also buried here are the victims of the **Boston Massacre** (see below) and the wife of Isaac Vergoose, who is believed to be **"Mother Goose"** of nursery rhyme fame. Note that gravestone rubbing, however tempting, is illegal in Boston's historic cemeteries.

   To continue on the Freedom Trail: Turn left as you leave the cemetery and continue 1½ blocks on Tremont Street.

Tremont St. at Bromfield St. Daily 9am–5pm (until 3pm in winter). T: Green or Red Line to Park St.

King's Chapel and Burying Ground   Architect Peter Harrison sent the plans for this Georgian-style building from Newport, Rhode Island, in 1749. Rather than replacing the existing wooden chapel, the granite edifice was constructed around it. Completed in 1754, it was the first Anglican church in Boston. George III sent gifts, as did Queen Anne and William and Mary, who presented the communion table and chancel tablets (still in use today) before the church was even built. The Puritan colonists had little use for the royal religion; after the Revolution, this became the first Unitarian church in the new nation. Today, the church conducts Unitarian Universalist services using the Anglican Book of Common Prayer.

Finds **Listen Up: The Audio Freedom Trail**

The **Freedom Trail Foundation** (© 617/357-8300; www.thefreedomtrail.org) rents handheld digital audio players, for use with or without headphones, that allow visitors to take a narrated tour of the Freedom Trail at their own pace. The 2-hour narrative includes interviews, sound effects, and music. Players rent for $15 (credit cards only); they're available at the Boston Common Visitor Center, 146 Tremont St., and can be dropped off there or at several other locations.

The **burying ground** ★★, on Tremont Street, is the oldest in the city; it dates to 1630. Among the scary colonial headstones (winged skulls are a popular decoration) are the graves of **John Winthrop,** the first governor of the Massachusetts Bay Colony; **William Dawes,** who rode with Paul Revere; **Elizabeth Pain,** the model for Hester Prynne in Nathaniel Hawthorne's novel *The Scarlet Letter;* and **Mary Chilton,** the first female colonist to step ashore on Plymouth Rock.

To continue on the Freedom Trail: Follow the trail back along Tremont Street and turn left onto School Street.

58 Tremont St. ℂ 617/523-1749. www.kings-chapel.org. Chapel: Year-round Sat 9am–4pm, summer Mon and Thurs–Fri 9am–4pm; check at entrance for up-to-date hours. $2 donation suggested. Services Wed 12:15pm, Sun 11am. Burying ground: Daily 8am–5:30pm (until 3pm in winter). T: Green or Blue Line to Government Center.

First Public School/Benjamin Franklin Statue   A colorful folk-art mosaic in the sidewalk marks the site of the first public school in the country. It was founded in 1634, 2 years before Harvard College. Samuel Adams, Benjamin Franklin, John Hancock, and Cotton Mather studied there. The original building (1645) was demolished to make way for the expansion of King's Chapel, and the school moved across the street. Now called Boston Latin School, the prestigious institution later moved to the Fenway neighborhood. Other alumni include Charles Bulfinch, Ralph Waldo Emerson, George Santayana, Arthur Fiedler, and Leonard Bernstein.

Behind the fence in the courtyard to your left is the **Benjamin Franklin statue,** the first portrait statue erected in Boston (1856). Franklin was born in Boston in 1706 and was apprenticed to his half-brother James, a printer, but they got along so poorly that in 1723 Benjamin ran away to Philadelphia. Plaques on the base of the statue describe Franklin's numerous accomplishments. The lovely granite building behind the statue is **Old City Hall** (1865), designed in Second Empire style by Arthur Gilman (who laid out the Back Bay) and Gridley J. F. Bryant. The administration moved to Government Center in 1969, and the building now houses commercial tenants.

To continue on the Freedom Trail: Follow School Street to Washington Street.

School St. at City Hall Ave. (between Tremont and Washington sts.). T: Blue or Orange Line to State.

Old Corner Bookstore Building   Built in 1718, this building stands on a plot of land that was once home to the religious reformer Anne Hutchinson, who was excommunicated and expelled from Boston in 1638 for heresy. In the middle of the 19th century, the little brick building held the publishing house of Ticknor & Fields, which effectively made this the literary center of America. Publisher James Fields, known as "Jamie," counted among his friends Henry Wadsworth Longfellow, James Russell Lowell, Henry David Thoreau, Ralph Waldo Emerson, Nathaniel Hawthorne, and Harriet Beecher Stowe. For many years this was the Globe Corner Bookstore, which is now in Harvard Square (p. 218).

To continue on the Freedom Trail: Turn right and walk 1 block.

3 School St. T: Blue or Orange Line to State.

Old South Meeting House ★   Look for the clock tower that tops this religious and political gathering place, best known as the site of an important event leading to the Revolution. On December 16, 1773, a restive crowd of several thousand, too big to fit into Faneuil Hall, gathered here. They were waiting for word from the governor about whether three ships full of tea—priced to undercut the cost of smuggled tea and force the colonists to trade with merchants approved by the Crown—would be sent back to England from Boston. The ships were not, and revolutionaries poorly disguised as Mohawks cast the tea into the harbor. The meeting house commemorates that uprising, the **Boston Tea Party.** You can even see a vial of the tea.

Originally built in 1670 and replaced by the current structure in 1729, the building underwent extensive renovations in the 1990s. In 1872, a devastating fire that destroyed most of downtown stopped at Old South, a phenomenon considered evidence of the building's power. An interactive multimedia exhibit, *Voices of Protest,* tells the story of the events that took place here.

The meeting house frequently schedules speeches, readings, panel discussions, and children's activities, often with a colonial theme. Each December, it stages a reenactment of the debate that led to the tea party. Call ahead or check the website for schedules.

To continue on the Freedom Trail: Exit through the gift shop and look across Milk Street to see **Benjamin Franklin's birthplace.** In a little house at 17 Milk St., Franklin was born in 1706, the 15th child of Josiah Franklin. The house is long gone, but look across at the second floor of what's now 1 Milk St. When the building went up after the fire of 1872, the architect guaranteed that the Founding Father wouldn't be forgotten: A bust and the words BIRTHPLACE OF FRANKLIN adorn the facade.

Now backtrack on Washington Street (passing Spring Lane, one of the first streets in Boston and originally the site of a real spring) to State Street.

310 Washington St. Ⓒ **617/482-6439.** www.oldsouthmeetinghouse.org. Admission $5 adults, $4 seniors and students, $1 children 6–18, free for children under 6. Freedom Trail ticket (with Old State House and Paul Revere House) $10 adults, $3 children. Daily Apr–Oct 9:30am–5pm; Nov–Mar 10am–4pm. T: Blue or Orange Line to State St.

Old State House   Built in 1713, this brick structure served as the seat of colonial government before the Revolution and as the state capitol until 1797. From its balcony, the Declaration of Independence was first read to Bostonians on July 18, 1776. In 1789, Pres. George Washington reviewed a parade from here. The exterior decorations are particularly interesting—the clock was installed in place of a sundial, and the gilded lion and unicorn are reproductions of the original symbols of British rule that were ripped from the facade and burned the day the Declaration of Independence was read.

Inside is the **Bostonian Society's museum** ★ of the city's history. The society was founded in 1881 to save this building, which was badly deteriorated and, incredibly, was about to be sold and shipped to Chicago. Exhibits include an introductory video on the history of the building, a meter that illustrates the proximity of the Blue Line subway (which makes the floor vibrate), and displays that focus on the Revolutionary period and more recent history.

To continue on the Freedom Trail: Leave the building, turn left, and walk half a block.

206 Washington St. Ⓒ **617/720-1713,** ext. 21. www.bostonhistory.org. Admission $5 adults, $4 seniors and students, $1 children 6–18, free for children under 6. Freedom Trail ticket (with Old South Meeting House and Paul Revere House) $10 adults, $3 children. Daily 9am–5pm. T: Blue or Orange Line to State.

Boston Massacre Site   A ring of cobblestones on a traffic island marks the location of the skirmish that helped consolidate the spirit of rebellion in the colonies. On March 5, 1770, angered at the presence of royal troops in Boston, colonists threw snowballs, garbage, rocks, and other debris at a group of redcoats. The soldiers panicked and fired into the crowd, killing five men. Their graves, including that of Crispus Attucks, the first black man to die in the Revolution, are in the Old Granary Burying Ground.

To continue on the Freedom Trail: Turn left onto Congress Street and walk down the hill. Faneuil Hall will be on your right.

State St. at Devonshire St. T: Blue or Orange Line to State.

Faneuil Hall ⚡ Built in 1742 (and enlarged using a Charles Bulfinch design in 1805), this building was a gift to the town from prosperous merchant Peter Faneuil. This "Cradle of Liberty" rang with speeches by orators such as Samuel Adams—whose statue stands outside the Congress Street entrance—in the years leading to the Revolution. Abolitionists, temperance advocates, and suffragists also used the hall as a pulpit. The upstairs is still a public meeting and concert hall, and downstairs holds retail space, all according to Faneuil's will. The grasshopper **weather vane,** the sole remaining detail from the original building, is modeled after the weather vane on London's Royal Exchange.

National Park Service rangers give **free 20-minute talks** every half-hour from 9am to 5pm in the second-floor auditorium. On the top floor is a small museum that houses the weapons collection and historical exhibits of the **Ancient and Honorable Artillery Company of Massachusetts.**

To continue on the Freedom Trail: Leave Faneuil Hall, cross North Street, and follow the trail through the "Blackstone Block." These buildings, among the oldest in the city, give a sense of the scale of 18th- and 19th-century Boston. In the park at the corner of North and Union streets are two sculptures of legendary Boston mayor (and Congressman, and federal prisoner) **James Michael Curley,** the basis for the protagonist of Edwin O'Connor's *The Last Hurrah.* Pause on Union Street.

Dock Sq. (Congress St. and North St.). 🅒 **617/242-5675.** Free admission. Daily 9am–5pm. T: Green or Blue Line to Government Center, or Orange Line to Haymarket.

The New England Holocaust Memorial ⚡⚡ Erected in 1995, these six glass towers spring up in the midst of attractions that celebrate freedom, reminding visitors of the consequences of a world without it. The pattern on the glass, which at first

---

Moments **Trail Mix**

Faneuil Hall Marketplace is a great spot for a break. Time your walk right, and it can be the starting point of a picnic lunch. Visit the **Quincy Market** food court for takeout, then head toward the water. Two good places to picnic are just across Atlantic Avenue. At the foot of State Street is **Long Wharf,** Boston's principal wharf since 1710 and a busy sightseeing-cruise dock. Pass the Marriott to reach the brick plaza at the end of the wharf. The granite building dates to 1846, and the plaza affords a great view of the harbor and the airport. Or stop at **Christopher Columbus Waterfront Park,** on the other side of the hotel, watch the action at the marina, and play in the playground.

As you walk from Faneuil Hall to the Paul Revere House, you'll find yourself in the midst of **Haymarket.** On Friday and Saturday, the bustling open-air market on Hanover and Blackstone streets consists of stalls piled high with produce, seafood, and flowers. Shoppers aren't allowed to touch anything they haven't bought, a rule you might learn from a hollering vendor or a cutthroat customer. It's a great scene and a favorite with photographers.

appears merely decorative, is actually 6 million random numbers, one for each Jew who died during the Holocaust. As you pass through, pause to read the inscriptions.

To continue on the Freedom Trail: The trail now passes through a lot of post–Big Dig construction—keep an eye out for signs pointing the way—and emerges in the North End. When you reach Cross Street, follow it to Hanover Street, turn left, and follow Hanover to Richmond Street. Turn right, go 1 block, and turn left.

Union St. between North and Hanover sts. ℂ 617/457-8755. www.nehm.org. T: Orange or Green Line to Haymarket.

Paul Revere House ⭐⭐⭐   One of the most pleasant stops on the Freedom Trail, this 2½-story wood structure presents history on a human scale. Revere was living here when he set out for Lexington on April 18, 1775, a feat immortalized in Henry Wadsworth Longfellow's poem "Paul Revere's Ride" ("Listen, my children, and you shall hear, of the midnight ride of Paul Revere"). The oldest house in downtown Boston, it was built around 1680, bought by Revere in 1770, and put to a number of uses before being turned into a museum in the early 20th century. It holds neatly arranged and identified 17th- and 18th-century furnishings and artifacts, including the famous Revere silver, considered some of the finest anywhere.

The thought-provoking tour is self-guided, with staff members around in case you have questions. The format allows you to linger on the artifacts that hold your interest. Revere had 16 children (he called them "my lambs")—eight with each of his two wives—and supported the family with a thriving silversmith's trade. At his home, you'll get a good sense of the risks he took in the events that led to the Revolutionary War.

Across the courtyard is the home of Revere's Hichborn cousins, the **Pierce/Hichborn House** ⭐. The 1711 Georgian-style home is a rare example of 18th-century middle-class architecture. It's suitably furnished and shown only by guided tour (usually twice a day at busy times). Call the Paul Revere House for schedules and reservations.

Before you leave North Square, look across the cobblestone plaza at **Sacred Heart Church.** It was established in 1833 as the Seamen's Bethel, a church devoted to the needs of the mariners who frequented the area. Wharves ran up almost this far in colonial days; in the 19th century, this was a notorious red-light district.

To continue on the Freedom Trail: The trail leaves the square on Prince Street and runs along Hanover Street past Clark Street. Before turning onto Prince Street, take a few steps down Garden Court Street and look for no. 4, on the right. The private residence was the birthplace of Rose Fitzgerald (later Kennedy).

19 North Sq. ℂ 617/523-2338. www.paulreverehouse.org. Admission $3 adults, $2.50 seniors and students, $1 children 5–17, free for children under 5. Freedom Trail ticket (with Old South Meeting House and Old State House) $10 adults, $3 children. Daily Apr 15–Oct 9:30am–5:15pm; daily Apr 1–14 and Nov–Dec 9:30am–4:15pm; Jan–Mar Tues–Sun 9:30am–4:15pm. Closed Jan 1, Thanksgiving, and Dec 25. T: Green or Orange Line to Haymarket, Blue Line to Aquarium, or Green or Blue Line to Government Center.

James Rego Square (Paul Revere Mall)   A pleasant little brick-paved park known as the Prado, the mall holds a famous equestrian statue of Paul Revere. Take time to read some of the **tablets** ⭐ on the left-hand wall that describe famous people and places in the history of the North End.

To continue on the Freedom Trail: Walk around the fountain and continue to Salem Street, heading toward the steeple of the Old North Church.

Hanover St. at Clark St. T: Green or Orange Line to Haymarket.

Moments Church Chat

One quick way to announce yourself as a tourist is to pause on Hanover Street between Prince and Fleet streets and proclaim that you see the Old North Church. The first house of worship you see is **St. Stephen's,** the only Charles Bulfinch–designed church still standing in Boston. It was Unitarian when it was dedicated in 1804. The next year, the congregation bought a bell from Paul Revere's foundry for $800. The design is a paragon of Federal-style symmetry. St. Stephen's became Roman Catholic in 1862 and was moved when Hanover Street was widened in 1870. During refurbishment in 1965, it regained its original appearance, with clear glass windows, white walls, and gilded organ pipes. It's one of the plainest Catholic churches you'll ever see.

Old North Church ✪   Officially named Christ Church, this is the oldest church building in Boston (1723). The building is in the style of Sir Christopher Wren. In the original steeple, sexton Robert Newman hung two lanterns on the night of April 18, 1775, to signal Paul Revere that British troops were setting out for Lexington and Concord in boats across the Charles River, not on foot ("One if by land, and two if by sea"). The steeple fell in hurricanes in 1804 and 1954; the current version is an exact copy of the original. The 190-foot spire, long a reference point for sailors, appears on navigational charts to this day. And how's this for a coincidence: Newman was a great-grandson of George Burroughs, one of the victims of the Salem witch trials of 1692.

Members of the Revere family attended this church (their plaque is on pew 54); famous visitors have included Presidents James Monroe, Theodore Roosevelt, Franklin D. Roosevelt, and Gerald R. Ford, and Queen Elizabeth II. There are markers and plaques throughout; note the bust of George Washington, reputedly the first memorial to the first president. The **gardens** ✪ on the north side of the church (dotted with more plaques) are open to the public. On the south side of the church, volunteers maintain an 18th-century garden. Proceeds from the quirky gift shop go to support the church.

Free tours of the church begin every 15 minutes. The 50-minute behind-the-scenes tour ($8 adults, $5 children under 17) includes visits to the steeple and the crypt. Tours are available on weekdays and on weekend afternoons from June to mid-August, and the rest of the year by appointment. Reservations are recommended.

To continue on the Freedom Trail: Cross Salem Street onto Hull Street and walk uphill toward Copp's Hill Burying Ground. On the left you'll pass 44 Hull St., a private residence that's the narrowest (10 ft. wide) house in Boston.

193 Salem St. ⊘ **617/523-6676.** www.oldnorth.com. $3 donation requested. Daily 9am–5pm. Sun services (Episcopal) 9 and 11am. T: Orange or Green Line to Haymarket.

Copp's Hill Burying Ground ✪   The second-oldest cemetery (1659) in the city is the burial place of Cotton Mather and his family, Robert Newman, and Prince Hall. Hall, a prominent member of the free black community that occupied the north slope of the hill in colonial times, fought at Bunker Hill and established the first black Masonic lodge. The highest point in the North End, Copp's Hill was the site of a windmill and of the British batteries that destroyed the village of Charlestown during the Battle of Bunker Hill on June 17, 1775. Charlestown is clearly visible (look for the masts of USS *Constitution*) across the Inner Harbor. No gravestone rubbing is allowed.

To continue on the Freedom Trail: Follow Hull Street down the hill to Commercial Street (note that there's no crosswalk on Commercial at the dangerous intersection with Hull) and follow the trail to North Washington Street and across the bridge. Follow signs and the trail to the Charlestown Navy Yard.

Off Hull St. near Snowhill St. Daily 9am–5pm (until 3pm in winter). T: Green or Orange Line to North Station.

USS *Constitution* ★★ *(Kids)* "Old Ironsides," one of the U.S. Navy's six original frigates, never lost a battle. The ship was constructed in the North End from 1794 to 1797 at a cost of $302,718, using bolts, spikes, and other fittings from Paul Revere's foundry. As the new nation built its naval and military reputation, the *Constitution* played a key role, battling French privateers and Barbary pirates, repelling the British fleet during the War of 1812, participating in 40 engagements, and capturing 20 vessels. The frigate earned its nickname during a battle on August 19, 1812, when shots from HMS *Guerriere* bounced off its thick oak hull as if it were iron. Today, the active-duty sailors who lead tours wear 1812 dress uniforms.

Retired from combat in 1815, the *Constitution* was rescued from destruction when Oliver Wendell Holmes's poem "Old Ironsides" launched a preservation movement in 1830. The frigate was completely overhauled for its bicentennial in 1997, when it sailed under its own power for the first time since 1881, drawing international attention. Tugs tow the *Constitution* into the harbor every **Fourth of July** for its celebratory "turnaround cruise" and for occasional events around the harbor. If you see TV helicopters circling over the water, wander down and take a look.

To continue on the Freedom Trail: Walk straight ahead to the museum entrance.

Charlestown Navy Yard. (C) **617/242-7511.** www.oldironsides.com. Free tours. Summer Tues–Sun 10am–3:30pm; winter Thurs–Sun 10am–3:30pm. T: Ferry from Long Wharf, or Green or Orange Line to North Station and 10-min. walk.

USS *Constitution* **Museum** *(Kids)* Just inland from the vessel, the museum features participatory exhibits that allow visitors to hoist a flag, fire a cannon, swing in a hammock, and learn more about the ship. The interactive computer displays and naval artifacts appeal to visitors of all ages. A display about the Barbary War (the only such exhibit in the United States) allows you to decide whether to risk a ship in the Mediterranean. The museum's collections include more than 3,000 items, arranged and interpreted in ways that put them in context. Each February and March, special displays and activities focus on ship models.

Also at the navy yard, **National Park Service** rangers ((C) **617/242-5601**) staff an **information booth** and give free 1-hour guided tours of the base.

To continue on the Freedom Trail: Follow the trail up Constitution Road, crossing Chelsea Street, and continue to the Bunker Hill Monument. A more interesting,

---

Tips **Security on "Old Ironsides"**

The Charlestown Navy Yard, home to USS *Constitution* and the Constitution Museum, is a heavily guarded area. Expect to have your bags searched at the gate or at the access point for "Old Ironsides," where you'll probably have to pass through a metal detector. And call ahead if the national terror alert is high; the navy yard closes to civilians at the first sign of a serious threat.

Tips **Trailing Off**

If you don't feel like retracing your steps at the end of the Freedom Trail, you have two public transit options. Return to the Charlestown Navy Yard for the **ferry** to Long Wharf, which leaves every half-hour from 6:45am to 8:15pm on weekdays (every 15 min. 6:45–9:15am and 3:45–6:45pm), and every half-hour on the quarter-hour from 10:15am to 6:15pm on weekends. The 10-minute trip costs $1.50, and the dock is an easy walk from Old Ironsides. Alternatively, walk to the foot of the hill; on Main Street, take **bus no. 92 or 93** to Haymarket (Green or Orange Line).

---

slightly longer route runs from Chelsea Street and Rutherford Avenue (back at the bridge) across City Square Park.

Off First Ave., Charlestown Navy Yard. ✆ 617/426-1812. www.ussconstitutionmuseum.org. Free admission; donations encouraged. Daily May–Oct 15 9am–6pm; Oct 16–Apr 10am–5pm. Closed Jan 1, Thanksgiving, and Dec 25. T: Ferry from Long Wharf (Blue Line Aquarium stop), or Green or Orange Line to North Station and 10-min. walk.

Bunker Hill Monument   The 221-foot granite obelisk honors the memory of the colonists who died in the Battle of Bunker Hill on June 17, 1775. The rebels lost the battle, but nearly half the British troops were killed or wounded, a loss that contributed to the redcoats' decision to abandon Boston 9 months later. The Marquis de Lafayette, the celebrated hero of the American and French revolutions, helped lay the monument's cornerstone in 1825. He is buried in Paris under soil taken from the hill. A punishing flight of 294 stairs leads to the top of the monument. There's no elevator, and although the views of the harbor and the northern portion of the Big Dig are good, the windows are quite small. The ranger-staffed lodge at the base of the monument holds dioramas and exhibits.

Monument Sq., Charlestown. ✆ 617/242-5641. www.nps.gov/bost. Free admission. Exhibits daily 9am–5pm; monument daily 9am–4:30pm. T: Ferry from Long Wharf (Blue Line Aquarium stop) to Navy Yard, or Orange Line to Community College.

3 More Museums & Attractions

Boston Public Library   The central branch of the city's library system is an architectural and intellectual monument. The original 1895 building, a National Historic Landmark designed by Charles F. McKim, is an Italian Renaissance–style masterpiece that fairly drips with art. The **lobby doors** are the work of Daniel Chester French (who also designed the Abraham Lincoln statue in the memorial in Washington, the *Minute Man* statue in Concord, and the John Harvard statue in Cambridge). The **murals** are by John Singer Sargent and Pierre Puvis de Chavannes, among others. Visit the lovely **courtyard** ✿ or peek at it from a window on the stairs. The adjoining addition, of the same height and material (pink granite), was designed by Philip Johnson and opened in 1972. The lobby holds changing exhibits. The restaurant, **Novel,** serves lunch and afternoon tea Monday through Friday, and **Sebastian's Map Room Café** is open 9am to 5pm Monday through Saturday.

Free **Art & Architecture Tours** (www.bpl.org/guides/tours.htm) begin Monday at 2:30pm, Tuesday and Thursday at 6pm, Friday and Saturday at 11am, with an additional tour October through May on Sunday at 2pm. Call ℭ **617/536-5400,** ext. 2216, to arrange group tours.

700 Boylston St., Copley Sq. ℭ **617/536-5400.** www.bpl.org. Free admission. Mon–Thurs 9am–9pm; Fri–Sat 9am–5pm; Sun (Oct–May only) 1–5pm. Closed Sun June–Sept and legal holidays. T: Green Line to Copley.

Commonwealth Museum/Massachusetts Archives The nearby Kennedy Library explores the history of one of Boston's most famous families; here, you might find your own clan's history. Neither collection is worth a trip on its own, but this is a worthwhile detour on the way to or from the Kennedy Library.

The **Commonwealth Museum** has videos, slide shows, and interactive exhibits on the state's people, places, and politics. Topics covered recently in the regularly changing exhibits include the archaeology of the Big Dig, the Civil War, and state history. In the same building, the state **archives** contain passenger lists for ships that arrived in Boston from 1848 to 1891; state census schedules that date to 1790; and documents, maps, and military and court records starting with the Massachusetts Bay Company (1628–29). Knowledgeable staff members are on hand to answer researchers' questions in person, by mail, or by phone.

220 Morrissey Blvd., Columbia Point. Museum: ℭ **617/727-9268**; www.state.ma.us/sec/mus. Archives: ℭ **617/ 727-2816**; www.state.ma.us/sec/arc. Free admission. Mon–Fri 9am–5pm; 2nd and 4th Sat of each month 9am–3pm. Closed legal holidays. T: Red Line to JFK/UMass; take free shuttle bus, which runs every 20 min.

Institute of Contemporary Art ⚝ In a former police station across from the Hynes Convention Center, the ICA is one of the least stuffy museums I've ever visited. It mounts rotating exhibits of 20th- and 21st-century art, including painting, sculpture, photography, and video and performance art. Its shows are among the most imaginative around, focusing on everything from baseball to an exploration of the concept of emotion. The museum also offers films, lectures, musical performances, poetry readings, and educational programs for children and adults.

The ICA's profile is on the rise. It's in the process of building a new museum at Fan Pier, on the South Boston waterfront near the federal courthouse. A $37 million project designed by the pioneering New York firm Diller Scofidio + Renfro, the new building is scheduled to open in 2006. Check at the current location or visit the website for details and updates.

955 Boylston St. ℭ **617/266-5152.** www.icaboston.org. Admission $7 adults, $5 seniors and students, free for children under 12; free to all Thurs 5–9pm. Tues–Wed and Fri noon–5pm; Thurs noon–9pm; Sat–Sun 11am–5pm. Closed Jan 1, July 4, Thanksgiving, Dec 25. T: Green Line B, C, or D to Hynes/ICA.

Larz Anderson Auto Museum The Larz Anderson Auto Museum occupies an 1888 carriage house modeled after a French château. Beginning in 1899, Larz and Isabel Anderson acquired the cars that form the core of the collection, now the country's oldest private assemblage of antique autos. The cars boast what was then the latest equipment, from a two-cylinder engine (in a 1901 Winton race car) to a full lavatory (in a 1906 CGV). Vehicles and memorabilia from the collection and from other sources are on display.

The museum (formerly the Museum of Transportation) has a good gift shop and frequently schedules special events such as concerts, lectures, and family programs. On most warm-weather Sundays, outdoor **lawn events** include displays of vehicles such as Corvettes, Cadillacs, Triumphs, European motorcycles, or Italian imports. Call to find out what's featured during your visit.

15 Newton St., Larz Anderson Park, Brookline. ℂ 617/522-6547. www.mot.org. Admission $5 adults; $3 seniors, students, and children 6–18; free for children under 6. Tues–Sun and Mon holidays 10am–5pm. Closed Jan 1, Thanksgiving, and Dec 25. T: Green Line D to Reservoir, then take bus no. 51 (Forest Hills); museum is 5 blocks from intersection of Newton and Clyde sts. Call for driving directions.

Mary Baker Eddy Library/Mapparium *Kids*   The Mary Baker Eddy Library, a research center with two floors of interactive and multimedia exhibits, opened in 2002. Its mission is to explore ideas such as liberty and spirituality through history, with a central role for Mary Baker Eddy, the founder of Christian Science. The library's most intriguing exhibit is the **Mapparium** ★, a unique hollow globe 30 feet across. A work of both art and history, it consists of a bronze framework that connects 608 stained-glass panels. Because sound bounces off the nonporous surfaces, the acoustics are as unusual as the aesthetics. As you cross the glass bridge just south of the equator, you'll see the political divisions of the world from 1932 to 1935, when the globe was constructed.

World Headquarters of the First Church of Christ, Scientist, 200 Mass. Ave. ℂ 888/222-3711 or 617/450-7000. www.marybakereddylibrary.org. Admission $5 adults; $3 seniors, students, and children 6–17. Tues–Fri and some Mon holidays 10am–9pm; Sat 10am–5pm; Sun 11am–5pm. Closed Jan 1, Thanksgiving, and Dec 25. MBTA: Green Line E to Symphony, Green Line B, C, or D to Hynes/ICA, or Orange Line to Mass. Ave.

Museum of Afro-American History ★★ *Kids*   The final stop on the **Black Heritage Trail** (p. 174), this museum offers a comprehensive look at the history and contributions of blacks in Boston and Massachusetts. It occupies the **Abiel Smith School** (1834), the first American public grammar school for African-American children, and the **African Meeting House,** 8 Smith Court. Changing and permanent exhibits use art, artifacts, documents, historic photographs, and other objects—including many family heirlooms—to explore an important era that often takes a back seat in Revolutionary War–obsessed New England. Children enjoy the interactive touch-screen displays and multimedia presentations, and the patient, enthusiastic staff helps them put the exhibits in context. The oldest standing black church in the United States, the meeting house opened in 1806; visitors in 2006 can expect to find bicentennial exhibits and events. William Lloyd Garrison founded the New England Anti-Slavery Society in this building, where Frederick Douglass made some of his great abolitionist speeches. Once known as the "Black Faneuil Hall," it also schedules lectures, concerts, and church meetings.

46 Joy St. ℂ 617/725-0022. www.afroammuseum.org. Free admission; donations encouraged. Memorial Day to Labor Day daily 10am–4pm; day after Labor Day to day before Memorial Day Mon–Sat 10am–4pm. Closed Jan 1, Thanksgiving, and Dec 25. MBTA: Red or Green Line to Park Street, or Red Line to Charles/MGH.

Moments **Eyes in the Skies**

For a smashing view of the airport, the harbor, and the South Boston waterfront, stroll along the harbor or Atlantic Avenue to Northern Avenue. On either side of this intersection are buildings with free observation areas. Be ready to show an ID to gain entrance. The first, on the 14th floor of Independence Wharf, 470 Atlantic Ave., is open daily from 11am to 5pm. The other, Foster's Rotunda, is on the ninth floor of 30 Rowes Wharf, in the Boston Harbor Hotel complex. It's open Monday to Friday from 11am to 4pm.

4 Historic Houses

The home in Boston imbued with the most history is the **Paul Revere House** (p. 167). A visit brings the legendary revolutionary to life. For information on the **Longfellow National Historic Site,** see p. 176.

On **Beacon Hill,** you'll find houses that are as interesting for their architecture as for their occupants. The south slope, facing Boston Common, has been a fashionable address since the 1620s; excellent tours of two houses (one on the north slope) focus on the late 18th and early 19th centuries. The architect of the homes was Charles Bulfinch; he also designed the State House, which sits at the hill's summit.

Historic New England (formerly the Society for the Preservation of New England Antiquities) owns and operates the Otis House Museum (see below) and dozens of other historic properties throughout New England. Museums all over the region have employed HNE's restoration techniques. Contact the organization (© **617/227-3956;** www.historicnewengland.org) for information on its properties, visiting hours and admission fees.

Gibson House Museum   In the Back Bay, the Gibson House is an 1859 brownstone that embodies the word "Victorian." You'll see decorations of all kinds, including family photos and portraits, petrified-wood hat racks, a sequined red-velvet pagoda for the cat, a Victrola, and an original icebox. Check ahead for the schedule of lectures and other special events.

137 Beacon St. © 617/267-6338. www.thegibsonhouse.org. Admission $7. Tours on the hour Wed–Sun 1–3pm. T: Green Line to Arlington.

John F. Kennedy National Historic Site   A property of the National Park Service, the 35th president's birthplace has been restored to appear as it did in 1917. The guided ranger-led tour discusses domestic life of the period and the roots of the Kennedy family. If you miss the last guided tour, ask about the self-guided option. One-hour walking tours of the neighborhood start at 12:45pm on weekends. Call ahead to double-check hours, which are set before each season.

83 Beals St., Brookline. © 617/566-7937. www.nps.gov/jofi. Tours $3 adults, free for children under 17. May–Oct Wed–Sun 10am–4:30pm. Tours every 30 min. 10am–3:30pm. Closed Nov–Apr. T: Green Line C to Coolidge Corner, then walk 4 blocks north on Harvard St. and turn right.

Nichols House Museum ⋆   A stroll around Beacon Hill can leave visitors pining to know what the stately homes look like inside. This is one of the only places to satisfy your curiosity. This 1804 home holds beautiful antique furnishings collected by several generations of the Nichols family. Its most prominent occupant, Rose Standish Nichols, was a suffragist and a pioneering landscape designer. Her legacy includes not just family heirlooms but objects she brought back from her many travels. Open days may vary, so call ahead.

55 Mount Vernon St. © 617/227-6993. www.nicholshousemuseum.org. Admission $7. May–Oct Tues–Sat noon–4pm; Nov–Apr Thurs–Sat noon–4pm; tours every 30 min. T: Red or Green Line to Park St.

Otis House Museum ⋆⋆   Legendary architect Charles Bulfinch designed this gorgeous 1796 mansion for Harrison Gray Otis, an up-and-coming young lawyer who later became mayor of Boston, and his wife, Sally. The restoration was one of the first in the country to use computer analysis of paint, and the result was revolutionary: It revealed that the walls were drab because the paint had faded, not because the colors started out dingy. Furnished in the style to which a wealthy family in the young

United States would have been accustomed, the Federal-style building is a colorful, elegant treasure. Guided tours (the only way to see the property) discuss the architecture of the house and post-Revolutionary social, business, and family life, and touch on the history of the neighborhood.

141 Cambridge St. ⓒ 617/227-3956. www.historicnewengland.org. Guided tour $8. Tours on the hour Wed–Sun 11am–4pm. T: Blue Line to Bowdoin (weekdays only), Green or Blue Line to Government Center, or Red Line to Charles/MGH.

5 African-American History

The 1.6-mile **Black Heritage Trail** covers sites on Beacon Hill that preserve the history of 19th-century Boston. The neighborhood was the center of the free black community, and the trail links stations of the Underground Railroad, homes of famous citizens, and the first integrated public school. You can take a free 2-hour guided tour with a ranger from the National Park Service's **Boston African American National Historic Site** (ⓒ 617/742-5415; www.nps.gov/boaf). Tours start at the **Robert Gould Shaw Memorial,** on Beacon Street across from the State House. They're available Monday through Saturday from Memorial Day to Labor Day, and by request at other times; call ahead for a reservation. Or go on your own, using a brochure (available at the Museum of Afro-American History and the Boston Common and State Street visitor centers) that includes a map and descriptions of the buildings. The only buildings on the trail that are open to the public are the **African Meeting House** and the **Abiel Smith School,** which make up the **Museum of Afro-American History** (p. 172). Check ahead for special programs in February.

The **Greater Boston Convention & Visitors Bureau** (ⓒ 800/SEE-BOSTON; www.bostonusa.com) compiles an annual African-American Heritage Destination Tour Planner. The Boston History Collaborative website **www.bostonfamilyhistory. net** lists resources for many ethnic groups, including African Americans.

Across the river, the **Cambridge African American Trail** (ⓒ 617/349-4683) focuses on significant sites in the history of the city's large black community. To buy

Focus on Women's History

The **Boston Women's Heritage Trail** (ⓒ 617/522-2872; www.bwht.org) creates walking tours with stops at homes, churches, and social and political institutions associated with women who made great contributions to society. Subjects include Julia Ward Howe, social reformer Dorothea Dix, the colonial religious leader Anne Hutchinson, and less famous Bostonians such as Phillis Wheatley, a slave who became the first African-American published poet, and abolitionist and feminist Lucy Stone. You can buy a guidebook at the National Park Service Visitor Center at 15 State St., at some local historic sites and bookstores, or by mail (check the website).

March is Women's History Month; special events include lectures, walking tours, museum events, and workshops. Check with the Greater Boston Convention & Visitors Bureau (ⓒ 800/SEE-BOSTON; www.bostonusa.com) for details.

the guide, visit the office at 831 Mass. Ave., download an order form from the website, or send a check for $3.50 (includes shipping), payable to the Cambridge Historical Society, to the **Cambridge Historical Commission,** 831 Mass. Ave., Cambridge, MA 02139 (www.ci.cambridge.ma.us/~historic).

6 Parks & Gardens

Green space is an important part of Boston's appeal, and the public parks are hard to miss. The world-famous **Emerald Necklace,** Frederick Law Olmsted's vision for a loop of green spaces, runs through the city. See p. 186 for information on seeing part or all of the Emerald Necklace with a Boston park ranger.

The best-known park, for good reason, is the spectacular **Public Garden** ★★★, bordered by Arlington, Boylston, Charles, and Beacon streets. Something lovely is in bloom at the country's first botanical garden at least half the year. The spring flowers are particularly impressive, especially if your visit happens to coincide with the first really warm days of the year. It's hard not to enjoy yourself when everyone around you seems ecstatic just to be seeing the sun.

For many people, the official beginning of spring coincides with the return of the **Swan Boats** ★★ (© **617/522-1966;** www.swanboats.com). The pedal-powered vessels—the attendants pedal, not the passengers—plunge into the lagoon on the Saturday before Patriots Day, the third Monday of April. Although they don't move fast, they'll transport you. They operate daily from 10am to 5pm in the summer, daily from 10am to 4pm in the spring, and weekdays noon to 4pm and weekends 10am to 4pm from Labor Day to mid-September. The cost for the 15-minute ride is $2.50 for adults, $2 for seniors, and $1 for children 2 to 15.

Across Charles Street is **Boston Common,** the country's first public park and the first site on the **Freedom Trail** (p. 160). The property was purchased in 1634 and officially set aside as public land in 1640, so if it seems a bit run-down (especially compared to the Public Garden), it's no wonder. The Frog Pond, where there really were frogs at one time, makes a pleasant spot to splash around in the summer and skate in the winter. At the Boylston Street side of the Common is the **Central Burying Ground,** where you can see the grave of famed portraitist Gilbert Stuart. There's also a bandstand where you might take in a free concert or play, and many beautiful shade trees.

The most spectacular garden in town is the **Arnold Arboretum** ★★, 125 Arborway, Jamaica Plain (© **617/524-1718;** www.arboretum.harvard.edu). One of the oldest parks in the United States, founded in 1872, it is open daily from sunrise to sunset. Its 265 acres contain more than 15,000 ornamental trees, shrubs, and vines from all over the world. In the spring, the grounds are ablaze with blossoming dogwood, azaleas, and rhododendrons, and the air fills with the dizzying scent of hundreds of varieties of lilacs, for which the arboretum is especially famous. This is definitely a place to take a camera—but not food. Lilac Sunday, in May, is the only time the arboretum allows picnicking.

There is no admission fee for this National Historical Landmark, which Harvard University administers in cooperation with the Boston Department of Parks and Recreation. To get there, take the MBTA Orange Line to the Forest Hills stop and follow signs to the entrance. The visitor center is open weekdays from 9am to 4pm, Saturday 10am to 4pm, and Sunday noon to 4pm. Call for information about educational programs.

7 Cambridge

Boston and Cambridge are so closely associated that many people believe they're the same—a notion that both cities' residents and politicians are happy to dispel. Cantabrigians are often considered more liberal and better educated than Bostonians, which is another idea that's sure to get you involved in a lively discussion. Take the Red Line across the river and see for yourself.

For a good overview, begin at the main Harvard T entrance. Follow our Harvard Square walking tour (p. 206), or set out on your own. At the **information booth** (© 800/862-5678 or 617/497-1630) in the middle of Harvard Square at the intersection of Mass. Ave., John F. Kennedy Street, and Brattle Street, trained volunteers dispense maps and brochures and answer questions Monday through Saturday from 9am to 5pm and Sunday from 1 to 5pm. From mid-June to Labor Day, guided tours explore the entire old Cambridge area. Check at the booth for rates, meeting places, and times, or call ahead. If you prefer to sightsee on your own, you can buy the Cambridge Historical Commission's *Revolutionary Cambridge* walking guide ($2).

Whatever you do, spend some time in **Harvard Square.** It's a hodgepodge of college and high school students, professors and instructors, commuters, street performers, and sightseers. Near the information booth are two well-stocked newsstands, **Nini's Corner** and **Out of Town News,** and the **Harvard Coop** bookstore. Stores and restaurants line all three streets that spread out from the center of the square and the streets that intersect them. If you follow **Brattle Street** to the residential area just outside the square, you'll arrive at a part of town known as **"Tory Row"** because the residents were loyal to King George during the Revolution.

The ravishing yellow mansion at 105 Brattle St. is the **Longfellow National Historic Site** ⚘ (© 617/876-4491; www.nps.gov/long), the longtime home of Henry Wadsworth Longfellow (1804–1882). The poet first lived here as a boarder in 1837. When he and Fanny Appleton married in 1843, her father made the house a wedding present. The furnishings and books in the stately home are original to Longfellow, who lived here until his death, and his descendants. During the siege of Boston in 1775–76, the house served as the headquarters of Gen. George Washington, with whom Longfellow was fascinated. On a tour—the only way to see the house—you'll learn about the history of the building and its famous occupants.

The house is usually open June through October Wednesday through Sunday from 10am to 4:30pm, but always check ahead. Tours begin at 10:30 and 11:30am, and 1, 2, 3, and 4pm. Admission is $3 for adults, free for children under 17.

Farther west, near where Brattle Street and Mount Auburn Street intersect, is **Mount Auburn Cemetery** (see the box titled "Celebrity Cemetery"). It's a pleasant but long walk; you might prefer to drive or take a bus from Harvard station.

HARVARD UNIVERSITY

Our Harvard Square walking tour (p. 206) describes many of the buildings you'll see on the Harvard campus. Free student-led tours leave from the **Events & Information Center** in Holyoke Center, 1350 Mass. Ave. (© 617/495-1573). They operate during the school year twice a day on weekdays and once on Saturday, except during vacations, and during the summer four times a day Monday through Saturday. Call for exact times; reservations aren't necessary. The Events & Information Center has maps, illustrated booklets, and self-guided walking-tour directions, as well as a bulletin

Harvard Square Attractions

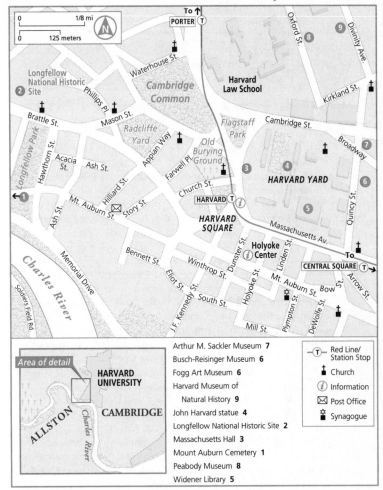

Arthur M. Sackler Museum **7**
Busch-Reisinger Museum **6**
Fogg Art Museum **6**
Harvard Museum of
    Natural History **9**
John Harvard statue **4**
Longfellow National Historic Site **2**
Massachusetts Hall **3**
Mount Auburn Cemetery **1**
Peabody Museum **8**
Widener Library **5**

ⓣ — Red Line/
    Station Stop
✝ Church
ⓘ Information
✉ Post Office
✡ Synagogue

board where flyers publicize campus activities. You might want to check out the university website (www.harvard.edu) before you visit.

The best-known part of the university is **Harvard Yard,** which consists of two large quadrangles. Daniel Chester French's **John Harvard statue,** a rendering of one of the school's original benefactors, is in the Old Yard, which dates to the college's founding in 1636. Most first-year students live in the dormitories here—even in the school's oldest building, **Massachusetts Hall** (1720). The other side of the Yard (sometimes called Tercentenary Theater because the college's 300th-anniversary celebration was held there) is home to the imposing **Widener Library,** named after a Harvard graduate who perished when the *Titanic* sank.

Celebrity Cemetery

Three important colonial burying grounds—Old Granary, King's Chapel, and Copp's Hill—are in Boston on the Freedom Trail (see "The Freedom Trail," earlier in this chapter), but the most famous cemetery in the area is in Cambridge.

Mount Auburn Cemetery 🌲, 580 Mount Auburn St. (📞 617/547-7105; www.mountauburn.org), the final resting place of many well-known people, is also famous simply for existing. Dedicated in 1831, it was the first of America's rural, or garden, cemeteries. The establishment of burying places removed from city centers reflected practical and philosophical concerns. Development was encroaching on urban graveyards, and the ideas associated with Transcendentalism and the Greek revival (the word *cemetery* derives from the Greek for "sleeping place") dictated that communing with nature take precedence over organized religion. Since the day it opened, Mount Auburn has been a popular place to retreat and reflect.

Visitors to this National Historic Landmark find history and horticulture coexisting with celebrity. The graves of Henry Wadsworth Longfellow, Oliver Wendell Holmes, Julia Ward Howe, and Mary Baker Eddy are here, as are those of Charles Bulfinch, James Russell Lowell, Winslow Homer, Transcendentalist leader Margaret Fuller, and abolitionist Charles Sumner. In season you'll see gorgeous flowering trees and shrubs (the Massachusetts Horticultural Society had a hand in the design). Stop at the office or front gate to pick up brochures and a map. You can rent an audiotape tour ($7; a $15 deposit is required) and listen in your car or on a portable tape player; there's a 60-minute driving tour and two 75-minute walking tours. The **Friends of Mount Auburn Cemetery** conduct workshops and lectures and coordinate walking tours. Call the main number for topics, schedules, and fees.

The cemetery is open daily from 8am to 5pm October through April, 8am to 7pm May through September; admission is free. Animals and recreational activities such as jogging, biking, and picnicking are not allowed. MBTA bus nos. 71 and 73 start at Harvard station and stop near the cemetery gates; they run frequently on weekdays and less often on weekends. By car (5 min.) or on foot (30 min.), take Mount Auburn Street or Brattle Street west from Harvard Square; just after the streets intersect, the gate is on the left.

Also on campus are two engaging museum complexes:

Harvard Museum of Natural History and Peabody Museum of Archaeology & Ethnology 🌲 *Kids*   These fascinating museums house the university's collections of items and artifacts related to the natural world. The world-famous academic resource offers interdisciplinary programs and exhibitions that tie in elements of all the associated fields. On weekends, staffed "Investigation Stations" help visitors learn through hands-on activities. You'll certainly find something interesting here, be it a dinosaur skeleton, a hunk of meteorite, a Native American artifact, or the Glass Flowers.

The **Glass Flowers** ✸✸✸ are 3,000 models of more than 840 plant species devised between 1887 and 1936 by the German father-and-son team of Leopold and Rudolph Blaschka. You might have heard about them, and you might be skeptical, but it's true: They look real. Children love the **zoological collections** ✸✸, where dinosaurs share space with preserved and stuffed insects and animals that range in size from butterflies to giraffes. The **mineralogical collections** are the most specialized but can be just as interesting as the others, especially if gemstones hold your interest.

The **Peabody Museum of Archaeology & Ethnology** ✸ boasts the **Hall of the North American Indian,** where 500 artifacts representing 10 cultures are on display, and is home to the only surviving artifacts positively attributed to the Lewis and Clark expedition. Photographs, textiles, pottery, and art and crafts of all descriptions fill the galleries.

Harvard Museum of Natural History: 26 Oxford St. ✆ **617/495-3045.** www.hmnh.harvard.edu. Peabody Museum: 11 Divinity Ave. ✆ **617/496-1027.** www.peabody.harvard.edu. Admission to both $7.50 adults, $6.50 seniors and students, $5 children 3–18, free for children under 3; free to all until noon Sun year-round and Wed 3–5pm Sept–May. Harvard Hot Ticket (see "The Harvard Hot Ticket" above) $10 adults, $8 seniors and students. Daily 9am–5pm. T: Red Line to Harvard. Cross Harvard Yard, keeping John Harvard statue on right, and turn right at Science Center. First left is Oxford St.

Harvard University Art Museums ✸   The Fogg Art Museum, the Busch-Reisinger Museum, and the Arthur M. Sackler Museum house more than 200,000 works, from ancient sculptures to contemporary photos. The exhibit spaces also serve as teaching and research facilities. If you prefer to explore with a guide, take a tour of the Fogg weekdays at 11am, of the Busch-Reisinger weekdays at 1pm (both year-round), or of the Sackler at 2pm weekdays September through June, Wednesdays only in July and August.

The **Fogg Art Museum** (32 Quincy St., near Broadway) centers on an impressive 16th-century Italian stone courtyard. Each of the 19 galleries displays something different—17th-century Dutch and Flemish landscapes, 19th-century British and American paintings and drawings, French paintings and drawings from the 18th century through the Impressionist period, contemporary sculpture, and more. Changing exhibits often draw on the museum's extensive collections of paintings, drawings, prints, and photos.

The **Busch-Reisinger Museum** in Werner Otto Hall (enter through the Fogg) concentrates on the painting, sculpture, and decorative art of northern and central Europe, specifically Germany. Particularly notable are the early-20th-century collections, including works by Klee, Feininger, Kandinsky, and artists and designers associated with the Bauhaus.

The **Arthur M. Sackler Museum** (485 Broadway, at Quincy St.) houses Asian, ancient, Islamic, and Later Indian art. Here you'll find internationally renowned Chinese jades, superb Roman sculpture, Greek vases, Korean ceramics, Japanese woodblock

---

Value **The Harvard Hot Ticket**

One ticket covers admission to Harvard's art museums and natural-history museums (and to the Semitic Museum, which is free anyway). You don't have to visit them all in a day, either—the pass is good for a year. It costs $10 for adults and $8 for seniors and students.

prints, and Persian miniature paintings and calligraphy. From August 1 through November 27, 2005, the Sackler will mount a special exhibition uniting the university's holdings of works by **Edgar Degas.**

32 Quincy St. and 485 Broadway. (℗ **617/495-9400.** www.artmuseums.harvard.edu. Admission to all 3 museums $6.50 adults, $5 seniors and students, free for children under 18; free to all until noon Sat. Harvard Hot Ticket (see box) $10 adults, $8 seniors and students. Mon–Sat 10am–5pm; Sun 1–5pm. Closed major holidays. T: Red Line to Harvard. Cross Harvard Yard diagonally from the T station and cross Quincy St., or turn your back on the Coop and follow Mass. Ave. to Quincy St., then turn left.

MASSACHUSETTS INSTITUTE OF TECHNOLOGY (MIT)

The public is welcome at the Massachusetts Institute of Technology campus, a mile or so from Harvard Square, across the Charles River from Beacon Hill and the Back Bay. Visit the **Information Office,** 77 Mass. Ave. (℗ **617/253-4795**), to take a free guided tour (weekdays at 10am and 2pm) or to pick up a copy of the *Walk Around MIT* map and brochure. At the same address, the **Hart Nautical Galleries** (open daily 9am–8pm) contain ship and engine models that illustrate the development of marine engineering.

MIT's campus is known for its art and architecture. The excellent **outdoor sculpture** collection includes works by Picasso and Alexander Calder, and notable modern buildings include designs by Frank Gehry, Eero Saarinen, and I. M. Pei. Gehry designed the **Stata Center** (http://web.mit.edu/evolving/stata), a curvilinear landmark that opened on Vassar Street off Main Street in 2004. Visit the information desk on the ground floor to pick up a pamphlet describing a self-guided tour.

Engaging holography displays are the hallmark of the **MIT Museum,** 265 Mass. Ave. (℗ **617/253-4444;** http://web.mit.edu/museum), where you'll also find works in more conventional media. The museum is open Tuesday through Friday from 10am to 5pm, and weekends from noon to 5pm; it's closed on major holidays. Admission is $5 for adults, $2 for seniors, and $1 for students and children 5 to 18. The school's contemporary art repository, the **List Visual Arts Center,** 20 Ames St. (℗ **617/253-4680;** http://web.mit.edu/lvac), is open Tuesday through Sunday from noon to 6pm, until 8pm on Friday. Admission is free.

To get to MIT, take the MBTA Red Line to Kendall/MIT. The scenic walk from the Back Bay takes you along Mass. Ave. over the river straight to the campus. By car from Boston, cross the river at the Museum of Science, Cambridge Street, or Mass. Ave. and follow signs to Memorial Drive, where you can usually find parking during the day.

8 Boston Neighborhoods to Explore

Boston is a city of neighborhoods, some of which I've described in talking about the Freedom Trail (see "The Freedom Trail," earlier in this chapter) and in the walking tours in chapter 9. Here are several other areas that are fun to explore. Bear in mind that many of the buildings you will see are private homes, not tourist attractions. See chapter 7 for dining suggestions and chapter 10 for shopping tips.

Impressions

For we must consider that we shall be as a city upon a hill. The eyes of all people are upon us . . .

—John Winthrop, "A Model of Christian Charity" (sermon), 1630

Welcome to the North End

The Paul Revere House and the Old North Church are the best-known buildings in the **North End** ✸✸✸, Boston's "Little Italy" (although it's *never* called that). Home to natives of Italy and their assimilated children, numerous Italian restaurants and private social clubs, and many historic sights, this is one of the oldest neighborhoods in the city. It was home in the 17th century to the **Mather family** of Puritan ministers, who certainly would be shocked to see the merry goings-on at the festivals and street fairs that take over different areas of the North End on weekends in July and August.

The Italians (and their yuppie neighbors who have made inroads since the 1980s) are only the latest immigrant group to dominate the North End. In the 19th century, this was an Eastern European Jewish enclave and later an Irish stronghold. In 1894, Rose Fitzgerald, mother of Pres. John F. Kennedy, was born on Garden Court Street and baptized at St. Stephen's Church.

Modern visitors might be more interested in a Hanover Street *caffè*, the perfect place to have coffee or a soft drink and feast on sweets. **Mike's Pastry** ✸✸✸, 300 Hanover St. (☏ **617/742-3050;** www.mikespastry.com), is a bakery that does a frantic takeout business and has tables where you can sit down and order one of the confections on display in the cases. Mike's claim to fame is its cannoli (tubes of crisp-fried pastry filled with sweetened ricotta cheese); the cookies, cakes, and other pastries are excellent, too. You can also sit and relax at **Caffè dello Sport** or **Caffè Vittoria**, on either side of Mike's.

Before you leave the North End, stroll down toward the water and see whether there's a **bocce** game going on at the courts on Commercial Street near Hull Street. The European pastime is both a game of skill and an excuse to hang around and shoot the breeze—in Italian and English—with the locals (mostly men of a certain age). It's so popular that the neighborhood has courts both outdoors, in the Langone Playground at Puopolo Park, and indoors, at the back of the Steriti Rink, 561 Commercial St.

BEACON HILL ✸✸✸

The original Boston settlers, clustered around what are now the Old State House and the North End, considered Beacon Hill far distant. Today the distance is a matter of atmosphere; climbing "the Hill" is like traveling back in time. Lace up your walking shoes (the brick sidewalks gnaw at anything fancier, and driving is next to impossible), wander the narrow streets, and admire the brick and brownstone architecture.

At Beacon and Park streets is a figurative high point (literally, it's *the* high point): Charles Bulfinch's magnificent **State House.** The 60-foot **monument** at the rear illustrates the hill's original height, before the top was shorn off to use in 19th-century landfill projects. **Beacon and Mount Vernon streets** run downhill to commercially dense **Charles Street,** but if ever there was an area where there's no need to head in a straight line, it's this one. Your travels might take you past the former homes of Louisa May Alcott (10 Louisburg Sq.), Henry Kissinger (1 Chestnut St.), Julia Ward Howe

---

(Tips **A Different Voice**

Mytown multicultural youth walking tours (© **617/536-2891;** www.mytowninc. com) offers tours led by a local high school student. The Youth Guide program trains participants in historical research and encourages them to put a personal spin on their narration. The result is a uniquely fascinating take on the city. Tours ($10) operate from late April to October; call for tour details, meeting times, and reservations.

(13 Chestnut St.), Edwin Booth (29A Chestnut St.), and Robert Frost (88 Mount Vernon St.). One of the oldest black churches in the country, the **African Meeting House,** is at 8 Smith Court.

These days, Alcott probably wouldn't be able to afford even the rent for a home on **Louisburg Square** (say "Lewis-burg"), better known since the 2004 presidential campaign as the home of John Kerry. Twenty-two homes where a struggling writer would more likely be an employee than a resident surround the lovely park. The iron-railed square is open only to tenants with keys.

Your wandering will probably lead you down to Charles Street. After you've had your fill of the shops and restaurants, you might want to investigate the architecture of the **"flats,"** between Charles Street and the Charles River. Built on landfill, the buildings here are younger than those higher up, but many are just as eye-catching. MTV fans might recognize the converted firehouse at Mount Vernon and River streets as a former *Real World* location (it's also a one-time *Spenser: For Hire* set).

T: Red Line to Charles/MGH, Green Line to Park Street, or Blue Line to Bowdoin (weekdays only).

THE SOUTH END ⊀⊀

One of Boston's most diverse neighborhoods is also one of its largest, but fans of Victorian architecture won't mind the sore feet they'll have after trekking around the South End.

The neighborhood was laid out in the mid–19th century, before the Back Bay. While the newer area's grid echoes the boulevards of Paris, the South End tips its hat to London. The main streets are broad, and pocket parks dot the side streets. Late-20th-century gentrification saw many South End brownstones reclaimed from squalor and converted into luxury condominiums, driving out many longtime residents and making construction materials as widespread as falling leaves. Even on the few remaining run-down buildings, you'll see wonderful details.

With Back Bay Station to your left, walk down **Dartmouth Street,** crossing Columbus Avenue. Proceed on Dartmouth and explore some of the streets that extend to the left, including **Chandler, Lawrence, and Appleton streets.** This area is known as **Clarendon Park.** Turn left on any of these streets and walk to **Clarendon Street.** Its intersection with Tremont Street is the part of the South End you're most likely to see if you're not out exploring. This is the area where businesses and restaurants surround the **Boston Center for the Arts** (p. 234). The BCA's **Cyclorama** building (the interior is dome-shaped), at 539 Tremont St., is listed on the National Register of Historic Places. Here you can see a show, have a meal, or continue your expedition, perhaps to Shawmut Avenue or Washington Street. There you can wander and explore all the way to Mass. Ave. From there, take the no. 1 bus to the Back Bay or into Cambridge, or the Orange Line downtown.

T: Orange Line to Back Bay, or Green Line to Copley.

JAMAICA PLAIN ⚓

You can combine a visit to the **Arnold Arboretum** (p. 175) with a stroll around Jamaica Pond or along Centre Street. Culturally diverse Jamaica Plain abounds with interesting architecture and open space. The pond is especially pleasant in good weather, when people walk, run, skate, fish, picnic, and sunbathe. Many of the 19th-century mansions overlooking the pond date to the days when families fled the oppressive heat downtown and moved to the "country" for the summer.

After you've had your fill of nature (or before you set out), Centre Street makes a good destination for wandering and snacking. The AIDS Action Committee's excellent resale shop, **Boomerangs,** 716 Centre St. (© **617/524-5120**), is worth a look for upscale merchandise and reasonable prices. Another favorite destination is **JP Licks Homemade Ice Cream,** 674 Centre St. (© **617/524-6740**). Across the street from the T stop is the **Dogwood Café,** 3712 Washington St. (© **617/522-7997**), a family-friendly bar and restaurant with plenty of beers on tap and tasty pizza.

T: Orange Line to Forest Hills.

9 Especially for Kids

What can the children do in Boston? A better question might be "What *can't* the children do in Boston?" Just about every major attraction in the city either is specifically designed to appeal to youngsters or can easily be adapted to do so.

I wouldn't ordinarily make such an insulting suggestion, but experience tells me that some parents need reminding: Allowing your kids some input while you're planning your trip and incorporating suggestions (especially from teenagers) cuts down on eye-rolling and sighing. And the college tour, whale watch, or day trip that you wouldn't have considered may turn out to be one of the highlights of your vacation.

The following attractions are covered extensively elsewhere in this chapter; here's the boiled-down version for busy parents.

Tips **More Kid Stuff**

For more suggestions, check (or let the kids check) elsewhere in this book. Chapter 11 lists nightlife destinations for all ages. Before night falls (and sometimes afterward), the whole family can have a great time at the **Hard Rock Cafe** (food and music), **Jillian's Boston** (pool and all manner of arcade and virtual-reality games), *Shear Madness* (audience-participation theater), **Blue Man Group** (performance art), and the **Puppet Showplace Theater.**

Turn to chapter 10 for shopping recommendations—**Beadworks,** the **CambridgeSide Galleria** mall, **Curious George Goes to WordsWorth, Pearl Art & Craft Supplies,** and the various **college bookstores** can be almost as fun as toy stores.

Finally, check chapter 12 for information about day trips. Fun destinations include **Salem, Plymouth,** and (for *Little Women* fans) **Concord.**

Destinations with something for every member of the family include **Faneuil Hall Marketplace** (☎ **617/338-2323;** p. 151) and the **Museum of Fine Arts** (☎ **617/ 267-9300;** p. 157), which offers special weekend and after-school programs.

Hands-on exhibits and large-format films are the headliners at the **New England Aquarium** (☎ **617/973-5200;** p. 159), where you'll find the Simons IMAX Theatre, and at the **Museum of Science** (☎ **617/723-2500;** p. 158), home to the Mugar Omni Theater as well as the Hayden Planetarium.

You might get your hands on a baseball at a **Red Sox game** (p. 197) or the **Sports Museum of New England** (☎ **617/624-1234;** p. 197).

The allure of seeing people the size of ants draws young visitors to the **Prudential Center Skywalk** (☎ **617/859-0648;** p. 158). And they can see actual ants—although they might prefer the dinosaurs—at the **Harvard Museum of Natural History** (☎ **617/495-3045;** p. 178).

Older children who have studied modern American history will enjoy a visit to the **John F. Kennedy Presidential Library and Museum** (☎ **617/929-4523;** p. 156). And kids interested in cars will like the **Larz Anderson Auto Museum** (☎ **617/522- 6547;** p. 171).

Middle-schoolers who enjoyed Esther Forbes's *Johnny Tremain* might get a kick out of the **Paul Revere House** (☎ **617/523-2338;** p. 167). Young visitors who have read Robert McCloskey's classic *Make Way for Ducklings* will relish a visit to the **Public Garden** (p. 175), and fans of E. B. White's *The Trumpet of the Swan* certainly will want to ride on the **Swan Boats** (☎ **617/522-1966;** p. 175). Considerably less tame (and much longer) are **whale watches** (p. 190).

Note: At press time, the **Boston Tea Party Ship & Museum** (☎ **617/269-7150;** www.bostonteapartyship.com) was under renovation and scheduled to reopen in 2006. The expanded museum complements full-size replicas of the three merchant ships (the *Beaver, Eleanor,* and *Dartmouth*) that were raided during the colonial uprising in December 1773. Call ahead to see whether this attraction has reopened; it makes an entertaining stop on the way to or from the Children's Museum.

WALKING TOURS

Boston By Foot (☎ 617/367-2345, or 617/367-3766 for recorded information; www.bostonbyfoot.com) has a special walk, **"Boston By Little Feet,"** that's geared to children 6 to 12 years old. The 60-minute walk gives a child's-eye view of the architecture along the Freedom Trail and of Boston's role in the American Revolution. Children must be accompanied by an adult, and a map is provided. Tours run from May through October and begin at the statue of Samuel Adams on the Congress Street side of Faneuil Hall, Saturday at 10am, Sunday at 2pm, and Monday at 10am, rain or shine. The cost is $8 per person.

The **Historic Neighborhoods Foundation** (☎ 617/266-5669) offers a 90-minute **"Make Way for Ducklings" tour** ($8 adults, $6 children, free for children under 5). The tour follows the path of the Mallard family described in Robert McCloskey's famous book and ends at the Public Garden. Reservations are required. Every year on Mother's Day, Historic Neighborhoods organizes the Ducklings Day Parade.

Blue Hills Trailside Museum *Kids* At the foot of Great Blue Hill, a 20-minute drive south of Boston, this museum is fun for all ages and especially popular with the under-10 set. Here you'll see replicas of the natural habitats found in the area, displays about Native Americans, and live animal exhibits. Resident animals include owls, honeybees, otters, foxes, snakes, opossum, and turtles. Children can feed the ducks and turkeys. Other activities include climbing the lookout tower and hiking around the 7,500-acre Blue Hills Reservation recreation area. On weekends, there's story time at 11am and natural-history programs at 12:30 and 2pm. Special events and family programs change with the seasons; call ahead to register.

1904 Canton Ave., Milton. © 617/333-0690. www.massaudubon.org. Admission $3 adults, $2 seniors, $1.50 children 3–12, free for children under 3 and Massachusetts Audubon Society members. Wed–Sun and Mon holidays 10am–5pm. By car, take I-93 south to Exit 2B (Rte. 138 north).

Children's Museum ★★ *Kids*   As you approach the Children's Museum, don't be surprised to see adults suddenly being dragged by the hand when their young companions realize how close they are and start running. You know that the museum is near when you see the 40-foot-high red-and-white milk bottle out front. It makes both children and adults look small in comparison—which is probably part of the point. No matter how old, everyone behaves like a little kid at this delightful museum.

Children under 11 are the museum's target audience. They can stick with their adults or wander on their own, learning, doing, and role-playing. A two-story-high maze, the **New Balance Climb & Construction Zone,** incorporates motor skills and problem-solving. Other favorite hands-on exhibits include **Grandparents' Attic,** a souped-up version of dress-up; physical experiments (such as creating giant soap bubbles) in **Science Playground;** and **Boats Afloat,** which has an 800-gallon play tank and a replica of the bridge of a working boat. You can explore the **Think Tank,** which encourages creative thinking with puzzles, games, and optical illusions; **Boston Black,** which celebrates Boston's black history and culture; and a Japanese house from Kyoto (Boston's sister city). Children under 4 and their caregivers have a special room, **Playspace,** that's packed with toys and activities.

Call or surf ahead for information about traveling exhibitions—public-TV characters often drop by—and special programs. And be sure to check out the excellent gift shop (as if you have a choice).

300 Congress St. (Museum Wharf). © 617/426-8855. www.bostonkids.org. Admission $9 adults, $7 children 2–15 and seniors, $2 children age 1, free for children under 1; Fri 5–9pm $1 for all. Sat–Thurs 10am–5pm; Fri 10am–9pm. Closed Thanksgiving, Dec 25, and until noon Jan 1. T: Red Line to South Station. From South Station walk north on Atlantic Ave. 1 block (past Federal Reserve Bank), turn right onto Congress St., walk 2 blocks (across bridge). Call for information about discounted parking.

Franklin Park Zoo *Kids*   The Franklin Park Zoo is an enjoyable, engaging attraction but not a can't-miss experience—mostly because of its distance from downtown Boston. From June to September, you can visit the popular, colorful **Butterfly Landing** enclosure. On the **Outback Trail,** you can see kangaroos, wallabies, emus, and cockatoos. **Serengeti Crossing** is home to zebras, ibex, ostriches, and wildebeests. Other installations house cheetahs, lions, snow leopards, and African wild dogs. The **African Tropical Forest** exhibit is a sprawling complex where you'll see more than 50 species of animals. This is the domain of the Western lowland gorillas, which appear to be roaming free in an approximation of their natural habitat. If you're traveling with animal-mad youngsters, the **Children's Zoo** is both entertaining and educational.

Schedule at least half a day for a visit to the zoo. Franklin Park is 40 minutes from downtown by public transportation, and the walk from the main gate and parking area to the entrance is fairly long, especially for those with little legs.

1 Franklin Park Rd. © 617/541-LION. www.zoonewengland.org. Admission $9.50 adults, $8 seniors, $5 children 2–15, free for children under 2; Butterfly Landing admission (with zoo admission only) $1. Apr–Sept Mon–Fri

10am–5pm, Sat–Sun and holidays 10am–6pm; Oct–Mar daily 10am–4pm. T: Orange Line to Forest Hills or Red Line to Andrew, then bus no. 16 to the main entrance. Call for driving directions.

10 Organized Tours

ORIENTATION TOURS

GUIDED WALKING TOURS   Even if you usually prefer to explore on your own, I heartily recommend a walking tour with **Boston By Foot** ★★, 77 N. Washington St. (© **617/367-2345,** or 617/367-3766 for recorded information; www.bostonby foot.com). From May to October, the nonprofit educational corporation conducts historical and architectural tours that focus on particular neighborhoods or themes. The rigorously trained guides are volunteers who encourage questions. Buy tickets ($10 adults, $8 children 6–12) from the guide; reservations are not required. The 90-minute tours take place rain or shine.

Note: All excursions from Faneuil Hall start at the statue of Samuel Adams on Congress Street.

The **Heart of the Freedom Trail** tour starts at Faneuil Hall daily at 10am. Tours of **Beacon Hill** begin at the foot of the State House steps on Beacon Street weekdays at 5:30pm, Saturday at 10am, and Sunday at 2pm. **Boston Underground** looks at subterranean technology, including the subway and the depression of the Central Artery. It starts at Faneuil Hall Sunday at 2pm. Other tours and meeting places are **Victorian Back Bay,** on the steps of Trinity Church, 10am Friday through Sunday and 5:30pm Tuesday and Thursday; the **North End,** at Faneuil Hall, 2pm Friday and Saturday; and **Literary Landmarks,** at Borders, 10–24 School St., 2pm Saturday.

On the last Sunday of each month, a special tour ($12) covers a particular subject or area. In addition, special theme tours—they include "Great Women of Boston" and "Art Deco Boston"—and off-season tours for groups of 10 or more ($10 per person) can be scheduled.

The **Boston Park Rangers** (© **617/635-7383;** www.ci.boston.ma.us/parks) offer free guided walking tours. The best-known focus is the **Emerald Necklace,** a loop of green spaces designed by pioneering American landscape architect Frederick Law Olmsted, including Boston Common, the Public Garden, the Commonwealth Avenue Mall, the Muddy River in the Fenway, Olmsted Park, Jamaica Pond, the Arnold Arboretum, and Franklin Park. The full walk takes 6 hours; a typical offering is a tour of one of the sites. Call or surf ahead for schedules.

"DUCK" TOURS   The most unusual and enjoyable way to see Boston is with **Boston Duck Tours** ★★★ (© **800/226-7442** or 617/267-DUCK; www.boston ducktours.com). The tours, offered April through November only, are pricey but great

---

Finds **Behind the Scenes at the BSO**

From October through early May, free volunteer-led tours of **Symphony Hall,** 301 Mass. Ave. (© **617/266-1492;** www.bso.org), take visitors all around the landmark building and relate the Boston Symphony Orchestra's fascinating history. The 1-hour tours start on Wednesday at 4:30pm, except during the last 3 weeks of December, and on the first Saturday of each month at 1:30pm. Reservations aren't necessary; meet in the lobby at the Mass. Ave. entrance. For information about performances, see p. 235.

Moments   **Moon River . . . & Harbor**

Fire up the camera as you approach the water. Every **bridge** that crosses the river between Boston and Cambridge affords an excellent perspective. If your travels take you to the area around the Esplanade or Kendall Square (T: Red Line to Charles/MGH or Kendall/MIT), wander out onto the **Longfellow Bridge,** especially at twilight—the views of the river are splendid, and if you hit it just right, the moon appears to shine out of the Hancock Tower.

In warm weather, check the papers for the time of moonrise and stroll down to the plaza at the end of **Long Wharf** (T: Blue Line to Aquarium). The full moon appears to rise out of the Boston Harbor Islands, and because it's so close to the horizon, it looks huge. For astronomical reasons, this only works in the summer, but boy, is it cool.

---

fun. In a casual survey of local travel experts I conducted for the 2005 edition of this book, a Duck Tour was the most popular thing to do with out-of-towners. Sightseers board a "duck," a reconditioned World War II amphibious landing craft, behind the Prudential Center on Huntington Avenue or at the Museum of Science. The 80-minute narrated tour begins with a quick but comprehensive jaunt around the city. Then the duck lumbers down a ramp, splashes into the Charles River, and goes for a spin around the basin.

Tickets, available at the Prudential Center, the Museum of Science, and Faneuil Hall, are $25 for adults, $22 for seniors and students, $16 for children 3 to 11, and $3 for children under 3. Tours run every 30 or 60 minutes from 9am to 30 minutes before sunset, and they usually sell out. You can buy tickets online or in person. Try to buy same-day tickets early in the day, or ask about the limited number of tickets available starting 5 days in advance. Reservations are accepted only for groups of 20 or more. No tours December through March.

TROLLEY TOURS   The ticket-sellers who clamor for your business wherever tourists gather will claim that no visit is complete without a day on a trolley. For many people, this is simply not true, but it can be—say, if you're unable to walk long distances, short on time, or traveling with children. Because Boston is so pedestrian-friendly, a trolley tour isn't the best choice for the able-bodied and unencumbered making a long visit. A narrated tour on a trolley (actually a bus chassis with a trolley body) can give you an overview of the city before you focus on specific attractions, or you can use the all-day pass to hit as many places as possible in 8 hours or so. In some neighborhoods, notably the North End, the trolleys stop some distance from the attractions—don't believe a ticket-seller who tells you otherwise.

The business is extremely competitive, with various firms offering different stops in an effort to distinguish themselves from the rest. All cover the major attractions and offer informative narratives and anecdotes in their 90- to 120-minute tours; most offer free reboarding if you want to visit the attractions. Each tour is only as good as its guide, and quality varies widely—every few years a TV station or newspaper runs an "exposé" of the wacky information a tour guide is passing off as fact. Have a grain of salt ready. If you have time, you might even chat up guides in the waiting area and choose the one you like best.

Trolley tickets cost $22 to $29 for adults and $15 or less for children. Most companies offer online discounts, and you may find discount coupons at visitor information centers and hotel-lobby brochure racks. Boarding spots are at hotels, historic sites, and tourist information centers. Busy waiting areas are near the New England Aquarium, the Park Street T stop, and the corner of Boylston Street and Charles Street South, across from Boston Common. Each company paints its cars a different color. They include orange-and-green **Old Town Trolley Tours** (𝄐 **617/269-7150;** www. trolleytours.com); **Beantown Trolleys** (𝄐 **800/343-1328** or 617/720-6342; www. grayline.com), which say "Gray Line" but are red; and silver **CityView Trolleys** (𝄐 **617/363-7899;** www.cityviewtrolleys.com). The **Discover Boston Trolley Tours** (𝄐 **617/742-1440;** www.discoverbostontours.com) vehicle is white; its narration is available translated into Japanese, Spanish, French, German, and Italian.

DOUBLE-DECKER BUS TOURS   The **Charles Riverboat Company** (𝄐 **617/ 621-3001;** www.charlesriverboat.com) offers 60-minute narrated tours of Cambridge and Boston on a London-style double-decker bus. Tours begin and end at Harvard Square; tickets cost $15 for adults, $13 for seniors, and $6 for children under 13.

SIGHTSEEING CRUISES

Take to the water for a taste of Boston's rich maritime history or a daylong break from walking and driving. You can cruise around the harbor or go all the way to Provincetown. The **sightseeing cruise** ★★ season runs from **April through October,** with spring and fall offerings often restricted to weekends. Check websites for discount coupons before you leave home. If you're traveling in a large group, call ahead for information about reservations and discounted tickets. If you're prone to seasickness, check the size of the vessel for your tour before buying tickets; larger boats provide more cushioning and comfort than smaller ones.

   Tip: Before taking a cruise just for the sake of taking a cruise, weigh the investment of time and money against your group's interests. Especially if kids are along, you might be better off with an excursion that targets a destination—the Charlestown Navy Yard (see the box titled "On the Cheap"), the Boston Harbor Islands (see the box titled "A Vacation in the Islands" on p. 195), or Boston Light (see the box titled "Trip the Light Fantastic" on p. 189)—than with a pricey "cruise to nowhere" with narration that the children are ignoring anyway.

   The largest company is **Boston Harbor Cruises,** 1 Long Wharf (𝄐 **877/SEE-WHALE** or 617/227-4321; www.bostonharborcruises.com). Ninety-minute **historic sightseeing cruises,** which tour the Inner and Outer harbors, depart daily from Long Wharf at 11am, 1, 3, and 6 or 7pm (the sunset cruise), with extra excursions at busy times. Tickets are $18 for adults, $16 for seniors, and $13 for children 4 to 12; tickets for the sunset cruise are $2 more. The 45-minute **USS *Constitution* cruise** takes you around the Inner Harbor and docks at the Charlestown Navy Yard so that you can go ashore and visit Old Ironsides. Tours leave Long Wharf hourly from 10:30am

---

Value **On the Cheap**

You don't have to take a tour to take a cruise. The MBTA runs a **ferry** that connects Long Wharf and the Charlestown Navy Yard. It costs $1.50, is included in the MBTA Boston Visitor Pass, and makes a good final leg of the Freedom Trail.

Finds   Trip the Light Fantastic

North America's oldest lighthouse, **Boston Light** 🌟🌟, is the only lighthouse in the country that's still staffed (by the Coast Guard). Built on **Little Brewster Island** in 1716, it fell to the British in 1776 and was rebuilt in 1783. Excursions to the 102-foot lighthouse include a narrated cruise, 90 minutes to explore the island, and a chance to climb the spiral stairs to the top (you must be 50 in. tall). The 3½-hour tours leave from the Moakley Courthouse at Fan Pier and from the UMass-Boston student center in Dorchester. From early June to mid-October, trips leave from Fan Pier Saturday at 10am and 2pm and Sunday at 2pm, and from UMass-Boston Friday at 2pm. Between July 4th and Labor Day, there are additional departures from Fan Pier on Sunday at 10am and from UMass-Boston Thursday and Friday at 10am. Tickets cost $27 for adults, $23 for seniors and students, and $17 for children 6 to 12; trips are free for children under 6. Only 32 people may take each tour; reservations (📞 **617/223-8666;** www.bostonislands.com) are recommended.

---

to 4:30pm, and on the hour from the Navy Yard from 11am to 5pm. The cruise is $12 for adults, $11 for seniors, and $9 for children.

Another large operation, **Massachusetts Bay Lines** (📞 **617/542-8000;** www.massbaylines.com), offers 55-minute **harbor tours** from Memorial Day to Columbus Day, with limited service through the end of October. Cruises leave Rowes Wharf on the hour from 11am to 6pm (there's no 6pm cruise after Labor Day); the price is $11 for adults, $8 for children and seniors. The 90-minute sunset cruise leaves nightly at 7pm from Memorial Day to September 1, and at 6pm through mid-October. The 90-minute moonlight cruise leaves at 8:45pm on Friday and Saturday from mid-June to early September; call for times in early summer and fall. Sunset and moonlight cruises costs $17 for adults, $13 for seniors and children.

The **Charles Riverboat Company** (📞 **617/621-3001;** www.charlesriverboat.com) offers 60-minute narrated cruises around the **lower Charles River basin.** Boats leave the CambridgeSide Galleria mall at 10 and 11:15am, 12:30, 1:45, 3, and 4:15pm daily June through August and on weekends in May and September. Sunset cruises run daily; call to confirm times. Tickets (cash only) cost $10 for adults, $9 for seniors, and $6 for children 2 to 12.

DAY TRIPS   Two companies serve **Provincetown** 🌟🌟🌟, at the tip of Cape Cod. On a day trip, you'll have time for world-class people-watching, strolling around the novelty shops and art galleries, lunching on seafood, and—if you're quick—a trip to the famous beaches. However, you'll have to forgo the hopping gay nightlife scene unless you've planned a longer excursion. (For in-depth coverage of Provincetown and other Cape Cod locales, consult *Frommer's Cape Cod, Nantucket & Martha's Vineyard* or *Frommer's New England.*)

Bay State Cruise Company (📞 **866/90-FERRY** or 617/748-1428; www.baystatecruises.com) operates conventional and high-speed service to Provincetown. Trips leave from Commonwealth Pier at the World Trade Center, 200 Seaport Blvd. To get to the pier, take the Silver Line bus from South Station, the $10 water taxi (📞 **617/422-0392;** www.citywatertaxi.com) from locations around the harbor, or a regular taxi (when you reserve your cruise, ask the clerk for the best way to reach the pier from your hotel).

M/V *Provincetown II* sails Friday through Sunday from late June through early September. It leaves at 9:30am for the 3-hour trip to Provincetown, at the tip of Cape Cod. The return trip leaves at 3:30pm, giving you 3 hours for shopping and sightseeing in P-town. Same-day round-trip fares are $29 for adults, $23 for seniors, and $19 for children 3 to 12. Bringing a bike costs $5 extra each way. **High-speed service** on the *Provincetown III* takes 90 minutes and operates 3 times a day from late May to early October. The round-trip fare is $59 for adults, $53 for seniors, and $48 for children, plus $5 each way for your bike. Reservations are recommended.

Boston Harbor Cruises, 1 Long Wharf (© **877/SEE-WHALE** or 617/227-4321; www.bostonharborcruises.com), operates catamarans that make the trip in just 90 minutes. They operate daily Memorial Day through Columbus Day, twice a day Monday through Wednesday and three times daily Thursday to Sunday, with extra runs on summer weekends. The round-trip fare is $59 for adults, $54 for seniors, and $49 for children 4 to 12.

For lighthouse fanatics, Boston Harbor Cruises also runs a 5-hour **Northern Lights** cruise that goes as far north as Gloucester. It starts at 10am on Saturday only from late May to late September and costs $47 for adults, $45 for seniors, $42 for children 4 to 12. This is an excellent way to see the coast, but it's a long time to be on the water. If you want to explore a lighthouse, you'll be better off on a trip to Boston Light (see the box titled "Trip the Light Fantastic").

WHALE WATCHING

For whale-watching trips from Cape Ann, see the box titled "A Whale of an Adventure" on p. 277.

The **New England Aquarium** (© **617/973-5200** for information, 617/973-5206 for tickets; www.newenglandaquarium.org; p. 159) runs **whale watches** ★★ daily from May through mid-October and on weekends in April and late October. You'll travel several miles out to sea to Stellwagen Bank, the feeding ground for the whales as they migrate from Newfoundland to Provincetown. Allow 3½ to 5 hours. Tickets are $29 for adults, $26 for seniors and college students, $23 for youths 12 to 18, and $20 for children 3 to 11. Children must be 3 years old and at least 30 inches tall. Reservations are strongly recommended; you can also buy tickets online, subject to a service charge.

With its onboard exhibits and vast experience, the aquarium offers the best whale watches in Boston. If they're booked, other companies offer whale watches: **Boston Harbor Cruises** (© **877/SEE-WHALE** or 617/227-4321; www.bostonharborcruises. com), which has a high-speed catamaran that trims the excursion time to 3 hours total; and **Massachusetts Bay Lines** (© **617/542-8000;** www.massbaylines.com).

SPECIALTY TOURS

BOSTON HISTORY COLLABORATIVE　The offerings of the nonprofit **Boston History Collaborative** (© **617/350-0358;** www.bostonhistorycollaborative.org) include several trails presented as guided and self-guided walking tours, longer excursions by bus and boat, and information-packed websites.

Boston By Sea (www.bostonbysea.org) offers an entertaining 100-minute boat trip around the harbor. Subtitled "A Seafaring Adventure through Boston's Past," the excursion includes an account of the city's maritime legacy, flag raising, and sea chanteys. Tickets cost $18 for adults, $11 for children. For schedules and reservations, contact **Massachusetts Bay Lines** (✆ **617/542-8000;** www.massbaylines.com).

The 20-mile **Literary Trail** (www.lit-trail.org) links sites in Boston, Cambridge, and Concord that are associated with authors and poets such as Emerson, Thoreau, Longfellow, and Louisa May Alcott, among others. If you don't want to explore on your own, a 3½-hour guided trolley tour starts at 9am on the second Saturday of every month. It costs $30 for adults, $26 for children under 12. Tours leave from Omni Parker House, 60 School St.

The **Innovation Odyssey** (www.innovationodyssey.com) covers locations in Boston and Cambridge associated with the area's rich legacy of scientific discovery and invention. The bus tour leaves at 1:40pm on the second Saturday of each month from the Boston's Museum of Science, and at 2pm from 28 State St., across the street from the Old State House. Tours costs $25 for adults, $15 for students, $10 for children under 12, and $50 for families.

The History Collaborative organizes its **Boston Family History** information (www.bostonfamilyhistory.net) by ethnic group. The comprehensive website describes specialized walking tours and includes links to research tools.

FOR HISTORY BUFFS   Historic New England ✿ (✆ **617/227-3956;** www. historicnewengland.org) offers a fascinating tour that describes and illustrates life in the mansions and garrets of Beacon Hill in 1810. The 2-hour program, "Magnificent and Modest," costs $10 and starts at the Otis House Museum, 141 Cambridge St., at 11am on Saturdays from mid-May to October. The price includes a tour of the museum, and reservations are recommended.

FOR ARCHITECTURE BUFFS   The **Boston Center for Adult Education** (✆ **617/267-4430;** www.bcae.org) offers guided walking tours led by academic experts. The focus might be as specific as Copley Square or as general as "the Anglophile's Boston." The center is the country's oldest continuing-ed institution, and tours ($22–$40 for nonmembers) are part of the regular course offerings. Surf ahead for descriptions and registration info.

The **Historic Neighborhoods Foundation** (✆ **617/266-5669;** www.historic-neighborhoods.org) offers walking tours of various neighborhoods, including Beacon Hill, the North End, and the Waterfront. Schedules change with the season, and reservations are required, so call ahead or visit the website. The programs highlight points

---

⟨Moments **Written in Stone**

As you explore Boston, you might notice that nearly every block in the central part of the city contains a plaque commemorating some long-gone person, event, or even place ("on this site stood . . ."). Each one tells a little story, not just in its text but also in its context. A marker describing the Molasses Flood of 1919 (on Commercial St. near Hull St.) recalls the days when manufacturing and industry dominated an area that's now the residential North End and scenic waterfront. A plaque honoring the first Catholic Mass in Boston (on School St. near Borders, across the street from the Freedom Trail) doesn't seem like a big deal now, but in a Puritan city, toleration of "popery" couldn't have come easily. Look around as you walk around—history is everywhere, just waiting for you to discover it.

of interest in each neighborhood while covering history, architecture, and land development. Tours usually cost $10 to $15; check ahead for schedules and meeting places.

FOR ART-HISTORY MAJORS   Galleries and museums are the focus of **Boston Art Tours** (© **617/732-3920;** www.bostonarttours.com). Founder Marina Veronica is an art historian and educator who brings a contagious enthusiasm to her standard and customized tour offerings. Group tours include excursions for teens, families, and gay, straight, and Jewish singles. Call or surf ahead for rates, which start at $40 for adults, and reservations, which are required.

FOR CRIMINAL-JUSTICE MAJORS   Free guided tours of the **John Joseph Moakley Federal Courthouse,** 1 Courthouse Way (© **617/748-4185** or 617/748-4125; www.discoveringjustice.org), show off the waterfront building's dramatic architecture and introduce visitors to the workings of the justice system. You may even see part of a trial. Tours begin at 1pm on Tuesdays June through August, and are available to individuals and groups by appointment only Tuesday through Thursday from 9am to 4pm throughout the year (reserve a month in advance).

The courthouse is on Fan Pier, off Old Northern Avenue across the Fort Point Channel from the Coast Guard building at 408 Atlantic Ave. You can walk from downtown or take the Silver Line bus from South Station. To enter the heavily guarded courthouse, adults must show two forms of ID (one of which must have a photo), and everyone must surrender his or her cellphone. You don't have to take a tour to enter—local office workers often visit the second-floor cafeteria, which has decent food and a breathtaking view.

FOR SHUTTERBUGS   The unusual offerings of **PhotoWalks** (© **617/851-2273;** www.photowalks.com) combine narrated walking tours with photography tips. On a 2-hour stroll around Beacon Hill, the Public Garden, or the Freedom Trail, visitors learn to look at Boston from (literally) a different angle—that of a creative photographer. Adults pay $20, students with ID $15, and children under 12 $5. Tours run several times a week from April through October, and by appointment during the winter. Call or surf ahead for reservations.

FOR HORROR-MOVIE FANS   Ghosts & Gravestones (© **617/269-3626;** www.ghostsandgravestones.com) covers burial grounds and other shiver-inducing areas in a trolley and on foot, with a guide dressed as a gravedigger. The 2-hour tour starts at dusk on weekends in May, Wednesday to Monday from June through September, and nightly in October. It costs $30 for adults and $18 for children under 13. Reservations are required.

FOR FOODIES   A neighborhood resident offers **North End Market Tours** (© **617/523-6032;** www.northendmarkettours.com), 3½-hour excursions that stop at many of the shops in the legendary Italian-American stronghold. Tours include product tastings, shopping and cooking tips, and plenty of local lore. They cost $49 per person, which must be paid in advance.

Old Town Trolley (© **617/269-7010;** www.historictours.com) offers the 3-hour **Boston Chocolate Tour** on weekends from January through mid-April. The $60 tour includes three restaurants noted for their chocolate desserts; reservations are required.

11 Outdoor Pursuits

The **Department of Conservation & Recreation** (© **617/626-1250;** www.state.ma.us/dcr) oversees outdoor activities on public lands across the state through its divisions of Urban Parks & Recreation and State Parks & Recreation. (The Division of Urban Parks & Recreation replaced the Metropolitan District Commission, a name that still appears on many signs.) The incredibly helpful website includes descriptions of properties and activities, and has a planning area to help you make the most of your time.

BEACHES

The beaches in Boston proper are not worth the trouble. Besides being bone-chilling, Boston Harbor water is subject to being declared unsafe for swimming. If you want to swim, book a hotel with a pool. If you want the sand-between-your-toes experience, visit the North Shore or Walden Pond in Concord. See chapter 12 or consult the DCR (see the introduction to this section) for information on suburban beaches.

BIKING

Even expert cyclists who feel comfortable with Boston's layout (a tiny group) will be better off in Cambridge, which has bike lanes, or on the area's many bike paths. State law requires that children under 12 wear helmets. Bicycles are forbidden on buses and the Green Line at all times and during rush hours on the other lines of the subway system.

On summer Sundays from 11am to 7pm, a flat 1½-mile stretch of **Memorial Drive** ✦ in Cambridge, from Western Avenue to the Eliot Bridge (Central Sq. to west Cambridge), closes to cars. It's also popular with pedestrians and in-line skaters, and it can get quite crowded. The **Dr. Paul Dudley White Charles River Bike Path** ✦✦ is an 18-mile circuit that begins at Science Park (near the Museum of Science) and runs along both sides of the river as far as Watertown. You can enter and exit at many points along the way. Bikers share the path with joggers and in-line skaters, especially in Boston near the Esplanade and in Cambridge near Harvard Square. The DCR (see the introduction to this section) maintains this path and the 5-mile **Pierre Lallement Bike Path,** in Southwest Corridor Park, which starts behind Copley Place and runs through the South End and Roxbury along the route of the MBTA Orange Line to Franklin Park. The 11-mile **Minuteman Bikeway** ✦✦ (www.minutemanbikeway. org) starts at Alewife station at the end of the Red Line in Cambridge. It runs through Arlington and Lexington to Bedford along an old railroad bed and is a wonderful way to reach the historic sites in Lexington.

Rental shops require you to show a driver's license or passport and leave a deposit using a major credit card. Most charge around $5 an hour, with a minimum of at least 2 hours, or a flat daily rate of about $30. They include **Back Bay Bicycles,** 366 Commonwealth Ave., near Mass. Ave. (© **617/247-2336;** www.backbaybicycles. com), and **Community Bicycle Supply,** 496 Tremont St., near East Berkeley Street (© **617/542-8623;** www.communitybicycle.com). Across the river, try **Cambridge Bicycle,** 259 Mass. Ave. (© **617/876-6555;** www.oldroads.com/cb.html), near MIT. For additional information, contact **MassBike** (© **617/542-BIKE;** www.massbike.org).

GOLF

You won't get far in the suburbs without seeing a golf course, and given the sport's popularity, you won't be the only one looking. If possible, opt for the lower prices and smaller crowds that you'll find on weekdays. The **Massachusetts Golf Association** (© **800/356-2201** or 774/430-9100; www.mgalinks.org) represents more than 400 golf courses around the state. It has a searchable online database and will send you a list of courses on request.

One of the best public courses in the area, **Newton Commonwealth Golf Course,** 212 Kenrick St., Newton (© **617/630-1971;** www.sterlinggolf.com), is a challenging 18-hole Donald Ross design. It's 5,305 yards from the blue tees, par is 70, and greens fees are $28 on weekdays and $35 on weekends.

Within the city limits is the legendary 6,009-yard **William J. Devine Golf Course,** in Franklin Park, Dorchester (© **617/265-4084;** www.sterlinggolf.com). As a Harvard student, Bobby Jones sharpened his game on the 18-hole, par-70 course, which is managed by the city parks department. Greens fees are $26 on weekdays and $34 on weekends.

Less challenging but with more of a neighborhood feel is the 9-hole, par-35 **Fresh Pond Golf Course,** 691 Huron Ave., Cambridge (© **617/349-6282;** www.freshpond golf.com). The recently refurbished 3,161-yard layout adjoins the Fresh Pond Reservoir, and there's water on four holes. It charges $20, or $30 to go around twice, on weekdays; $24 and $36, respectively, on weekends.

GYMS

If your hotel doesn't have a health club, the concierge or front desk staff can recommend one nearby and possibly give you a pass good for free or discounted admission. Guests at the **Ritz-Carlton, Boston Common,** have the use of the over-the-top facilities at the 100,000-square-foot Sports Club/LA (guests at the original Ritz pay $20), which is otherwise closed to nonmembers. Other hotels with good health clubs (see chapter 6) include the **Boston Harbor Hotel,** the **Four Seasons Hotel,** the **Hilton Boston Logan Airport,** and the **Royal Sonesta Hotel.**

The "Y" offers the best combination of facilities and value. The **Wang YMCA of Chinatown,** 8 Oak St. W., off Washington St. (© **617/426-2237**), is close to downtown; the **Central Branch YMCA,** 316 Huntington Ave. (© **617/536-7800**), is near Symphony Hall. A 1-day pass costs $10 and includes the use of the pool, gym, weight room, and fitness center. Closer to downtown, **Crunch,** 17 Winter St. (© **617/338-9001;** www.crunch.com), sells a $19 day pass that includes access to equipment as well as its extensive roster of fun classes. **Fitcorp** (© **617/375-5600;** www.fitcorp.com) charges $20 for a guest pass and offers well-equipped facilities but no pool. It has branches at 1 Beacon St. (© **617/248-9797**), near Government Center; 125 Summer St. (© **617/261-4855**), in the Financial District; and in the Prudential Center (© **617/262-2050**).

HIKING

For information about hiking in state parks and forests, visit **www.massparks.org**. The **Boston Harbor Islands** offer great hiking; circling the largest island, Peddocks, takes half a day. See the box, "A Vacation in the Islands," p. 195.

The **Bay Circuit Trail & Greenway** is a 200-mile corridor of open space that curves around Boston from Newburyport, near the New Hampshire border, to Kingston Bay, north of Plymouth. The ribbon of conservation land touches on 50 cities and towns; it comes closest to the areas covered in this book when it cuts through **Concord** along the north shore of Walden Pond (see chapter 12). For information, contact the nonprofit **Bay Circuit Alliance,** 3 Railroad St., Andover, MA 01810 (© **978/470-1982;** www.baycircuit.org).

ICE SKATING & IN-LINE SKATING

The skating rink at the Boston Common **Frog Pond** ☆☆ (© **617/635-2120;** www. cityofboston.gov/parks) is an extremely popular cold-weather destination. It's an open

Finds   A Vacation in the Islands

Majestic ocean views, hiking trails, historic sites, rocky beaches, nature walks, campsites, and picnic areas abound in New England. To find them all together, head east (yes, east) of Boston to the **Boston Harbor Islands** (© 617/223-8666; www.bostonislands.com). The national park area's unspoiled beauty is a welcome break from the urban landscape, and the islands are not well known, even to many longtime Bostonians. Thirty-four islands dot the Outer Harbor, and at least a half dozen are open for exploring, camping, swimming, and more. Bring a sweater or jacket. Plan a day trip or even an overnight trip, but note that only Georges Island has fresh water, and management strongly suggests bringing your own.

Ferries run to **Georges Island,** home of Fort Warren (1833), which held Confederate prisoners during the Civil War. You can investigate on your own or take a ranger-led tour. The island has a visitor center, refreshment area, fishing pier, picnic area, and wonderful view of Boston's skyline. Allow at least half a day, longer if you plan to take the free water taxi to **Lovell, Peddocks, Bumpkin,** or **Grape Island,** all of which have picnic areas and campsites. Lovell Island also has the remains of a fort (Fort Standish).

Harbor Express (© 617/222-6999; www.harborexpress.com) serves Georges Island from Long Wharf and Fan Pier; the trip takes 30 minutes, and round-trip tickets are $10 for adults, $9 for seniors, and $7 for children 4 to 12. Cruises depart daily on the hour from 10am to 5pm in the summer, less frequently in the spring and fall. In the off-season, check ahead for winter wildlife excursions (scheduled occasionally). Water taxis and admission to the islands are free.

A public-private National Park Partnership administers the Boston Harbor Islands National Recreation Area (www.nps.gov/boha). For more information, visit the website, consult the staff at the **kiosk on Long Wharf,** or contact the **Friends of the Boston Harbor Islands** (© 617/740-4290; www.fbhi. org). The Friends coordinate a variety of cruises on and around the harbor throughout the summer and fall; check ahead for details.

surface with an ice-making system and a clubhouse. Admission is $3 for adults and free for children under 14; skate rental costs $7 for adults, $5 for kids. The rink gets unbelievably crowded on weekend afternoons, so try to go in the morning or on a weekday.

Cambridge's **Charles Hotel** (© 617/234-8008; www.charleshotel.com) has a small ice rink off the lobby. It's open weekdays from 3 to 8pm, weekends from 10am to 8pm. Admission is $5 for adults, $3 for children under 12; skate rental costs $5.

A favorite spot for in-line skaters is the **Esplanade,** between the Back Bay and the Charles River. It continues onto the bike path that runs to Watertown and back (p. 193), but after you leave the Esplanade, the pavement isn't totally smooth, which can lead to mishaps. Your best bet is to wait for a Sunday in the summer, when **Memorial Drive** ⟨ near Harvard Square in Cambridge closes to traffic from 11am to

7pm. It's a perfect surface. Unless you're confident of your ability and your knowledge of Boston traffic, stay off the streets.

To rent skates or blades, visit the **Beacon Hill Skate Shop,** 135 Charles St. S. (© **617/482-7400**), not far from the Esplanade. Expect to pay about $15 a day. The **InLine Club of Boston's** website (www.sk8net.com) offers up-to-date event and safety information.

JOGGING

The **Dr. Paul Dudley White Charles River Bike Path** ★★ is also a jogging route. The 18-mile loop along the water is extremely popular because it's car-free (except at intersections), scenic, and generally safe. The bridges that connect Boston and Cambridge allow for circuits of various lengths. Be careful around abutments, where you can't see far ahead. Don't jog at night, and try not to go alone. Visit the DCR website (see the introduction to this section) to view a map that gives distances. If the river's not convenient, the concierge or desk staff at your hotel probably can provide a map with suggested jogging routes. As in any other city, stay out of park areas at night.

SAILING

Sailboats fill the Charles River basin all summer and skim across the Inner Harbor in all but the coldest weather. Your options during a short stay aren't especially cost-effective, but they are fun.

The best deal is with **Community Boating,** 21 David Mugar Way, on the Esplanade (© **617/523-1038;** www.community-boating.org). Visitors pay $100 for 2 days of unlimited use in the Charles River Basin, a gorgeous but congested patch of water between the Back Bay and Cambridge's Kendall Square. The oldest public sailing facility in the country offers lessons and boating programs for children and adults from April through November. The fleet includes 13- to 23-foot sailboats as well as Windsurfers and kayaks. The **Boston Sailing Center,** Lewis Wharf, off Atlantic Avenue (© **617/227-4198;** www.bostonsailingcenter.com), offers lessons for sailors of all ability levels. The center is open year-round (even for "frostbite" racing in the winter). The least expensive 30-day mini-membership costs $350.

TENNIS

Public courts are available throughout the city at no charge. Well-maintained courts that seldom get busy until after work are at several spots on the Southwest Corridor Park in the **South End** (there's a nice one near **West Newton St.**). The courts on **Boston Common** and in **Charlesbank Park,** overlooking the river next to the bridge to the Museum of Science, are more crowded during the day. To find the court nearest you, ask the concierge or desk staff at your hotel or visit the DCR website (www.state.ma.us/dcr).

12 Spectator Sports

Boston is a great sports town, and at press time, in mid-2005, eastern Massachusetts is the center of the North American sports universe. Red Sox fans are high on their beloved team's first World Series championship in 86 years, and the New England Patriots (who play in suburban Foxboro) are celebrating their third Super Bowl victory in 4 years. Fans are also passionate about college sports, particularly hockey, in which the Division I schools are fierce rivals.

The **TD Banknorth Garden** (Causeway St.; © **617/624-1000** for events line or 617/931-2000 for Ticketmaster; www.tdbanknorthgarden.com), is open for tours on the hour from 11am to 3pm daily, depending on the arena schedule. On the fifth- and sixth-floor concourses, the **Sports Museum of New England** (© **617/624-1235;** www.sportsmuseum.org) celebrates local teams and athletes of all ages—especially the Celtics and Bruins, who play in the building. Tickets cost $6 for adults, $4 for seniors and children 6 to 17, free for children under 6. Always call ahead; there's no access during events. *Note:* Visitors may not bring any bags, including backpacks and brief-cases, into the arena.

BASEBALL

The 2004 World Series champion **Boston Red Sox** play at **Fenway Park** ★★★, home of the 2004 World Series champion Boston Red Sox. Redundant and repetitive? Oh, yeah. Get used to it.

The Red Sox were an obsession with fans all over the world long before they snapped an 86-year dry spell and (maybe you heard about this) won the 2004 World Series. Jokes about pigs flying and hell freezing over are passé by now, but you still might catch the true believers pinching themselves.

The Sox play from early April to early October, later if they make the playoffs. The quirkiness of the oldest park in the major leagues (1912) only adds to the mystique. A hand-operated scoreboard fronts the 37-foot left-field wall, or "Green Monster." Watch carefully during a pitching change—the left fielder from either team might suddenly disappear into a door in the wall to cool off. The seats are narrow, uncomfortable, and gratifyingly close to the field, and the concession items are more varied than they once were, though definitely not cheaper. The Red Sox franchise changed hands in 2002, and the new owners have invested so much in the existing structure that rumors of its impending demolition have quieted down. The most obvious change is the addition of seats and standing room in a new section *above* the Green Monster.

Practical concerns: Compared with its modern brethren, Fenway is tiny. Tickets are the most expensive in the majors—a few upper bleacher seats go for $12, but most are in the $23-to-$85 range. They go on sale in December; order early. Forced to choose between seats in a low-numbered grandstand section—say, 10 or below—and in the bleachers, go for the bleachers. They can get rowdy during night games, but the view is better from there than from deep in right field. Monster seats top out at $120 and go on sale by lottery in batches throughout the season; check the website. A limited number of same-day standing-room tickets are available before each game, and fans sometimes return presold tickets (especially if a rainout causes rescheduling). It can't hurt to check, particularly if the team isn't playing well.

The **Fenway Park ticket office** (© **877/REDSOX-9;** www.redsox.com; T: Green Line B, C, or D to Kenmore, or D to Fenway) is at 4 Yawkey Way, near the corner of

---

Moments **Play Ball!**

Fenway Park tours (© 617/226-6666) include a walk on the warning track, a stop in the press box, and a visit to the Red Sox Hall of Fame. Tours start on the hour from 9am to 4pm (or 3 hr. before game time, whichever is earlier) daily, year-round. There are no tours on holidays or before day games. Admission is $12 for adults, $11 for seniors, and $10 for children under 15.

Brookline Avenue. Tickets for people with disabilities and in no-alcohol sections are available. Smoking is not allowed in the park.

BASKETBALL

Sixteen National Basketball Association championship banners hang from the ceiling of the TD Banknorth Garden, testimony to the glorious history of the **Boston Celtics.** Unfortunately, the most recent is from 1986. The Celtics play from early October to April or May; when a top contender is visiting, you might have trouble getting tickets. Prices are as low as $10 for some games and top out at $150 ($750 for floor seats). For information, call the TD Banknorth Garden (© **617/624-1000;** www.nba.com/celtics); for tickets, contact Ticketmaster (© **617/931-2000;** www. ticketmaster.com). To reach the TD Banknorth Garden, take the MBTA Green or Orange Line or commuter rail to North Station. *Note:* Spectators may not bring any bags, including backpacks and briefcases, into the arena.

FOOTBALL

The **New England Patriots** (© **800/543-1776;** www.patriots.com) were playing to standing-room-only crowds even before they won three Super Bowls in 4 years (2002, 2004, and 2005). The Pats play from August through December or January at Gillette Stadium on Route 1 in Foxboro, about a 45-minute drive south of Boston. Tickets ($59–$125, the most expensive in the league) sell out well in advance, often as part of season-ticket packages. Call or check the website for information on individual ticket sales and public-transit options.

   Boston College, another tough ticket, is New England's only Division I-A college team. The Eagles play at Alumni Stadium in Chestnut Hill (© **617/552-3000;** www. bceagles.collegesports.com). The area's Division I-AA teams are **Harvard University,** Harvard Stadium, North Harvard Street, Allston (© **617/495-2211;** www.gocrimson. com), and **Northeastern University,** Parsons Field, Kent Street, Brookline (© **617/ 373-4700;** www.gonu.com).

GOLF TOURNAMENTS

The major tours have changed their schedules several times in recent years; at least one usually gets within an hour of downtown Boston. Over Labor Day weekend, the **PGA Tour** (www.pgatour.com) visits the Tournament Players Club of Boston, which is actually in Norton (© **508/285-3200;** www.thetpcofboston.com). The senior golfers on the **Champions Tour** (www.pgatour.com) swing by every June or July, landing at Nashawtuc Country Club in Concord (© **978/369-3457;** www.nashawtuc.com). The **Women's Senior Golf Tour** (www.wsgtour.com) stops at Granite Links Golf Club in Quincy (© **617/296-7600;** www.granitelinksgolfclub.com) in August. Check ahead for exact dates and other information, including whether the **LPGA** (www.lpga.com) will return to eastern Massachusetts. The *Globe* and *Herald* regularly list numerous amateur events for fun and charity.

HOCKEY

The **Boston Bruins,** one of the NHL's original six teams, are exciting but incredibly expensive to watch. Tickets for many games sell out early despite being among the priciest ($19–$155) in the league. For information, call the TD Banknorth Garden (© **617/624-1000;** www.bostonbruins.com); for tickets, contact Ticketmaster (© **617/931-2000;** www.ticketmaster.com). To reach the TD Banknorth Garden, take the MBTA Green or Orange Line or commuter rail to North Station. *Note:* Spectators may not bring any bags, including backpacks and briefcases, into the arena.

Budget-minded fans who don't have their hearts set on seeing a pro game will be pleasantly surprised by the quality of local **college hockey** ✦. Even for sold-out games, standing-room tickets are usually available the night of the game. Women's games don't sell out. The local teams regularly hit the national rankings; they include **Boston College,** Conte Forum, Chestnut Hill (© **617/552-3000;** www.bceagles. collegesports.com); **Boston University,** Agganis Arena, 928 Commonwealth Ave. (© **617/353-3838;** www.bu.edu/athletics); **Harvard University,** Bright Hockey Center, North Harvard Street, Allston (© **617/495-2211;** www.gocrimson.com); and **Northeastern University,** Matthews Arena, St. Botolph Street (© **617/373-4700;** www.gonu.com). These four are the Beanpot schools, whose men's teams play a tradition-steeped tournament on the first 2 Mondays of February at the TD Banknorth Garden.

HORSE RACING

Suffolk Downs ✦, 111 Waldemar Ave., East Boston (© **617/567-3900;** www. suffolkdowns.com), is one of the best-run smaller tracks in the country. The legendary Seabiscuit raced here; a marker commemorates his storied career. In addition to extensive simulcasting options day and night year-round, the live racing season runs from April to November. General admission on live racing days is $2; otherwise, admission is free. The Grade 2 Massachusetts Handicap takes place on a Saturday in late spring or early summer.

The day's entries appear in the *Globe* and *Herald.* The track is off Route 1A, about 2 miles north of Logan Airport. The MBTA Blue Line has a Suffolk Downs station; wait for the shuttle bus or walk about 10 minutes to the track entrance.

THE MARATHON

Every year on Patriots Day—the third Monday in April—the **Boston Marathon** ✦✦✦ rules the roads from suburban Hopkinton to Copley Square in Boston. Cheering fans line the entire route. An especially nice place to watch is tree-shaded Commonwealth Avenue between Kenmore Square and Mass. Ave., but you'll be in a crowd wherever you stand, particularly near the finish line in front of the Boston Public Library. For information about qualifying, contact the **Boston Athletic Association** (© **617/236-1652;** www.bostonmarathon.org).

ROWING

In late October, the **Head of the Charles Regatta** ✦ (© **617/868-6200;** www.hocr. org) attracts more rowers than any other crew event in the country. Some 4,000 oarsmen and oarswomen race against the clock for 4 miles from the Charles River basin to the Eliot Bridge in west Cambridge. Hundreds of thousands of spectators socialize and occasionally watch the action, which runs nonstop on Saturday afternoon and all day Sunday.

Spring crew racing is more exciting than the "head" format; the course is 1¼ miles, and races last just 5 to 7 minutes. Men's and women's collegiate events take place on Saturday mornings in April and early May in the Charles River basin. You'll have a perfect view of the finish line from Memorial Drive between the MIT boathouse and the Hyatt Regency Cambridge hotel. To find out who's racing, check the Friday *Globe* sports section.

SOCCER

The **New England Revolution** (© 877/438-7387; www.revolutionsoccer.net) of Major League Soccer plays at Gillette Stadium on Route 1 in Foxboro from April through September. Tickets cost $16 to $32 and are available through Ticketmaster (© 617/931-2000; www.ticketmaster.com).

Check the Women's United Soccer Association website (www.wusa.com) before you visit to see whether the league has resumed play; the **Boston Breakers** are the local franchise.

9

Boston Strolls

Walking is the best way to see Boston. The narrow, twisting streets that make driving such a headache are a treat for pedestrians, who are never far from something worth seeing. The central city is compact—walking quickly from one end to the other takes about an hour—and abounds with historically and architecturally interesting buildings and neighborhoods.

In this chapter you'll find a tour of Boston's **Back Bay** and one of **Harvard Square** in Cambridge. For information on Boston's most famous walking tour, the 3-mile **Freedom Trail** ★★★, see chapter 8.

Be sure to wear comfortable shoes, and if you're not inclined to pay designer prices for designer water, bring your own bottle and fill it at your hotel.

WALKING TOUR 1   THE BACK BAY

Start:	The Public Garden (T: Green Line to Arlington).
Finish:	Copley Square.
Time:	2 hours if you make good time, 3 if you detour to the Esplanade, and longer if you do a lot of shopping.
Best Time:	Any time before late afternoon.
Worst Time:	Late afternoon, when people and cars pack the streets. And don't attempt the detour on July 4th, when concertgoers jam the neighborhood. This walk is mostly outdoors, so if the weather is bad, you may find yourself in lots of shops. You decide whether that makes an overcast day a "best" or "worst" time.

The Back Bay is the youngest neighborhood in central Boston, the product of a massive landfill project that transformed the city from 1835 to 1882. It's flat, symmetrical, logically designed—the names of the cross streets go in alphabetical order—and altogether anomalous in Boston's crazy-quilt geography.

Begin your walk in the:

❶ Public Garden
Before the Back Bay was filled in, the Charles River flowed right up to Charles Street, which separates Boston Common from the Public Garden. On the night of April 18, 1775, British troops bound for Lexington and Concord boarded boats to Cambridge ("two if by sea") at the foot of the Common and set off across what's now the Public Garden.

Explore the lagoon, the trees and other flora, and the statuary. Take a ride on the **Swan Boats** (mid-Apr to mid-Sept), and then make your way toward the corner of Charles and Beacon streets.

A short distance away, inside the Public Garden (listen for the cries of delighted children), you'll see a 35-foot strip of cobblestones topped with the bronze figures that immortalize Robert McCloskey's book:

❷ *Make Way for Ducklings*

Installed in 1987 and wildly popular since the moment they were unveiled, Nancy Schön's renderings of Mrs. Mallard and her eight babies are irresistible. Mrs. Mallard is 38 inches tall, making her back a bit higher than a tricycle seat, but that doesn't keep people of all ages from climbing on. If you don't know the story of the Mallards' perilous trip to meet Mr. Mallard at the lagoon, ask one of the parents or children you'll find here.

The city bought the site of the Public Garden from private interests in 1824. Planting began in 1837, but it wasn't until the late 1850s that Arlington Street was built and the land permanently set aside. George F. Meacham executed the design.

Cross the lagoon using the little suspension bridge and look for the statue of:

❸ George Washington

Unveiled in 1875, this was Boston's first equestrian statue. It stands 38 feet tall and is considered an excellent likeness of the first president of the United States, an outstanding horseman. The artist, Thomas Ball, was a Charlestown native who worked in Italy. Among his students was noted sculptor Daniel Chester French. Pass through the gate onto Arlington Street. Before you begin exploring in earnest, this is a good place to detour.

TAKE A BREAK
Turn right and walk up Arlington Street to Beacon Street. On your right across the busy intersection is **Cheers**, 84 Beacon St. (✆ 617/227-9605; www.cheersboston.com), originally the Bull & Finch Pub. The food is quite tasty, but remember two things: The bar looks nothing like its TV offspring (you'll find a replica of the set at Faneuil Hall Marketplace), and the patrons generally consist of people from everywhere else in the universe except Boston.

Alternatively, turn right on Beacon Street and walk 1 long block to Charles Street. You can pick up food to go at **Panificio**, 144 Charles St. (✆ 617/227-4340), or **Cafe Vanille**, 70 Charles St. (✆ 617/523-9200). This street is also a promising place for a **shopping** break (see chapter 10).

When you've found something to eat, backtrack along Beacon Street past Arlington Street to Embankment Road and turn right. Take the Arthur Fiedler Footbridge across Storrow Drive to the Esplanade, and unpack your food near the giant head of:

❹ Arthur Fiedler

Installed in 1985, this sculpture by Ralph Helmick consists of sheets of aluminum that eerily capture the countenance of the legendary conductor of the Boston Pops, who died in 1979. The amphitheater to the right is the **Hatch Shell**, where the Pops perform free during the week leading up to and including July 4th.

When you're ready, retrace your steps to the corner of Arlington Street and Commonwealth Avenue. This is the:

❺ Boston Center for Adult Education

Constructed in 1904 as a private home, this building, at 5 Commonwealth Ave., gained a huge ballroom in 1912. If the ornate ballroom is not in use for a class or

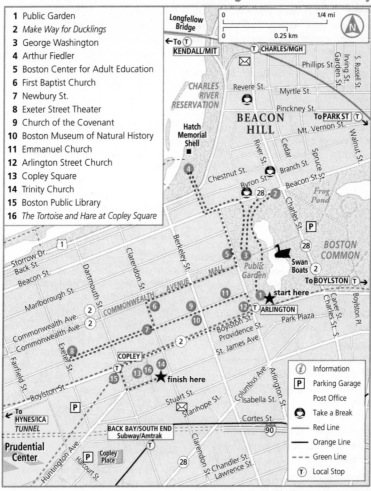

1 Public Garden
2 *Make Way for Ducklings*
3 George Washington
4 Arthur Fiedler
5 Boston Center for Adult Education
6 First Baptist Church
7 Newbury St.
8 Exeter Street Theater
9 Church of the Covenant
10 Boston Museum of Natural History
11 Emmanuel Church
12 Arlington Street Church
13 Copley Square
14 Trinity Church
15 Boston Public Library
16 *The Tortoise and Hare at Copley Square*

Information
Parking Garage
Post Office
Take a Break
Red Line
Orange Line
Green Line
Local Stop

a function (it's popular for weddings), you're welcome to have a look. The BCAE (℡ 617/267-4430; www.bcae.org), established in 1933, is the oldest continuing-education institution in the country.

You're now on the 8-block **Commonwealth Avenue Mall.** This graceful promenade is the centerpiece of architect Arthur Gilman's design of the Back Bay. The mall is 100 feet wide (the entire street is 240 ft.) and stretches to Kenmore

Square. The elegant Victorian mansions on either side—almost all divided into apartments or in commercial or educational use—are recognized as a great asset, but the attitude toward the apparently random collection of sculpture along the mall is hardly unanimous. Judge for yourself as you inspect the art, starting with **Alexander Hamilton** across Arlington Street from **George Washington.** The most moving sculpture is at Dartmouth

Street. The **Vendome Memorial** honors the memory of the nine firefighters who lost their lives in a blaze at the Hotel Vendome in 1972.

Two blocks from the Public Garden, at 110 Commonwealth Ave., at the corner of Clarendon Street, is the:

❻ First Baptist Church

Built from 1870 to 1872 of Roxbury puddingstone, it originally housed the congregation of the Brattle Street Church (Unitarian), which had been downtown, near Faneuil Hall.

At Clarendon Street or Dartmouth Street, turn left and walk 1 block to:

❼ Newbury Street

Commonwealth Avenue is the architectural heart of the Back Bay, and Newbury Street is the commercial center. Take some time to roam around here (see chapter 10 for pointers), browsing in the galleries, window-shopping at the boutiques, and watching the chic shoppers.

Walk down Newbury St. to Exeter St. At 26 Exeter St. is the building that was once the:

❽ Exeter Street Theater

Designed in 1884 as the First Spiritualist Temple, it was a movie house from 1914 to 1984. Once known for the crowds flocking to *The Rocky Horror Picture Show,* it's now the home of a TGI Friday's restaurant.

When you're ready to continue your stroll (or when your credit cards cry for mercy), turn back toward the Public Garden and seek out three of Newbury Street's oldest buildings, starting with the:

❾ Church of the Covenant

This Gothic revival edifice at 67 Newbury St. was designed by Richard Upjohn and completed in 1867. The stained-glass windows are the work of Louis Comfort Tiffany.

Across the street, set back from the sidewalk at 234 Berkeley St., an opulent store occupies an opulent setting. Now the clothing emporium Louis Boston, this is the original home of the:

❿ Boston Museum of Natural History

A forerunner of the Museum of Science, it was built according to William Preston's French Academic design. The 1864 structure was originally two stories high and has its original roof, preserved when the building gained a third floor.

Cross Newbury Street again and continue walking toward the Public Garden. On your left, at 15 Newbury St., is:

⓫ Emmanuel Church

The first building completed on Newbury Street, this Episcopal church ministers through the arts, so there might be a concert (classical to jazz, solo to orchestral) going on during your visit. Check ahead (*©* **617/536-3355;** www.emmanuel-boston.org) for schedules.

Now you're almost back at the Public Garden. On your left is the original **Ritz-Carlton** (1927).

Turn right onto Arlington Street and walk 1 block. On your right, at 351 Boylston St., is the:

⓬ Arlington Street Church

This is the oldest church in the Back Bay, completed in 1861. An interesting blend

---

Fun Fact **The Shape of Things to Come**

The **First Baptist Church** is a fine building, but the design is notable mainly because its creators went on to much more famous projects. The architect, **H. H. Richardson,** is best known for nearby **Trinity Church.** The artist who created the frieze, which represents the sacraments, was **Frédéric Auguste Bartholdi,** who designed the **Statue of Liberty.**

of Georgian and Italianate details, it's the work of architect Arthur Gilman, who laid out this whole neighborhood. Here you'll find more Tiffany stained glass. Step inside to see the pulpit that was in use in 1788 when the congregation worshipped downtown on Federal Street.

Follow Boylston Street away from the Public Garden. Two blocks up is:

⑬ Copley Square

Enjoy the fountain and visit the farmers' market, which operates Tuesday and Friday afternoons from July through November.

Overlooking the square is one of the most famous church buildings in the United States. This is:

⑭ Trinity Church

H. H. Richardson's Romanesque masterpiece, completed in 1877, is to your left. The church, 206 Clarendon St. (② **617/ 536-0944;** www.trinitychurchboston. org), was built on 4,502 pilings driven into the mud that was once the Back Bay. The building is undergoing extensive renovations. Brochures and guides are available to help you find your way around a building considered one of the finest examples of church architecture in the country. Admission is free; tours cost $5. It's open daily from 8am to 6pm. Friday organ recitals begin at 12:15pm.

Across Dartmouth Street is the:

⑮ Boston Public Library

The work of architect Charles Follen McKim and many others, the Renaissance revival building was completed in 1895 after 10 years of construction. Its design reflects the significant influence of the Bibliothèque Nationale in Paris. Wander up the steps to check out the building's impressive interior (see p. 170 for more details). **Daniel Chester French** designed the doors.

Head across the street to Copley Square. In a sense, you've come full circle; as at the Public Garden, you'll see a playful and compelling sculpture:

⑯ *The Tortoise & Hare* at Copley Square

This is another work by Nancy Schön. Designed to signify the end of the **Boston Marathon** (the finish line is on Boylston St. between Exeter and Dartmouth sts.). It was unveiled for the 100th anniversary of the event in 1996.

From here you're in a good position to set out for any other part of town or walk a little way in any direction and continue exploring. Copley Place and the Shops at Prudential Center are nearby, Newbury Street is 1 block over, and there's a Green Line T station at Boylston and Dartmouth streets.

Start: Harvard Square (T: Red Line to Harvard).

Finish: John F. Kennedy Park.

Time: 2 to 4 hours, depending on how much time you spend in shops and museums.

Best Time: Almost any time during the day. The Harvard University Art Museums are free on Saturday morning; the natural history museums are free on Sunday morning year-round and on Wednesday from 3 to 5pm during the school year.

Worst Time: The first full week of June. You might have trouble gaining admission to Harvard Yard during commencement festivities. The ceremony is Thursday morning; without a ticket, you won't be allowed in.

Popular impressions to the contrary, Cambridge is not exclusively Harvard. In fact, even Harvard Square isn't exclusively Harvard. During a walk around the area, you'll see historic buildings and sights, interesting museums, and notable architecture on and off the university's main campus.

Leave the T station by the main entrance (take the ramp to the turnstiles, then take the escalators) and emerge in the heart of:

❶ Harvard Square

Town and gown meet at this lively intersection, where you'll get a taste of the improbable mix of people drawn to the crossroads of Cambridge. To your right is the landmark **Out of Town News** kiosk. It stocks newspapers and magazines from all over the world and tons of souvenirs (beefed up when the rise of the Internet cut into the demand for non-virtual journalism). At the booth (© **800/862-5678**) in front of you, you can request information about the area. Step close to it so that you're out of the flow of pedestrian traffic and look around.

The store across Mass. Ave. is the **Harvard Coop.** It rhymes with *hoop*—say "co-op" and risk being taken for a Yalie. On the far side of the intersection,

at the corner of John F. Kennedy and Brattle streets, is a sign reading DEWEY CHEETHAM & HOWE (say it out loud) on the third floor of the brick building. National Public Radio's "Car Talk" originates here.

Turn around so that the Coop is at your back and walk half a block, crossing Dunster Street. Across the way, at 1341 Mass. Ave., you'll see:

❷ Wadsworth House

Most of the people waiting for the bus in front of this yellow wood building probably don't know that it was built in 1726 as a residence for Harvard's fourth president—but then, neither do most Harvard students. Its biggest claim to fame is a classic: George Washington slept here.

Cross the street and go left. Follow the outside of the brick wall past one gate until you see another T exit. Turn right and use Johnston Gate to enter:

Impressions

One emerged, as one still does, from the subway exit in the Square and faced an old red-brick wall behind which stretched, to my fond eye, what remains still the most beautiful campus in America, the Harvard Yard. If there is any one place in all America that mirrors better all American history, I do not know of it.

—Theodore H. White, *In Search of History*, 1978

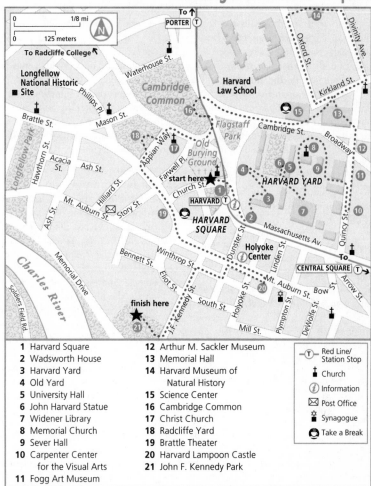

1	Harvard Square	12	Arthur M. Sackler Museum
2	Wadsworth House	13	Memorial Hall
3	Harvard Yard	14	Harvard Museum of
4	Old Yard		Natural History
5	University Hall	15	Science Center
6	John Harvard Statue	16	Cambridge Common
7	Widener Library	17	Christ Church
8	Memorial Church	18	Radcliffe Yard
9	Sever Hall	19	Brattle Theater
10	Carpenter Center	20	Harvard Lampoon Castle
	for the Visual Arts	21	John F. Kennedy Park
11	Fogg Art Museum		

Ⓣ — Red Line/ Station Stop
✝ Church
ⓘ Information
✉ Post Office
✡ Synagogue
☕ Take a Break

❸ Harvard Yard

This is the oldest part of "the Yard." It was a patch of grass with animals grazing on it when Harvard College was established in 1636 to train young men for the ministry. It wasn't much more when the Continental Army spent the winter of 1775–76 here. Harvard is the oldest college in the country, with the most competitive admissions process, and if you suggest aloud that it's not the best, you might encounter the attitude that inspired the saying, "You can always tell a Harvard man, but you can't tell him much."

Harvard, a private institution since 1865, includes the college and 10 graduate and professional schools. It owns more than 400 buildings in Boston and Cambridge; some of the most interesting surround this quad.

The classroom and administration buildings and dormitories here make up the:

④ Old Yard

To your right is **Massachusetts Hall.** Built in 1720, this National Historic Landmark is the university's oldest surviving building. First-year students share the building with the first-floor office of the university president (or perhaps it's the other way around), whom they traditionally invite upstairs for tea once a year. To your left, across from "Mass. Hall," is **Harvard Hall,** a classroom building constructed in 1765. Turn left and walk along Harvard Hall. You'll come to matching side-by-side buildings, **Hollis** and **Stoughton halls.** Hollis dates to 1763 (Stoughton "only" to 1805) and has been home to many students who went on to great fame, among them Ralph Waldo Emerson, Henry David Thoreau, and Charles Bulfinch. Almost hidden across the tiny lawn between these two buildings is **Holden Chapel,** a Georgian-style gem built in 1745. It has been an anatomy lab, a classroom building, and, of course, a chapel, and it is now home to the Harvard Glee Club.

Cross the Yard to the building opposite the gate where you entered. This is:

⑤ University Hall

Designed by Charles Bulfinch and constructed of granite quarried in nearby Chelmsford, the 1813 structure is the college's main administration building. In 1969, students protesting the Vietnam War occupied it.

University Hall is best known as the backdrop of the:

⑥ John Harvard Statue

This is one of the most photographed objects in the Boston area. Daniel Chester French designed it in 1884.

Walk around University Hall into the adjoining quad. This is still the Yard, but it's the **"New Yard,"** sometimes called **Tercentenary Theater** because the college's 300th-anniversary celebration was held here. Commencement and other university-wide ceremonies take place here.

On your right is:

⑦ Widener Library

The centerpiece of the world's largest university library system was built in 1913 as a memorial to Harry Elkins Widener, Harvard class of 1907. Legend has it that he died when the *Titanic* sank in 1912 because he was unable to swim 50 yards to a lifeboat, and his mother donated $2 million for the library on the condition that every undergraduate prove his ability to swim 50 yards. Today the library holds more than 3 million volumes, including 3,500 rare volumes collected by Harry Elkins Widener, on 50 miles of shelves. Don't even think about swiping Harry's Gutenberg Bible. The last person to try, in 1969, gained access from above but couldn't climb out. With the 70-pound Bible in his knapsack, he fell six stories to the courtyard below.

Horace Trumbauer of Philadelphia designed the library. His primary design assistant was Julian Francis Abele, a student of architecture at the University of Pennsylvania and the first black graduate

---

Fun Fact Nothing But the Truth

The likeness of **John Harvard** outside University Hall is known as the "Statue of Three Lies" because the inscription reads "John Harvard/Founder/1638." In fact, the college was founded in 1636; Harvard (one of many benefactors) didn't establish it, but donated money and his library; and this isn't John Harvard anyway. No portraits of him survive, so the model for this benevolent-looking bronze gentleman was, according to various accounts, either his nephew or a student.

Moments **Pssst . . . Check This Out**

As you cross Harvard Yard, stand with Memorial Church behind you and turn left toward **Sever Hall**. The front door is in a "whispering gallery." Stand on one side of the arch, station a friend or willing passerby on the opposite side, and speak softly into the facade. Someone standing next to you can't hear you, but the person at the other side of the arch can.

of L'Ecole des Beaux Arts in Paris. For security reasons, access to the lobby—which sits within view of the locked memorial room that holds Widener's collection—may be restricted. Check to see if you're allowed to take a peek, or just stop at the top of the outside staircase and enjoy the view.

Facing the library is:

⑧ Memorial Church

Built in 1931, the church is topped with a tower and weather vane 197 feet tall. You're welcome to look around this Georgian revival–style edifice unless services are going on, or to attend them if they are. Morning prayers run daily from 8:45 to 9am, and the Sunday service is at 11am. Weddings and funerals also take place here. The entrance is on the left. On the south wall, toward the Yard, panels bear the names of Harvard alumni who died in the world wars, Korea, and Vietnam. One is Joseph P. Kennedy Jr., the president's brother, class of 1938.

With Memorial Church behind you, turn left toward:

⑨ Sever Hall

H. H. Richardson, architect of Boston's Trinity Church, designed this classroom building (1880). Surveys of architects and designers consistently name the deceptively simple structure one of the professionals' favorite buildings in the Boston area. Notice the gorgeous brickwork that includes roll moldings around the doors, the fluted brick chimneys, and the arrangement of the windows.

Facing Sever Hall, turn right and go around to the back. The building on your right is Emerson Hall, which appeared in the movie *Love Story* as Barrett Hall, named after the family of Ryan O'Neal's character. Cross this quad and exit through the gate onto Quincy Street.

On your right on the other side of the street, at 24 Quincy St., is the:

⑩ Carpenter Center for the Visual Arts

Art exhibitions occupy the lobby, the Harvard Film Archive shows movies in the basement (pick up a schedule on the main floor), and the concrete-and-glass building is itself a work of art. Opened in 1963, it was designed by the Swiss-French architect Le Corbusier and the team of Sert, Jackson, and Gourley. It's the only Le Corbusier design in North America.

Just up Quincy Street, opposite the gate you used to leave the Yard, is the:

⑪ Fogg Art Museum

Founded in 1895, the museum has been at 32 Quincy St. since the building was completed in 1927. The Fogg's excellent collection of painting, sculpture, and decorative art runs from the Middle Ages to the present. See chapter 8 for a description of the Fogg, the Busch-Reisinger Museum, and the next stop on our walk.

Turn right as you leave the museum (or left if you're facing it) and cross Broadway to reach the:

⑫ Arthur M. Sackler Museum

The British architect James Stirling (who described this area as an "architectural zoo") designed the Sackler, at 485 Broadway. It houses the university's spectacular collection of Asian art.

Continue on Quincy Street. As you cross Cambridge Street, watch out for confused drivers emerging from the underpass to your left. Covering the block between Cambridge and Kirkland streets is:

⑬ Memorial Hall

This imposing Victorian structure, known to students as "Mem Hall," was completed in 1874. Enter from Cambridge Street and investigate the hall of memorials, a transept where you can read the names of the Harvard men who died fighting for the Union during the Civil War—but not of their Confederate counterparts. (The name of Col. Robert Gould Shaw, Matthew Broderick's character in the movie *Glory,* is halfway down on the right.) To the right is **Sanders Theatre,** prized as a performance space and lecture hall for its excellent acoustics and clear views. To the left is **Annenberg Hall.** It's a dining hall that's closed to visitors, but you might be able to sneak a look at the gorgeous stained-glass windows. Harvard graduates William Ware and Henry Van Brunt won a design competition for Memorial Hall, which was constructed for a total cost of $390,000 (most of it donated by alumni). The colorful tower is a replica of the original, which was destroyed by fire in 1956 and rebuilt in 1999.

Facing in the same direction you were when you entered, walk through the transept and exit onto Kirkland Street. Turn left and take the first right, onto Oxford Street. One block up on the right, at 26 Oxford St., you'll see an entrance to the:

⑭ Harvard Museum of Natural History

Adjoining the Peabody Museum of Archaeology & Ethnology at 11 Divinity Ave., the Museum of Natural History entertainingly presents the university's collections and research relating to the natural world. See p. 178 for a full description.

Leave through the back door of 11 Divinity Ave. and look around. Across the street at 6 Divinity Ave. is the **Semitic Museum** (✆ 617/495-4631), where the second- and third-floor galleries hold displays of archaeological artifacts and photographs from the Near and Middle East. Horace Trumbauer, the architect of Widener Library, designed the building next door, 2 Divinity Ave. It's home to the Harvard-Yenching Institute, which promotes East Asian studies and facilitates scholar-exchange programs. For every person who can tell you that, there are several thousand who know this building for the pair of **Chinese stone lions** flanking the front door.

Turn right and return to Kirkland Street, then go right. At the intersection of Kirkland and Oxford streets, at Zero Oxford St., is the university's:

⑮ Science Center

The 10-story monolith is said to resemble a Polaroid camera (Edwin H. Land, founder of the Polaroid Corporation, was one of its main benefactors). The Spanish architect Josep Luis Sert designed the Science Center, which opened in 1972. Sert, the dean of the university's Graduate School of Design from 1953 to 1969, was a disciple of Le Corbusier (who designed the Carpenter Center for the Visual Arts). On the plaza between the Science Center and the Yard is the **Tanner Rock Fountain,** a group of 159 New England boulders arranged around a small fountain. Since 1985 this has been a favorite spot for students to relax and watch unsuspecting passersby get wet: The fountain sprays a fine mist, which begins slowly and gradually intensifies.

TAKE A BREAK
The **main level of the Science Center** is open to the public and has several options if you want a soft drink, gourmet coffee, or sandwich. Go easy on the sweets, though, in anticipation of the next break.

Leave the Science Center near the fountain and turn right. Keeping the underpass on your left, follow the walkway for the equivalent of 1½ blocks as it curves around to the right. The Harvard Law School campus is on your right. You're back at Mass. Ave. Cross carefully to:

⑯ Cambridge Common

Memorials and plaques dot this well-used plot of greenery and bare earth. Follow the sidewalk along Mass. Ave. to the left, and after a block or so you'll walk near or over horseshoes embedded in the concrete. This is the path William Dawes, Paul Revere's fellow alarm-sounder, took from Boston to Lexington on April 18, 1775. Turn right onto Garden Street and continue following the Common for 1 block. On your right you'll see a monument marking the place where General George Washington took control of the Continental Army on July 3, 1775. The elm under which he reputedly assumed command is no longer standing.

Cross Garden Street and backtrack to Zero Garden St. This is:

⑰ Christ Church

Peter Harrison of Newport, Rhode Island (also the architect of King's Chapel in Boston), designed the oldest church in Cambridge, which opened in 1760. Note the square wooden tower. Inside the vestibule you can still see bullet holes made by British muskets. At one time the church was used as the barracks for troops from Connecticut, who melted down the organ pipes to make ammunition. The graveyard on the Mass. Ave. side of the building, the **Old Burying Ground,** is the oldest in Cambridge, dating to 1635.

Facing the church, turn right and follow Garden Street to the next intersection. This is Appian Way. Turn left and take the first right into:

⑱ Radcliffe Yard

Radcliffe College was founded in 1879 as the "Harvard Annex" and named for Ann Radcliffe, Lady Mowlson, Harvard's first female benefactor. Undergraduate classes merged with Harvard's in 1943, Radcliffe

graduates first received Harvard degrees in 1963, and Harvard officially assumed responsibility for educating undergraduate women in 1977. Radcliffe was an independent corporation until 1999; it's now the university's Radcliffe Institute for Advanced Study. After you've strolled around, return to Appian Way and turn right. You'll emerge on Brattle Street.

The **Longfellow National Historic Site,** 105 Brattle St. (✆ **617/876-4491;** www.nps.gov/long; p. 176), makes an interesting detour and adds about an hour to your walk. If you don't detour, turn left and continue walking along Brattle Street. Excellent shops are on both sides of the street.

TAKE A BREAK
Hi-Rise at the Blacksmith House, 56 Brattle St. (✆ **617/492-3003),** a branch of a well-known local artisan bread company, handles the baking for this legendary house, made famous by a Longfellow poem. "Under the spreading chestnut tree," stuff yourself with delectable pastry.

Across the street, at 40 Brattle St., is the:

⑲ Brattle Theater

Opened in 1890 as Brattle Hall, the theater was founded by the Cambridge Social Union and used as a venue for cultural entertainment. It became a movie hall in 1953 and gained a reputation as Cambridge's center for art films.

You're now in the **Brattle Square** part of Harvard Square. You might see street performers, a protest, a speech, or more shopping opportunities. Facing Dickson Brothers Hardware, cross Brattle Street, bear right, and follow the curve of the building all the way around the corner so that you're to Mount Auburn Street. Stay on the left-hand side of the street as you cross John F. Kennedy, Dunster, Holyoke, and Linden streets. On your left between

---

Fun Fact Play It, Sam

The **Brattle Theater,** one of the oldest independent movie houses in the country, started the *Casablanca* revival craze, which explains the name of the restaurant in the basement.

Dunster and Holyoke streets is **Holyoke Center,** an administration building designed by Josep Luis Sert that has commercial space on the ground floor.

The corner of Mount Auburn and Linden streets offers a good view of the:

⑳ Harvard Lampoon Castle
Constructed in 1909, designed by Wheelwright & Haven (architects of Boston's Horticultural Hall), and listed on the National Register of Historic Places, this is the home of Harvard's undergraduate humor magazine, the *Lampoon.* The main tower resembles a face, with windows as the eyes, nose, and mouth, topped by what looks like a miner's hat. The *Lampoon* and the daily student newspaper, the *Crimson,* share a long history of reciprocal pranks and vandalism. Elaborate security measures notwithstanding, *Crimson* editors occasionally make off with the bird that you might see atop the castle (it looks like a crane but is actually an ibis), and *Lampoon* staffers have absconded with the huge wooden president's chair from the *Crimson.*

You'll pass the *Crimson* on your right if you detour to the **Harvard Book Store** (turn left onto Plympton St. and follow it to the corner of Mass. Ave.). Otherwise, cross Mount Auburn Street and walk away from Holyoke Center on Holyoke Street or Dunster Street to get a sense of some of the rest of the campus.

Turn right on Winthrop Street or South Street, and proceed to Kennedy Street. Turn left and follow Kennedy St. toward the Charles River. On your right at Memorial Drive is:

㉑ John F. Kennedy Park
In the 1970s, when the search was on for a site for the Kennedy Library, this lovely parcel of land was an empty plot near the MBTA train yard (the Red Line then ended at Harvard). Traffic concerns led to the library's being built in Dorchester, but the **Graduate School of Government** and this adjacent park bear the president's name. Walk away from the street to enjoy the fountain, which is engraved with excerpts from JFK's speeches. This is a great place to take a break and plan the rest of your day.

Shopping

If you turned straight to this chapter, you're in good company: Surveys of visitors to Boston consistently show that shopping is the most popular activity, beating museum-going by a comfortable margin.

Boston-area shopping represents a tempting blend of classic and contemporary. Boston and Cambridge boast tiny boutiques and sprawling malls, esoteric bookshops and national chain stores, classy galleries and snazzy secondhand-clothing outlets.

This chapter concentrates on only-in-Boston businesses, and it includes many national (and international) names that are worth a visit. I'll point you to areas that are great for shop-hopping and toward specific destinations that are great for particular items.

1 The Shopping Scene

One of the best features of shopping in Massachusetts is that there's **no sales tax** on clothing priced below $175 or on food items. All other items are taxed at 5% (as are restaurant meals and takeout food). Just about every store will ship your purchases home for a fee, but if the store is part of a chain that operates in your home state, you'll probably have to pay that sales tax. Be sure to ask.

In the major shopping areas, stores usually open at 10am and close at 6 or 7pm Monday through Saturday. On Sunday, most open at 11am or noon and close at 5 or 6pm, but some don't open at all. Closing time may be later on 1 night a week, usually Wednesday or Thursday. Malls keep their own hours (noted below), and some smaller shops open later. Days and hours can vary in winter. If a store sounds too good to pass up, call to make sure it's open before heading out.

GREAT SHOPPING AREAS

The area's premier shopping district is Boston's **Back Bay,** where dozens of classy galleries, shops, and boutiques make **Newbury Street** a world-famous destination. Nearby, the **Shops at Prudential Center** and **Copley Place** (linked by an enclosed walkway across Huntington Ave.) bookend a giant retail complex that includes the posh department stores **Neiman Marcus, Lord & Taylor,** and **Saks Fifth Avenue.** The adjacent **South End,** though less commercially dense, boasts a number of art galleries and quirky shops.

Another popular destination is **Faneuil Hall Marketplace.** The shops, boutiques, and pushcarts at Boston's busiest attraction sell everything from cosmetics to costume jewelry, sweaters to souvenirs.

If the hubbub at Faneuil Hall and in the Back Bay overwhelms you, stroll over to Beacon Hill. Picturesque **Charles Street,** at the foot of the hill, is a short but commercially dense street noted for its excellent gift shops and antiques dealers.

One of Boston's oldest shopping areas is **Downtown Crossing,** a traffic-free pedestrian mall along Washington, Winter, and Summer streets near Boston Common. Here you'll find two major department stores (**Filene's** and **Macy's**), tons of smaller clothing and shoe stores, Swedish fashion phenomenon **H&M**, food and merchandise pushcarts, outlets of two major bookstore chains (**Barnes & Noble** and **Borders**), and the original **Filene's Basement** (see "Discount Shopping," later in this chapter).

Harvard Square in Cambridge, with its bookstores, boutiques, and T-shirt shops, is about 15 minutes from downtown Boston by subway. Despite the neighborhood association's efforts, chain stores have swept over "the Square." You'll find a mix of national and regional outlets, and more than a few persistent independent retailers.

For a less generic experience, stroll from Harvard Square along shop-lined **Mass. Ave.** toward **Porter Square** to the north or **Central Square** to the southeast. Another neighborhood with a well-deserved reputation for shopping variety is Brookline's **Coolidge Corner,** which is worth a trip (on the Green Line C train).

2 Shopping A to Z

Here I've singled out establishments that I especially like and neighborhoods that suit shoppers interested in particular types of merchandise. Addresses are in Boston unless otherwise indicated.

ANTIQUES & COLLECTIBLES

No antiques hound worthy of the name will leave Boston without an expedition along both sides of **Charles Street** ★★, with a detour to **River Street** (parallel to Charles, 1 block closer to the river). Also see the listing for the auction house **Skinner,** under "Art," below.

Boston Antique Cooperative I & II ★   Merchandise from Europe, Asia, and the United States fills these shops. They specialize in furniture and accessories, 17th- to 19th-century paintings, vintage photographs, jewelry, silver, textiles, and porcelain, but you might come across just about anything. 119 Charles St. © **617/227-9810** or 617/227-9811. www.bostonantiqueco-op.com. T: Red Line to Charles/MGH.

Bromfield Pen Shop ★   This shop's selection of antique pens will thrill any collector. It also sells new pens—including Mont Blanc, Pelikan, Waterman, and Omas—gifts, and the full Filofax line. Closed Sunday. 5 Bromfield St. © **617/482-9053.** www.bromfieldpenshop.com. T: Red or Orange Line to Downtown Crossing.

Danish Country Antique Furniture ★   Owner James Kilroy specializes in Scandinavian furnishings dating from the 1700s onward. In this mahogany-intensive neighborhood, the light woods are a visual treat. You'll also see folk art, clocks, Royal Copenhagen porcelain, and antique Chinese furniture and home accessories. 138 Charles St. © **617/227-1804.** T: Red Line to Charles/MGH.

Shreve, Crump & Low ★★   "Shreve's," a Boston institution founded in 1796, is famous for jewelry, china, silver, crystal, and watches. The antiques department specializes in 18th- and 19th-century American and English furnishings, British and American silver, and Chinese porcelain. 330 Boylston St. © **800/225-7088** or 617/267-9100. T: Green Line to Arlington.

Upstairs Downstairs Antiques ★★★ *Finds*   It's a cliché to say that antiques remind you of your grandmother's furniture. Here that's less trite because the merchandise

Back Bay Shopping

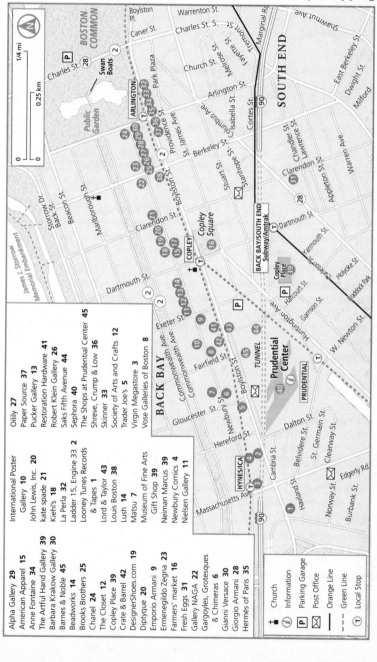

Alpha Gallery **29**
American Apparel **15**
Anne Fontaine **34**
The Artful Hand Gallery **39**
Barbara Krakow Gallery **30**
Barnes & Noble **45**
Beadworks **14**
Brooks Brothers **25**
Chanel **24**
The Closet **12**
Copley Place **39**
Crate & Barrel **42**
DesignerShoes.com **19**
Diptyque **20**
Emporio Armani **9**
Ermenegildo Zegna **23**
Farmers' market **16**
Fresh Eggs **31**
Gallery NAGA **22**
Gargoyles, Grotesques
& Chimeras **6**
Gianni Versace **30**
Giorgio Armani **28**
Hermès of Paris **35**

International Poster
Gallery **10**
John Lewis, Inc. **20**
kate spade **21**
Kiehl's **18**
La Perla **32**
Ladder 15, Engine 33 **2**
Looney Tunes Records
& Tapes **1**
Lord & Taylor **43**
Louis Boston **38**
Lush **14**
Matsu **7**
Museum of Fine Arts
Gift Shop **39**
Neiman Marcus **39**
Newbury Comics **4**
Nielsen Gallery **11**

Oilily **27**
Paper Source **37**
Pucker Gallery **13**
Restoration Hardware **41**
Robert Klein Gallery **26**
Saks Fifth Avenue **44**
Sephora **40**
The Shops at Prudential Center **45**
Shreve, Crump & Low **36**
Skinner **33**
Society of Arts and Crafts **12**
Trader Joe's **5**
Virgin Megastore **3**
Vose Galleries of Boston **8**

✝ Church
ⓘ Information
Ⓟ Parking Garage
⊠ Post Office
--- Orange Line
--- Green Line
Ⓣ Local Stop

215

displays are room arrangements that change with the seasons. From huge sideboards to delicate side tables to books and doilies, it's more evocative than a madeleine. 93 Charles St. ☎ 617/367-1950. T: Red Line to Charles/MGH.

ART

The greatest concentration of galleries lines **Newbury Street,** at street level and above; budget some time for exploring. Browsers and questions are welcome. Most galleries are open Tuesday through Saturday or Sunday from 10 or 11am to 5:30 or 6pm. Exhibitions typically change once a month. For specifics, visit individual websites or pick up a copy of the free monthly *Gallery Guide,* available at galleries and many businesses along Newbury Street.

The up-and-coming **SoWa district**—short for "south of Washington Street"—centers on Bernard Toale Gallery (see below). The Back Bay and South End don't have a monopoly, either; real estate prices being what they are, artists tend to crop up in even the unlikeliest-looking areas.

An excellent way to see artists at work is to visit during neighborhood **open studio** days. Artists' communities throughout the Boston area stage the weekend events once or twice a year. You might be asked for a contribution to a charity in exchange for a map of the studios. Check listings in the *Globe* and *Herald* or visit www.cityofboston. gov/arts for information.

Alpha Gallery ⭐ The Alpha Gallery specializes in contemporary American paintings, sculpture, and works on paper, as well as modern master paintings and prints. This is a family business: Director Joanna E. Fink is founder Alan Fink's daughter. Closed Sunday and Monday. 14 Newbury St., 2nd floor. ☎ 617/536-4465. www.alphagallery.com. T: Green Line to Arlington.

Barbara Krakow Gallery ⭐ This prestigious gallery, established more than 30 years ago, specializes in paintings, sculptures, drawings, and prints created after 1945. Closed Sunday and Monday. 10 Newbury St., 5th floor. ☎ 617/262-4490. www.barbarakrakow gallery.com. T: Green Line to Arlington.

Bernard Toale Gallery ⭐ One of the Boston area's best-known galleries was a pioneer in the "SoWa" (south of Washington St.) section of the South End in the late '90s. It shows exclusively contemporary art, in every medium and by artists at all stages of their careers. Closed Sunday and Monday; closed August except by appointment. 450 Harrison Ave. (between Randolph and Thayer sts.). ☎ 617/482-2477. www.bernardtoale gallery.com. T: Orange Line to New England Medical Center or Back Bay; 15-min. walk. Or Silver Line bus from Temple Pl. (Downtown Crossing).

Gallery NAGA ⭐⭐ In the neo-Gothic Church of the Covenant, Gallery NAGA exhibits contemporary paintings, photography, and studio furniture, often by New England artists. A stop here is a must if you want to see holography (trust me, you do). Closed Sunday and Monday. 67 Newbury St. ☎ 617/267-9060. www.gallerynaga.com. T: Green Line to Arlington.

Gargoyles, Grotesques & Chimeras ⭐⭐ *Finds* Gargoyles of all sizes decorate this intentionally gloomy space. You'll see plaster reproductions of details on famous cathedrals and other buildings, religious icons, non-gargoyle home decorations, and haunting photographs that set the gothic mood. The doors usually open daily around 3pm, but hours vary, so call ahead. 262 Newbury St. ☎ 617/536-2362. T: Green Line B, C, or D to Hynes/ICA.

Haley & Steele ✪   If you prefer traditional art to contemporary, this is the place. The century-old business specializes in maritime, military, botanical, ornithological (think Audubon), and historical prints, as well as 19th-century oil paintings and British sporting prints. Closed Sunday. 91 Newbury St. ✆ 617/536-6339. www.haleysteele. com. T: Green Line to Arlington.

International Poster Gallery ✪✪✪ *(Finds)*   Yes, posters are art—as you'll see before you even cross the threshold of this extraordinary gallery. It features extensive collections of French, Swiss, Soviet, and Italian vintage posters, and thousands of other posters, including originals from around the world. The accommodating staff will comb its databases (cyber and cerebral) to help you find the exact image you want. The theme of the works on display changes three or four times a year. Prices start at $50, with most between $500 and $2,000. 205 Newbury St. ✆ 617/375-0076. www.international poster.com. T: Green Line to Copley.

Nielsen Gallery ✪   Owner Nina Nielsen personally selects the contemporary artists who exhibit in her gallery (which opened in 1963), and she has great taste. You might see the work of a young, newly discovered talent or that of a more established artist. Closed Sunday and Monday. 179 Newbury St. ✆ 617/266-4835. www.nielsengallery. com. T: Green Line to Copley.

Pucker Gallery ✪✪   The eclectic offerings at this 35-plus-year-old gallery include African, Asian, Inuit, and Israeli art; contemporary paintings, prints, drawings, sculpture, and ceramics by regional and international artists; and excellent photographs. The staff is eager to discuss the art, which spreads over five floors. 171 Newbury St. ✆ 617/ 267-9473. www.puckergallery.com. T: Green Line to Copley.

Robert Klein Gallery ✪   For 19th- to 21st-century photography, head here. Among the dozens of artists represented are Diane Arbus, Robert Mapplethorpe, Man Ray, and Ansel Adams. Closed Sunday and Monday. 38 Newbury St., 4th floor. ✆ 617/267-7997. www.robertkleingallery.com. T: Green Line to Arlington.

Skinner   *Antiques Roadshow* fans, this one's for you: The show's rotating cast of appraisers includes staff members from New England's best-known auction house. Skinner mounts about 60 auctions a year in Boston (usually on weekends) and suburban Bolton. Visitors can bid or observe. You might see fine art, antiques, collectibles, jewelry, furniture, ceramics, textiles, rugs, or even musical instruments. Call or check the website for information about buying a catalog, or just show up. Heritage on the Garden (Boylston and Arlington sts.), 63 Park Plaza. ✆ 617/350-5400. www.skinnerinc.com. T: Green Line to Arlington.

Vose Galleries of Boston ✪   One of Vose's specialties is Hudson River School paintings—fitting, because the business and the mid-19th-century movement are about the same age. The Vose family (now in its fifth generation) runs the oldest continuously operating gallery in the United States, which opened in 1841. You'll see works of the Boston School and American Impressionists among the 18th-, 19th-, and early-20th-century American paintings, as well as contemporary pieces by American realists. Closed Sunday. 238 Newbury St. ✆ 617/536-6176. www.vosegalleries.com. T: Green Line to Copley or Green Line B, C, or D to Hynes/ICA.

BOOKS

The Boston area is a book-lover's paradise. It's an important stop on most author tours; check the local papers or stop by any store that sells new books for details on **readings and book-signings.**

Finds Fired Up

A good souvenir is something you'd never find anywhere else, and a **Boston Fire Department T-shirt** is a great one. They cost about $15 at most neighborhood firehouses. The handiest for out-of-towners are Engine 8, Ladder 1, on Hanover Street at Charter Street in the North End (off the Freedom Trail), and Ladder 15, Engine 33, on Boylston Street at Hereford Street in the Back Bay (near the Hynes Convention Center).

Barnes & Noble The downtown branch of the national chain carries a large selection of local-interest titles and has a huge periodicals section. The similarly well-stocked Prudential Center location boasts both a lively pickup scene and plenty of kids' events. Barnes & Noble runs the bookstore operations at Boston University, Harvard, and MIT (see "College Merchandise," below). 395 Washington St. ✆ 617/426-5502. www.barnesandnoble.com. T: Red or Orange Line to Downtown Crossing. Shops at Prudential Center, 800 Boylston St. ✆ 617/247-6959. T: Green Line E to Prudential, Green Line to Copley, or Green Line B, C, or D to Hynes/ICA. 325 Harvard St., Brookline. ✆ 617/232-0594. T: Green Line C to Coolidge Corner.

Borders Two levels of books and one of music, plus a cafe, author appearances, and musical performances, make the sprawling Downtown Crossing store a popular destination. The comfy-cozy ambience of the Cambridge location makes it a good refuge when you've had enough of the mall. 10–24 School St. ✆ 617/557-7188. www.bordersstores. com. T: Orange or Blue Line to State. CambridgeSide Galleria mall, Cambridge. ✆ 617/679-0887. T: Green Line to Lechmere.

Brattle Book Shop ★★ Bibliophiles who start here might not get any other shopping done. This marvelous store near Macy's buys and sells used, rare, and out-of-print titles, and second-generation owner Kenneth Gloss does free appraisals. Be sure to check the carts out front for good deals on books of all ages. Closed Sunday. 9 West St. ✆ 800/447-9595 or 617/542-0210. www.brattlebookshop.com. T: Red or Orange Line to Downtown Crossing or Green Line to Park St.

Brookline Booksmith ★★★ The huge, varied selection makes this store a polymath's dream. The employees have excellent taste—look for their recommendations. Named the best bookstore in the country by *Publishers Weekly* in 1998, Brookline Booksmith boasts a great gift-and-card section, offers a small but choice used-book selection in the basement, and stages tons of events. 279 Harvard St., Brookline. ✆ 617/566-6660. www.brooklinebooksmith.com. T: Green Line C to Coolidge Corner.

Curious George Goes to WordsWorth Here you'll find a superlative selection of children's books and gifts, including toys, stuffed animals, and games. Check downstairs for items that suit older kids, with an emphasis on old and new classics. The odd name? This store is a spin-off of now-defunct WordsWorth Books, a longtime Harvard Square favorite. 1 John F. Kennedy St. ✆ 617/498-0062. T: Red Line to Harvard.

Globe Corner Bookstore ★ This overstuffed store (offspring of the dear departed original on the Freedom Trail) carries huge selections of travel guides and essays, maps, atlases, and globes. Check ahead for special events, such as the annual adventure-travel lecture series. 28 Church St., Cambridge. ✆ 617/497-6277. www.globecorner. com. T: Red Line to Harvard.

Harvard Book Store ★★   *Publishers Weekly*'s 2002 Bookseller of the Year attracts shoppers to its main level with an excellent scholarly selection and discounted best-sellers. The basement is the draw for those in the know: Prices on remainders are good, and used paperbacks (many bought for classes and hardly opened) are 50% off their original prices. Check ahead for information on readings and other special events. 1256 Mass. Ave., Cambridge. ☎ 800/542-READ or 617/661-1515. www.harvard.com. T: Red Line to Harvard.

Rand McNally Map & Travel Store   Armchair travelers who get as far as Faneuil Hall Marketplace can go 1 block more for guides, maps, games, software, travel accessories, and a great variety of globes. 84 State St. ☎ 617/720-1125. www.randmcnally.com. T: Orange or Blue Line to State.

Schoenhof's Foreign Books ★   The oldest foreign-language bookseller in the country stocks volumes for adults and children in more than 50 languages. It also carries dictionaries and language-learning materials for 700-plus languages and dialects, plus gift items. The multilingual staff schedules book-discussion groups in various languages and arranges special orders at no extra charge. Closed Sunday. 76A Mt. Auburn St., Cambridge. ☎ 617/547-8855. www.schoenhofs.com. T: Red Line to Harvard.

COLLEGE MERCHANDISE

The big names are BU and Harvard (you'll see Boston College merchandise downtown, too), but why stop there? Look like an insider with a T-shirt from the **Emerson College Book Store,** 80 Boylston St. (☎ 617/728-7700; T: Green Line to Boylston); the **MIT Coop,** 3 Cambridge Center (☎ 617/499-3200; T: Red Line to Kendall/ MIT); the **Northeastern University Bookstore,** 360 Huntington Ave. (☎ 617/373-2286; T: Green Line E to Northeastern); or the **Suffolk University Bookstore,** 148 Cambridge St., Beacon Hill (☎ 617/227-4085; T: Blue Line to Bowdoin or Green Line to Government Center).

Barnes & Noble at Boston University   The BU crest, terrier mascot, or name appears on at least a floor's worth of clothing and just about any other item with room for a logo. The book selection is huge, and the author series (☎ 617/236-7448) brings writers to campus year-round. 660 Beacon St. ☎ 617/267-8484. www.bu.bkstore.com. T: Green Line B, C, or D to Kenmore.

The Harvard Coop ★   The Coop (rhymes with *hoop*), or Harvard Cooperative Society, is student-oriented but not a run-of-the-mill college bookstore. You'll find Harvard insignia merchandise, stationery, prints, and posters. As at BU, Barnes & Noble runs the book operation. 1400 Mass. Ave., Cambridge. ☎ 617/499-2000. www.thecoop. com. T: Red Line to Harvard.

CRAFT GALLERIES

The Artful Hand Gallery ★   The Artful Hand specializes, as you might guess, in handcrafted items by an excellent roster of artists. It shows and sells wonderful jewelry, ceramics, blown glass, wood pieces (including boxes), and sculpture, plus furniture, folk art, and books. Copley Place. ☎ 617/262-9601. T: Orange Line to Back Bay or Green Line to Copley.

Society of Arts and Crafts ★★   Contemporary American work is the focus at the oldest nonprofit craft organization in the country. The jewelry, furniture, home accessories, glass, ceramics, and fiber art range from practical to purely decorative; the second floor holds a gallery that mounts four shows a year. 175 Newbury St. ☎ 617/266-1810. www.societyofcrafts.org. T: Green Line to Copley.

CRAFT SUPPLIES

The Art Store   The extensive selection of art supplies and equipment, plus the unusual gift items, almost make up for the unoriginal name and steep (at least compared to Pearl, the other big national name in this market) prices. In the Landmark Center, 401 Park Dr. ℂ **617/247-3322**. www.artstore.com. T: Green Line D to Fenway.

Paper Source ★★   Gorgeous paper (writing and wrapping), cards, pens, ink, stamps, books, stickers, gifts, and custom invitations make these well-organized stores magnets for anyone with a thing for stationery. Be sure to check out the handmade paper from around the world. A crafty friend swears by the Boston location, but all three are delightful. www.paper-source.com. 338 Boylston St. ℂ **617/536-3444**. T: Green Line to Arlington. 1810 Mass. Ave., Cambridge. ℂ **617/497-1077**. T: Red Line to Porter. 1361 Beacon St., Brookline. ℂ **617/264-2800**. T: Green Line C to Coolidge Corner.

Pearl Art & Craft Supplies ★   The Central Square branch of the national discount chain stocks everything you need to do it yourself, from pens and pencils to stamps and stencils to cards and canvas. 579 Mass. Ave., Cambridge. ℂ **617/547-6600**. www.pearlpaint.com. T: Red Line to Central.

Windsor Button   The name doesn't come close to telling the whole story. This 70-year-old shop does stock thousands of buttons, from utilitarian to ultra-fancy, as well as ribbon, trim, and needlework kits. It's equally beloved for its enormous notions selection, full range of yarn and knitting and crochet patterns and accessories, and helpful staff. Closed Sunday. 35 Temple Place. ℂ **617/482-4969**. www.windsorbutton.com. T: Red or Green Line to Park St., or Orange Line to Downtown Crossing.

DEPARTMENT STORES

Filene's   Filene's (say "Fie-*leen's*") is a full-service department store with all the usual trappings plus a terrific cosmetics department. The original Filene's Basement (see "Discount Shopping," below) is still downstairs, under separate management. 426 Washington St. ℂ **617/357-2100**. www.filenes.com. T: Red or Orange Line to Downtown Crossing.

Lord & Taylor   Despite the strong New York association, Lord & Taylor is a Boston favorite for special-occasion outfits. Great seasonal sales, superb costume jewelry, and a wide selection of men's and women's sportswear make it a good stop even if you don't need something to wear to a wedding. 760 Boylston St. ℂ **617/262-6000**. www.lordandtaylor.com. T: Orange Line to Back Bay or Green Line to Copley.

Tips **Present at the Creation: Craft Shows**

New England is a hotbed of fine crafts, and the Boston area affords many opportunities to explore the latest trends in every imaginable medium and style. Prominent artisans often have exclusive relationships with galleries; an excellent way to get an overview is to attend a show and sale. The best-known exhibitions are prestigious weekend events that benefit nonprofit organizations. **Crafts at the Castle** (ℂ **617/523-6400**, ext. 5987; www.artfulgift.com/catc) takes place in late November or early December at the Castle, an exhibition space on Columbus Avenue at Arlington Street. **CraftBoston** (ℂ **617/266-1810**; www.craftboston.org) is in April or May at the World Trade Center.

Macy's   Across Summer Street from Filene's stands New England's largest store. It bears the hallmarks of the New York flagship, such as excellent selections of housewares, china, and silver. 450 Washington St. ℂ **617/357-3000**. www.macys.com. T: Red or Orange Line to Downtown Crossing.

Neiman Marcus   Here you'll find the trappings of true luxury, including exceptional cosmetics and unique accessories, at Texas-size prices. 5 Copley Place. ℂ **617/536-3660**. www.neimanmarcus.com. T: Orange Line to Back Bay or Green Line to Copley.

Saks Fifth Avenue   This is another classy New York name noted for its fashion and cosmetics. Don't forget to check out the shoe collections. If you aren't up for tangling with mall crowds, enter from Ring Road. Prudential Plaza, 786 Boylston St. ℂ **617/262-8500**. www.saksfifthavenue.com. T: Green Line to Copley or Orange Line to Back Bay.

DISCOUNT SHOPPING

DSW Shoe Warehouse   Here you'll find two large floors of discounted women's and men's shoes, boots, sandals, and sneakers. Check the clearance racks for the real deals. 385 Washington St. ℂ **617/556-0052**. www.dswshoe.com. T: Red or Orange Line to Downtown Crossing.

Eddie Bauer Outlet   Not what you might expect from an outlet—the prices aren't breathtaking, but the quality and selection are good. 500 Washington St. ℂ **617/423-4722**. www.eddiebaueroutlet.com. T: Red or Orange Line to Downtown Crossing.

Filene's Basement ★★★ *Value*   New England's most famous discount retailer opened in 1908 (it's now a subsidiary of a Midwestern chain). Its celebrated automatic markdowns apply only at this location, the original. With the rise of competing chains, deals worth bragging about have become harder to find than they once were, but they're just as rewarding when you do discover them. I happen to love this sort of thing, but if you don't, you might find that battling the no-holds-barred crowds isn't worth the payoff—the aisles are pretty wild at busy times.

The automatic-markdown policy (25% off the already-discounted price after 2 weeks on the selling floor, up to 75% after 8 weeks) applies to everything from lingerie to overcoats. The most ego-boosting finds are designer and other top-quality clothes and shoes at a fraction of their original prices. Try to beat the lunchtime crowds and check the papers for early opening times during special sales—notably the $249 wedding-dress blowout. 426 Washington St. ℂ **617/348-7848**. www.filenesbasement.com. T: Red or Orange Line to Downtown Crossing.

FASHION

Also see "Shoes & Boots" and "Vintage & Secondhand Clothing" later in this chapter.

ADULTS

The **Back Bay** is New England's top destination for high-end boutiques and if-you-have-to-ask-you-can't-afford-it designer shops. **Newbury Street** in particular is a retail fantasyland. Bring your platinum card to **Chanel,** 15 Arlington St., in the Ritz-Carlton, Boston (ℂ **617/859-0055**); **Ermenegildo Zegna,** 39 Newbury St. (ℂ **617/424-6657**); **Gianni Versace,** 12 Newbury St. (ℂ **617/536-8300**); **Hermès of Paris,** 22 Arlington St. (ℂ **617/482-8707**); **kate spade,** 117 Newbury St. (ℂ **617/262-2632**); and **La Perla,** 250 Boylston St. (ℂ **617/423-5709**).

American Apparel ★★   A leading light of the anti-sweatshop movement, American Apparel is so sincere that you might expect the clothes to be the fabric equivalent of Brussels sprouts. But the women's and men's T-shirts, underwear, and other fashionable knits—all manufactured in downtown L.A.—are fun, gorgeous, or both. 138 Newbury St. ℂ 617/536-4768. www.americanapparel.net. T: Green Line to Arlington.

Anne Fontaine ⭐ This was the first U.S. outlet for the designer's "perfect white blouse collection from Paris." I wanted to laugh, but then I saw for myself—almost every item *is* a perfect (for one reason or another) white blouse. Prices start at $80. Closed Sunday. Heritage on the Garden (Boylston and Arlington sts.), 318 Boylston St. ℂ 617/423-0366. www.annefontaine.com. T: Green Line to Arlington.

Brooks Brothers Would-be "proper Bostonians" head here for blue blazers, gray flannels, seersucker suits, and less conservative business and casual wear for men and women. Brooks is the only place for exactly the right preppy shade of pink button-down oxford shirts—something I've never seen at the outlet stores. www.brooksbrothers. com. 46 Newbury St. ℂ 617/267-2600. T: Green Line to Arlington. 75 State St. ℂ 617/261-9990. T: Orange or Blue Line to State.

Dakini ⭐ Come here for fleece in every form, from shearling-like jackets to velvety gloves, high-fashion women's separates to kids' pullovers. You'll see casual warm-weather fashions as well, but the locally made fleece clothing is the star of the show. Although it's not cheap, it's top quality, and the regular sales can make you feel both toasty and thrifty. 1704 Mass. Ave., Cambridge. ℂ 617/864-7661. www.dakini.com. T: Red Line to Porter.

Giorgio Armani Here you'll find Armani's sleek, sophisticated men's and women's clothing in an elegant setting. If your taste and budget are less grand, head down the street to **Emporio Armani,** 210–214 Newbury St. (ℂ 617/262-7300; T: Green Line to Copley), which carries sportswear, jeans, evening wear, and home accessories. 22 Newbury St. ℂ 617/267-3200. www.giorgioarmani.com. T: Green Line to Arlington.

H&M ⭐ The Swedish discount-fashion juggernaut is a terrific place to look for cheap, stylish clothing and accessories for women, men, and kids. 350 Washington St. ℂ 617/482-7001. www.hm.com. T: Red or Orange Line to Downtown Crossing.

Jean Therapy Designer dungarees are the raison d'être of this posh boutique in a fancy hotel. Jean Therapy prides itself on its discriminating selection and on customer service so good that it eases the stress of checking out your own butt in public. Closed Monday except by appointment. In the Hotel Commonwealth, 524 Commonwealth Ave. ℂ 617/266-6555. www.jean-therapy.com. T: Green Line B, C, or D to Kenmore.

Louis Boston Louis (pronounced "Louie's") enjoys a well-deserved reputation for offering cutting-edge New York style in a traditional Boston setting. The ultra-prestigious store sells men's designer suits, handmade shirts, silk ties, and Italian shoes; the women's fashions are equally elegant. The merchandise represents a mix of big names, emerging stars, and the celebrated house label. Also on the premises are an "apothecary" department, a full-service salon, and a restaurant that serves lunch and dinner. 234 Berkeley St. ℂ 800/225-5135 or 617/262-6100. www.louisboston.com. T: Green Line to Arlington.

Matsu ⭐ The female staff members at many Newbury Street businesses have that certain something—they're fashionable but not trendy, tasteful but never boring. When I quiz them about where they shop, this name comes up over and over. Possibly the calmest place on Newbury Street, this Japanese-influenced boutique carries fashion, accessories, and gift items. 259 Newbury St. ℂ 617/266-9707. T: Green Line B, C, or D to Hynes/ICA.

CHILDREN

Calliope ★★ *(Finds)*   The must-see window displays at this Harvard Square shop use stuffed animals, clothes, and toys to illustrate sayings and proverbs, often twisted into hilarious puns. The merchandise inside is equally delightful. You'll find clothing and accessories, European shoes, and unusual gifts, including a huge selection of plush animals. 33 Brattle St., Cambridge. © 617/876-4149. T: Red Line to Harvard.

Oilily   At this end of Newbury Street, even kids must be *au courant*. Lend a hand with a visit to the Boston branch of the chichi international chain, which specializes in brightly colored clothing and accessories for kids and women. The store stages several fashion shows a year; call ahead if you hope to catch one. 32 Newbury St. © 617/247-2386. www.oililyusa.com. T: Green Line to Arlington.

Saturday's Child ★   Never mind the nursery rhyme—"Saturday's child works hard for a living," my foot. You won't want your little angel lifting a finger in these precious (in both senses of the word) outfits. You'll also find top-quality shoes, accessories, and toys here. Closed Sunday. 1762 Mass. Ave., Cambridge. © 617/661-6402. T: Red Line to Porter.

FOOD & CANDY

At press time, the legendary **Penzeys** (© 800/741-7787; www.penzeys.com) chain was poised to venture into the Boston area. The Wisconsin-based purveyor of spices, herbs, flavorings, and spice rubs was gearing up to open at 1293 Mass. Ave. Arlington. To get there, take the Red Line to Harvard or Porter and take the no. 77 bus to Arlington—but call first to be sure the shop is open.

Cardullo's Gourmet Shoppe   A veritable United Nations of fancy food, this Harvard Square landmark carries specialties (including beer, wine, and a huge variety of candy) from just about everywhere. If you can't afford the big-ticket items, order a tasty sandwich to go. 6 Brattle St., Cambridge. © 617/491-8888. T: Red Line to Harvard.

Dairy Fresh Candies ★★ *(Finds)*   This North End hole-in-the-wall is crammed with sweets and other delectables, from nuts and dried fruit to imported Italian specialties. Before sweet tooth–oriented holidays (especially Easter), it's irresistible. There's also a fine gourmet-condiment selection. The store is too small for turning children loose, but they'll be happy they waited outside when you return with fuel for the Freedom Trail. 57 Salem St. © 800/336-5536 or 617/742-2639. www.dairyfreshcandies.com. T: Green or Orange Line to Haymarket.

Tips An Outlet Excursion

If you can't get through a vacation without some outlet shopping, the fact that you left the car at home doesn't have to stop you. **Brush Hill Tours** (© 800/343-1328; www.brushhilltours.com) operates daily service to **Wrentham Village Premium Outlets** (© 508/384-0600; www.premiumoutlets.com), a huge complex about 45 minutes south of Boston. Its dozens of outlet stores include—and this is merely scratching the surface—Anne Klein, Banana Republic, Barneys New York, Kenneth Cole, Nike, Polo, Ralph Lauren, Reebok, Timberland, Tommy Hilfiger, and Versace. Shoppers leave Boston between 9:30 and 10am; the return trip departs at 5pm. The round-trip fare is $33 for adults, $16 for children 5 to 11; reservations are required.

Savenor's Market 🛪 Savenor's is the perfect place to provision yourself before a concert or movie on the nearby Esplanade (or a really pricey cookout; Kobe beef, anyone?). And it's *the* local purveyor of exotic meats—if you crave buffalo or rattlesnake, this is the place. 160 Charles St. ⓒ 617/723-6328. www.savenorsmarket.com. T: Red Line to Charles/MGH.

Trader Joe's 🛪🛪🛪 This celebrated California-based retailer stocks a great selection of prepared foods, cheese, nuts, baked goods, natural and organic products, and other edibles, all at excellent prices. Get a preview on the website or just ask devotees—they can't shut up about it. The Cambridge location (which sells alcohol, as does the Brookline store) is a good place to stop for picnic provisions if you're driving. www.traderjoes.com. 899 Boylston St. ⓒ 617/262-6505. T: Green Line B, C, or D to Hynes/ICA. 1317 Beacon St., Brookline. ⓒ 617/278-9997. T: Green Line C to Coolidge Corner. 748 Memorial Dr., Cambridge. ⓒ 617/491-8582.

GIFTS & SOUVENIRS

Boston has dozens of shops and pushcarts that sell T-shirts, hats, and other souvenirs. At the stores listed here, you'll find gifts that say Boston without actually *saying* "Boston" all over them. Remember to check out museum shops for unique items, including crafts and games. Particularly good outlets include those at the **Museum of Fine Arts,** the **Museum of Science,** the **Isabella Stewart Gardner Museum,** the **Concord Museum,** and the **Peabody Essex Museum** in Salem. The online-only merchandise of the **Boston Public Library** (www.bpl.org) incorporates images from the library's vast holdings, including historic maps, photos, and even sports memorabilia—and you don't have to take up space in your carry-on to get your souvenirs home.

Black Ink 🛪🛪 The wacky wares here defy categorization, but they all fit comfortably under the umbrella of "oh, cool." Rubber stamps, stuffed animals, and offbeat books caught my eye recently; greeting cards and retro toys are equally appealing. 101 Charles St. ⓒ 617/723-3883. T: Red Line to Charles/MGH. 5 Brattle St., Cambridge. ⓒ 617/497-1221. T: Red Line to Harvard.

Cross 🛪 The Rhode Island–based pen company's first retail outlet proves that good things come in small packages. The tiny store carries a surprisingly large selection of beautiful stationery and cards, gift items such as journals and picture frames, office accessories, and, of course, pens. Zero Brattle St., Cambridge. ⓒ 617/868-7020. www.cross.com. T: Red Line to Harvard.

Joie de Vivre 🛪🛪🛪 *Finds* When I'm stumped for a present for a person who has everything, I head to this delightful little shop, which has been here for over 2 decades. Joie de Vivre's selection of gifts and toys for adults and sophisticated children is beyond compare. The kaleidoscope collection alone is worth the trip; you'll also find jewelry, note cards, puzzles, music boxes, and even salt and pepper shakers. 1792 Mass. Ave., Cambridge. ⓒ 617/864-8188. T: Red Line to Porter.

Museum of Fine Arts Gift Shop 🛪 For those without the time or inclination to visit the museum, these satellite shops carry posters, prints, cards and stationery, books, educational toys, scarves, mugs, T-shirts, and reproductions of jewelry in the museum's collections. You might even be inspired to pay a call on the real thing. www.mfa.org/shop. Copley Place. ⓒ 617/536-8818. T: Orange Line to Back Bay or Green Line to Copley. South Market Building, Faneuil Hall Marketplace. ⓒ 617/720-1266. T: Green or Blue Line to Government Center.

HOME & GARDEN

Abodeon My notes say "groovy, retro, vintage"—was it the mid-20th-century furniture and home accessories? The classic kitchen equipment and tableware? The "stay tuned, *Laugh-In* will be right back" vibe? This place is great for browsing—and hey, it made me use the word "groovy." 1731 Mass. Ave., Cambridge. © **617/497-0137**. T: Red Line to Porter.

Crate & Barrel This is wedding-present heaven, packed with contemporary and classic housewares. The merchandise, from juice glasses and linen napkins to top-of-the-line knives and roasting pans, boasts items to suit any budget. The Boylston Street location (which also stocks the full line of housewares) and the Mass. Ave. store carry furniture and home accessories. www.crateandbarrel.com. South Market Building, Faneuil Hall Marketplace. © **617/742-6025**. T: Green or Blue Line to Government Center. 777 Boylston St. © **617/262-8700**. T: Green Line to Copley. 48 Brattle St., Cambridge. © **617/876-6300**. T: Red Line to Harvard. 1045 Mass. Ave., Cambridge. © **617/547-3994**. T: Red Line to Harvard.

Diptyque 🌟 I'm not a candle person, but even I admire the subtly fragrant offerings at this Parisian outpost. The shop carries other scented products, such as soaps and room sprays, and other brands, but if you're looking for a hostess gift with off-the-charts snob appeal, you can't go wrong with a Diptyque candle ($45). 123 Newbury St. © **617/351-2430**. www.diptyqueusa.com. T: Green Line to Copley.

Fresh Eggs 🌟🌟 *(Finds)* Venture into the South End for the latest in stylish home accessories, an irresistible assortment of classic designs and light-hearted touches. From kitchen gadgets to imported linens to tabletop accessories, everything is fun and functional. Closed Monday. 58 Clarendon St. © **617/247-8150**. T: Orange Line to Back Bay.

Koo De Kir 🌟 In the heart of 19th-century Beacon Hill, Koo De Kir is a splash of modern style. Owner Kristine Irving has a great eye, and her selection of contemporary home accessories, furniture, lighting, sculpture, and gifts ranges from classics-to-be to downright whimsical. 65 Chestnut St. (at Charles St.). © **617/723-8111**. www.koodekir.com. T: Red Line to Charles/MGH.

Restoration Hardware This national chain specializes in old-fashioned style at new-fashioned prices. The merchandise runs more to home accessories, toys, and furniture than to hardware (although there's plenty of that, too) and makes for great browsing. 711 Boylston St. © **617/578-0088**. www.restorationhardware.com. T: Green Line to Copley.

JEWELRY

For information on Boston's best-known jewelry emporium, **Shreve, Crump & Low,** see "Antiques & Collectibles," earlier in this chapter.

Beadworks The jewelry at these shops will suit you exactly—you make it yourself. Prices for the dazzling variety of raw materials start at 5¢ a bead, findings (hardware) are available, and you can assemble your finery at the in-store worktable. Beadworks also carries ready-made pieces and schedules jewelry-making workshops; check ahead for details. www.beadworksboston.com. 167 Newbury St. © **617/247-7227**. T: Green Line to Copley. 23 Church St., Cambridge. © **617/868-9777**. T: Red Line to Harvard.

High Gear Jewelry 🌟 The biggest jewelry snob I know makes up excuses to visit the North End just so she can stop in here. Don't be put off by the sign saying that this eye-catching shop around the corner from the Paul Revere House (on the Freedom Trail) is a wholesale outlet. Retail shoppers are welcome to peruse the impressive

---

Tips   Flying Lobsters

Why go to the trouble of sending a postcard? Send a lobster instead. **James Hook & Co.,** 15 Northern Ave. at Atlantic Avenue (℗ **617/423-5500;** T: Red Line to South Station), and **Legal Sea Foods Fresh by Mail,** Logan Airport Terminal B and C (℗ **800/343-5804,** 617/568-2811, or 617/568-2800; www.sendlegal.com; T: Blue Line to Airport), do overnight shipping.

---

selection of reasonably priced costume jewelry, watches, and hair accessories. 139 Richmond St. ℗ **617/523-5804.** T: Green or Orange Line to Haymarket.

John Lewis, Inc. ★★ *Finds*   John Lewis's imaginative women's and men's jewelry—crafted on the premises—suits both traditional and trendy tastes. The wide selection of silver, gold, and platinum items and unusual colored stones add to the museum-like shop's appeal. The pieces that mark you as a savvy Bostonian are earrings, necklaces, and bracelets made of hammered metal circles. Closed Sunday and Monday. 97 Newbury St. ℗ **617/266-6665.** www.johnlewisinc.com. T: Green Line to Arlington.

MALLS & SHOPPING CENTERS

CambridgeSide Galleria   This three-level mall houses two large department stores—**Filene's** (℗ **617/621-3800**) and **Sears** (℗ **617/252-3500**)—and more than 100 specialty stores. Pleasant but quite generic, it might be the bargaining chip you need to lure your teenager to the nearby Museum of Science.

There's trendy sportswear at **Abercrombie & Fitch** (℗ 617/494-1338), electronics at **Cambridge SoundWorks** (℗ 617/225-3900) and the **Apple Store** (℗ 617/225-0442), casual clothing at **J. Crew** (℗ 617/225-2739), and music and appliances at **Best Buy** (℗ 617/225-2004). The mall also has a branch of **Borders** (℗ 617/679-0887), three restaurants, a food court, and seating along a pleasant canal.

Strollers and wheelchairs are available. Open Monday through Saturday from 10am to 9:30pm, Sunday from 11am to 7pm. 100 CambridgeSide Place, Cambridge. ℗ **617/621-8666.** www.shopcambridgeside.com. T: Green Line to Lechmere, or Red Line to Kendall/MIT and free shuttle bus (every 10–20 min.). Garage parking from $1/hr.

Copley Place   Copley Place has set the standard for upscale shopping in Boston since 1985. Connected to the Westin and Marriott hotels and the Prudential Center, it's a crossroads for office workers, out-of-towners, and enthusiastic consumers. You can while away a couple of hours or a whole day shopping and dining here and at the adjacent Shops at the Prudential Center (see below) without ever going outdoors.

Some of Copley Place's 100-plus shops will be familiar from the mall at home, but this is emphatically not a suburban shopping complex that happens to be in the city. You'll see famous stores that don't have another branch in Boston, including **Christian Dior** (℗ 617/927-7577), **Gucci** (℗ 617/247-3000), **Louis Vuitton** (℗ 617/437-6519), and **Tiffany & Co.** (℗ 617/353-0222), and a suitably classy "anchor" department store, **Neiman Marcus** (℗ 617/536-3660). Also here are the **Artful Hand Gallery** (p. 219) and a **Museum of Fine Arts Gift Shop** (p. 224). At press time, rumors were flying about **Barneys New York** taking over the space that once held a multiplex; check at your hotel to see whether they were true.

Open Monday through Saturday from 10am to 9pm, Sunday from 11am to 7pm. Some stores have longer or shorter hours, and most restaurants are open through late evening. 100 Huntington Ave. ℂ **617/369-5000**. www.shopcopleyplace.com. T: Orange Line to Back Bay or Green Line to Copley. Discounted validated parking with purchase.

Faneuil Hall Marketplace ★★   The original festival market hall is both wildly popular and widely imitated, so Faneuil Hall Marketplace changes constantly to appeal to visitors as well as to locals wary of its touristy reputation. The original part of **Faneuil Hall** itself dates to 1742, and the lower floors preserve the building's retail roots. The **Quincy Market Colonnade,** in the central building, houses a gargantuan selection of food and confections. The bars and restaurants always seem to be crowded, and the shopping is terrific, if generic.

In and around the five buildings, the shops combine "only in Boston" with "only at every mall in the country." **Marketplace Center** and the ground floors of the **North Market** and **South Market buildings** have lots of chain outlets. Most of the unique offerings are under the Quincy Market canopies, where crafts and gifts spill off dozens of **pushcarts,** and upstairs and downstairs in the market buildings.

Shop hours are Monday through Saturday from 10am to 9pm and Sunday from noon to 6pm. The Colonnade opens earlier, and most bars and restaurants close later. If you must drive, many businesses offer a discount at the 75 State St. Garage; there's also parking in the Government Center garage off Congress Street and the marketplace's crowded garage off Atlantic Avenue. Between North, Congress, and State sts. and Atlantic Ave. ℂ **617/338-2323**. www.faneuilhallmarketplace.com. T: Green or Blue Line to Government Center or Orange Line to Haymarket.

The Shops at Prudential Center   The main level of the city's second-tallest tower holds this sprawling complex. In addition to **Saks Fifth Avenue** (ℂ **617/262-8500**), there are dozens of shops and boutiques, a large **Barnes & Noble** (p. 218), a food court, a post office, and five restaurants, including Legal Sea Foods and The Cheesecake Factory. **Krispy Kreme Doughnuts** (ℂ **617/262-5531;** www.krispykreme.com) can satisfy your sugar cravings. Also here are Boston's branch of **Sephora** (p. 229) and one of just four retail outlets for the upscale office and home accessories that **Levenger** (ℂ **800/667-8934** or 617/536-3434; www.levenger.com) calls "tools for serious readers." Vendors sell gifts, souvenirs, and novelty items off carts and kiosks in the arcades, the Greater Boston Convention & Visitors Bureau operates an **information booth,** and there's outdoor space in front if you need some fresh air.

Hours are Monday through Saturday from 10am to 9pm, Sunday from 11am to 6pm. Restaurant hours vary. 800 Boylston St. ℂ **800/SHOP-PRU**. www.prudentialcenter.com. T: Green Line E to Prudential, Green Line to Copley, Orange Line to Back Bay, or Green Line B, C, or D to Hynes/ICA. Discounted validated parking with purchase.

Moments **Sports Memorabilia**

Faneuil Hall Marketplace's abundant photo ops don't stop with the colorful crowds. Focus on the sculptures in the area between the South Canopy of Quincy Market and the South Market building. Try to pull the cigar away from Celtics legend **Red Auerbach** (he doesn't mind if you perch on his lap). Then compare your tiny sneakers to **Larry Bird's** clodhoppers or marathon legend **Bill Rodgers's** running shoes, captured in bronze right next to Red.

MARKETS

Massachusetts farmers and growers under the auspices of the state **Department of Food and Agriculture** (© 617/227-3018) dispatch trucks filled with whatever's in season to the heart of the city from July through November. Depending on the time of year, you'll have your pick of berries, herbs, tomatoes, squash, pumpkins, apples, corn, and more, all fresh and reasonably priced. In Boston, stop by City Hall Plaza on Monday or Wednesday (T: Green or Blue Line to Government Center) or Copley Square on Tuesday or Friday (T: Green Line to Copley or Orange Line to Back Bay). In Cambridge, head to Parking Lot 5, a block from Mass. Ave., in Central Square on Monday (T: Red Line to Central).

MUSIC

Looney Tunes Records & Tapes   Where there are college students, there are pizza places, copy shops, and used-CD (and record) stores. Looney Tunes specializes in classical, jazz, and rock, and sells tons of other tunes at excellent prices. 1106 Boylston St. © 617/247-2238. T: Green Line B, C, or D to Hynes/ICA. 1001 Mass. Ave., Cambridge © 617/876-5624. T: Red Line to Harvard.

Newbury Comics   You'll find a wide selection of CDs, tapes, posters, gifts, novelty items, T-shirts—and, of course, comics—at the branches of this funky chain. The music is particularly cutting-edge, with lots of independent labels and imports. www.newbury.com. 332 Newbury St. © 617/236-4930. T: Green Line B, C, or D to Hynes/ICA. 1 Washington Mall, off State St. at Washington St. © 617/248-9992. T: Orange or Blue Line to State. 36 John F. Kennedy St., Cambridge © 617/491-0337. T: Red Line to Harvard.

Tower Records   The mega-chain carries records, tapes, CDs, videos, periodicals, and books. 95 Mount Auburn St., Cambridge © 617/876-3377. www.towerrecords.com. T: Red Line to Harvard.

Virgin Megastore   The entertainment preview system! The plasma-screen TVs! The interactive kiosks! The cafe! And, oh yeah, the music—a huge selection, as befits a 40,000-square-foot store, including a notable classical section. Virgin is a can't-miss destination for the limited-attention-span set. 360 Newbury St. (at Mass. Ave.). © 617/896-0950. www.virginmega.com. T: Green Line B, C, or D to Hynes/ICA.

PERFUME & COSMETICS

Colonial Drug ★★ *(Finds)*   The perfume counter at this family business puts the "special" in "specialize." You can choose from more than 1,000 fragrances—plus cosmetics, soap, and countless other body-care products—with the help of the gracious staff members. They remain unflappable even during Harvard Square's equivalent of rush hour, Saturday afternoon. No credit cards; closed Sunday. 49 Brattle St., Cambridge. © 617/864-2222. T: Red Line to Harvard.

Kiehl's ★   Lots of trends originate in New York, but few of them develop this kind of cult following. Customers wax evangelical over the skin, hair, and body products from Kiehl's ("since 1851"), which straddle the line between cosmetics and pharmaceuticals. 112 Newbury St. © 617/247-1777. www.kiehls.com. T: Green Line to Copley.

Lush ★★★   Of all the lotions-and-potions purveyors that have found their way to Boston over the past few years, this is my favorite. It smells great—without that overwhelming wall of scent that greets you at so many other shops—and the enthusiastic staff is entirely attitude-free. U.K.-based Lush specializes in fresh, organic, natural products, notably "bath bombs" (solid bubble bath) and solid shampoo priced by the pound. 166 Newbury St. ℭ 617/375-5874. www.lush.com. T: Green Line to Copley.

Sephora ⭐ This European phenomenon is a *fashionista* magnet. You'll find an encyclopedic, international selection of manufacturers and products in a well-lit, well-organized space overflowing with testers. Everything is self-service, and the staff provides as much help as you want. Shops at Prudential Center, 800 Boylston St. ℭ 617/262-4200. www.sephora.com. T: Green Line E to Prudential, Green Line to Copley, or Green Line or B, C, or D to Hynes/ICA.

SHOES & BOOTS

Also see the listing for **DSW Shoe Warehouse** under "Discount Shopping," earlier in this chapter.

Berk's Shoes "Trendy" is inadequate to describe the wares at this Harvard Square institution. College students and people who want to look like them come here to stock up on whatever's fashionable right this red-hot minute. 50 John F. Kennedy St. ℭ 888/GO-BERKS or 617/492-9511. www.berkshoes.com. T: Red Line to Harvard.

DesignerShoes.com ⭐ Here you'll find women's shoes in sizes 10½ to 14 (with wide and narrow widths from size 8 or 9). If you're in this neglected demographic, you'll glory in the selection, which ranges from sensible to sexy, with plenty of options in between. 125 Newbury St., 4th floor. ℭ 888/371-SHOE or 617/247-0202. www.designershoes.com. T: Green Line to Copley.

Helen's Leather Shop ⭐ Homesick Texans visit Helen's just to gaze upon the boots. Many are handmade from exotic leathers, including ostrich, buffalo, and snakeskin. The shop carries brands such as Lucchese and Tony Lama, along with a large selection of other leather goods, Western shirts, belts and buckles, and Stetson hats. Closed Tuesday. 110 Charles St. ℭ 617/742-2077. www.helensleather.com. T: Red Line to Charles/MGH.

TOYS & GAMES

A number of businesses listed earlier in this chapter are good places to look for toys. They include most of the shops under "Gifts & Souvenirs," **Curious George Goes to WordsWorth** (see "Books"), and **Calliope** (see "Fashion").

The Games People Play ⭐ Just outside Harvard Square, this 30-plus-year-old business carries enough board games (foreign as well as domestic) to outfit every country, summer, and beach house in New England. There are puzzles, playing cards, role-playing games, and chess and backgammon sets, too. 1100 Mass. Ave., Cambridge. ℭ 800/696-0711 or 617/492-0711. T: Red Line to Harvard.

Stellabella Toys A large space that's both retro (lots of wooden toys) and modern (no guns), Stellabella is a welcoming destination for parents and kids alike. It carries everything from baby strollers to craft supplies and costumes for big kids, and the friendly staff can lend a hand if you need help maintaining your status as the cool aunt or uncle. 1360 Cambridge St., Cambridge. ℭ 617/491-6290. T: Red Line to Central; 10-min. walk on Prospect St.

VINTAGE & SECONDHAND CLOTHING

The Closet This is the not-very-secret weapon of many a chic shopper. One of Boston's best consignment shops, it offers "gently worn" designer clothing for women and men at drastically reduced prices. 175 Newbury St. ℭ 617/536-1919. T: Green Line to Copley.

The Garment District ⭐ You're hitting the clubs and you want to look cool, but you have almost no money. You'll be right at home among the shoppers here, paying great prices for a huge selection of contemporary and vintage clothing, costumes, and accessories. Merchandise on the first floor is sold (no kidding) by the pound. 200 Broadway, Cambridge. © 617/876-5230. www.garmentdistrict.com. T: Red Line to Kendall/MIT.

Oona's ⭐⭐ From funky accessories and costume jewelry to vintage dresses nice enough to get married in, Oona's carries an extensive selection of "experienced clothing" at good prices. The Harvard Square stalwart celebrated its 30th anniversary in 2003. 1210 Mass. Ave., Cambridge. © 617/491-2654. T: Red Line to Harvard.

11

Boston After Dark

Countless musicians, actors, and comedians went to college or got their start in the Boston area, and it's a great place to check out rising stars and promising unknowns. You might get an early look at the next Branford Marsalis, Denis Leary, Bonnie Raitt, or Yo-Yo Ma. And you'll certainly be able to enjoy the work of many established artists.

The nightlife scene is, to put it mildly, not exactly world-class—you can be home from a night on the town when your friends in New York are still drying their hair. Closing time for clubs is 2am, which means packing a lot into 4 hours or so.

Massachusetts **state law forbids smoking** in all workplaces—including bars,

clubs, and restaurants. The tobacco taboo has created a parallel universe on the state's sidewalks, even in unbearable weather.

For up-to-date entertainment listings, consult the "Calendar" section of Thursday's *Boston Globe,* the "Edge" section of Friday's *Boston Herald,* and the Sunday arts sections of both papers. Three free publications, available at newspaper boxes around town, publish nightlife listings: the weekly *Boston Phoenix* and the biweekly *Stuff@Night* (a *Phoenix* offshoot) and *Improper Bostonian.* The *Phoenix* website (**www.bostonphoenix.com**) archives the paper's season-preview issues; especially before a summer or fall visit, it's a valuable planning tool.

GETTING TICKETS

Some companies and venues sell tickets over the phone or the Internet; many will refer you to a ticket agency. The major agencies that serve Boston, **Ticketmaster** (✆ 617/ 931-2000; www.ticketmaster.com), **Next Ticketing** (✆ 617/423-NEXT; www.next ticketing.com), and **Tele-Charge** (✆ 800/447-7400 or TTY 888/889-8587; www. telecharge.com), calculate service charges per ticket, not per order. To avoid the fee— and possible losses if your plans change and you can't get your money back—visit the box office in person. *Tip:* If you wait until the day before or day of a performance, you'll sometimes have access to tickets that were held back for some reason and have just gone on sale.

1 The Performing Arts

PERFORMANCE VENUES

The **Hatch Shell** on the Esplanade (✆ 617/727-5215) is an amphitheater best known for the Boston Pops' Fourth of July concerts. On many summer nights, free music and dance performances and films take over the stage, to the delight of crowds on the lawn. (T: Red Line to Charles/MGH, or Green Line to Arlington.)

Bank of America Pavilion One of the most pleasant venues in the area, this giant white tent encloses a 5,000-seat pavilion. It schedules pop, rock, country, rap, folk, and jazz on evenings from May through September. Check ahead for information about

Boston After Dark

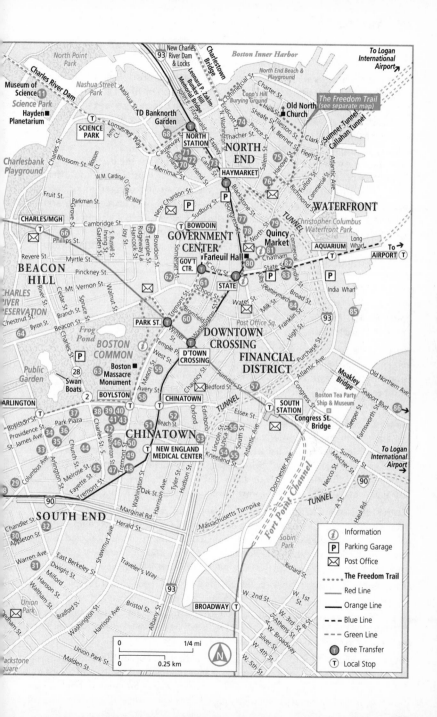

Value Let's Make a Deal

Yankee thrift gains artistic expression at the **BosTix** booths at Faneuil Hall Marketplace, on the south side of Faneuil Hall (T: Green or Blue Line to Government Center or Orange Line to Haymarket), and in Copley Square at the corner of Boylston and Dartmouth streets (T: Green Line to Copley or Orange Line to Back Bay). Same-day tickets to musical and theatrical performances are half price, subject to availability. You must pay cash in person, and there are no refunds or exchanges. Check the board or the website for the day's offerings.

BosTix (© **617/482-2849** for information; www.artsboston.org) also offers full-price advance tickets; discounts on more than 100 theater, music, and dance events; and tickets to museums, historic sites, and attractions in and around town. The booths are also Ticketmaster outlets. Both are open Tuesday through Saturday from 10am to 6pm (half-price tickets go on sale at 11am), and Sunday from 11am to 4pm. The Copley Square location is also open Monday from 10am to 6pm.

water transportation and shuttle service from South Station. 290 Northern Ave., South Boston. © **617/728-1600** or 617/931-2000 (Ticketmaster). www.bankofamericapavilion.com. T: Silver Line bus from South Station.

Berklee Performance Center   The Berklee College of Music's theater features professional artists (many of them former Berklee students, both alumni and dropouts), instructors, and students. Offerings are heavy on jazz and folk, with plenty of other options. 136 Mass. Ave. © **617/747-8890**. www.berkleebpc.com. T: Green Line B, C, or D to Hynes/ICA.

Boston Center for the Arts   Multiple performance spaces and an anything-goes booking policy make the BCA a leading venue for contemporary theater, music and dance performances, and visual arts exhibitions. The BCA and the Huntington Theatre Company (see "Theater," below) are partners in the Theatre Pavilion, which incorporates 350- and 200-seat theaters, that opened in 2004. 539 Tremont St. © **617/426-5000** or 617/426-2787 (box office). www.bcaonline.org. T: Orange Line to Back Bay.

Cutler Majestic Theatre   A popular dance and music performance space, the recently restored Cutler Majestic is the home stage of several small arts companies. The gorgeous 1903 theater also books Emerson College student productions and touring opera and ballet companies. 219 Tremont St. © **800/233-3123** (Tele-Charge) or 617/824-8000 (information). www.maj.org. T: Green Line to Boylston or Orange Line to Chinatown.

New England Conservatory's Jordan Hall   NEC's concert hall books students, faculty members, and professionals. It presents classical instrumental and vocal soloists, chamber music, and jazz; student and faculty performances are frequent and free. 290 Huntington Ave. © **617/585-1260** or 617/585-1122 (concert line). www.newenglandconservatory.edu/jordanhall. T: Green Line E to Symphony, or Orange Line to Mass. Ave.

Orpheum Theater   Although it's old (the building went up in 1852) and cramped, the Orpheum offers an intimate setting for big-name performers. It books both top local acts and international icons, recently including Ashlee Simpson and Bob Dylan (not together—but if that's not a wide range, I don't know what is). 1 Hamilton Place (off

Tremont St., across from Park St. Church). (C) **617/679-0810** or 617/931-2000 (Ticketmaster). www.tea partyconcerts.com. T: Red or Green Line to Park St.

Sanders Theatre   A landmark space in Harvard's Memorial Hall, Sanders Theatre is a lecture hall and performance venue that schedules big names in classical, folk, and world music, as well as student performances. 45 Quincy St. (at Cambridge St.), Cambridge. (C) **617/496-2222**. www.fas.harvard.edu/~memhall. T: Red Line to Harvard.

Symphony Hall   Acoustically perfect Symphony Hall, which celebrated its 100th anniversary in 2000, is the home of the **Boston Symphony Orchestra** and the **Boston Pops.** When they're away, top-notch classical and chamber music artists from elsewhere take over. For information on free tours of Symphony Hall, see p. 186. 301 Mass. Ave. (at Huntington Ave.). (C) **617/266-1492** or 617/CONCERT (program information). SymphonyCharge (C) **888/ 266-1200** or 617/266-1200. www.bostonsymphonyhall.org. T: Green Line E to Symphony, or Orange Line to Mass. Ave.

TD Banknorth Garden   This state-of-the-art facility is home to the Bruins (hockey), the Celtics (basketball), the circus (in Oct), ice shows (at least twice a year), and touring rock and pop artists of all stripes. Concerts are in the round or in the arena stage format. Causeway St. (C) **617/624-1000** (events line) or 617/931-2000 (Ticketmaster). www.tdbanknorthgarden.com. T: Orange or Green Line to North Station.

Tweeter Center for the Performing Arts   When a mainstream act's summer schedule says "Boston," that often means this bucolic setting about an hour south of town. A sheltered (it has a roof but no sides) auditorium surrounded by a lawn, the Tweeter Center features rock, alternative, folk, pop, country, reggae, and light classical artists. Shows go on rain or shine. 885 S. Main St. (Rte. 140), Mansfield. (C) **508/339-2333** or 617/931-2000 (Ticketmaster). http://tweetercenter.com/boston.

Wang Theatre   Also known as the Wang Center, this Art Deco palace is home to **Boston Ballet** performances (except *The Nutcracker* which performs at the new Opera House), and it books numerous and varied national companies. On some Monday evenings, it reverts to its roots as a movie theater and shows classic films on an enormous screen—free. 270 Tremont St. (C) **800/447-7400** (Tele-Charge) or 617/482-9393. www.wang center.org. T: Green Line to Boylston, or Orange Line to New England Medical Center.

CLASSICAL MUSIC

Boston Symphony Orchestra ★★★   The Boston Symphony, one of the world's greatest, was founded in 1881. The repertoire includes contemporary music, but classical is the BSO's calling card—you might want to schedule your trip to coincide with a particular performance or with a visit by a celebrated guest artist. Illustrious conductor James Levine, who remains artistic director of New York City's Metropolitan Opera, became music director in 2004.

Tips **Music Under the Sky & Stars**

The **Boston Landmarks Orchestra** ((C) **617/520-2200**; www.landmarksorchestra. org) performs free classical concerts in parks around town, including Boston Common, on weekend afternoons and evenings in July and August. The goal of the "greatest hits" repertoire is to demystify classical music and call attention to the historic settings.

Tips   A Major Music Festival in the Bucolic Berkshires

When the Boston Symphony Orchestra goes on summer vacation, it goes to Tanglewood (© 413/637-5165 or 617/266-1492 out of season; www.bso.org), in Lenox, Massachusetts, a 2½-hour drive from Boston. Weekend concerts sell out in advance, but tickets to weeknight performances and Saturday morning rehearsals are usually available at the box office. If you can't get a seat inside, bring a blanket and picnic on the lawn. (Consult *Frommer's New England* for in-depth coverage of western Massachusetts.)

The season runs from October to April, with performances most Tuesday, Thursday, and Saturday evenings; Friday afternoons; and some Friday evenings. Explanatory talks (included in the ticket price) begin 30 minutes before the curtain rises. If you aren't able to get tickets in advance, check at the box office for returns from subscribers 2 hours before show time. A limited number of same-day **rush tickets** (one per person) are available for Tuesday and Thursday evening and Friday afternoon programs. Some Wednesday evening and Thursday morning rehearsals are open to the public. Symphony Hall, 301 Mass. Ave. (at Huntington Ave.). © 617/266-1492 or 617/CONCERT (program information). SymphonyCharge © 888/266-1200 or 617/266-1200. www.bso.org. Tickets $27–$105. Rush tickets $8 (on sale Fri 9am; Tues, Thurs 5pm). Rehearsal tickets $16. T: Green Line E to Symphony, or Orange Line to Mass. Ave.

Boston Pops ★★   From early May to early July, members of the Boston Symphony Orchestra lighten up. Tables and chairs replace the floor seats at Symphony Hall, and drinks and light refreshments are served. Under the direction of conductor Keith Lockhart, the Pops plays a range of music from light classical to show tunes to popular (hence the name), often with celebrity guest stars. Performances are Tuesday through Sunday evenings. Special holiday performances in December ($31–$107) usually sell out well in advance, but it can't hurt to check; tickets go on sale in late October.

The regular season ends with a week of **free outdoor concerts at the Hatch Shell** on the Esplanade along the Charles River. It includes the traditional **Fourth of July concert.** Performing at Symphony Hall, 301 Mass. Ave. (at Huntington Ave.). © 617/266-1492 or 617/CONCERT (program information). SymphonyCharge © 888/266-1200 or 617/266-1200. www.bso.org. Tickets $37–$72 for tables; $16–$43 for balcony seats. T: Green Line E to Symphony, or Orange Line to Mass. Ave.

Handel & Haydn Society ★★   The Handel & Haydn Society uses period instruments and techniques in its orchestral and choral performances, yet it's as cutting-edge as any other ensemble in town. Established in 1815, it's the oldest continuously performing arts organization in the country. The company prides itself on its creative programming of "historically informed" concerts, which it stages year-round, with most performances at Symphony Hall and Jordan Hall.

H&H was the first American group to perform Handel's *Messiah,* in 1818, and has made it an annual holiday tradition since 1854. If you'll be in town in December, check for ticket availability as soon as you start planning your trip. 300 Mass. Ave. © 617/266-3605. www.handelandhaydn.org. Tickets $30–$77. T: Green Line E to Symphony, or Orange Line to Mass. Ave.

ADDITIONAL OFFERINGS

The repertoire of the **Boston Lyric Opera** (✆ 800/447-7400 Tele-Charge, 617/542-6772, or 617/542-4912 for tickets; www.blo.org) includes classical and contemporary works. The season runs from October to May. Performances are at the Shubert Theatre, 265 Tremont St. Tickets cost $34 to $159; student rush tickets are half price.

Boston Baroque (✆ 617/484-9200; www.bostonbaroque.org), a Grammy-nominated period orchestra with a chamber chorus, performs at Jordan Hall and Sanders Theatre. Tickets cost $22 to $63.

CONCERT & PERFORMANCE SERIES

The starriest names in classical music, dance, theater, jazz, and world music appear as part of the **Bank of America Celebrity Series** (✆ 617/482-2595 or 617/482-6661 for Celebrity Charge; www.celebrityseries.org). It's a subscription series that also offers tickets to individual events, which go on sale in September. Performances take place at Symphony Hall, Jordan Hall, the Wang and Shubert theaters, and other venues.

World Music (✆ 617/876-4275; www.worldmusic.org) showcases top-flight musicians, dance troupes, and other performers from around the world. Shows (60 a year) are at the Somerville Theater, the Berklee Performance Center, Sanders Theatre, the Cutler Majestic Theatre, and other venues.

The **Isabella Stewart Gardner Museum,** 280 The Fenway (✆ 617/734-1359; www.gardnermuseum.org; T: Green Line E to Museum), features soloists, local students, chamber music, and jazz in the Tapestry Room. Performances are Saturday and Sunday at 1:30pm from late September to early May. Tickets (including museum admission) are $20 adults, $14 seniors, $10 students with ID, $5 children 5 to 17. Children under 5 not admitted. See p. 156 for a full museum listing.

FREE (& ALMOST FREE) CONCERTS

Radio stations sponsor free outdoor music all summer. Specifics change frequently, but you can count on hearing oldies, pop, jazz, and classical music at various convenient venues, including City Hall Plaza, Copley Square, and the Hatch Shell, at lunch, after work, and in the evening. Check the papers when you arrive, listen to a station that sounds good to you, or just follow the crowds.

Students and faculty members at two prestigious musical institutions perform frequently during the academic year; admission is usually free. For information, contact the **New England Conservatory of Music,** 290 Huntington Ave. (✆ 617/585-1100; www.newenglandconservatory.edu/concerts), or the **Longy School of Music,** 1 Follen St., Cambridge (✆ 617/876-0956, ext. 500; www.longy.edu). Also check listings for the particulars of student performances at other area colleges; most are free or cheap, and the quality is often quite high.

Fridays at Trinity   This landmark church features 30-minute organ recitals by local and visiting artists on Fridays at 12:15pm. Ongoing renovation may affect this series; check ahead. Trinity Church, 206 Clarendon St., Copley Sq. ✆ 617/536-0944. www.trinitychurchboston. org. $5 donation suggested. T: Green Line to Copley, or Orange Line to Back Bay.

King's Chapel Noon Hour Recitals   Organ, instrumental, and vocal solos fill this historic building with music and make for a pleasant break along the Freedom Trail. Concerts are at 12:15pm on Tuesday. 58 Tremont St. ✆ 617/227-2155. $3 donation requested. T: Red or Green Line to Park St.

DANCE

The best-known offering by Jose Mateo's **Ballet Theatre of Boston** (© 617/262-0961; www.ballettheatre.org) is *The Nutcracker,* performed in December at the Sanctuary Theatre, 400 Harvard St., Cambridge. Although Boston Ballet's production has more impressive sets, BTB's has a reputation as a good "starter" ballet. Tickets run $15 to $35.

Boston Ballet ★★   Boston Ballet's reputation seems to jump a notch every time someone says, "So it's not just *The Nutcracker.*" The country's fourth-largest dance company performs the holiday staple from Thanksgiving to New Year's at the **Opera House,** 539 Washington St. During the rest of the season (Oct–May), it presents an eclectic mix of classic story ballets and contemporary works at the **Wang Theatre.** Because the Wang was originally a movie theater, the pitch of the seats makes the top two balconies less than ideal for ballet. Paying more for a better seat is a good investment. Performing at the Wang Theatre, 270 Tremont St., and the Opera House, 539 Washington St. © **800/447-7400** (Tele-Charge) or 617/695-6955. www.bostonballet.org. Tickets $39–$98. Student rush tickets (1 hr. before curtain) $15, except for The Nutcracker. T: Green Line to Boylston.

THEATER

Local and national companies, professional and amateur actors, and classic and experimental drama combine to make the local theater scene a lively one. Call or surf ahead, or check the papers or BosTix (see "Let's Make a Deal," on p. 234) after you arrive.

Boston is one of the last cities for pre-Broadway tryouts, allowing an early look at a classic (or a classic flop) in the making. It's also a popular destination for touring companies of established hits. The promoter is often **Broadway in Boston** (© 617/880-2400; www.broadwayinboston.com). You'll find most of the shows headed to or coming from Broadway in the Theater District, at the **Colonial Theatre,** 106 Boylston St. (© 617/426-9366); the **Opera House,** 539 Washington St. (© 617/880-2400); the **Shubert Theatre,** 265 Tremont St. (© 617/482-9393); the **Wang Theatre,** 270 Tremont St. (© 617/482-9393); and the **Wilbur Theater,** 246 Tremont St. (© 617/423-4008).

The excellent local theater scene boasts the **Huntington Theatre Company,** which performs at the Boston University Theatre, 264 Huntington Ave. (© 617/266-0800; www.huntingtontheatre.org), and the **American Repertory Theatre,** or ART, which makes its home at Harvard University's **Loeb Drama Center,** 64 Brattle St., Cambridge (© 617/547-8300; www.amrep.org). Both stage classic and contemporary productions.

The **Lyric Stage,** 140 Clarendon St. (© 617/437-7172; www.lyricstage.com), mounts contemporary and modern works in an intimate second-floor setting. The

---

(*Finds*   **A Summer Theater Treat**

The **Commonwealth Shakespeare Company** ★★★ (© 617/532-1252; www.commonwealthshakespeare.org) performs free on Boston Common Tuesday through Sunday nights in July and early August. Bring a picnic and blanket, rent a chair ($5 or so) if you don't want to sit on the ground, and enjoy the sunset and a high-quality performance. The company is about half Equity actors, the sets are spectacular—and it's free!

Finds Dessert Alert

I don't want to boss you around; I'm here to suggest. So I *suggest* that before or after the theater, you run right over to **Finale**. It serves glorious desserts—fruit desserts, pastry desserts, dessert wines, and, best of all, chocolate desserts. Yes, it's a tad expensive. No, this is not a balanced meal. But the sweet tooths (sweet teeth?) who flock here don't want to hear it. Branches are in the Theater District at 1 Columbus Ave. (© 617/423-3184; www.finaledesserts.com), in the pointy end of the Park Plaza Building, and at 30 Dunster St., Harvard Square (© 617/441-9797). They also serve some real food, such as salads and pizzas, but the desserts are the real draw.

Copley Theatre, 225 Clarendon St. (© 617/266-7262), stages revues, concerts, and one-person shows. The **Stuart Street Playhouse,** 200 Stuart St., in the Radisson Hotel Boston (© 617/426-4499; www.stuartstreetplayhouse.com), often books one-person shows. **Jimmy Tingle's Off Broadway,** 255 Elm St., Davis Sq., Somerville (© 617/591-1616; www.jtoffbroadway.com), is a 200-seat space where you'll often find the owner/comedian/actor/social critic performing.

The Loeb also features student productions, and other college options include Suffolk University's **C. Walsh Theatre,** 55 Temple St., Beacon Hill (© 617/573-8680); various performance spaces at **MIT** (© 617/253-4003; web.mit.edu/arts) and **Boston University** (© 617/266-0800); and Northeastern's **Blackman Theater,** 360 Huntington Ave. (© 617/373-2247).

FAMILY THEATER/AUDIENCE PARTICIPATION

Charles Playhouse *(Kids)*   The off-Broadway sensation **Blue Man Group** ✪✪ began selling out as soon as it arrived on the Charles Playhouse's Stage I in 1995. Famous for reducing even the most eloquent theatergoer to one-syllable sputtering, the trio of cobalt-colored entertainers backed by a rock band uses music, percussion, food, and audience members in its performance. It's not recommended for children under 8, but older kids will love it. Shows are at 8pm Wednesday and Thursday; 7pm Friday; 4, 7, and 10pm Saturday; and 2 and 5pm Sunday (check ahead for extra performances during the holidays). Tickets are available at the box office and through Ticketmaster.

Shear Madness ✪, on Stage II (downstairs), is the longest-running nonmusical play in theater history. Since January 1980, the zany "comic murder mystery" has turned the stage into a unisex hairdressing salon. The show's never the same twice; one of the original audience-participation productions, the play changes at each performance as spectator-investigators question suspects, reconstruct events, and then name the murderer. Performances are Tuesday through Friday at 8pm, Saturday at 6:30 and 9:30pm, and Sunday at 3 and 7:30pm. 74 Warrenton St. © 617/426-6912 (Blue Man Group) and 617/426-5225 (Shear Madness). www.blueman.com and www.shearmadness.com. Blue Man Group $53 and $43; Shear Madness $34. T: Green Line to Boylston.

Le Grand David and His Own Spectacular Magic Company ✪ *(Kids)*   Three generations of magicians make up this company, a nationally acclaimed troupe of illusionists that has delighted families since 1977. Le Grand David has received national attention for his sleight-of-hand and has performed at Easter parties at the White House. The ever-changing 2-hour shows, directed by master magician Marco the

---

Tips **Got a Light? Not So Fast!**

Massachusetts state law forbids smoking in all workplaces, including bars, night-clubs, and restaurants. The only exception in Boston is hard to reach, and it'll cost you. It's the Houlihan's in **Logan Airport Terminal E,** and to get there, you need a plane ticket—for an international flight.

Magi, take place on Sunday afternoon and Thursday evening at two historic theaters in Beverly, about 40 minutes from Boston by car. Cabot Street Cinema Theater, 286 Cabot St., Beverly; and Larcom Theatre, 13 Wallis St., Beverly. ✆ 978/927-3677. www.legranddavid.com. Tickets $18 adults, $12 children under 12.

Puppet Showplace Theatre *Kids*   The Puppet Showplace presents favorite fables, ethnic legends, and folktales and fairy tales from around the world. Professional pup-peteers put on creative, engaging shows year-round in a lovely 100-seat theater. The theater displays historic puppets and puppet posters, offers puppet-making workshops, and sells toy puppets. Family performances take place on weekends, with shows for tod-dlers on weekdays. Adult-oriented "Puppets at Night" shows run at the theater and other local venues. Call for schedules and reservations. 32 Station St., Brookline. ✆ 617/731-6400. www.puppetshowplace.org. Tickets $8.50 for children's shows, $12–$20 for adult shows. T: Green Line D to Brookline Village.

2 The Club & Music Scene

The Boston-area club scene is multifaceted and constantly changing, and somewhere out there is a good time for anyone, regardless of age, musical taste, or budget. Check the "Calendar" section of Thursday's *Globe,* the "Edge" section of Friday's *Herald,* the *Phoenix, Stuff@Night,* or the *Improper Bostonian* while you're making plans.

Many nightclubs are along **Lansdowne Street,** near Boston's Kenmore Square, and on **Boylston Place,** off Boylston Street near Boston Common. The center of the local live-music universe is **Central Square** in Cambridge. Rowdy college bars and clubs abound near the intersection of Harvard and Brighton avenues in **Allston** (T: Green Line B to Harvard Ave.). That makes club-hopping easy, but it also means that students run wild on weekends. If you don't feel like dealing with swarms of teenagers, students, and recent college grads, stick to slightly more upscale and isolated nightspots. If you do like teenagers (or you are one), seek out a place where admission is 18- or 19-plus. Policies change regularly, sometimes from night to night, so call ahead.

A night on the town in Boston and Cambridge is relatively brief: Most bars close by 1am, clubs close at 2am, and the T shuts down around 12:30am (though Night Owl bus service—assuming it survives the MBTA budget process—runs till 2:30am on Fri and Sat nights). The drinking age is 21; a valid driver's license or passport is required as proof of age, and the law is strictly enforced, especially near college campuses.

COMEDY CLUBS

The Comedy Connection at Faneuil Hall ★★   A large room with a clear view from every seat, the oldest original comedy club in town (established in 1978) draws top-notch talent from near and far. Big-name national acts lure enthusiastic crowds, and the opening acts are often just as funny but not as famous—yet. There's one show a night Sunday through Thursday, two shows Friday and Saturday (times vary, so call ahead for specifics). The cover charge seldom tops $15 during the week but jumps for big names appearing on weekends. 245 Quincy Market Place (2nd floor, off the rotunda). © 617/ 248-9700. www.comedyconnectionboston.com. Cover $12–$45. T: Green or Blue Line to Government Center, or Orange Line to Haymarket. Validated parking available.

The Comedy Studio ★★ *Finds*   Nobody here is a sitcom star—yet. With a stellar reputation for searching out undiscovered talent, the no-frills Comedy Studio draws a savvy crowd of comedy connoisseurs, college students, and network scouts. It's not just setup-punchline-laugh, either; sketches and improv spice up the standup. Check ahead for singles night, known as "Luvs2Laff." Shows are Tuesday through Sunday at 8pm. At the Hong Kong restaurant, 1238 Mass. Ave., Cambridge. © 617/661-6507. www.thecomedy studio.com. Cover $7–$10. T: Red Line to Harvard.

Improv Asylum   The posters that catch your eye on the Freedom Trail might draw you back to the North End later for raucous improv and sketch comedy in a subterranean setting. Performances are Wednesday through Sunday evenings, and buying tickets in advance is recommended. 216 Hanover St. © 617/263-6887. www.improvasylum.com. Tickets $15–$20. T: Green or Orange Line to Haymarket. Validated parking available.

DANCE CLUBS

Most clubs enforce a **dress code** that forbids athletic wear, sneakers, jeans, and ball caps on everyone, as well as tank tops on men. Some places require that men wear a shirt with a collar, or even a jacket. Check ahead to make sure you don't wind up spending the evening on the sidewalk instead of the dance floor. While you're checking out websites, note that some clubs will let you put your name on the VIP list online. Can't hurt, might help.

Avalon ★★★   A cavernous multilevel space with a full concert stage, private booths and lounges, large dance floors, and a spectacular light show, Avalon is either great fun or sensory overload. The club books concerts, usually in the early evening (Gavin DeGraw, Toots and the Maytals, and Joss Stone have played recently); when the stage is not in use, DJs take over.

Friday is **"Avaland,"** with national and international names in the DJ booth and costumed house dancers on the floor. On Saturday (suburbanites' night out), expect more mainstream dance music. The crowd here is in their 20s to 30s, slightly older than the crowd at Axis (see below). Open Thursday (international night) to Sunday (gay night) from 10pm to 2am. 15 Lansdowne St. © 617/262-2424 or 617/423-NEXT (for tickets). www.avalon boston.com. Cover $5–$20. T: Green Line B, C, or D to Kenmore.

Axis   Progressive rock at bone-rattling volume and "creative dress"—break out the leather—attract a young crowd. There are special nights for alternative rock, house, techno, soul, and funk. Axis also schedules international DJs and occasional concerts;

Tips **Cinderella Goes Clubbing**

At press time, MBTA **Night Owl bus service** was operating on Friday and Saturday nights until 2:30am. Budget cuts were threatening the service; if it's still operating when you visit, you can ride it on popular bus routes and on supplemental routes that parallel the subway lines. The fare is $1.50 in coins. For info and schedules, contact the MBTA (© **800/392-6100** or 617/222-3200; www.mbta.com).

really hot stuff turns up on the Avalon website (see above). Open Monday (gay night) and Thursday through Saturday from 10pm to 2am. 13 Lansdowne St. ☎ **617/262-2437.** Cover $5–$15. T: Green Line B, C, or D to Kenmore.

The Big Easy Buttoned-up Boston meets let-it-all-hang-out New Orleans—look out. This large space has a balcony (great for people-watching), billiard room, dance floor, and live bands or top local DJs playing anything from soul to alternative. The lower level is the **Sugar Shack;** on both levels, the crowd is on the young (collegiate and post-) side. No ripped jeans or athletic shoes. 1 Boylston Place. ☎ 617/351-7000. www. bigeasyboston.com. Cover $8–$10. T: Green Line to Boylston.

The Rack Across the street from Faneuil Hall Marketplace, this enormous space is nominally an upscale pool hall (with 22 tournament-size tables), but it's far better known as a hot nightspot. You can order food from 11am to 1am and maybe do a little stargazing—pro athletes turn up periodically. In good weather, the action spills onto the patio. 24 Clinton St. (at North St.). ☎ 617/725-1051. www.therackboston.com. T: Green or Blue Line to Government Center, or Orange Line to Haymarket.

The Roxy ★★ This former hotel ballroom boasts excellent DJs and all sorts of live music, a huge dance floor, a stage, and a balcony (perfect for checking out the action below). Occasional concerts and boxing cards take good advantage of the sight lines. Offerings change regularly, so call or surf for the latest schedule. Open 9pm (entertainment starts at 10pm) Thursday through Saturday, and some Wednesdays and Sundays. In the Tremont Boston hotel, 279 Tremont St. ☎ 617/338-7699. www.roxyplex.com. Cover $10–$20. T: Green Line to Boylston or Orange Line to New England Medical Center.

ECLECTIC

Johnny D's Uptown Restaurant & Music Club ★★★ *Finds* This family-owned and -operated establishment is one of the best places in the area for live music. You'll kick yourself if you don't at least check the lineup while you're in town. Johnny D's draws a congenial all-ages crowd for acts on international tours as well as acts that haven't been out of eastern Massachusetts. The music ranges from zydeco to rock, rockabilly to jazz, blues to ska. The veggie-friendly food's good, too; try the weekend brunch. This place is worth a long trip, but it's only two stops past Harvard on the Red Line (about a 15-min. ride at night). Open daily from 11:30am to 1am. Brunch starts at 9am on weekends; dinner runs from 4:30 to 9:30pm Tuesday through Saturday, with lighter fare until 11pm. 17 Holland St., Davis Sq., Somerville. ☎ 617/776-2004 or 617/ 776-9667 (concert line). www.johnnyds.com. Cover $3–$20, usually $8–$12. T: Red Line to Davis.

Lizard Lounge ★★ In the basement of the Cambridge Common restaurant, this way-cool, cozy-but-not-cramped room features well-known local rock and folk musicians who play right in the middle of the floor. The Lizard Lounge draws a postcollegiate-and-up crowd (Harvard Law School is next door). Shows are daily at 8 and 9:30pm; Sunday is open-mike poetry jam night. 1667 Mass. Ave., Cambridge. ☎ 617/547-0759. Cover for late show $5–$12. T: Red Line to Harvard.

T.T. the Bear's Place ★ This friendly no-frills spot generally attracts a young crowd, but 30-somethings will feel comfortable, too. Bookings—three or four per night—range from cutting-edge alternative rock and roots music to ska and funk shows to up-and-coming pop acts. New bands predominate early in the week, with more established artists (recently, Scissor Sisters and Damien Rice) on weekends. Open until 1am on weeknights, 2am on weekends. 10 Brookline St., Cambridge. ☎ 617/492-0082 or 617/492-BEAR (concert line). www.ttthebears.com. Cover $5–$12. T: Red Line to Central.

The Western Front ☆   A 30-ish friend swears by this legendary reggae club for one reason: "You're never the oldest one there." Open since 1968 (hey! the club is 30-something, too), it's a casual spot on a nondescript street south of Central Square. Integrated crowds flock here for world-beat music, blues, and especially reggae. Open Wednesday (jazz night) through Saturday from 8pm to 2am; live entertainment begins at 8:30 or 9pm. 343 Western Ave., Cambridge. ℂ 617/492-7772. www.thewesternfront club.com. Cover $5–$10. T: Red Line to Central.

Zeitgeist Gallery   "Eclectic" doesn't begin to capture the vibe at this place, which schedules a huge variety of music (folk, jazz, improvisational, rock, soul, world, and more), performance art, films, poetry, and other forms of self-expression nearly every night. As the name indicates, it's also an art gallery (open Tues–Sun from 1–7pm). 1353 Cambridge St., Cambridge. ℂ 617/567-6060. www.zeitgeist-gallery.org. Cover free–$10. T: Red Line to Central; 10-min. walk on Prospect St.

FOLK

Boston is one of the only cities where folk musicians consistently sell out large venues that usually book rock and pop performers. If an artist you want to see is touring, check ahead for Boston-area dates. The annual **Boston Folk Festival** (ℂ 617/287-6911; www.bostonfolkfestival.org) is a 2-day event in mid-September on the UMass-Boston campus in Dorchester.

The music listings in the "Calendar" section of Thursday's *Globe* include information about **coffeehouses,** the area's main outlets for folk. The streets around **Harvard Square** are another promising venue—Tracy Chapman is just one famous graduate of the scene.

Also see the **Lizard Lounge** (p. 242).

Club Passim ☆☆☆   Passim has launched more careers than the mass production of acoustic guitars—Joan Baez, Shawn Colvin, and Tom Rush started out here, and this is where you'll find Arlo Guthrie when he's in town. In a basement on the street between Harvard Coop buildings, this legendary coffeehouse (which doesn't serve alcohol) enjoys an international reputation built on more than 30 years of nurturing new talent and showcasing established musicians. Patrons who have been regulars since day one mix with college students. There's live music nightly, and coffee and vegetarian food until 10:30pm. Tuesday is open-mike night. Open Sunday through Thursday from 11am to 11pm, Friday and Saturday from 11am to midnight. Most shows start at 8pm. 47 Palmer St., Cambridge. ℂ 617/492-7679. www.clubpassim.org. Cover $5–$25; most shows $15 or less. T: Red Line to Harvard.

JAZZ & BLUES

If you're partial to these genres, consider timing your visit to coincide with the *Boston Globe* Jazz & Blues Festival (ℂ 617/929-3460; https://bostonglobe.com/promotions/jazzfest), usually scheduled in late June or July. Constellations of jazz and blues stars (large and small) appear at events, some of them free, many of them outdoors. The festival wraps up with a free Sunday-afternoon program at the Hatch Shell (p. 231).

Two restaurants that offer jazz along with excellent food are **Bob the Chef's Jazz Café** (p. 132) and **Les Zygomates** (p. 123).

On summer Thursdays at 6pm, the **Boston Harbor Hotel** (ℂ 617/491-2100; www.bhh.com) sponsors free performances on the "Blues Barge," which floats in the water behind the hotel.

Cantab Lounge ⚓ Follow your ears to this friendly neighborhood bar, which attracts a lively three-generation crowd. When the door swings open at night, deafening music—usually blues, rock, folk, or bluegrass—spills out. If Little Joe Cook and the Thrillers are on the schedule, don't miss them. Downstairs is the Third Rail, which schedules poetry on Wednesday, improv on Thursday, and DJs on weekends. 738 Mass. Ave., Cambridge. ℂ 617/354-2685. Cover $3–$8. T: Red Line to Central.

Regattabar ⚓⚓⚓ The Regattabar's selection of local and international jazz artists is often considered the best in the area—a title that Scullers Jazz Club (see below) is happy to dispute. Buckwheat Zydeco, Irma Thomas, Joe Lovano, and Madeleine Peyroux have appeared recently. The large third-floor room holds about 200 and, unfortunately, sometimes gets a little noisy. Buy tickets in advance or try your luck at the door an hour before show time. Open Tuesday through Saturday and some Sundays, with one or two performances per night. In the Charles Hotel, 1 Bennett St., Cambridge. ℂ 617/661-5000 or 617/395-7757 for tickets. www.regattabarjazz.com. Tickets $12–$35. T: Red Line to Harvard.

Ryles Jazz Club ⚓ This popular spot, which doubles as a barbecue joint, books a wide variety of blues, jazz, R&B, world beat, and Latin in two rooms. Both levels offer excellent music and a friendly atmosphere. Sunday jazz brunch runs from 10am to 3pm. Open Tuesday through Sunday at 5pm; shows start at 9pm. 212 Hampshire St., Inman Sq., Cambridge. ℂ 617/876-9330. www.ryles.com. Cover for music $7–$15. T: Red Line to Central, 10-min. walk.

Scullers Jazz Club ⚓⚓⚓ Overlooking the Charles River, Scullers is a lovely, comfortable room with a top-notch sound system. It books acclaimed singers and instrumentalists—recent notables include Tower of Power, Abbey Lincoln, Nicholas Payton, and Al Jarreau. Patrons tend to be more hard-core than the crowds at the Regattabar, but it depends on who's performing. There are usually two shows a night Tuesday through Saturday; the box office is open Monday through Saturday from 11am to 6pm. Ask about dinner packages ($47–$75 per person), which include preferred seating and a three-course meal, and overnight packages (from $99). In the Doubletree Guest Suites hotel, 400 Soldiers Field Rd. ℂ 617/562-4111. www.scullersjazz.com. Tickets $15–$50. Validated parking available.

Wally's Cafe ⚓ This Boston institution, near a busy corner in the South End, opened in 1947. It draws a notably diverse crowd—black, white, straight, gay, affluent, indigent. Live jazz, by local ensembles, students and instructors from the Berklee College of Music, and the occasional international star (recently, Roy Haynes), starts every night at 9pm. Open daily until 2am. 427 Mass. Ave. ℂ 617/424-1408. www.wallyscafe.com. No cover; 1-drink minimum. T: Orange Line to Mass. Ave.

> **Tips Rock of Ages**
>
> Bring your driver's license or passport when you go club-hopping, no matter how old you think you look—you must be 21 to drink alcohol, and the law is strictly enforced. Most bouncers won't risk a fine or license suspension, especially at 18-plus shows.

ROCK

Bill's Bar Long known as the only real hangout on Lansdowne Street, Bill's has a friendly atmosphere and a great beer menu. In recent years it has shifted from neighborhood bar to live-music destination back to neighborhood bar, keeping live reggae on Sunday. Open nightly from 9pm to 2am. 5½ Lansdowne St. ℂ 617/421-9678. www.billsbar.com. Cover $5–$10. T: Green Line B, C, or D to Kenmore.

Kids **Theme a Little Theme**

The **Hard Rock Cafe,** 131 Clarendon St. (📞 **617/424-ROCK;** www.hardrock.com), is a fun link in the fun chain—just ask the other visitors in line with you. The two-level space boasts a guitar-shaped bar and stained-glass windows that glorify rock stars. You'll see memorabilia of Jimi Hendrix, Elvis Presley, Madonna, local favorites Aerosmith and the Cars, and others. The kid-friendly menu features salads, burgers, and sandwiches, including the legendary "pig sandwich."

The Middle East ⭐⭐⭐   The best rock club in the area books an impressive variety of progressive and alternative artists in two rooms (upstairs and downstairs) every night. Showcasing top talent as well as bands with local roots and international reputations, it's a popular hangout that gets crowded, hot, and *loud*. The Middle East is the heart of a complex that incorporates the **Corner,** a former bakery that features acoustic artists most of the time and belly dancers on Sundays and Wednesday. And **ZuZu** (📞 **617/492-9181**) is a Middle Eastern restaurant that has its own music schedule and gallery space with rotating art exhibits. All shows are 18-plus; the age of the crowd varies with the performer. 472–480 Mass. Ave., Central Sq., Cambridge. 📞 **617/864-EAST** or 617/931-2000 (Ticketmaster). www.mideastclub.com. Cover $7–$15. T: Red Line to Central.

Paradise Rock Club ⭐   Hard by the Boston University campus, the medium-size Paradise draws enthusiastic, student-intensive crowds for top local rock and alternative performers. You might see national names (lately, Marianne Faithfull and Johnny Winter) who want a relatively small venue and others who aren't ready to headline a big show on their own (Ray LaMontagne, Jump Little Children, and, uh, Minnie Driver). Most shows are 18-plus. You must be 21 to drink alcohol, an iron-clad policy here; don't forget your ID. 967 Commonwealth Ave. 📞 **617/562-8800** or 617/423-NEXT for tickets. www. teapartyconcerts.com. T: Green Line B to Pleasant St.

Toad ⭐⭐ *Value*   Essentially a bar with a stage, this narrow space (the high ceiling helps a little) draws a savvy three-generation clientele attracted by the local big-name performers—rock, rockabilly, and sometimes blues—and the lack of cover. Toad enjoys good acoustics but not much elbow room—a plus when restless musicians wander into the crowd. 1912 Mass. Ave., Cambridge. 📞 **617/497-4950** (info line). T: Red Line to Porter.

3 The Bar Scene

Bostonians had some quibbles with the TV show *Cheers,* but no one complained that the concept was implausible. From the Littlest Bar (a closet-size downtown watering hole) to the original Cheers bar (formerly the Bull & Finch), neighborhood bars occupy a vital niche. This tends to be a fairly insular scene—as a stranger, don't assume that you'll get a warm welcome. This is one area where you can and probably should judge a book by its cover: If you peek in and see people who look like you and your friends, give it a whirl.

BARS & LOUNGES

Casablanca ⭐⭐   Students and professors jam this legendary Harvard Square watering hole, especially on weekends. You'll find excellent food (p. 145), an excellent jukebox, and excellent eavesdropping. 40 Brattle St., Cambridge. 📞 **617/876-0999**. T: Red Line to Harvard.

Cheers (Beacon Hill)   If you're out to impersonate a native, try not to be shocked when you enter "the *Cheers* bar" and the inside looks nothing like the bar on the TV show. (A spin-off in Faneuil Hall Marketplace fills that niche—see the listing below.) Formerly the Bull & Finch Pub, this really is a neighborhood bar, but it's far better known for attracting legions of out-of-towners, who find good pub grub and plenty of souvenirs. There's food from 11am to 11:45pm and a kids' menu ($4–$5). 84 Beacon St. ℂ 617/227-9605. www.cheersboston.com. T: Green Line to Arlington.

Cheers (Faneuil Hall Marketplace)   Blatantly but good-naturedly courting fans of the sitcom, this bar's interior is an exact replica of the *Cheers* TV set. It serves pub fare until 11:45pm and schedules live entertainment on weekend nights. Memorabilia on display includes Sam Malone's Red Sox jacket. Go ahead, you know you want to. Quincy Market Building, South Canopy, Faneuil Hall Marketplace. ℂ 617/227-0150. www.cheersboston.com. Cover $5 for live entertainment. T: Green or Blue Line to Government Center, or Orange Line to Haymarket.

Coyote Ugly   This New York–based chain gained fame thanks to the movie of the same name. The staff consists of no-nonsense babes with a penchant for dancing on the bar—but if you don't know that already, this might not be the place for you. 234 Friend St. ℂ 617/854-7300. www.coyoteuglysaloon.com. T: Green or Orange Line to North Station.

DeLux Cafe 🌟🌟   Ultracool but never obnoxious about it, the DeLux is one of the classiest dives around. The funky decor, selection of microbrews, and veggie-friendly ethnic menu attract a cross-section of the neighborhood, from off-duty chefs to yuppies. Part of the appeal is the decor, a scrapbook of 20th-century pop culture (posters, photos, postcards, and such)—check out the Elvis shrine. 100 Chandler St. ℂ 617/338-5258. T: Orange Line to Back Bay.

The Fours   One of Boston's best and best-known sports bars, the Fours is about one football field away from the TD Banknorth Garden. Festooned with sports memorabilia and TVs, it's a madhouse before Celtics and Bruins games—and a promising place to pick up an extra ticket. 166 Canal St. ℂ 617/720-4455. T: Green or Orange Line to North Station.

Game On! Sports Cafe   Yes, it's actually in Fenway Park, and no, you can't just sneak into the stands. The overgrown sports bar and restaurant boasts the latest techno toys, including high-def TVs and a booming sound system, on two deafeningly loud levels of a onetime bowling alley. On game days, the line stretches out the door and down the street toward the left-field wall. 82 Lansdowne St. ℂ 617/351-7001. www.gameonboston.com. T: Green Line D to Fenway or B, C, or D to Kenmore.

Green Street Grill 🌟🌟   This Central Square hangout isn't the entertaining dive it once was, but it still draws a savvy crowd for live blues, rock, and jazz. There's also excellent food (p. 148). 280 Green St., Cambridge. ℂ 617/876-1655. www.thegreenstreetgrill.com. T: Red Line to Central.

Grendel's Den 🌟   A vestige of pre-franchise Harvard Square, this cozy subterranean space is *the* place to celebrate turning 21. Recent grads and grad students dominate, but Grendel's has been so popular for so long that it also gets its share of Gen Y's parents. The food is tasty, with loads of vegetarian dishes, and the fireplace enhances the comfy atmosphere. 89 Winthrop St., Cambridge. ℂ 617/491-1160. www.grendels den.com. T: Red Line to Harvard.

Harvard Gardens   A Beacon Hill standby, Harvard Gardens is a neighborhood favorite. In this neighborhood, that means students, yuppies, and medical professionals

(Mass. General Hospital is across the street). It's more lounge than tavern, with plenty of beers on tap, great margaritas, and food until 11pm (midnight on weekends). *320 Cambridge St.* ☎ **617/523-2727.** T: Red Line to Charles/MGH.

The Hong Kong ⚡ This fun hangout is a retro Chinese restaurant on the first floor, a bar on the second floor, and a small dance club on the third floor. It's also the home of the scorpion bowl, a rum-based concoction that has contributed to the destruction of countless Ivy League brain cells. Nevertheless, you might see Harvard football players here. Never mind how I know. *1238 Mass. Ave., Cambridge* ☎ **617/864-5311.** T: Red Line to Harvard.

Hooters What can I say? The tank tops are tight, the shorts are short, the beer is cold, and the chicken wings are the culinary equivalent of the articles in *Playboy.* *222 Friend St.* ☎ **617/557-4555.** www.hooters.com. T: Green or Orange Line to North Station.

The Place ⚡ Is it a Financial District hangout? A sports bar on (pardon the word choice) steroids, with flat-screen TVs all over? An after-work destination for bankers and lawyers and the men and women who love them? Yes, yes, and yes. *2 Broad St.* ☎ **617/523-2081.** www.theplaceboston.com. Cover $5 Thurs–Sat after 9pm. T: Orange or Blue Line to State. Validated parking available.

The Purple Shamrock Across the street from Faneuil Hall Marketplace, the Purple Shamrock packs in wall-to-wall tourists of all ages. This is a rowdy, fun place that schedules DJs and cover bands. *1 Union St.* ☎ **617/227-2060.** www.irishconnection.com. Cover $5–$10 Thurs–Sat. T: Green or Blue Line to Government Center, or Orange Line to Haymarket.

Radius The high-tech bar at this hot, *haute* restaurant offers almost everything the dining room does—the chic crowd, the noise, the perfect martinis—without the sky-high food bill. *8 High St.* ☎ **617/426-1234.** T: Red Line to South Station.

Top of the Hub ⚡⚡⚡ Boasting a panoramic view of greater Boston, Top of the Hub is 52 stories above the city; the view is especially beautiful at sunset. It's an elegant destination and a favorite with couples out on a big date or celebrating a special occasion. Take a turn around the dance floor or just enjoy the live jazz and the late-night menu, which features superb desserts. Dress is casual but neat (no jeans). Open until 1am Sunday through Wednesday, 2am Thursday through Saturday. You must have a photo ID to enter the building. *Prudential Center, 800 Boylston St.* ☎ **617/536-1775.** www.selectrestaurants.com. T: Green Line E to Prudential. Validated parking available.

21st Amendment A Beacon Hill standby, this tavern looks like a regular old neighborhood bar and restaurant—unless the Legislature is in session. Then it turns into an annex of the State House, just across the street, and the entertainment value of the

---

⎛ *Tips* **Bowled Over**

The hottest nightlife destination in town is, of all things, a bowling alley. **Kings,** 10 Scotia St. (☎ **617/266-BOWL;** www.backbaykings.com), is a 25,000-sq.-ft. complex in a former movie theater. It has 20 bowling lanes (4 of them private) and an eight-table billiards room. The complex also includes a branch of the Cambridge restaurant **Jasper White's Summer Shack** (p. 147). Scotia Street is off Dalton Street, across from the Hynes Convention Center. Open until 2am daily; patrons must be 21 after 6pm.

conversation jumps dramatically. (In case you were absent that day, the 21st Amendment repealed Prohibition.) 150 Bowdoin St. ℂ 617/227-7100. T: Red Line to Park Street.

Via Matta This chic Italian restaurant's equally stylish bar and divine wine list make this a perfect place to recharge after an afternoon of hard work or hard shopping—Newbury Street is 3 blocks away. 79 Park Plaza (Arlington St. and Columbus Ave.). ℂ 617/422-0008. www.viamattarestaurant.com. T: Green Line to Arlington.

Whiskey Park New York wannabes congregate outside the Boston incarnation of the posh national chain. A dark, plush space with wood and copper accents, Whiskey Park packs in the black-clad 20-somethings who line up outside to seek admission. Be sure to check out the space-age restrooms (on the lower level). In the Boston Park Plaza Hotel, 64 Arlington St. ℂ 617/542-1482. www.midnightoilbars.com. T: Green Line to Arlington.

BREWPUBS

Boston Beer Works Across the street from Fenway Park, this cavernous space is frantic before and after Red Sox games. Don't plan to be able to hear anything your friends are saying. It has a full food menu and 14 brews on tap, including excellent bitters and ales. Especially good are the cask-conditioned offerings, seasoned in wood until they're as smooth as fine wine. The sweet-potato fries make a terrific snack. A branch near **North Station,** at 110 Canal St. (ℂ **617/896-BEER**), is smaller but equally loud. Open daily from 11:30am to 1am. 61 Brookline Ave. ℂ **617/536-BEER.** www.beerworks.net. T: Green Line B, C, or D to Kenmore.

John Harvard's Brew House ★★ This subterranean Harvard Square hangout pumps out terrific English-style brews in a clublike setting (try to find the sports figures in the stained-glass windows) and prides itself on its food. The beer selection changes regularly; it includes at least one selection from each "family" (ambers, porters, seasonals, and more), all brewed on the premises. Order a sampler if you can't decide. Open Sunday through Thursday from 11:30am to midnight, Friday and Saturday till 2am, with food service until 11:30pm. 33 Dunster St., Cambridge. ℂ 617/868-3585. www.johnharvards.com. T: Red Line to Harvard.

HOTEL BARS & LOUNGES

Many popular nightspots are associated with hotels and restaurants (see chapters 6 and 7); as a rule, these are the only watering holes in town where you don't have to shout to be heard. The following are particularly agreeable, albeit expensive, places to while away an hour or three.

The Atrium The floor-to-ceiling windows of this ground-floor room across the street from Faneuil Hall Marketplace allow for great people-watching. The Atrium also offers champagne by the glass, live piano music on weeknights, and cushy furnishings that

---

Finds **The Classiest Pickup Joint in Town**

On the first Friday of each month, the **Museum of Fine Arts,** 465 Huntington Ave. (ℂ 617/267-9300; www.mfa.org), becomes a spirited nightlife destination. From 5:30 to 9:30pm, music, a cash bar, and a crowd of 20- and 30-somethings liven up the galleries. General admission to the museum ($13 after 5pm) includes admission to "firstfridays."

encourage lingering. Open daily until midnight. In the Millennium Bostonian Hotel, 26 North St. © **617/523-3600**. T: Green or Blue Line to Government Center, or Orange Line to State.

Boston Harbor Hotel ★ You have two appealing options on the ground floor: **Intrigue** looks like a comfortable living room, serves food all day, and boasts a harbor view; and the businesslike **Rowes Wharf Bar,** which makes a serious martini. Rowes Wharf (entrance on Atlantic Ave.). © **617/439-7000**. T: Red Line to South Station.

The Bristol ★★★ This is a perfect choice after the theater, after work, or after anything else. An elegant room with soft lounge chairs, a fireplace, and fresh flowers, it features a fabulous Viennese Dessert Buffet on Friday and Saturday from 9pm to midnight. There's live jazz every evening. Food is available until 11:30pm (12:30am Fri–Sat). In the Four Seasons Hotel, 200 Boylston St. © **617/351-2037**. T: Green Line to Arlington.

Oak Bar ★★ This paneled, high-ceilinged room feels like an old-fashioned men's club—but one that welcomes women. The lighting is muted, the leather seating soft and welcoming, and the raw bar picture-perfect. There's live entertainment on weekends. Proper dress (no jeans, shorts, or sneakers) is required. Open Sunday through Thursday until midnight, Friday and Saturday until 1am. In the Fairmont Copley Plaza Hotel, 138 St. James Ave. © **617/267-5300**. www.theoakroom.com. T: Green Line to Copley, or Orange Line to Back Bay.

IRISH BARS
The Black Rose Purists might sneer at the Black Rose's touristy location, but performers don't. Sing along with the authentic entertainment at this jam-packed pub and restaurant at the edge of Faneuil Hall Marketplace. You might even be able to make out the tune on a fiddle over the din. 160 State St. © **617/742-2286**. www.irishconnection.com. Cover $3–$5. T: Orange or Blue Line to State.

The Burren ★ The expatriate Irish community seems to find the Burren an antidote to homesickness, and you will, too. There's traditional music in the front room, acoustic rock in the large back room, and good food. Bonus: Loud commiserating (still!) about the smoking ban. 247 Elm St., Somerville. © **617/776-6896**. www.burren.com. Cover (back room only) $5–$10. T: Red Line to Davis.

The Grand Canal No, it's not Italian. This is an atmospheric pub and restaurant with an excellent beer selection, good food, a 12-foot TV screen, and Irish or rock cover bands or DJs Thursday through Saturday nights. (By the way, the Grand Canal connects Dublin to the Shannon River.) 57 Canal St. © **617/523-1112**. www.somerspubs.com. Cover $5 for music. T: Green or Orange Line to Haymarket or North Station.

Mr. Dooley's Boston Tavern ★★ Sometimes an expertly poured Guinness is all you need. If one of the nicest bartenders in the city pours it, and you enjoy it in an authentically decorated room, so much the better. This Financial District spot offers a wide selection of imported beers on tap, live Irish music, and a menu of pub favorites at lunch and dinner. 77 Broad St. © **617/338-5656**. www.somerspubs.com. Cover (Fri–Sat only) $3–$5. T: Orange Line to State or Blue Line to Aquarium.

GAY & LESBIAN BARS & CLUBS
In addition to the clubs listed here, some mainstream venues schedule a weekly gay night. On Sunday, **Avalon** (p. 241) plays host to the largest gathering of gay men in town. Also check out Monday nights at **Axis** (p. 241). Wednesday night at **Aria**, 246 Tremont St. (© **617/338-7080**) is known as "Sanctuary" and welcomes both men

and women. On Saturday, women congregate at the **Ekco Lounge,** 41 Essex St., in Chinatown (© **617/338-8283**). For up-to-date listings, check *Bay Windows,* the *Improper Bostonian,* and the *Phoenix.*

Fritz This popular South End hangout is a neighborhood favorite that serves brunch on weekends. The friendly crowd bonds over sports—there's even a satellite dish. In the Chandler Inn Hotel, 26 Chandler St. © **617/482-4428.** T: Orange Line to Back Bay.

Jacques ★ The only drag venue in town, Jacques draws a friendly crowd of gay and straight patrons who mix with the "girls" and sometimes engage in a shocking activity— that's right, disco dancing. The eclectic entertainment includes live music (on weekends), performance artists, and, of course, drag shows. Open daily from noon to midnight. 79 Broadway, Bay Village. © **617/426-8902.** www.jacquescabaret.com. Cover $6–$8. T: Green Line to Arlington.

Man-Ray The area's best goth scene is at Man-Ray, which has regular fetish nights and an appropriately gloomy atmosphere. Thursday is "Campus" night, when the crowd is 19-plus and mostly men; the Friday dress code calls for gothic or fetish attire. Open Wednesday until 1am, Thursday through Saturday until 2am. 21 Brookline St., Cambridge. © **617/864-0400.** www.manrayclub.com. Cover $8–$12. T: Red Line to Central.

Paradise Not to be confused with the Boston rock club (well, you can, but it won't be quite the same experience), the Paradise attracts an all-ages male crowd. There's a stripper every evening. Thursday is college night. Open Sunday through Wednesday until 1am, Thursday through Saturday until 2am. 180 Mass. Ave., Cambridge. © **617/494-0700.** www.paradisecambridge.com. T: Red Line to Central, 10-min. walk.

209 at Club Café ★★ This fun South End spot draws a chic crowd of men and women for conversation (the noise level is reasonable), dining, live music in the front room, and video entertainment in the back room. Thursday is the busiest night. Open daily until 2am; the kitchen serves lunch weekdays, Sunday brunch, and dinner nightly. 209 Columbus Ave. © **617/536-0966.** www.clubcafe.com. T: Green Line to Arlington, or Orange Line to Back Bay.

4 More Entertainment Options

COFFEEHOUSES & TEA SALONS

As in most other American cities, you won't get far without seeing a Starbucks. I'll submit to the passive-aggressive counter routine if it ends in a frozen drink, but for coffee, tea, and hanging out, there are plenty of less generic options. Many are in the North End (see chapter 7); other favorites are listed here. At all of them, hours are long, and loitering is encouraged—these are good places to bring your journal.

Algiers Café & Restaurant ★ Middle Eastern food and music, plain and flavored coffees, and the legendary atmosphere make this a classic Harvard Square hangout. Your "quick" snack or drink (try the mint coffee) might turn into a longer stay as the sociologist in you studies the resident and would-be intellectuals. This is a good spot to eavesdrop while you sample terrific soups, sandwiches, homemade sausages, falafel, and hummus. 40 Brattle St., Cambridge. © **617/492-1557.** T: Red Line to Harvard.

BeanTowne Coffee House A splash of the bohemian in a buttoned-up office-retail complex, this is a good stop before or after a film at the Kendall Square Cinema. There's only one problem—it's too popular. If a table empties, move in fast. 1 Kendall Sq., Cambridge. © **617/621-7900.** T: Red Line to Kendall.

Someday Café ★ If you lived near the Somerville Theater, you might not even bother furnishing the living room—you could hang out here. The coffee and tea selections are impressive, and there's great lemonade in summer, cider in winter, and brownies all the time. 51 Davis Sq., Somerville. ✆ 617/623-3323. T: Red Line to Davis.

Tealuxe Tealuxe pulls in the connoisseurs with its selection of 100-plus teas (dispensed by unfortunately named "tea-tenders"). The Harvard Square location is the original in the chain, which thrives on a combination of hard-to-find selections and comfortable atmosphere. www.tealuxe.com. 108 Newbury St. ✆ 617/927-0400. T: Green Line to Arlington. Also at Zero Brattle St., Cambridge. ✆ 617/441-0077. T: Red Line to Harvard.

1369 Coffee House ★ A long, narrow room with a colorful clientele, the 1369 offers excellent baked goods, a dazzling selection of premium teas and coffees, and great people-watching. The namesake original location is at 1369 Cambridge St., Inman Square (✆ **617/576-1369**). 757 Mass. Ave., Central Sq., Cambridge. ✆ **617/576-4600**. T: Red Line to Central.

Trident Booksellers & Café ★★ This Back Bay institution offers a view of the funkier end of Newbury Street, a browsing-friendly book selection, occasional author events, and a casual, New Age-y atmosphere. The draw for the digital set is free Wi-Fi access throughout the premises. Open until midnight daily. 338 Newbury St. ✆ 617/267-8688. www.tridentbookscafe.com. T: Green Line B, C, or D to Hynes/ICA.

POOL PLUS

Plenty of bars have pool tables, but at Boston's relatively upscale billiards palaces, drinking is what you do while you're playing pool, rather than the other way around.

Boston Billiard Club A large, clubby space decorated with brass sconces and a mahogany bar, this club has 55 tables, tasty bar food, and full liquor service. If you don't want to wait for a table, ask about reserving a private room (from $30/hr.). Like other establishments in this neighborhood, it's a madhouse on Red Sox game days and nights. Open daily from noon to 2am. On Wednesday, free lessons run from 7:30 to 9pm. 126 Brookline Ave. ✆ 617/536-POOL. www.bostonbilliardclub.com. Weekend evenings $13/hr. for 2 players, $2/hr. for each extra person. Daytime and weeknight discounts. T: Green Line B, C, or D to Kenmore or D to Fenway.

Flat Top Johnny's ★★ A spacious, loud room with a bar and 12 red-topped tables, Flat Top Johnny's has a funky neighborhood feel despite being in a rather sterile office-retail complex. Open weekdays noon to 1am, weekends 3pm to 1am. 1 Kendall Sq., Cambridge. ✆ 617/494-9565. www.flattopjohnnys.com. Mon–Sat $12/hr., Sun $6/hr. T: Red Line to Kendall/MIT.

Jillian's Boston ★ *Kids* The owners of Jillian's revived Boston's interest in pool and continue to make the most of advances in entertainment technology. The 70,000-square-foot complex, which anchors the Lansdowne Street strip, offers billiards in a 52-table pool parlor, a virtual-reality movie ride, Texas hold 'em (for fun, not profit), and tons of interactive games and sports. The 250-game video midway includes classic arcade games. There are dartboards, a table tennis area, foosball, a dance club, five full bars, and a restaurant. If you can't scare up some fun here, check your pulse. Open Monday through Saturday from 11am to 2am, Sunday from noon to 2am. Children under 18 accompanied by an adult are admitted before 8pm. 145 Ipswich St. ✆ 617/437-0300. www.jilliansboston.com. $12/hr. for 1–2 people, $14 for 3 or more. Valet parking available Wed–Sun after 6pm, except during Red Sox games. T: Green Line B, C, or D to Kenmore.

FILMS

Free Friday Flicks at the Hatch Shell ★★★ (© 617/727-5215) are family films shown on a large screen in the amphitheater on the Esplanade. On the lawn in front of the Hatch Shell, hundreds of people picnic until the sky grows dark and the credits roll. In the last few years, the films have tended toward recent releases (no big thrill for anyone with a Netflix subscription), but a few classics usually crop up, and the movie is only part of the experience.

Tip: Bring sweaters in case the breeze off the river grows chilly.

True revival houses—they feature lectures and live performances in addition to foreign and classic films—include the **Brattle Theater,** 40 Brattle St., Cambridge (© 617/876-6837; www.brattlefilm.org; T: Red Line to Harvard), and the **Coolidge Corner Movie Theater,** 290 Harvard St., Brookline (© 617/734-2500; www. coolidge.org; T: Green Line C to Coolidge Corner). The Coolidge also schedules midnight shows. Classic and foreign films are the tip of the iceberg at the quirky **Harvard Film Archive,** 24 Quincy St., Cambridge (© 617/495-4700; www.harvardfilmarchive. org; T: Red Line to Harvard), which also shows student films.

For first-run independent and foreign films, head to the **Kendall Square Cinema,** 1 Kendall Sq., Cambridge (© 617/499-1996; www.landmarktheatres.com; T: Red Line to Kendall/MIT). The best movie theater in the immediate Boston area, it offers discounted parking in the adjoining garage. Second-run current releases at discount prices are the usual fare at the **Somerville Theater,** 55 Davis Sq. (© 617/625-5700; www.somervilletheatreonline.com; T: Red Line to Davis), which sometimes schedules concerts, too. A great place to see mainstream releases is the 19-screen **Loews Boston Common,** 175 Tremont St. (© 617/423-3499; T: Green Line to Boylston), which has stadium seating and digital sound.

LECTURES & READINGS

The Thursday *Globe* "Calendar" section is the best place to check for listings of lectures, readings, and talks on a wide variety of subjects, often at local colleges and libraries. Many are free or charge a small fee. Most of the bookstores listed in chapter 10 sponsor author readings; check their websites or in-store displays, or call ahead.

5 Late-Night Bites

To be frank, Boston's late-night scene needs to climb a couple of notches to reach pathetic, and Cambridge's wee-hour diversions are even skimpier. The only plus is that just about every cab driver out cruising knows how to reach the places that are still open. If you're out and about in the late evening, especially on weekends, you have it a bit easier: Hit a restaurant (see chapter 7) that keeps relatively late hours. They include **Brasserie Jo,** the lounge at **Troquet, Davio's, Jacob Wirth,** and **Pizzeria Regina.**

Two promising late-night destinations are near the Theater District and Chinatown. The **South Street Diner,** 178 Kneeland St. (© 617/350-0028; www.south streetdiner.com), is a traditional hash joint with a wine and beer license; it's open 24 hours. The upscale **News Restaurant & Lounge,** 150 Kneeland St. (© 617/426-6397; www.newsboston.com), is open until 4am during the week and round the clock on weekends. Besides the entertaining patrons, diversions include abundant periodicals, flat-screen TVs, and Internet access. A number of **Chinatown** restaurants (see chapter 7) don't close until 3 or 4am. Asking for "cold tea" might—*might*—get you a teapot full of beer. The hottest scene is at **Ginza Japanese Restaurant,** 14 Hudson St. (© 617/338-2261). In the North End, **Caffe Pompei,** 280 Hanover St. (© 617/ 523-9438), draws European club-hoppers and neighborhood shift workers until 3:30am. And if you have a car, make like a college student and road-trip to the **International House of Pancakes** at 1850 Soldiers Field Rd. in Brighton (© 617/787-0533). It's open 24 hours daily.

12

Side Trips from Boston

In addition to being, in Oliver Wendell Holmes's words, "the hub of the solar system," Boston is the hub of a network of delightful excursions. The destinations in this chapter—**Lexington** and **Concord,** the **North Shore** and **Cape Ann,** and **Plymouth**—make fascinating, manageable day trips and offer enough diversions to fill several days.

Like Boston, the suburbs are home to many attractions that rely heavily on aid from outside sources. Admission fees in this chapter are current at press time, but the domino effect of corporate mergers and government budget cuts may have nudged prices higher by the time you visit. If you're on a tight budget, call ahead.

1 Lexington & Concord

The shooting stage of the Revolutionary War began here, and parts of the towns still look much as they did in April 1775, when the fight for independence began. Start your visit in **Lexington,** where colonists and British troops first clashed. Spend some time at **Minute Man National Historical Park,** on the border with **Concord,** investigating the battle that raged there. Decide for yourself where the "shot heard round the world" rang out—bearing in mind that **Ralph Waldo Emerson,** who wrote those words, lived in Concord. Emerson's house and **Louisa May Alcott's** nearby family home are just two of the fascinating destinations in this area.

Some attractions close from November to March or mid-April, opening after **Patriots Day,** the third Monday in April. Information about both towns is available from the **Greater Merrimack Valley Convention & Visitors Bureau,** 9 Central St., Suite 201, Lowell, MA 01852 (© **978/459-6150;** www.merrimackvalley.org).

LEXINGTON ⟨★
6 miles NW of Cambridge, 9 miles NW of Boston

A country village turned prosperous suburb, Lexington takes great pride in its history. It's a pleasant town with some engaging destinations, but it lacks the atmosphere and abundant attractions of nearby Concord. Being sure to leave time for a tour of the Buckman Tavern, you can schedule as little as a couple of hours to explore downtown Lexington, possibly en route to Concord; a visit can also fill a half or full day. The town contains part of **Minute Man National Historical Park** (see "Exploring the Area" in the "Concord" section, below), which is definitely worth a visit.

British troops marched from Boston to Lexington late on April 18, 1775 (no need to memorize the date; you'll hear it everywhere). Tipped off, patriots Paul Revere and William Dawes rode ahead to sound the warning. Members of the local militia, known as "Minutemen" for their ability to assemble quickly, were waiting at the **Buckman Tavern.** John Hancock and Samuel Adams, leaders of the revolutionary movement,

---

Tips **Poetry in Motion**

Before you visit Lexington and Concord, you might want to read **"Paul Revere's Ride,"** Henry Wadsworth Longfellow's classic but historically questionable poem that dramatically chronicles the events of April 18 and 19, 1775.

---

were sleeping (or trying to) at the nearby **Hancock-Clarke House.** The warning came around midnight, followed about 5 hours later by some 700 British troops, en route to Concord, where they planned to destroy the rebels' military supplies. Ordered to disperse, the colonists—fewer than 100, and some accounts say 77—stood their ground. Nobody knows who started the shooting, but when it was over, eight militia members lay dead, including a drummer boy, and 10 were wounded.

ESSENTIALS

GETTING THERE   From downtown Boston, take Storrow Drive or Memorial Drive to Route 2. Take Route 2 from Cambridge through Belmont, exit at Route 4/225, and follow signs to the center of Lexington. Or take Route 128 (I-95) to Exit 31A and follow the signs. Massachusetts Avenue—the same "Mass. Ave." you saw in Boston and Cambridge—runs through Lexington. There's metered parking on the street and in several municipal lots, and free parking at the National Heritage Museum and the National Historical Park.

The **MBTA** (© **617/222-3200;** www.mbta.com) runs bus routes nos. 62 (Bedford) and 76 (Hanscom) to Lexington from Alewife station, the last stop on the Red Line. The one-way fare is 90¢, and the trip takes about 25 minutes. Buses leave every hour during the day and every half-hour during rush periods, Monday through Saturday, with no service on Sunday. They pass the Munroe Tavern and the National Heritage Museum, if you prefer not to walk from the center of town. There's no public transit between Lexington and Concord, but the seasonal Liberty Ride tour connects the towns.

VISITOR INFORMATION   The **Chamber of Commerce Visitor Center,** 1875 Mass. Ave., Lexington, MA 02420 (© **781/862-2480;** www.lexingtonchamber.org), distributes sketch maps and information. It's open daily from 9am to 5pm (10am–4pm Dec–Mar).

SEEING THE SIGHTS

Minute Man National Historical Park is in Lexington, Concord, and Lincoln (see "Concord," below).

Start your visit to Lexington at the **visitor center,** on the town common, better known as the Battle Green. It's open daily from 9am to 5pm (10am–4pm Dec–Mar). A **diorama** and accompanying narrative illustrate the Battle of Lexington. The *Minuteman* statue on the Green is of Capt. John Parker, who commanded the militia. When the British confronted his troops, Parker called: "Stand your ground. Don't fire unless fired upon, but if they mean to have a war, let it begin here!" Allow about 30 minutes to look around the visitor center and the Green.

Three important destinations in Lexington were among the country's first **historic houses** when restoration of them began in the 1920s. The **Lexington Historical Society** (© **781/862-1703;** www.lexingtonhistory.org) operates all three. Currently headquartered in the Munroe Tavern, the society is in the process of restoring a building on

Lexington

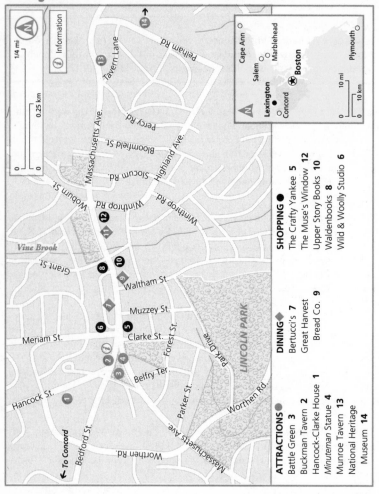

ATTRACTIONS ●
Battle Green **3**
Buckman Tavern **2**
Hancock-Clarke House **1**
Minuteman Statue **4**
Munroe Tavern **13**
National Heritage
Museum **14**

DINING ◆
Bertucci's **7**
Great Harvest
Bread Co. **9**

SHOPPING ●
The Crafty Yankee **5**
The Muse's Window **12**
Upper Story Books **10**
Waldenbooks **8**
Wild & Woolly Studio **6**

Depot Square (downtown, off Mass. Ave. near the Battle Green) that will hold exhibits, offices, and a gift shop.

The **Buckman Tavern** 🏠🏠, 1 Bedford St., built around 1710, is the only building still on the Green that was there on April 19, 1775. If time is short and you have to pick just one house to visit, make it this one. The interior of the tavern has been restored to approximate its appearance on the day of the battle. The Minutemen gathered here to await word of British troop movements, and they brought their wounded here after the conflict. The tour of the tavern, by costumed guides, is educational and entertaining.

Within easy walking distance, the **Hancock-Clarke House,** 36 Hancock St., is where Samuel Adams and John Hancock were staying when Paul Revere arrived. They fled to nearby Woburn. The 1698 house, furnished in colonial style, contains Lexington Historical Society's museum.

Tips **Touring Lexington and Concord**

The **Liberty Ride** (© 781/862-0500, ext. 702; www.libertyride.us) is a narrated bus tour that connects the attractions in both towns and the Concord commuter rail station. It operates from 10am to 3pm daily July through Columbus Day; check ahead for schedules and to confirm that it's running before you plan on it. The fare (good for a full day) is $20 for adults, $10 for children 5 to 17, free for children under 5. There's free parking at the museum and the park visitor center, and your ticket entitles you to discounts at local businesses.

The British took over the **Munroe Tavern** ★, 1332 Mass. Ave. (about 1 mile from the Green), to use as their headquarters and, after the battle, as their field hospital. The building (1690) holds many fascinating artifacts. The furniture, carefully preserved by the Munroe family, includes the table and chair President George Washington used when he dined here in 1789. The historically accurate gardens in the rear (free admission) are beautifully planted and maintained.

A guided tour (30–45 min.) is the only way to see each of the houses. The Buckman Tavern is open daily from Patriots Day weekend through October; tours start every half-hour from 10am to 4pm. The Hancock-Clarke House and the Munroe Tavern are open weekends from Patriots Day weekend through April and daily from May through October. Tours of the Hancock-Clarke House start on the hour from 11am to 2pm; tours of the Munroe Tavern start at 3pm. Admission for adults is $5 for one house, $8 for two, and $10 for all three; for children 6 to 16, $3 for one house, $5 for two, and $7 for three. Call for information about group tours, which are offered by appointment.

The fascinating exhibits at the **National Heritage Museum** ★★, 33 Marrett Rd., Route 2A, at Mass. Ave. (© 781/861-6559; www.monh.org), explore American history and culture. The museum makes an entertaining complement to the colonial focus of the rest of the town. The installations in the six exhibition spaces change regularly; you can start with another dose of the Revolution, the permanent exhibit **Lexington Alarm'd.** Other topics of exhibits have ranged from Paul Revere to U.S. Route 1 to early photos of Elvis, Dylan, and the Beatles. The museum schedules lectures, concerts, and family programs, and the cafe in the atrium serves lunch Tuesday through Saturday. Admission is free. The museum (formerly the Museum of Our National Heritage) is open Monday through Saturday from 10am to 5pm, Sunday from noon to 5pm; it's closed January 1, Thanksgiving, and December 24 and 25. The Scottish Rite of Freemasonry sponsors the museum.

SHOPPING

A stroll along **Mass. Ave.** near the center of town won't disappoint. Start at the **Muse's Window,** 1656 Mass. Ave. (© 781/274-6873), an excellent crafts gallery. As you head back toward the Green, check out **Waldenbooks,** 1713 Mass. Ave. (© 781/862-7870); **Upper Story Books,** 1730 Mass. Ave. (© 781/862-0999); and the **Crafty Yankee,** 1838 Mass. Ave. (© 781/861-1219). One of the best-known yarn shops in eastern Massachusetts is **Wild & Woolly Studio,** 7A Meriam St., off Mass. Ave. (© 781/861-7717).

WHERE TO DINE

If you're not continuing to Concord, which has more interesting dining options, Lexington offers some pleasant choices. The fresh soups and sandwiches at the cafe at the **National Heritage Museum** (see above) are popular for lunch; it's open Tuesday through Saturday from 11:30am to 2:30pm. **Bertucci's,** 1777 Mass. Ave. (© **781/ 860-9000**), is a branch of the family-friendly pizzeria chain. For a muffin or scone and a hot drink, seek out Lexington's branch of **Great Harvest Bread Co.,** 1736 Mass. Ave. (© **781/861-9990**).

CONCORD ✸✸✸

18 miles NW of Boston, 15 miles NW of Cambridge, 6 miles W of Lexington

Concord (say "conquered") revels in its legacy as a center of groundbreaking thought and its role in the country's political and intellectual history. The first official battle of the Revolutionary War took place in 1775 at the North Bridge (now part of Minute Man National Historical Park); less than a century later, Concord was an important literary and intellectual center. A visit can easily fill a day; if your interests are specialized or time is short, a half-day excursion is reasonable. For an excellent overview of town history, start at the **Concord Museum.**

After just a little time in this lovely town, you might find yourself adopting the local attitude toward two famous residents: **Ralph Waldo Emerson,** who comes across as a respected uncle figure, and **Henry David Thoreau,** everyone's favorite eccentric cousin. The contemplative writers wandered the countryside and did much of their work in Concord, forming the nucleus of a group of important writers who settled in the town. By the mid–19th century, Concord was the center of the Transcendentalist movement. Sightseers can tour the former **homes of Emerson, Thoreau, Nathaniel Hawthorne,** and **Louisa May Alcott** and visit their graves at **Sleepy Hollow Cemetery.**

ESSENTIALS

GETTING THERE From Lexington, take Route 2A west from Mass. Ave. (Route 4/225) at the National Heritage Museum; follow the BATTLE ROAD signs. From Boston and Cambridge, take Route 2 into Lincoln and stay in the right lane. Where the main road makes a sharp left, go straight onto Cambridge Turnpike. Signs that point to HISTORIC CONCORD lead downtown. To go straight to Walden Pond, use the left lane, take what's now Route 2/2A another mile or so, and turn left onto Route 126. There's parking throughout town and at the attractions.

The **commuter rail** (© **617/222-3200;** www.mbta.com) takes about 45 minutes from North Station in Boston, with a stop at Porter Square in Cambridge. The round-trip fare is $10. There is no bus service from Boston to Concord, and no transportation (other than the seasonal Liberty Ride tour) between Lexington and Concord. The station is about three-quarters of a mile over flat terrain from the town center.

VISITOR INFORMATION The **Chamber of Commerce,** 15 Walden St., Suite 7, Concord, MA 01742 (© **978/369-3120;** www.concordchamberofcommerce.org), maintains a visitor center at 58 Main St., next to Middlesex Savings Bank, 1 block south of Monument Square. It's open daily 9:30am to 4:30pm from April through October; public restrooms in the same building are open year-round. Guided walking tours are available. Group tours are available by appointment. The chamber office at 100 Main St. is open year-round Monday through Friday; hours vary, so call ahead. Websites with visitor information include **www.concordnet.org** and **www.concordma.com.**

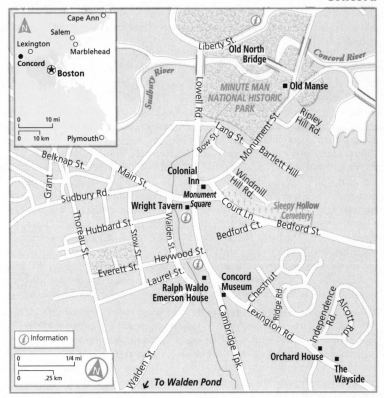

EXPLORING THE AREA

Minute Man National Historical Park ★★ *Kids* This 970-acre park preserves the scene of the first Revolutionary War battle at Concord on (all together now) April 19, 1775. After the skirmish at Lexington, the British continued to Concord in search of stockpiled arms (which militia members had already moved). Warned of the advance, the colonists prepared to confront the troops. The Minutemen crossed the North Bridge, evading the regulars standing guard, and waited on a hilltop for reinforcements. The British searched nearby homes and burned any guns they found. The colonials saw the smoke and, mistakenly thinking that the troops were torching the town, attacked the soldiers at the bridge. The gunfire that ensued is remembered as "the shot heard round the world," the opening salvo of the Revolution.

The park is open daily, year-round. A visit can take as little as half an hour for a jaunt to the North Bridge (a reproduction) or as long as half a day or more, if you stop at both visitor centers and perhaps participate in a ranger-led program. Travelers in 2005–06 may not be able to cross the bridge because a replacement will be under construction. To reach the bridge, follow Monument Street out of Concord Center until you see the parking lot on the right. Park and walk a short distance to the bridge, stopping along the unpaved path to read the narratives and hear the audio presentations.

On one side of the bridge is a plaque commemorating the British soldiers who died in the Revolutionary War; on the other is Daniel Chester French's famed *Minute Man* **statue.**

You can also start at the **North Bridge Visitor Center** ★, 174 Liberty St., off Monument Street (© **978/369-6993;** www.nps.gov/mima), which overlooks the Concord River and the bridge. A diorama and video program illustrate the battle, and exhibits include uniforms, weapons, and tools of colonial and British soldiers. Park rangers are on duty if you have questions. Outside, picnicking is allowed, and the scenery is lovely, especially in the fall. The center is open daily from 9am to 5pm (until 4pm in winter) and is closed January 1 and December 25.

At the Lexington end of the park is the **Minute Man Visitor Center** ★, off Route 2A, about ½ mile west of I-95 Exit 30B (© **781/674-1920;** www.nps.gov/mima). This area of the park includes the first 4 miles of the Battle Road, the route the defeated British troops took as they left Concord. At the visitor center, you'll see a fascinating multimedia program about the Revolution, informational displays, and a 40-foot mural illustrating the battle. On summer weekends, rangers lead tours of the park (call ahead for times). The **Battle Road Trail,** a 5½-mile interpretive path, carries pedestrian, wheelchair, and bicycle traffic. Panels and granite markers along the trail display information about the military, social, and natural history of the area. In season, this center is open daily, but schedules vary. Call ahead (use the phone number for the North Bridge Visitor Center, above, if there's no answer here) for open days and hours.

Walden Pond State Reservation ★★ The conservation movement started here, in a small wooden structure where a misunderstood social activist moved to "live deliberately." A pile of stones marks the site of the cabin where Henry David Thoreau lived from 1845 to 1847. Today the picturesque park is an extremely popular destination for walking (a path circles the pond), swimming, and fishing. Although crowded, it's well-preserved and insulated from development, making it less difficult than you might expect to imagine Thoreau's experience. Call for the schedule of ranger-led interpretive programs. No dogs or bikes are allowed. In good weather, the parking lot fills early every day—call before setting out because the rangers turn away visitors if the park has reached capacity (1,000).

915 Walden St. (Rte. 126). © **978/369-3254.** www.mass.gov/dcr. Free admission. Parking $5. Daily 8am–sunset. From downtown, take Walden St. (Rte. 126) south, cross Rte. 2, and follow signs to the parking lot.

Museums & Literary Sites

Concord Museum ★★ (Kids) Just when you're (understandably) suspecting that everything interesting in this area started on April 18, 1775, and ended the next day, this superb museum sets you straight. It's a great place to start your visit to the town.

The **History Galleries** ★★ explore the question "Why Concord?" Artifacts, murals, films, maps, documents, and other exhibits illustrate the town's changing

---

Moments **Row, Row, Row Your Boat**

Pretend you're Henry David Thoreau and take to the Concord River. The **South Bridge Boathouse,** 496 Main St. (© **978/369-9438**), just over half a mile west of the town center, will rent you a canoe for about $13 an hour on weekends, less on weekdays.

roles. It has been a Native American settlement, Revolutionary War battleground, 19th-century intellectual center, and focal point of the 20th-century historic preservation movement. Items on display include silver from colonial churches, a fascinating collection of embroidery samplers, 19th-century clocks (Concord was a center of clock making), and rooms furnished with period furniture and textiles. Explanatory text places the objects in context. One of the **lanterns** immortalized by Longfellow in "Paul Revere's Ride" ("one if by land, two if by sea") is on display. You'll also see the contents of **Ralph Waldo Emerson's study,** arranged the way it was at his death in 1882, and a large collection of **Henry David Thoreau's belongings.**

Pick up a **family activity pack** ★ as you enter; kids can use the games and reproduction artifacts (including a quill pen and powder horn) to get a hands-on feel for life in the past. The museum also offers changing exhibits in the New Wing, special events such as "tea and tour" (call for reservations), and an outstanding gift shop.

Cambridge Turnpike at Lexington Rd. ℭ **978/369-9609** (recorded info) or 978/369-9763. www.concordmuseum. org. Admission $8 adults, $7 seniors and students, $5 children under 16. June–Aug daily 9am–5pm; Apr–May and Sept–Dec Mon–Sat 9am–5pm, Sun noon–5pm; Jan–Mar Mon–Sat 11am–4pm, Sun 1–4pm. Closed Easter, Thanksgiving, and Dec 25. Parking allowed on road. Follow Lexington Rd. out of Concord Center and bear right at museum onto Cambridge Tpk.; entrance is on left.

The Old Manse ★ The engaging history of this home touches on the military and the literary, but it's mostly the story of a family. The Rev. William Emerson built the Old Manse in 1770 and watched the Battle of Concord from the yard. He died during the Revolutionary War, and for almost 170 years the house was home to his widow, her second husband (Rev. Ripley), their descendants, and two famous friends. Nathaniel Hawthorne and his bride, Sophia Peabody, moved in after their marriage in 1842 and stayed for 3 years. As a wedding present, Henry David Thoreau sowed a vegetable garden; today, a re-creation of that garden is part of a self-guided tour of the grounds. This is also where William's grandson Ralph Waldo Emerson wrote the essay "Nature." On the guided tour (the only way to visit the house), you'll see mementos and memorabilia of the Emerson and Ripley families and of the Hawthornes, who scratched notes on two windows with Sophia's diamond ring.

269 Monument St. (at North Bridge). ℭ 978/369-3909. www.thetrustees.org. Guided tour $7.50 adults, $6.50 seniors and students, $5 children 6–12, $22 families. Mid-Apr–Oct Mon–Sat 10am–5pm, Sun and holidays noon–5pm (last tour at 4:30pm). Closed Nov–mid-Apr. From Concord Center, follow Monument St. to North Bridge parking lot (on right); Old Manse is on left.

Orchard House ★★★ **Kids** *Little Women* (1868), Louisa May Alcott's best known and most popular work, was written and set at Orchard House. Seeing the Alcotts' home brings the author and her family to life for legions of female visitors and their pleasantly surprised male companions. Fans won't want to miss the excellent tour (the only way to explore the house), copiously illustrated with heirlooms. Serious buffs can check ahead for information on special events and holiday programs, some of which require reservations.

Louisa's father, Amos Bronson Alcott, was a writer, educator, and philosopher, and the leader of the Transcendentalist movement. He created Orchard House by joining and restoring two homes on 12 acres of land that he bought in 1857. The family lived here from 1858 to 1877, socializing in the same circles as Emerson, Thoreau, and Hawthorne.

Other family members served as the models for the characters in *Little Women.* Anna ("Meg"), the eldest, was an amateur actress, and May ("Amy") was a talented artist. Elizabeth ("Beth"), a gifted musician, died before the family moved to this house. Their mother, the social activist Abigail May Alcott, frequently assumed the role of family breadwinner—Bronson, Louisa wrote in her journal, had "no gift for money making."

Note: Call before visiting; an extensive preservation project was under way at press time and may still be going on when you're here.

399 Lexington Rd. ℂ **978/369-4118.** www.louisamayalcott.org. Guided tours $8 adults, $7 seniors and students, $5 children 6–17, $20 families. Apr–Oct Mon–Sat 10am–4:30pm, Sun 1–4:30pm; Nov–Mar Mon–Fri 11am–3pm, Sat 10am–4:30pm, Sun 1–4:30pm. Closed Jan 1–15, Easter, Thanksgiving, and Dec 25. Follow Lexington Rd. out of Concord Center and bear left at Concord Museum; house is on the left. Overflow parking lot is across the street.

Ralph Waldo Emerson House   This house offers an instructive look at the days when a philosopher could attain the status we now associate with rock stars. Emerson, also an essayist and poet, lived here from 1835 until his death, in 1882. He moved here after marrying his second wife, Lydia Jackson, whom he called Lydian; she called him Mr. Emerson, as the staff still does. The tour (the only way to enter the house) gives a good look at Emerson's personal side and at the fashionably ornate interior decoration of the time. You'll see original furnishings and some of Emerson's personal effects. (The contents of his study from the time of his death are in the Concord Museum; p. 260.)

28 Cambridge Tpk. ℂ **978/369-2236.** Guided tours $7 adults, $5 seniors and students. Call to arrange group tours (10 people or more). Mid-Apr to Oct Thurs–Sat 10am–4:30pm, Sun 1–4:30pm. Closed Nov to mid-Apr. Follow Cambridge Tpk. out of Concord Center; just before Concord Museum, house is on right.

Sleepy Hollow Cemetery ⍟   Follow the signs for AUTHOR'S RIDGE and climb the hill to the graves of some of the town's literary lights, including the Alcotts, Emerson, Hawthorne, and Thoreau. Emerson's bears no religious symbols; the marker is an uncarved quartz boulder. Thoreau is buried nearby; at his funeral in 1862, his old friend Emerson concluded his eulogy with these words: " . . . wherever there is knowledge, wherever there is virtue, wherever there is beauty, he will find a home." The cemetery was dedicated in 1855; observations of its 150th anniversary will take place in September 2005.

Entrance on Rte. 62 W. ℂ **978/318-3233.** www.concordnet.org. Daily 7am–dusk, weather permitting. Call ahead for wheelchair access. No buses allowed.

The Wayside ⍟   The Wayside was Nathaniel Hawthorne's home from 1852 until his death in 1864. The Alcotts also lived here (the girls called it "the yellow house"), as did Harriett Lothrop, who wrote the *Five Little Peppers* books under the pen name Margaret Sidney and owned most of the current furnishings. The Wayside is part of Minute Man National Historical Park, and the fascinating 45-minute ranger tour (the only way to see the house) illuminates the occupants' lives and the house's crazy-quilt architecture. The exhibit in the barn (free admission) consists of audio presentations and figures of Hawthorne, Louisa May and Bronson Alcott, and Sidney. Call ahead to double-check hours, which are subject to change.

455 Lexington Rd. ℂ **978/318-7863.** www.nps.gov/mima/wayside. Guided tours $4 adults, free for children under 17. May–Oct; open days and hours vary. Closed Nov–Apr. Follow Lexington Rd. out of Concord Center past Concord Museum and Orchard House. Park across the street.

NEARBY SIGHTS

DeCordova Museum and Sculpture Park ⍟⍟   Indoors and out, this amazing museum shows the work of American contemporary and modern artists, with an emphasis on living New England residents. The imaginative curatorial staff builds exhibits around themes as well as the work of individual artists—shows during the lifespan of this book will focus on (among other things) animals, horses, and the concept of narrative. The main building, on a leafy hilltop, overlooks a pond and the outdoor public sculpture park. The museum also has a sculpture terrace that displays the work of one sculptor per year. The prestigious **DeCordova Annual Exhibition,** from June through September, is a group show of recent work in various media by a select group of New England artists. Picnicking is allowed in the sculpture park; bring your lunch or buy it at the cafe (open Tues–Sun 11am–3pm). Free guided tours of the main galleries start at 1pm Thursday and 2pm Sunday, year-round; sculpture-park tours run May through October on weekends at 1pm. Be sure to check out the excellent gift shop.

51 Sandy Pond Rd., Lincoln. (© 781/259-8355. www.decordova.org. Admission $9 adults; $6 seniors, students, and children 6–12. Admission to sculpture park free when museum is closed. Museum: Tues–Sun and some Mon holidays 11am–5pm. Closed Jan 1, July 4, Thanksgiving, and Dec 25. Sculpture park: Daily daylight hours. From Rte. 2 E., take Rte. 126 south to Baker Bridge Rd. (1st left after Walden Pond). When it ends, go right onto Sandy Pond Rd.; museum is on the left. From I-95, take Exit 28B, follow Trapelo Rd. 2½ miles to Sandy Pond Rd., then follow signs.

Gropius House 🔭 Architect Walter Gropius (1883–1969), founder of the Bauhaus school of design, built this home for his family in 1938. Having taken a job at the Harvard Graduate School of Design, he worked with Marcel Breuer to design the hilltop house. He used traditional materials such as clapboard, brick, and fieldstone, with components then seldom seen in domestic architecture, including glass blocks and chrome (on the banisters). Breuer designed many of the furnishings, which were made for the family at the Bauhaus. Decorated as it was in the last decade of Gropius's life, the house affords a revealing look at his life, career, and philosophy. Call for information on special tours and workshops.

68 Baker Bridge Rd., Lincoln. (© 781/259-8098. www.historicnewengland.org. Guided tours $10 adults, $9 seniors, $5 students with ID and children. Tours on the hour June–Oct 15 Wed–Sun 11am–4pm; Oct 16–May Sat and Sun 11am–4pm. From Rte. 2 E., take Rte. 126 south to Baker Bridge Rd. (1st left after Walden Pond); house is on the right. From I-95, take Exit 28B, follow Trapelo Rd. to Sandy Pond Rd., go left onto Baker Bridge Rd.; house is on the left.

SHOPPING

Downtown Concord, off **Monument Square,** is a terrific shopping destination. Here you'll find the **Concord Toy Shop,** 4 Walden St. (© **978/369-2553**); the **Grasshopper Shop,** 36 Main St. (© **978/369-8295**), which carries women's clothing and accessories; jewelry and art at **Catseye,** 48 Monument Sq. (© **978/369-8377**); and the **Concord Bookshop,** 65 Main St. (© **978/371-2672**). The compact shopping district in **West Concord,** along Route 62, boasts the old-fashioned **West Concord 5 & 10,** 106 Commonwealth Ave. (© **978/369-9011**), which carries everything from light bulbs to lace.

WHERE TO STAY & DINE

Consider taking a **picnic** to the North Bridge, Walden Pond, or another spot that catches your eye. Stock up at **Nashoba Brook Bakery** (see below) or downtown at the **Cheese Shop,** 25–31 Walden St. (© **978/369-5778**).

Concord's Colonial Inn ★ The main building of the Colonial Inn has overlooked Monument Square since 1716. Like many historic inns, it's not luxurious, but it is comfortable, centrally located—and possibly home to a ghost. Additions since it became a hotel in 1889 have made the inn large enough to offer modern conveniences (including wireless Internet access) and small enough to feel friendly. It's popular with local businesspeople as well as vacationers, especially during foliage season. The 15 original guest rooms—one of which (no. 24) supposedly is haunted—are in great demand. Reserve early if you want to stay in the main inn, which is decorated (surprise, surprise) in colonial style. Rooms in the 1970 Prescott House have country-style decor, as do the one-, two-, and three-bedroom suites (available for long-term stays) in four freestanding buildings.

The inn has two lounges that serve light meals; ask for a table on the porch, and you'll have a front-row seat for the action on Monument Square. The lovely restaurant serves salads, sandwiches, and pasta at lunch and traditional American fare at dinner. Afternoon tea ($22) is served Friday through Sunday; reservations (© **978/369-2373**) are required.

48 Monument Sq., Concord, MA 01742. © **800/370-9200** or 978/369-9200. Fax 978/371-1533. www.concords colonialinn.com. 56 units (some with shower only). Apr–Oct $195–$225 main inn, $159–$189 Prescott House; Nov–Mar $165 main inn, $145 Prescott House. Long-term rates from $50/day. AE, DC, DISC, MC, V. **Amenities:** Restaurant (American); 2 lounges; bar with live jazz and blues on weekends; access to nearby health club ($10); concierge; tour desk; business center; same-day dry cleaning; executive-level rooms. Rooms for travelers with disabilities are available. *In room:* A/C, TV/DVD, wireless Internet access, coffeemaker, hair dryer, iron.

Nashoba Brook Bakery & Café ★★ AMERICAN The enticing variety of fresh artisan breads, scrumptious baked goods and pastries, and made-from-scratch soups, salads, and sandwiches makes this airy cafe a popular destination throughout the day. It offers a good break from the sightseeing circuit. The industrial-looking building off West Concord's main street backs up to little Nashoba Brook, which is visible through the glass back wall. Order and pick up at the counter, and then grab a seat along the window or near the children's play area. You can also order takeout—this is great picnic food—or a loaf of crusty bread. See p. 133 for information about the branch in Boston's **South End.**

152 Commonwealth Ave., West Concord. © **978/318-1999.** www.slowrise.com. Sandwiches $5–$6; salads $6–$8 per lb. MC, V. Mon–Fri 6am–6:30pm, Sat–Sun 8am–5pm. From Concord Center, follow Main St. (Rte. 62) west, across Rte. 2; bear right at traffic light in front of train station and go 3 blocks. To reach overflow parking, turn right onto Commonwealth Ave. and take first right into lot on Winthrop St.; walk across bridge over brook.

2 The North Shore & Cape Ann

The areas north of Boston abound with historic sights and gorgeous ocean vistas. Cape Ann is a rocky peninsula so enchantingly beautiful that when you hear the slogan "Massachusetts's *Other* Cape," you might forget what the first one was. Cape Ann and Cape Cod do share some attributes—scenery, shopping, seafood, and traffic. Its proximity to Boston and manageable scale make Cape Ann a wonderful day trip as well as a good choice for a longer stay.

The **Cape Ann Chamber of Commerce** information center (see "Gloucester," later in this chapter) is a good resource. The **North of Boston Convention & Visitors Bureau,** 17 Peabody Sq., Peabody, MA 01960 (© **800/742-5306** or 978/977-7760; www.northofboston.org), publishes a map and a visitor guide that covers 34 municipalities, including Salem, Marblehead, and Cape Ann. It also coordinates **ArtsNorth** (www. arts-north.org), which lists cultural venues throughout the area.

Tips **North of Boston: Road Rules**

The drive from Boston to Cape Ann on I-93 and Route 128 takes about an hour. A more leisurely excursion on Routes 1A, 129, 114, and 127 allows you to explore Marblehead and Salem. You can also follow Route 1 to I-95 and 128, but don't attempt it during rush hour. To go straight to Gloucester and Rockport—or to start there and work back—take I-93 north out of Boston. Where it turns into I-95 (signs point to New Hampshire and Maine), stay left and take Route 128 to the end. The last exit, no. 9, puts you in East Gloucester. To take Route 1A, leave downtown Boston through the Callahan or Ted Williams Tunnel. If you miss the tunnel and wind up on I-93, follow signs to Route 1 and pick up Route 1A in Revere.

If you can, drive a car to explore north of the city. Public transportation in this area is good, but it doesn't go everywhere, and in many towns the train station is some distance from the attractions. For the full day-trip experience, try to visit on a spring, summer, or fall weekday; traffic is brutal on warm weekends. Many areas are practically ghost towns from November through March, but all of the destinations in this chapter have enough of a year-round community to make an off-season excursion worthwhile.

MARBLEHEAD ✶✶✶
15 miles NE of Boston

Like an attractive person with a great personality, Marblehead has it all. Scenery, history, architecture, and shopping combine to make this one of the area's most popular day trips for both locals and visitors. It's even polite—many speed-limit signs say PLEASE. Allow at least a full morning, but be flexible because you might want to hang around.

One of the most picturesque neighborhoods in New England is **Old Town** ✶✶✶, where narrow, twisting streets lead down to the magnificent harbor that helps make this the self-proclaimed "Yachting Capital of America." As you walk around Old Town, you'll see plaques on the houses bearing the date of construction, as well as the names of the builder and original occupant—a history lesson without studying. Many of the houses have stood since before the Revolutionary War, when Marblehead was a center of merchant shipping. Two historic homes are open for tours (see "Exploring the Town," below).

ESSENTIALS
GETTING THERE   By car, take Route 1A north through Revere and Lynn; bear right at the signs for Nahant and Swampscott. Follow Lynn Shore Drive through Swampscott to Route 129, which runs into town. Or take I-93 or Route 1 to Route 128, then follow Route 114 through Salem into Marblehead. Parking is tough, especially in Old Town—grab the first spot you see.

MBTA (© **617/222-3200;** www.mbta.com) bus no. 441/442 runs from Haymarket (Orange or Green Line) to downtown Marblehead. During rush periods on weekdays, the no. 448/449 connects Marblehead to Downtown Crossing. The trip takes about an hour, and the one-way fare is $3.45.

Marblehead

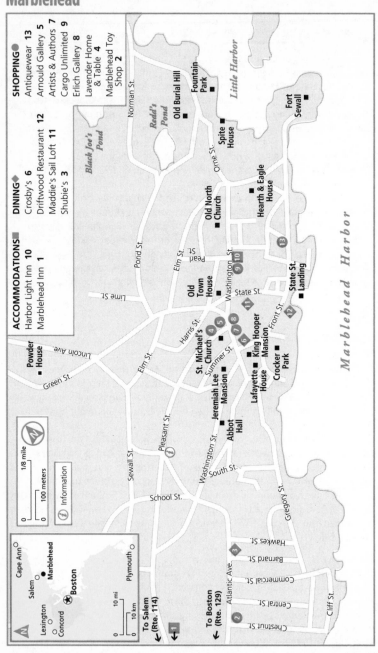

ACCOMMODATIONS■
Harbor Light Inn **10**
Marblehead Inn **1**

DINING◆
Crosby's **6**
Driftwood Restaurant **12**
Maddie's Sail Loft **11**
Shubie's **3**

SHOPPING●
Antiquewear **13**
Arnould Gallery **5**
Artists & Authors **7**
Cargo Unlimited **9**
Erlich Gallery **8**
Lavender Home & Table **4**
Marblehead Toy Shop **2**

Powder House

Green St.
Lincoln Ave.
Lime St.
Pond St.
Elm St.
Norman St.
Orne St.
Pearl St.
Elm St.
Harris St.
Washington St.
State St.
Front St.
Summer St.

Black Joe's Pond
Redd's Pond
Old Burial Hill
Fountain Park
Little Harbor
Spite House
Fort Sewall
Hearth & Eagle House
Old North Church
Old Town House
State St. Landing

St. Michael's Church
Jeremiah Lee Mansion
Abbot Hall
Lafayette House
King Hooper Mansion
Crocker Park

Pleasant St.
Sewall St.
Washington St.
South St.
School St.
Gregory St.
Hawkes St.
Barnard St.
Commercial St.
Central St.
Chestnut St.
Atlantic Ave.
Cliff St.

Marblehead Harbor

N
0   1/8 mile
0   100 meters
i Information

Cape Ann
Salem
Marblehead
Lexington
Concord
Boston
Plymouth
0   10 mi
0   10 km

To Salem (Rte. 114)
To Boston (Rte. 129)

266

VISITOR INFORMATION   The **Marblehead Chamber of Commerce,** 62 Pleasant St., Marblehead, MA 01945 (© **781/631-2868;** www.marbleheadchamber.org or www.visitmarblehead.com), is open weekdays from 9am to 5pm. The **information booth** (© **781/639-8469**), on Pleasant Street near Spring Street, is open mid-May through October, Monday to Friday noon to 5pm, Saturday and Sunday 10am to 6pm. The chamber publishes a visitor guide and map that includes a calendar of events; ask for a business directory or check the website if you want a description of a walking tour.

SPECIAL EVENTS   Sailing regattas take place in the outer harbor all summer, and **Race Week** in mid to late July attracts enthusiasts from all over the country. The **Christmas Walk,** on the first weekend in December, incorporates music, arts and crafts, shopping, and Santa Claus, who arrives by lobster boat.

EXPLORING THE TOWN

Marblehead is a wonderful place for aimless wandering; to add some structure, consult the walking tour described in the chamber of commerce's business directory. Whatever else you do, be sure to spend some time in **Crocker Park** ★★, on the harbor off Front Street. Especially in the warmer months, when boats jam the water nearly as far as the eye can see, the view is breathtaking. The park has benches and a swing, and it's a great place for a picnic. The view from **Fort Sewall,** at the other end of Front Street, is equally mesmerizing.

Just inland, the **Lafayette House** is at the corner of Hooper and Union streets. A corner of the private home was chopped off to make room for the passage of the Marquis de Lafayette's carriage when he visited the town in 1824. In Market Square on Washington Street, near the corner of State Street, is the **Old Town House,** in use for meetings and gatherings since 1727.

Abbot Hall   A 5-minute stop here (look for the clock tower) is just the ticket if you want to be able say you did some sightseeing. The town offices and historical commission share Abbot Hall with Archibald M. Willard's famous painting **The Spirit of '76** ★, on display in the Selectmen's Meeting Room. The thrill of recognizing the ubiquitous drummer, drummer boy, and fife player is the main reason to stop here. Cases in the halls contain objects and artifacts from the Marblehead Historical Society's collections.

Finds **For the Birds**

Marblehead Neck, an upscale neighborhood across the causeway from Devereux Beach, is home to a **Massachusetts Audubon Society bird sanctuary** (© **800/AUDUBON** or 781/259-9500; www.massaudubon.org). Turn east on Ocean Avenue south of downtown and follow it less than a mile until you see a small sign to the left at Risley Avenue. Park in the small lot and follow the path into the sanctuary, where you can see the varied species of birds that use the Atlantic flyway, especially in spring and fall. Admission is $3 for adults, $2 for seniors and children 3 to 12. To return to Marblehead proper, continue on Ocean Avenue, which becomes Harbor Avenue and forms a loop. En route, at the end of "the Neck," you can park near the decommissioned lighthouse and take in a breathtaking view.

Washington Sq. ⓒ 781/631-0528. Free admission. Nov–Apr Mon–Tues and Thurs 8am–5pm, Wed 7:30am–7:30pm, Fri 8am–1pm; May–Oct Mon–Tues and Thurs 8am–5pm, Wed 7:30am–7:30pm, Fri 8am–5pm, Sat 9am–6pm, Sun 11am–6pm. From the historic district, follow Washington St. up the hill.

Jeremiah Lee Mansion ★★ The excitement of seeing original hand-painted wallpaper in an 18th-century home is reason enough to visit this house, built in 1768 for a wealthy merchant and considered an extraordinary example of pre-Revolutionary Georgian architecture. Rococo woodcarving and other details complement historically accurate room arrangements, and ongoing restoration and interpretation by the Marblehead Museum & Historical Society place the 18th- and 19th-century furnishings and artifacts in context. The friendly guides welcome questions and are well versed in the history of the home and the town. The lawn and gardens are open to the public.

> **Fun Fact Architectural Details**
>
> On the hill between the Jeremiah Lee Mansion and Abbot Hall, notice the private homes at 185, 181, and 175 Washington St. These are other good examples of the architecture of the pre-Revolutionary period.

Across the street is a visitor center (free admission) that houses two galleries. One displays folk art by the noted Primitivist painter J.O.J. Frost, a Marblehead native; the other mounts changing exhibits, which will include a display of Early American decorative arts from October 2005 through spring 2006. Call ahead for the schedule of **summer walking tours** of Marblehead.

161 Washington St. ⓒ 781/631-1768. www.marbleheadmuseum.org. Guided tours $5 adults, $4.50 seniors and students. June to Oct Tues–Sat 10am–4pm. Closed Nov–May. Visitor center: 170 Washington St. Free admission. June–Oct Tues–Sat 10am–4pm; Nov–May Tues–Fri 10am–4pm. Follow Washington St. until it curves right and heads uphill toward Abbot Hall; mansion is on right.

King Hooper Mansion Shipping tycoon Robert Hooper got his nickname because he treated his sailors so well, but it's easy to think he was called King because he lived like royalty—his house has both a wine cellar and a ballroom. Around the corner from the home of Jeremiah Lee (whose sister was the second of Hooper's four wives), the 1728 King Hooper Mansion gained a Georgian addition in 1745. The period furnishings, though not original, give a sense of the life of an 18th-century merchant prince. The building houses the headquarters of the **Marblehead Arts Association,** which stages monthly exhibits, schedules classes and special events, and sells members' work in the gift shop. The mansion has a lovely garden; enter through the gate at the right of the house.

8 Hooper St. ⓒ 781/631-2608. www.marbleheadarts.org. Donation requested for tour. Tues–Sat 10am–4pm, Sun 1–5pm. Call ahead; no tours during private parties. Where Washington St. curves at the foot of hill near Lee mansion, look for the colorful sign.

SHOPPING
Marblehead is a legendary (or notorious, if you're on a budget) shopping destination. Shops, boutiques, and galleries abound in **Old Town** and on **Atlantic Avenue** and the east end of **Pleasant Street.** The most unusual shop in town is **Antiquewear,** 82 Front St. (ⓒ 781/639-0070), near the town pier, which sells 19th-century buttons ingeniously fashioned into women's and men's jewelry of all descriptions. Other good stops include **Arnould Gallery,** 111 Washington St. (ⓒ 781/631-6366); **Artists & Authors,** 108 Washington St. (ⓒ 781/639-0400; www.artists-authors.com), which carries rare

books and fine art; **Cargo Unlimited,** 82 Washington St. (© **781/631-1112;** www. cargounlimited.com), for home furnishings and accessories; **Erlich Gallery,** 96 Washington St. (© **781/631-1202**); **Lavender Home & Table,** 7 Pleasant St. (© **781/639-2238**), which specializes in French country wares; and the **Marblehead Toy Shop,** 44–48 Atlantic Ave. (© **781/631-9900**).

WHERE TO STAY
This is B&B heaven. Space considerations preclude listing the numerous small inns and bed-and-breakfasts, but the accommodations listings of the **Marblehead Chamber of Commerce,** 62 Pleasant St., Marblehead, MA 01945 (© **781/631-2868;** www. marbleheadchamber.org), include many of them. Check the website, call or write for a visitor guide, or consult one of the B&B agencies listed on p. 78.

Harbor Light Inn ★★   A stone's throw from the Old Town House, two Federal-era mansions make up this gracious inn. From the wood floors to the 1729 beams (in a third-floor room) to the swimming pool, it's both historic and relaxing. Rooms are comfortably furnished in period style, with some lovely antiques; most have canopy or four-poster beds. Eleven hold working fireplaces, and five of those have double Jacuzzis. VCRs and free video rentals are available. The best rooms, on the top floor at the back of the building, away from the street, have gorgeous harbor views. The undeniably romantic inn also attracts weekday business travelers with its wireless Internet access (included in the room rate) and meeting space.

58 Washington St., Marblehead, MA 01945. © **781/631-2186.** Fax 781/631-2216. www.harborlightinn.com. 21 units (some with shower only). $125–$245 double; $195–$295 suite. Rates include breakfast, afternoon refreshments, and use of bikes. Corporate rate available midweek. 2-night minimum stay weekends, 3-night minimum holiday and high-season weekends. AE, MC, V. Free parking. **Amenities:** Heated outdoor pool; access to nearby health club ($5); Jacuzzi; concierge; airport shuttle; in-room massage. *In room:* A/C, TV/VCR, wireless Internet access, hair dryer, iron, robes.

Marblehead Inn ★ *Kids*   This three-story Victorian mansion just outside the historic district is an all-suite inn. It's not as convenient and romantic as the Harbor Light Inn, but it offers better amenities and a more family-friendly atmosphere. Each attractively decorated unit contains a living room, bedroom, and workstation. This is a good choice for businesspeople making an extended stay, as well as families, who can make good use of the kitchenette (the inn supplies breakfast provisions). Most suites have Jacuzzis, and some have working fireplaces and small patios. The 1872 building has been an inn since 1923, and it once played host to Amelia Earhart.

264 Pleasant St. (Rte. 114), Marblehead, MA 01945. © **800/399-5843** or 781/639-9999. Fax 781/639-9996. www. marbleheadinn.com. 10 units (2 with shower only). $109–$219 double. Extra person $25. Children under 11 stay free in parent's room. Rates include continental breakfast. Winter discounts, corporate and long-term rates available. 2-night minimum stay busy weekends, 3-night minimum holiday weekends. AE, MC, V. Free parking. *In room:* A/C, TV/VCR, dataport, kitchenette, fridge, coffeemaker, hair dryer, umbrella.

WHERE TO DINE
You can stock up for a picnic at a number of places in Old Town. **Crosby's,** 118 Washington St. (© **781/631-1741**), is a full-service market with a large prepared-food section. **Shubie's,** 32 Atlantic Ave. (© **781/631-0149**), carries a good selection of specialty foods.

Driftwood Restaurant ★ DINER/SEAFOOD   At the foot of State Street, next to Clark Landing (the town pier), is an honest-to-goodness local hangout. Join the crowd at a table or the counter for generous portions of breakfast (served all day) or lunch.

Try pancakes or hash, chowder or a seafood roll—a hot dog bun filled with, say, fried clams or lobster salad. The house specialty, served on weekends and holidays, is fried dough, which is exactly as delicious and indigestible as it sounds.

63 Front St. ✆ **781/631-1145.** Main courses $3–$12; breakfast items less than $7. No credit cards. Daily 5:30am–2pm.

Maddie's Sail Loft SEAFOOD   Less than a block from the harbor, Maddie's is a friendly tavern that serves good steaks as well as excellent fresh seafood. The strong drinks are another attraction, especially during the summer boating season; this (or, alas, one of the private yacht clubs) is the place to search for that cute sailor you saw down by the water. There's live jazz on Thursday nights and a lively local scene year-round.

15 State St. ✆ **781/631-9824.** Main courses $9–$16. No credit cards. Mon–Sat 11:45am–2pm and 5–10pm; Sun 11:45am–4pm. Bar open until 11:30pm.

SALEM ★★
17 miles NE of Boston, 4 miles NW of Marblehead

Settled in 1626, 4 years before Boston, Salem later enjoyed international renown as a center of merchant shipping, but today it's famous around the world because of a 7-month episode in 1692. The witchcraft trial hysteria led to 20 deaths, 3-plus centuries of notoriety, countless lessons on the evils of prejudice, and innumerable bad puns ("Stop by for a spell" is a favorite slogan).

Unable to live down the association, and never forgetting the victims, Salem embraces its reputation. The high school sports teams are the Witches, and the *Salem Evening News* logo is a silhouette of a sorceress. The city abounds with witch-associated attractions, plus nearly as many reminders of Salem's seagoing legacy. Most are historically accurate, but you'll also see a fair number of goofy souvenirs and opportunistic tourist traps. An excellent antidote to the latter is the **Peabody Essex Museum.** Salem is a family-friendly destination that's worth at least a half-day visit (perhaps after a stop in Marblehead) and can easily fill a day.

ESSENTIALS
GETTING THERE   By car from Marblehead, follow Route 114 west. From Boston, take Route 1A north to Salem, being careful in Lynn, where the road turns left and immediately right. You can also take I-93 or Route 1 to Route 128 and then Route 114 into downtown Salem. There's metered street parking and a reasonably priced municipal garage across the street from the National Park Service Regional Visitor Center.

From Boston, the **MBTA** (✆ **617/222-3200;** www.mbta.com) operates commuter trains from North Station and bus no. 450 from Haymarket (Orange or Green Line). The train is more comfortable than the bus but runs less frequently. It takes 30 to 35 minutes; the round-trip fare is $7.50. The station is about 5 blocks from the downtown area. The one-way fare for the 35- to 55-minute bus trip is $3.45.

VISITOR INFORMATION   A good place to start your visit is the **National Park Service Regional Visitor Center,** 2 New Liberty St. (✆ **978/740-1650;** www.nps.gov/sama), open daily from 9am to 5pm. Exhibits highlight early settlement, maritime history, and the leather and textiles industries. The center also distributes brochures and pamphlets, including one that describes a **walking tour** of the historic district, and has an auditorium where a free film on Essex County provides an overview.

The city's Office of Tourism, **Destination Salem,** 54 Turner St., Salem, MA 01970 (✆ **877/SALEM-MA** or 978/744-3663; www.salem.org), produces and distributes a

Salem

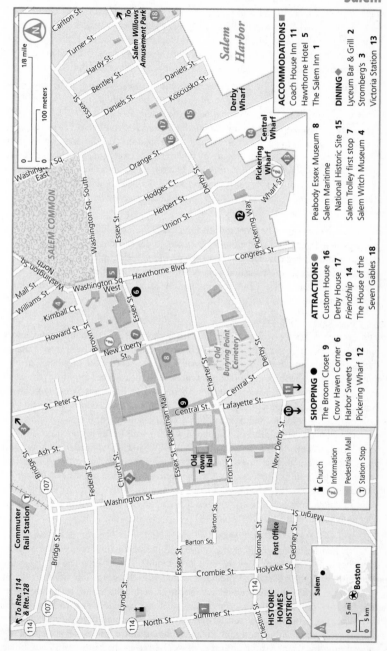

ACCOMMODATIONS ■
Coach House Inn **11**
Hawthorne Hotel **5**
The Salem Inn **1**

DINING ◆
Lyceum Bar & Grill **2**
Stromberg's **3**
Victoria Station **13**

ATTRACTIONS ●
Custom House **16**
Derby House **17**
Friendship **14**
The House of the
  Seven Gables **18**

Peabody Essex Museum **8**
Salem Maritime
  National Historic Site **15**
Salem Trolley first stop **7**
Salem Witch Museum **4**

SHOPPING ●
The Broom Closet **9**
Crow Haven Corner **6**
Harbor Sweets **10**
Pickering Wharf **12**

✚ Church
ℹ Information
▦ Pedestrian Mall
Ⓣ Station Stop

Salem Harbor

Derby Wharf

Central Wharf

Pickering Wharf

SALEM COMMON

Old Town Hall

Old Burying Point Cemetery

Commuter Rail Station

Post Office

HISTORIC HOMES DISTRICT

Salem
★ Boston

0   5 mi
0   5 km

1/8 mile
100 meters

free visitor guide that includes an excellent map. The **Salem Chamber of Commerce,** 63A Wharf St., Salem, MA 01970 (© **978/744-0004;** www.salem-chamber.org), maintains a large rack of brochures and pamphlets at its office on Pickering Wharf, and the staff is up on the latest events. It's open weekdays from 9am to 5pm. Salem has an excellent community website (www.salemweb.com) that includes a city guide.

GETTING AROUND   In the congested downtown area, **walking** is the way to go, but you might not want to hoof it to all the sights, especially if it's hot. At the Essex Street side of the visitor center, you can board the **Salem Trolley** ⋆ (© **978/744-5469;** www.salemtrolley.com) for a 1-hour narrated tour, and you can reboard as often as you like at any of the 12 stops. It's a good deal if you're spending the day and don't want to keep moving the car or carrying leg-weary children. The trolley operates from 10am to 5pm (last tour at 4pm) daily April through October; check ahead for hours in November. Tickets ($10 adults, $9 seniors, $5 children 5–14) are good all day; they're available onboard, at the Trolley Depot shop on the Essex Street pedestrian mall at Central Street, and at the Park Service visitor center.

SPECIAL EVENTS   The city's month-long Halloween celebration, **Haunted Happenings** ⋆⋆ (www.hauntedhappenings.org), includes parades, parties, tours, and a ceremony on the big day. During **Heritage Days,** a weeklong event in mid-August, the city celebrates its multicultural history with musical and theatrical performances, a parade, and fireworks. Contact Destination Salem (see "Visitor Information," above) for details.

EXPLORING THE TOWN

The historic district extends well inland from the waterfront. Many 18th-century houses, some with original furnishings, still stand. Ship captains lived near the water at the east end of downtown, in relatively small houses crowded close together. The captains' employers, the shipping company owners, built their homes away from the water (and the accompanying aromas). Many of them lived on **Chestnut Street** ⋆⋆, now a National Historic Landmark. Residents along the grand thoroughfare must, by legal agreement, adhere to colonial style in their decorating and furnishings. Ask at the visitor center for the pamphlet that describes a walking tour of the historic district.

By car or trolley, the **Salem Willows** (© **978/745-0251;** www.salemwillows.com) amusements are 5 minutes away; many signs point the way. The strip of rides and snack bars has a honky-tonk air, and the waterfront park is a good place to bring a picnic and wander along the shore. There's no admission fee; meter parking is available. To enjoy the great view without the arcades and rides, have lunch one peninsula over at **Winter Island Park.**

The House of the Seven Gables ⋆ *Kids*   Nathaniel Hawthorne's cousin lived here, and stories and legends of the house and its inhabitants inspired the author's 1851 book. If you haven't read the eerie novel, don't let that keep you away—begin your visit with the audiovisual program, which tells the story. The house, built by Capt. John Turner in 1668, holds six rooms of period furniture, including pieces referred to in the book, and a secret staircase. Tours include a visit to Hawthorne's birthplace (built before 1750 and moved to the grounds) and describe what life was like for the house's 18th-century inhabitants. The costumed guides can get a little silly as they mug for young visitors, but they're well versed in the history of the buildings and artifacts, and eager to answer questions. Also on the grounds, overlooking Salem

Harbor, are period gardens, the **Retire Beckett House** (1655), the **Hooper-Hathaway House** (1682), and a **counting house** (1830).

54 Turner St. (✆ **978/744-0991.** www.7gables.org. Guided tour of house and grounds $11 adults, $10 seniors, $7.25 children 5–12, free for children under 5. Surcharges may apply for special exhibitions. July–Oct daily 10am–7pm; Nov–June daily 10am–5pm. Closed 1st 3 weeks of Jan, Thanksgiving, and Dec 25. From downtown, follow Derby St. east 3 blocks past Derby Wharf.

Peabody Essex Museum ★★ *Kids*   The Peabody Essex Museum enjoys a flourishing national reputation for its impressive collections of art and cultural artifacts. Though sometimes overshadowed by Salem's every-witch-way reputation, the museum offers an engaging look at nearly 4 centuries in a fascinating seaport (yes, including the witchcraft trials). A huge expansion project completed in 2003 created new galleries and added a well-preserved 18th-century Qing dynasty house, **Yin Yu Tang,** that was shipped from China and reassembled. The new wing, designed by Moshe Safdie, allows the museum to display a significant proportion of its holdings for the first time.

The permanent collections blend "the natural and artificial curiosities" that Salem's sea captains and merchants brought back from around the world to the Peabody Museum (1799) with the local and domestic artifacts of the Essex Institute (1821), the county historical society. The displays help you understand the significance of each artifact, and interpretive materials (including interactive and hands-on activities) let children get involved. You might see objects related to the history of the port of Salem (including gorgeous furniture), the whaling trade, or the witchcraft trials. Other noteworthy collections include American, African, Indian, Asian, and East Asian art and objects; photography; and the practical arts and crafts of East Asian, Pacific Island, and Native American peoples. Portraits of area residents include Charles Osgood's omnipresent rendering of Nathaniel Hawthorne.

Special exhibitions during the period covered by this book include *The Taj Mahal* (Oct 15, 2005–Sept 2006) and *The Artful Teapot* (Nov 25, 2005–Mar 5, 2006).

Sign up for a fascinating tour of one or more of the museum's two dozen historic houses. The sites include the meticulously restored 1804 **Gardner-Pingree House** ★★, a magnificent Federal mansion where a notorious murder was committed in 1830. You can also take a guided or self-guided gallery tour. The museum cafe keeps the same hours as the museum, and the restaurant serves lunch Wednesday through Sunday and afternoon tea on weekends.

East India Sq. (✆ **866/745-1876** or 978/745-9500. www.pem.org. Admission $13 adults, $11 seniors, $9 students, free for children under 17. Yin Yu Tang admission $4 with museum admission. Surcharges may apply for special exhibitions. Daily 10am–5pm. Take Hawthorne Blvd. to Essex St., following signs for visitor center. Enter on Essex St. or New Liberty St.

Salem Maritime National Historic Site ★ *Kids*   An entertaining introduction to Salem's seagoing history, this complex includes an exciting attraction: a real live ship. The *Friendship* ★★ is a full-size replica of a 1797 East Indiaman merchant vessel, a three-masted 171-footer that disappeared during the War of 1812. The tall ship is a faithful replica with some concessions to the modern era, such as diesel engines. The **guided ranger tour** includes a tour of the ship.

With the decline of merchant shipping in the early 19th century, Salem's wharves fell into disrepair. In 1938, the National Park Service took over a small piece of the waterfront, **Derby Wharf.** It's now a finger of parkland extending into the harbor; part of the 9 acres is dotted with explanatory markers that make up the historic site.

> **Fun Fact** A Face in the Crowd
>
> On the traffic island across from the entrance to the **Salem Witch Museum** is a statue that's easily mistaken for a witch. It's really **Roger Conant,** who founded Salem in 1626.

On adjacent **Central Wharf** is a warehouse, built around 1800, that houses the orientation center. Tours, which vary seasonally, explore Salem's maritime history. Tours might include the **Derby House** (1762), a wedding gift to shipping magnate Elias Hasket Derby from his father, and the **Custom House** (1819). Legend (myth, really) has it that Nathaniel Hawthorne was working here when he found an embroidered scarlet "A." If you prefer to explore on your own, you can see the free film at the orientation center and wander around **Derby Wharf,** the **West India Goods Store,** the **Bonded Warehouse,** the **Scale House,** and Central Wharf.

174 Derby St. ℂ 978/740-1660. www.nps.gov/sama. Free admission. Guided tours $5 adults, $3 seniors and children 6–15. Daily 9am–5pm. Closed Jan 1, Thanksgiving, and Dec 25. Take Derby St. east; just past Pickering Wharf, Derby Wharf is on the right.

Salem Witch Museum ⭐⭐ (Kids)   This is one of the most memorable attractions in eastern Massachusetts—it's both interesting and scary. The main draw of the museum (a former church) is a three-dimensional audiovisual presentation with life-size figures. The show takes place in a huge room lined with displays that are lighted in sequence. The 30-minute narration tells the story of the witchcraft trials and the accompanying hysteria. The well-researched presentation tells the story accurately, if somewhat over-dramatically. One of the victims was crushed to death by rocks piled on a board on his chest—smaller kids might need a reminder that he's not real. The narration is available translated into French, German, Italian, Japanese, and Spanish. There's also a small exhibit that traces the history of witches, witchcraft, and witch hunts.

19½ Washington Sq., on Rte. 1A. ℂ 978/744-1692. www.salemwitchmuseum.com. Admission $6.50 adults, $6 seniors, $4.50 children 6–14. Daily July–Aug 10am–7pm; Sept–June 10am–5pm; check ahead for Oct hours. Closed Jan 1, Thanksgiving, and Dec 25. Follow Hawthorne Blvd. to the northwest corner of Salem Common.

SHOPPING

Pickering Wharf (ℂ 978/740-6990; www.pickeringwharf.com), at the corner of Derby and Congress streets, is a waterfront complex of shops, boutiques, restaurants, and condos. It's popular for strolling, snacking, and shopping, and the central location makes it a local landmark.

Several shops specialize in witchcraft accessories. Bear in mind that Salem is home to many practicing witches who take their beliefs very seriously. The **Broom Closet,** 3–5 Central St. (ℂ 978/741-3669), and **Crow Haven Corner,** 125 Essex St. (ℂ 978/745-8763), stock everything from crystals to clothing.

WHERE TO STAY

The busiest and most expensive time of year is Halloween week; reserve well in advance.

Coach House Inn   Built in 1879 for a ship's captain, this welcoming inn is in a historic district 2 blocks from the harbor and just a mile from downtown. It's a 20-minute walk or a 5-minute drive from the center of town, 9 blocks away. Salem State College is up the street. The three-story mansion was renovated in 2002. The good-size rooms are elegantly furnished with period antiques, four-poster beds, and Oriental rugs. All have high ceilings, and most have (nonworking) fireplaces. Breakfast arrives at your door in a basket—a nice perk if dining-room chitchat isn't your thing.

284 Lafayette St. (Rtes. 1A and 114), Salem, MA 01970. © 800/688-8689 or 978/744-4092. Fax 978/745-8031. www.coachhousesalem.com. 11 units, 9 with bathroom (2 with shower only). $115–$175 double; $170–$230 2-room suite. Rates include continental breakfast. Minimum 2- or 3-night stay weekends and holidays. AE, DISC, MC, V. Free parking. *In room:* A/C, TV, fridge, coffeemaker.

Hawthorne Hotel ★ *Kids* This historic hotel, built in 1925, is both convenient and comfortable. It books both vacationers and business travelers, and it's popular for functions. The six-story building is centrally located and well maintained, with a pleasant atmosphere and an ornate lobby that evokes the building's Roaring Twenties origins. The well-kept guest rooms are adequate in size and attractively furnished with reproduction Federal-style pieces. The best units, on the Salem Common (north) side of the building, have better views than rooms that face the street. Whatever direction you face, ask to be as high up as possible because the neighborhood is busy. If you're traveling with children, ask about "Family Fun" packages, which include discounted tickets to area museums.

18 Washington Sq. W. (at Salem Common), Salem, MA 01970. © 800/729-7829 or 978/744-4080. Fax 978/745-9842. www.hawthornehotel.com. 89 units (some with shower only). $104–$204 double; $204–$309 suite. Extra person $12. Children under 16 stay free in parent's room. Off-season discounts, senior discount, and weekend and other packages available. 2-night minimum stay May–Oct weekends. AE, DC, DISC, MC, V. Limited self-parking. Pets accepted; $15 fee. **Amenities:** Restaurant (American); tavern; exercise room; access to nearby heath club with pool; concierge; airport shuttle; business center; room service until 11pm; laundry service; same-day dry cleaning. Rooms for travelers with disabilities are available. *In room:* A/C, TV, wireless Internet access, hair dryer, iron.

Salem Inn ★★ The Salem Inn occupies the comfortable niche between too-big hotel and too-small B&B. Its clientele includes honeymooners as well as sightseers and families, and the variety of rooms means that the innkeepers can make a good match of guest and accommodations. The inn consists of three properties. The 1834 West House and the 1854 Curwen House, former homes of ship captains, are listed on the National Register of Historic Places. The best units are the honeymoon and family suites (which have kitchenettes) in the 1874 Peabody House. Guest rooms are large and tastefully decorated; some have fireplaces, canopy beds, and whirlpool baths. Guests of all three houses can relax in the peaceful rose garden at the rear of the main building.

7 Summer St. (Rte. 114), Salem, MA 01970. © 800/446-2995 or 978/741-0680. Fax 978/744-8924. www. saleminnma.com. 41 units (some with shower only). Nov–Sept $119–$149 double; $169–$229 suite; Oct $180–$210 double, $220–$285 suite. Rates include continental breakfast. Extra person $15–$25. Minimum stay 2–3 nights during special events and holidays. AE, DC, DISC, MC, V. Free parking. Pets accepted with prior arrangement; $15/night Nov–Sept, $25/night Oct. *In room:* A/C, TV, coffeemaker, hair dryer, iron.

Finds **Confection Connection**

Shops throughout New England sell the chocolate confections of **Harbor Sweets** ★★, Palmer Cove, 85 Leavitt St., off Lafayette Street (© **978/745-7648**; www.harborsweets.com). The retail store overlooks the floor of the factory. The deliriously good sweets are expensive, but candy bars and small assortments are available. Closed Sunday.

WHERE TO DINE

Pickering Wharf has a food court as well as a **Victoria Station** restaurant (© 978/ 744-7644; www.victoriastationinc.com), where the deck has a great view of the marina and the menu emphasizes seafood and traditional American dishes. The restaurant and cafe at the **Peabody Essex Museum** (p. 273) serve lunch.

Lyceum Bar & Grill ★★ CONTEMPORARY AMERICAN   The elegance of the Lyceum's high-ceilinged front rooms and glass-walled back rooms matches the sky-high quality of the food, which attracts local businesspeople and out-of-towners. Grilling is a favored cooking technique —try the signature grilled marinated portobello mushrooms. They're available as an appetizer and scattered throughout the menu—for example, in a delectable pasta dish with chicken, red peppers, and chard in Madeira sauce. Meat and fish dishes, such as pork tenderloin with mashed sweet potatoes or pan-seared swordfish with wild-mushroom risotto, are equally delicious. Try to save room for one of the traditional yet sophisticated desserts—the brownie sundae is out of this world.

> **Fun Fact Party Line**
>
> Alexander Graham Bell made the first long-distance telephone call from the building that now holds the Lyceum Bar & Grill.

43 Church St. (at Washington St.). © 978/745-7665. www.lyceumsalem.com. Reservations recommended. Main courses $7–$12 at lunch, $18–$29 at dinner. AE, DISC, MC, V. Mon–Fri 11:30am–3pm; Sun brunch 11am–3pm; daily 5:30–10pm. Validated parking available.

Stromberg's ★ *Kids* SEAFOOD   For generous portions of well-prepared seafood and a view of the water, seek out this popular spot next to the bridge to Beverly. Stromberg's is just far enough from downtown to make dropping in impractical; the clientele consists of both locals and in-the-know out-of-towners. You won't care that Beverly Harbor isn't the most exciting spot, especially if it's summer and you're out on the deck. The fish and clam chowders are excellent, daily specials are numerous, and there are more chicken, beef, and pasta options than you might expect. Crustacean lovers in the mood to splurge will fall for the world-class lobster roll.

2 Bridge St. (Rte. 1A). © 978/744-1863. www.strombergs.com. Reservations recommended at dinner. Main courses $7–$13 at lunch, $11–$19 at dinner; lobster market price. Children's menu $5. AE, DISC, MC, V. Sun and Tues–Thurs 11am–9pm; Fri–Sat 11am–10pm.

A DETOUR TO ESSEX

If you approach or leave Cape Ann on Route 128, head west on Route 133 to **Essex.** It's a beautiful little town known for Essex clams, salt marshes, a long tradition of ship-building, an incredible number of antiques shops, and one celebrated restaurant.

Legend has it that **Woodman's of Essex** ★★★, 121 Main St. (© 800/649-1773 or 978/768-6057; www.woodmans.com), was the birthplace of the fried clam in 1916. Today, the thriving family-owned eatery is a great spot to join legions of locals and visitors from around the world for lobster "in the rough," chowder, steamers, corn on the cob, onion rings, and (you guessed it) superb fried clams. The line is long, but it moves quickly and offers a good view of the regimented commotion in the food-preparation area. Eat in a booth, upstairs on the deck, or out back at a picnic table. Credit cards aren't accepted, but there's an ATM on the premises. You'll want to be well fed before you set off to explore the numerous antiques shops along Main Street.

Kids A Whale of an Adventure

The depletion of New England's fishing grounds has led to the rise of another important seagoing industry, **whale watching** ★★. The waters off the coast of Massachusetts are prime territory, and Gloucester is a center of whale-watching cruises. Stellwagen Bank, which runs from Gloucester to Provincetown about 27 miles east of Boston, is a rich feeding ground for the magnificent mammals. Species spotted in the area are mainly humpback, finback, and minke whales, who dine on sand eels and other fish that gather along the ridge. The whales often perform for their audience by jumping out of the water, and dolphins occasionally join the show. Naturalists onboard narrate the trip for the companies listed here, pointing out the whales and describing birds and fish that cross your path.

Whale watching is not particularly time- or cost-effective, especially if restless children are along, but it's so popular for a reason: The payoff is, literally and figuratively, huge. This is an "only in New England" experience that kids (and adults) will remember for a long time.

The season runs from April or May through October. Dress warmly—it's much cooler at sea than on land. Wear a hat and rubber-soled shoes, and take sunglasses, sunscreen, a hat, and a camera with plenty of film. If you're prone to motion sickness, take precautions because you'll be at sea for 3½ to 5 hours. If you plan to take Dramamine, take it before you depart.

This is an extremely competitive business—they'd deny it, but the companies are virtually indistinguishable. Most guarantee sightings, offer a morning and an afternoon cruise as well as deep-sea fishing excursions and charters, honor other firms' coupons, and offer AAA and AARP discounts. Check the local marinas for sailing times, prices ($34–$38 for adults, less for seniors and children), and reservations, which are strongly recommended.

In downtown Gloucester, **Cape Ann Whale Watch** (© 800/877-5110 or 978/283-5110; www.caww.com) is the best-known operation. Also downtown are **Capt. Bill's Whale Watch** (© 800/33-WHALE or 978/283-6995; www.captainbillswhalewatch.com) and **Seven Seas Whale Watch** (© 888/238-1776 or 978/283-1776; www.7seas-whalewatch.com). At the Cape Ann Marina, off Route 133, is **Yankee Whale Watch** (© 800/WHALING or 978/283-0313; www.yankeefleet.com).

Open daily in the summer from 11am to 10pm; winter, Sunday to Thursday from 11am to 8pm, Friday and Saturday 11am to 9pm.

GLOUCESTER ★★
33 miles NE of Boston, 16 miles NE of Salem

The ocean has been Gloucester's lifeblood since long before the first European settlement in 1623. The French explorer Samuel de Champlain called the harbor "Le Beauport" when he came across it in 1604, some 600 years after the Vikings. The harbor's configuration and proximity to good fishing gave it the reputation it enjoys to this day. If you read or saw *The Perfect Storm,* you'll have a sense of what to expect here.

Cape Ann

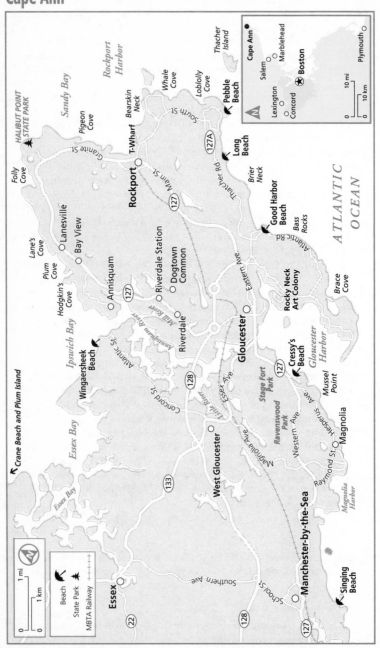

Thacher Island

ATLANTIC OCEAN

Sandy Bay

Rockport Harbor

Whale Cove

Loblolly Cove

Pebble Beach

Folly Cove

HALIBUT POINT STATE PARK

Pigeon Cove

Bearskin Neck

T-Wharf

Granite St.

Rockport

South St.

127A

Long Beach

Brier Neck

Lanesville

Bay View

Main St.

127

Good Harbor Beach

Thatcher Rd.

Bass Rocks

Atlantic Rd.

Lane's Cove

Plum Cove

Hodgkin's Cove

Annisquam

127

Riverdale Station

Dogtown Common

Eastern Ave.

Rocky Neck Art Colony

Brace Cove

Ipswich Bay

Mill River

Riverdale

Gloucester

Cressy's Beach

Gloucester Harbor

Mussel Point

Wingaersheek Beach

Atlantic St.

Annisquam River

Stage Fort Park

127

Crane Beach and Plum Island

Essex Bay

Concord St.

128

Essex Ave.

Little River

Ravenswood Park

Western Ave.

Hesperus Ave.

Magnolia

West Gloucester

Magnolia Ave.

Magnolia Harbor

Essex Bay

133

Raymond St.

Essex

22

Southern Ave.

School St.

128

Manchester-by-the-Sea

127

Singing Beach

Inset map

Cape Ann

Marblehead

Salem

Boston

Lexington

Concord

Plymouth

10 mi

10 km

0

Legend

1 mi

1 km

0

Beach

State Park

MBTA Railway

Gloucester (which rhymes with "roster") is a working city, not a cutesy tourist town. It's home to one of the last commercial fishing fleets in New England, an internationally celebrated artists' colony, a large Portuguese-American community, and just enough historic attractions. Allow at least half a day, perhaps combined with a visit to the tourist magnet of Rockport; a full day would be better, especially if you plan a cruise or whale watch.

ESSENTIALS

GETTING THERE   From Salem, follow Route 1A across the bridge to Beverly, pick up Route 127, and take it through Manchester (near, not on, the water) to Gloucester. From Boston, the quickest path is I-93 or Route 1 to Route 128, which runs directly to Gloucester. Route 128 is mostly inland; to take in more scenery, leave Route 128 at Manchester and continue to Gloucester on Route 127. There's street parking (metered and not), and a free lot on the causeway to Rocky Neck.

The **commuter rail** (© 617/222-3200; www.mbta.com) runs from Boston's North Station. The trip takes about an hour; the round-trip fare is $11. The station is across town from downtown, so allow time for getting to the waterfront area. The **Cape Ann Transportation Authority,** or CATA (© 978/283-7916; www. canntran.com), runs buses from town to town on Cape Ann and operates special routes during the summer.

VISITOR INFORMATION   The **Gloucester Tourism Office,** 22 Poplar St., Gloucester, MA 01930 (© 800/649-6839 or 978/281-8865; www.gloucesterma.com), operates the excellent Visitors Welcoming Center at Stage Fort Park, off Route 127 at Route 133. It's open during the summer daily from 9am to 5pm; closed in winter. The **Cape Ann Chamber of Commerce,** 33 Commercial St., Gloucester, MA 01930 (© 800/321-0133 or 978/283-1601; www.capeannvacations.com), is open year-round (summer weekdays 8am–6pm, Sat 10am–6pm, Sun 10am–4pm; winter weekdays 8am–5pm) and has a helpful staff. It also operates a seasonal information booth on Rogers Street at Harbor Loop. Call or write for the chamber's four-color map and brochure.

SPECIAL EVENTS   Gloucester holds festivals and street fairs that honor everything from clams to schooners on weekends throughout the summer—check in advance to find out what's up when you'll be in town. The best-known event is **St. Peter's Fiesta,** a colorful 4-day celebration at the end of June. The Italian-American fishing colony's festival has more in common with a carnival midway than a religious observation, but it's great fun. There are parades, games, music, food, sporting events, and, on Sunday, the blessing of the fleet.

Moments Down by the Sea

On Stacy Boulevard west of downtown Gloucester is a reminder of the sea's danger. Leonard Craske's bronze statue of the **Gloucester Fisherman,** known as "The Man at the Wheel," bears the inscription "They That Go Down to the Sea in Ships 1623–1923." Several hundred yards west is a memorial to the women and children who waited at home. As you take in the glorious view, consider this: More than 10,000 fishermen lost their lives during the city's first 300 years.

Moments   The Perfect Storm

Long after the release of the blockbuster movie, Sebastian Junger's best-selling book *The Perfect Storm* remains a popular reason to visit Gloucester. The thrilling but tragic true account of the "no-name" hurricane of 1991 centers on the ocean and a neighborhood tavern. The **Crow's Nest,** 334 Main St. (© **978/281-2965**), a bit east of downtown, is a no-frills place with a horseshoe-shaped bar and a crowd of regulars who seem amused that their hangout is a tourist attraction. The Crow's Nest plays a major role in Junger's story, but its ceilings weren't high enough for it to be a movie set—so the crew built an exact replica nearby. If you admired the movie's wardrobe design, check out the shirts and caps at **Cape Pond Ice,** 104 Commercial St., near the Chamber of Commerce (© **978/283-0174**; www. capepondice.com).

EXPLORING THE TOWN

Business isn't nearly what it once was, but fishing is still Gloucester's leading industry (as your nose will tell you). Tourism is a very close second, and the city is an exceptionally welcoming destination—residents seem genuinely happy to see out-of-towners and to offer directions and insider info. The **"Gloucester Maritime Trail"** brochure, available at visitor centers, describes four excellent self-guided tours.

Stage Fort Park, off Route 127 at Route 133, offers an excellent view of the harbor and has a busy snack bar (summer only). It's a good spot for picnicking, swimming, or playing on the cannons in the Revolutionary War fort.

To reach **East Gloucester,** follow signs as you leave downtown or go directly from Route 128, Exit 9. On East Main Street, you'll see signs for the world-famous **Rocky Neck Art Colony** ★★, the oldest continuously operating art colony in the country. Park in the lot on the tiny causeway and head west along Rocky Neck Avenue, which abounds with studios, galleries, restaurants, and people. The draw is the presence of working artists, not just shops that happen to sell art. Most galleries are open daily in the summer 10am to 10pm.

The prestigious **North Shore Arts Association,** 197 E. Main St. (© **978/283-1857;** www.northshoreartsassoc.org), was founded in 1922 to showcase local artists' work. The exhibits are worth a visit before or after your excursion across the causeway. The building is open late May through Columbus Day, Monday through Saturday from 10am to 5pm, Sunday noon to 5pm. Admission is free.

Also in East Gloucester, the **Gloucester Stage Company** ★, 267 E. Main St. (© **978/ 281-4099;** www.gloucesterstage.com), is one of the best repertory troupes in New England. Founder and artistic director Israel Horovitz, a prizewinning playwright and screenwriter, schedules six plays a season (June to mid-Sept).

NARRATED CRUISES   For information on whale watches, see the box "A Whale of an Adventure" (p. 277).

Moby Duck Tours ★ (© **978/281-DUCK;** www.mobyduck.com) are 55-minute sightseeing expeditions that travel on land (20 min.) before plunging into the water (35 min.). They're just the right length for kids, who delight in the transition from street to sea. The amphibious vehicles leave from **Harbor Loop** downtown. Tickets (cash only) cost $16 for adults, $14 for seniors, and $10 for children under 12. Tours operate daily from Memorial Day to Labor Day and on weekends in September, departing hourly from 10am through 4pm (weather permitting).

The schooner **Thomas E. Lannon** ★ (© **978/281-6634;** www.schooner.org) is a gorgeous reproduction of a Gloucester fishing vessel. The 65-foot tall ship sails from Seven Seas Wharf downtown; 2-hour excursions ($33 for adults, $30 for seniors, $25 for children under 17) leave about four times daily from mid-June to mid-September, less often on weekends from mid-May to mid-June and mid-September to mid-October. Reservations are recommended. The company also offers music and dining cruises, including lobster bakes on Friday, and "storytelling sails."

Beauport (Sleeper-McCann House) ★★

Historic New England, which operates Beauport, describes it as a "fantasy house," and that's putting it mildly. Interior designer Henry Davis Sleeper used his seaside summer home as a retreat and as a repository for his vast collection of American and European decorative arts and antiques. From 1907 to 1934, he decorated the 40 rooms, most of which are open to the public, to illustrate literary and historical themes. The entertaining tour concentrates more on the gorgeous house and rooms in general than on the countless objects on display. You'll see architectural details rescued from other buildings, magnificent arrangements of colored glassware, an early American kitchen, the "Red Indian Room" (with a majestic view of the harbor), and "Strawberry Hill," the master bedroom. Check ahead to see if there's a special event (afternoon tea, specialty tour, or evening concert) while you're in town. Note that the house is closed on summer weekends.

75 Eastern Point Blvd. © 978/283-0800. www.historicnewengland.org. Guided tour $10 adults, $9 seniors, $5 students and children 6–12. Tours on the hour June to mid-Sept Mon–Fri 10am–4pm; mid-Sept to Oct 15 daily 10am–4pm. Closed Oct 16–May and summer weekends. Take E. Main St. to Eastern Point Blvd. (a private road), continue ½ mile to house, park on left.

Cape Ann Historical Museum ★

This meticulously curated museum makes an excellent introduction to Cape Ann's history and artists. It devotes an entire gallery to the extraordinary work of **Fitz Hugh Lane** ★★★, the Luminist painter whose light-flooded canvases show off the best of his native Gloucester. The nation's largest collection of his paintings and drawings is here. Other galleries feature works on paper by 20th-century artists such as Maurice Prendergast and Milton Avery, work by other contemporary artists, and granite-quarrying tools and equipment. There's also an outdoor sculpture court. On display in the maritime and fisheries galleries are entire vessels (including one about the size of a station wagon that crossed the Atlantic), exhibits on the fishing industry, ship models, and historic photographs and models of the Gloucester waterfront. The **Capt. Elias Davis House** (1804), decorated and furnished in Federal style with furniture, silver, and porcelains, is part of the museum.

27 Pleasant St. © 978/283-0455. www.capeannhistoricalmuseum.org. Admission $6.50 adults, $6 seniors, $5 students, free for children under 6. Mar–Jan Tues–Sat 10am–5pm, Sun 1–4pm. Closed Feb. Follow Main St. west through downtown and turn right onto Pleasant St.; museum is 1 block up on right. Metered parking on street or in lot across street.

SHOPPING

Rocky Neck (see "Exploring the Town," above) offers great browsing. Downtown, **Main Street** between Pleasant and Washington streets is a good destination. Agreeable stops include **Mystery Train,** 178 Main St. (© **978/281-8911;** www.mysterytrain records.com), which carries a huge variety of used LPs, CDs, tapes, and videos; **Ménage Gallery,** 134 Main St. (© **978/283-6030**), which shows varied works by artists and artisans, including gorgeous furniture; and the **Dogtown Book Shop,** 2 Duncan St. (© **978/281-5599**), noted for its used and antiquarian selection.

WHERE TO STAY
Gloucester abounds with B&Bs; for guidance, check with the Cape Ann Chamber of Commerce (© **978/283-1601**) or consult one of the agencies listed on p. 78.

Atlantis Oceanfront Motor Inn   This motor inn with an outdoor pool sits across the street from the water, affording stunning views from every window. It doesn't have the resort feel of the neighboring Bass Rocks Ocean Inn, but the views are the same. The well-maintained, good-size guest rooms are decorated in comfortable, contemporary style. Each room has a terrace or balcony and a small table and chairs. Second-floor accommodations are slightly preferable because the view is a little better.

125 Atlantic Rd., Gloucester, MA 01930. © **800/732-6313** or 978/283-0014. Fax 978/281-8994. www.atlantismotor inn.com. 40 units (some with shower only). Late June to Labor Day $150–$180 double; spring and fall $125–$155 double. Extra person $8. Children under 12 stay free in parent's room. Minimum stay may be required. Off-season midweek

North Shore Beaches

North of Boston, sandy beaches complement the predominantly rocky coastline. Things to know: The water is *cold* (optimistic locals say "refreshing"). Parking can be scarce, especially on weekends, and pricey—as much as $20 per car. If you can't set out early, wait until midafternoon and hope that the people who arrived in the morning have had their fill. During the summer, lifeguards are on duty from 9am to 5pm at larger public beaches. Surfing is generally permitted outside of those hours. The beaches listed here all have bathhouses and snack bars. Swimming or not, watch out for greenhead flies in July and August. They don't sting—they take little bites of flesh. Bring or buy insect repellent.

The best-known North Shore beach is **Singing Beach** ⋆⋆, off Masconomo Street in Manchester-by-the-Sea. Because it's accessible by public transportation, it attracts the most diverse crowd—car-less singles, local families, and other beach bunnies of all ages. They walk ½ mile on Beach Street from the train station to find sparkling sand and lively surf. Take the commuter rail (© **617/222-3200;** www.mbta.com) from Boston's North Station.

Nearly as famous and popular is **Crane Beach** ⋆, off Argilla Road in Ipswich, part of a 1,400-acre barrier beach reservation. Fragile dunes and a white sand beach lead down to Ipswich Bay. The surf is calmer than that at less sheltered Singing Beach, but it's still quite chilly. Pick up Argilla Road south of Ipswich Center near the intersection of Routes 1A and 133. Also on Ipswich Bay is Gloucester's **Wingaersheek Beach** ⋆, on Atlantic Street off Route 133. It has its own exit (no. 13) off Route 128, about 15 minutes away on winding roads with low speed limits. When you finally arrive, you'll find beautiful white sand, a glorious view, and more dunes. Because these beaches are harder to get to, they attract more locals—but also lots of day-tripping families. At the east end of Route 133, the beaches and snack bar in Gloucester's easily accessible **Stage Fort Park** are popular local hangouts.

discounts available. AE, MC, V. Closed Nov to mid-Apr. 128 to the end (Exit 9, East Gloucester), turn left onto Bass Ave. (Rte. 127A), and follow it ½ mile. Turn right and follow Atlantic Rd. **Amenities:** Coffee shop (breakfast only); heated outdoor pool. *In room:* A/C, TV, dataport, coffeemaker.

Best Western Bass Rocks Ocean Inn   A family operation since 1946, the Bass Rocks Ocean Inn offers gorgeous ocean views, a heated pool, and modern accommodations. Across the road from the rocky shore, the sprawling, comfortable two-story motel contains spacious guest rooms. A Colonial Revival mansion built in 1899 and known as the "wedding-cake house" holds the office and public areas, including a billiard room and a library. The guest rooms are up-to-date, but overall the property feels like an old-fashioned resort, which distinguishes it from the neighboring Atlantis. Each guest room has sliding glass doors that open onto a balcony or patio, and a king bed or two double beds. Second-floor rooms have slightly better views. In the afternoon, the staff serves coffee, tea, lemonade, and chocolate-chip cookies.

107 Atlantic Rd., Gloucester, MA 01930. ℂ **800/WESTERN** or 978/283-7600. Fax 978/281-6489. www.bestwestern.com/bassrocksoceaninn. 48 units. Late June to Sept $170–$285 double; spring and fall $125–$210 double. Extra person $8. Children under 12 stay free in parent's room. Rollaway or crib $12. Rates include continental breakfast, afternoon refreshments, and use of bikes. Minimum 3-night stay summer weekends, some spring and fall weekends. AE, DC, DISC, MC, V. Closed Nov to late Apr. Follow Rte. 128 to the end (Exit 9, East Gloucester), turn left onto Bass Ave. (Rte. 127A), and follow it ½ mile. Turn right and follow Atlantic Rd. **Amenities:** Heated outdoor pool; game room. *In room:* A/C, TV/VCR, high-speed Internet access, fridge, coffeemaker, hair dryer, iron.

WHERE TO DINE

See "A Detour to Essex," on p. 276, for information about the celebrated **Woodman's of Essex,** which is about 20 minutes from downtown Gloucester. The Stage Fort Park snack bar, the **Cupboard** (ℂ **978/281-1908**), serves excellent fried seafood and blue-plate specials in the summer. **Lobsta Land,** 10 Causeway St., near Exit 12 off Route 128 (ℂ **978/281-0415**), is a summer-only destination for familiar and unusual seafood dishes and amazing french fries. If you're in town just for a day, consider sticking around for dinner at the **Franklin Cape Ann,** 118 Main St. (ℂ **978/283-7888**). It serves excellent bistro cuisine daily from 5pm to midnight (but unfortunately not at lunch).

The Gull Restaurant ★★ *Kids* SEAFOOD/AMERICAN   Floor-to-ceiling windows show off the Annisquam River from almost every seat at the Gull. This big, friendly restaurant is known for prime rib as well as seafood and is a popular breakfast destination. Large portions at reasonable prices draw locals, visitors, boaters, and families. The seafood chowder is famous (with good reason), appetizers tend toward bar food, and the french fries are terrific. Fish is available in just about any style. Ask about daily specials, which run from simple lobster (market price) to sophisticated fish and meat dishes. At lunch, there's an extensive sandwich menu.

75 Essex Ave. (Rte. 133), at Cape Ann Marina. ℂ 978/281-6060. Reservations recommended for parties of 8 or more. Main courses $5–$13 at lunch, $8–$22 at dinner; breakfast items less than $8. DISC, MC, V. Daily May–mid-Oct 6am–9pm. Closed mid-Oct–Apr. Take Rte. 133 west from intersection with Rte. 127, or take Rte. 133 east from Rte. 128.

Halibut Point Restaurant SEAFOOD/AMERICAN   A local legend for its chowders and burgers, Halibut Point is a friendly tavern that serves generous portions of good food. The "Halibut Point Special"—$12.50 for a cup of chowder, a burger, and a beer—hits the high points. Although the clam chowder is terrific, the spicy Italian fish chowder is also so good that some people come to Gloucester just for a bowlful of that. There's also a raw bar. Main courses are simple (mostly sandwiches) at lunch and more elaborate at dinner. Be sure to check the specials board—you didn't come all this way to a fishing port not to have fresh fish, did you?

289 Main St. ℂ **978/281-1900.** Main courses $5–$12 at lunch, $9–$17 at dinner. AE, DISC, MC, V. Daily 11:30am–11pm.

ROCKPORT
40 miles NE of Boston, 7 miles N of Gloucester

This lovely little town at the tip of Cape Ann was settled in 1690. Over the years it has been an active fishing port, a center of granite excavation and cutting, and a thriving summer community whose specialty appears to be selling fudge and refrigerator magnets to out-of-towners. Rockport is an entertaining half-day trip, perhaps combined with a visit to Gloucester.

There's more to Rockport than just gift shops. It's home to a lovely state park, and it's popular with photographers, painters, jewelry designers, and sculptors. Winslow Homer, Fitz Hugh Lane, and Childe Hassam are among the famous artists who have captured the local color. At times, however, especially on summer weekends, you'll be hard pressed to find much local color in this tourist-weary destination. But for every year-round resident who seems genuinely startled when legions of people with cameras around their necks descend on Rockport each June, there are dozens who are proud to show off their town.

Out of season, especially January through mid-April, Rockport is pretty but somewhat desolate, though some businesses stay open and keep reduced hours.

ESSENTIALS
GETTING THERE   Rockport is north of Gloucester along Route 127 or 127A. At the end of Route 128, turn left at the signs for Rockport to take Route 127, which is shorter but more commercial. To take Route 127A, which runs along the east coast of Cape Ann, continue on Route 128 until you see the sign for East Gloucester and turn left. Parking is next to impossible, especially on summer Saturday afternoons. Make one loop around downtown and then head to the free parking lot on Upper Main Street (Rte. 127). The shuttle bus to downtown costs $1.

The **commuter rail** (ℂ **617/222-3200;** www.mbta.com) runs from Boston's North Station. The trip takes 60 to 70 minutes, and the round-trip fare is $12. The station is about 6 blocks from the downtown waterfront. The **Cape Ann Transportation Authority,** or CATA (ℂ **978/283-7916**), runs buses from town to town on Cape Ann.

VISITOR INFORMATION   The **Rockport Chamber of Commerce and Board of Trade,** 22 Broadway (ℂ **888/726-3922** or 978/546-6575; www.rockportusa.com), is open daily in summer from 9am to 5pm and winter weekdays from 10am to 4pm. The chamber operates an information booth on Upper Main Street (Rte. 127) from mid-May to October. It's about a mile from the town line and a mile from downtown—look for the WELCOME TO ROCKPORT sign on the right as you head north. At either location, ask for the pamphlet *Rockport: A Walking Guide,* which contains a good map and descriptions of three short walking tours. At press time, the chamber was weighing a merger with the Cape Ann Chamber of Commerce (see "Gloucester," earlier in this chapter); check either website to see how the decision has affected visitor services.

SPECIAL EVENTS   The **Rockport Chamber Music Festival** (ℂ **978/546-7391;** www.rcmf.org) takes place during the month of June at the Rockport Art Association, 12 Main St. It's a good excuse to see the lovely town before the tourist season gets wild.

In addition to performances and family concerts (tickets $20–$30 adults, free for youth 18 and under), events include free lectures and discussions. Check ahead for 25th-anniversary celebrations throughout 2006.

The annual **Christmas pageant,** on Main Street in early December, is a crowded, kid-friendly event with carol singing and live animals.

EXPLORING THE TOWN

The most famous sight in Rockport has something of an "Emperor's New Clothes" aura—it's a wooden fish warehouse on the town wharf, or T-Wharf, in the harbor. The barn-red shack known as **Motif No. 1** is the most frequently painted and photographed object in a town filled with lovely buildings and surrounded by breathtaking rocky coastline. The color certainly catches the eye against the neutrals of the seascape, but you might find yourself wondering what the big deal is. Originally constructed in 1884 and destroyed during the blizzard of 1978, Motif No. 1 was rebuilt using donations from residents and tourists. It stands on the same pier as the original, duplicated in every detail and reinforced to withstand storms.

Nearby is a phenomenon whose popularity is easier to explain. **Bearskin Neck,** named after an unfortunate ursine visitor who drowned and washed ashore in 1800, has perhaps the highest concentration of gift shops anywhere. It's a narrow peninsula with one main street (South Rd.) and several alleys crammed with galleries, snack bars, antiques shops, and ancient houses. The peninsula ends in a plaza with a magnificent water view.

Throughout the town, more than two dozen **art galleries** ✦ display the works of local and nationally known artists. The **Rockport Art Association,** 12 Main St. (℃ **978/ 546-6604;** www.rockportartassn.org), sponsors major exhibitions and special shows. It's open daily mid-morning to late afternoon in the summer (except on Sun, when it opens at noon); in the winter, it's open mid-morning to late afternoon Tuesday through Saturday and noon to late afternoon Sunday.

To get a sense of the power of the sea, take Route 127 north of town to the tip of Cape Ann. Turn right on Gott Avenue to reach **Halibut Point State Park** ✦✦ (℃ **978/546-2997;** www.state.ma.us/dcr/parks/halb.htm). The park is a great place to wander around and admire the gorgeous scenery. On a clear day, you can see Maine. It has a staffed visitor center, walking trails, and tidal pools. Swimming in the water-filled quarries is absolutely forbidden. You can climb around on giant boulders on the rocky beach or climb to the top of the World War II observation tower. Guided quarry tours and stone-splitting demonstrations take place on summer Saturdays at 10am. Call ahead for information about other special programs, scheduled from May through September. The park is open daily, year-round, from dawn to dusk; parking costs $2 from Memorial Day to Columbus Day.

If the mansions of Gloucester were too plush for you, or if you want some recycling tips, visit the **Paper House,** 52 Pigeon Hill St., Pigeon Cove (℃ **978/546-2629;** www. rockportusa.com/paperhouse). A genuinely wacky attraction, it was built in 1922 entirely out of 100,000 newspapers—walls, furniture, even a newspaper-covered piano. Every item is made from papers of a different period. It's open daily April through October from 10am to 5pm (closed Nov–Mar). Admission is $1.50 for adults, $1 for children. Follow Route 127 north out of downtown about 1½ miles until you see signs at Curtis Street pointing to the left, then go left on Pigeon Hill Street.

SHOPPING

Bearskin Neck is the obvious place to start. Dozens of little shops stock clothes, gifts, toys, jewelry, souvenirs, inexpensive novelties, and expensive handmade crafts and paintings. Another enjoyable stroll is along **Main** and **Mount Pleasant streets.** Good stops include the nonprofit **Toad Hall Bookstore,** 47 Main St. (✆ **978/546-7323**); **New England Goods,** 57 Main St. (✆ **978/546-9677**), where the stock is exclusively local; and **Willoughby's,** 20 Main St. (✆ **978/546-9820**), a women's clothing and accessories shop.

Two of my favorite stops are retro delights. Downtown, you can watch taffy being made at **Tuck's Candy Factory,** 7 Dock Sq. (✆ **800/569-2767** or 978/546-6352), a local landmark since the 1920s. Near the train station, **Crackerjacks,** 27 Whistlestop Mall, off Railroad Avenue (✆ **978/546-1616**), is an old-fashioned variety store with a great crafts department.

WHERE TO STAY

When Rockport is busy, it's very busy—and when it's not, it's practically empty. The town's dozens of B&Bs fill in good weather and empty or even close in the winter. Make summer reservations well in advance or cross your fingers and call the Chamber of Commerce (p. 284) to ask about cancellations.

If you're traveling by train, call ahead to request pick-up at the Rockport station, which most lodgings in town offer at no charge.

Captain's Bounty Motor Inn This modern, newly renovated motor inn is on the water. In fact, it's almost *in* the water and nearly as close to the center of town as to the harbor. Each room in the three-story building overlooks the water and has its own balcony and sliding glass door. Rooms are spacious and soundproofed, with good cross-ventilation but no air-conditioning. Each has a microwave and fridge in case you want to eat some meals in. The best units are on the adults-only top floor. Although it's hardly plush and the pricing structure is a bit peculiar (note the charge for children), you can't beat the location. Kitchenette units are available.

1 Beach St., Rockport, MA 01966. ✆ **978/546-9557.** Fax 978/546-9993. www.captainsbountymotorinn.com. 24 units. Late May to late Sept $140 double, $155 efficiency, $170 efficiency suite; spring and fall $90–$110 double, $95–$115 efficiency, $100–$125 efficiency suite. Extra adult $10; $5 for each child over 5. 10% senior discount available. Minimum 2-night stay weekends, 3-night stay holiday weekends. MC, V. Closed Nov–Mar. Pets allowed in off season only; $10/night. *In room:* TV, fridge, coffeemaker.

Inn on Cove Hill (Caleb Norwood, Jr., House) ✸ This attractive Federal-style inn was built in 1771 using the proceeds of pirates' gold found nearby. Although it's just 2 blocks from the town wharf, the inn is set back from the road and has a hideaway feel. Guest rooms are decorated in period style; most have colonial furnishings and handmade quilts, and some have canopy beds. Innkeeper Betsy Eck overhauls one room each winter. Water views from the back of the house are worth the climb on the narrow stairs that lead to the third floor. The generous breakfast is served in the dining room or, in good weather, in the pleasant garden. A harbor-view apartment across the street is available for long-term (1 week or more) stays.

37 Mount Pleasant St., Rockport, MA 01966. ✆ **888/546-2701** or 978/546-2701. Fax 978/546-1095. www.innoncove hill.com. 7 units (some with shower only). $100–$165 double. Extra person $25. Rates include continental breakfast. 2-night minimum June–Oct weekends. Off-season discounts available. MC, V. *In room:* A/C, TV, no phone.

Sandy Bay Motor Inn ✦   About half a mile from downtown Rockport, this modern motor inn offers comfortable accommodations and a variety of recreational facilities at a good price. One of the largest lodgings in town, it's a sprawling two-story complex with attractively landscaped grounds on a hill next to Route 127, which is busy during the day but not at night. Still, units that face away from the unattractive road are preferable. Guest rooms are large and conventionally furnished—nothing fancy, but well maintained and large enough to hold a cot. There are six two-bedroom units; if you don't need that much space, you can book an efficiency and eat some meals in.

183 Main St. (Rte. 127), Rockport, MA 01966. ℭ 800/437-7155 or 978/546-7155. 79 units (some with shower only). Mid-June to early Sept $120–$165 double or efficiency; spring and fall $100–$130 double or efficiency; winter $85–$115 double or efficiency. Extra adult $10. Each child $4. Cot $6. Minimum 2-night stay summer weekends. AE, MC, V. Pets accepted; $50 deposit. **Amenities:** Restaurant (breakfast only); heated indoor pool; putting green; 2 outdoor tennis courts; whirlpool; saunas. Rooms for travelers with disabilities are available. *In room:* A/C, TV.

WHERE TO DINE

At press time, Rockport was in the midst of a roaring battle over lifting the town-wide ban on selling and serving alcoholic beverages. If the "dry" spell has ended by the time you visit, expect restaurants to be keeping longer hours. If the ban stands, you'll still be able to BYOB, usually subject to a corking fee.

The birthplace of the fried clam, **Woodman's of Essex** (see "A Detour to Essex," on p. 276), is about half an hour from Rockport.

Off Bearskin Neck, the **Portside Chowder House,** 7 Tuna Wharf (ℭ **978/546-7045**) serves delicious fresh chowder, fresh seafood, salads, and sandwiches in its harbor-view dining room.

Brackett's Oceanview Restaurant SEAFOOD/AMERICAN   The dining room at Brackett's has a gorgeous view of the water. The nautical decor suits the seafood-intensive menu, which offers enough variety to make this a good choice for families—burgers are always available. The service is friendly, and the fresh seafood is quite good, if not particularly adventurous. Try the moist, plump codfish cakes if you're looking for a traditional New England dish or go for something with Cajun spices if you're looking for something out of the ordinary. The most exciting offerings are on the extensive dessert menu, where anything homemade is a great choice.

25 Main St. ℭ **978/546-2797.** www.bracketts.com. Reservations recommended at dinner. Main courses $7–$20 at lunch, $10–$26 at dinner. AE, DC, DISC, MC, V. Mid-Apr to Memorial Day Wed–Sun 11:30am–8pm; Memorial Day to Oct Sun–Fri 11:30am–8pm, Sat 11:30am–9pm. Closed Nov to mid-Apr.

The Greenery ✦ SEAFOOD/AMERICAN   The Greenery could get away with serving so-so food because of its great location at the head of Bearskin Neck—but it doesn't. The cafe at the front serves delicious light fare to stay or to go; the dining rooms, at the back, boast great views of the harbor. The food ranges from tasty quiche at lunch to lobster at dinner to steamers and fresh-caught fish anytime. As in any town with a fishing fleet, check out the daily specials. All baking is done in-house, which explains the lines at the front counter for muffins and pastries. When the restaurant is busy, the usually cheerful service tends to drag. This is a good place to launch a picnic lunch on the beach and an equally good spot for lingering over coffee and dessert and watching the action around the harbor.

15 Dock Sq. ℭ **978/546-9593.** Reservations recommended at dinner. Main courses $7–$12 at lunch, $10–$22 at dinner; breakfast items $2–$7. AE, DC, DISC, MC, V. Spring–fall daily 8am–9:30pm; call for winter hours.

3 Plymouth ★★

40 miles SE of Boston

Everyone educated in the United States knows at least a little about Plymouth—about how the Pilgrims, fleeing religious persecution, left Europe on the *Mayflower* and landed at Plymouth Rock in December 1620. Many also know that the Pilgrims endured disease and privation, and that just 51 people from the original group of 102 celebrated the first Thanksgiving in 1621 with Squanto, a Pawtuxet Indian associated with the Wampanoags, and his cohorts.

What you won't know until you visit is how small everything was. The *Mayflower* (a replica) seems perilously tiny, and when you contemplate how dangerous life was at the time, it's hard not to marvel at the settlers' accomplishments. One of their descendants' accomplishments is this: Plymouth is in many ways a model destination, where the 17th century coexists with the 21st, and most historic attractions are both educational and fun. Tourists positively jam the downtown area in the summer, but the year-round population is so large that Plymouth feels more like the working community it is than like a warm-weather day-trip destination. It's a manageable 1-day excursion from Boston, particularly enjoyable if you're traveling with children. It also makes a good stop between Boston and Cape Cod.

ESSENTIALS

GETTING THERE By car, follow the Southeast Expressway (I-93) south from Boston to Route 3. Take Exit 6A and then Route 44 east and follow signs to the historic attractions. The trip from Boston takes 45 to 60 minutes if it's not rush hour. Take Exit 5 to the **Regional Information Complex** for maps, brochures, and information. To go directly to **Plimoth Plantation,** take Exit 4. There's metered parking throughout town.

The **commuter rail** (© 617/222-3200; www.mbta.com) serves Cordage Park, on Route 3A north of downtown, from Boston's South Station four times a day on weekdays and three times a day on weekends (at other times, service is to nearby Kingston).

Tips **A Presidential History Twofer**

A worthwhile detour en route to Plymouth is the **Adams National Historical Park** in Quincy, about 10 miles south of Boston. The park preserves the birthplaces of Presidents John Adams and John Quincy Adams, the house where four generations of the family lived, and eight other buildings associated with the political dynasty. A trolley connects the buildings, which are open for guided tours daily from 9am to 5pm in season (Patriots Day through Veterans Day). Admission is $3 for adults, free for children under 16. The grounds and the visitor center, 1250 Hancock St. (© **617/770-1175;** www.nps.gov/adam), are open in the winter Tuesday through Friday 10am to 4pm. The center is across the street from the Quincy Adams stop on the Red Line; call or surf ahead for driving directions.

Plymouth

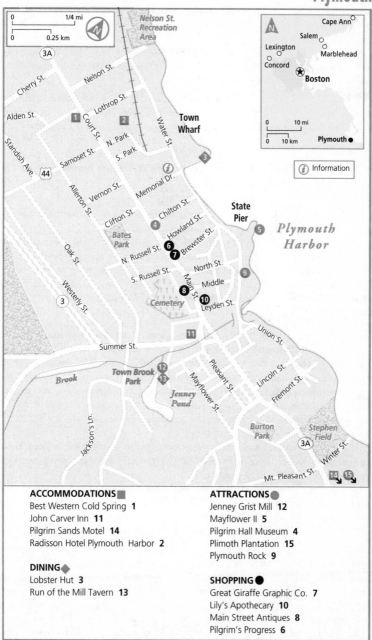

0 1/4 mi
0 0.25 km

3A

Cherry St.
Nelson St.
Lothrop St.
Alden St.
Court St.
N. Park
S. Park
Samoset St.
Standish Ave.
44
Allerton St.
Vernon St.
Clifton St.
Memorial Dr.
Chilton St.
Howland St.
Oak St.
Bates Park
N. Russell St.
Brewster St.
Westerly St.
3
S. Russell St.
Main St.
Middle
North St.
Cemetery
Leyden St.
Summer St.
Union St.
Town Brook Park
Brook
Jenney Pond
Jackson's Ln.
Mayflower St.
Pleasant St.
Lincoln St.
Fremont St.
Burton Park
3A
Stephen Field
Winter St.
Mt. Pleasant St.

Nelson St. Recreation Area

Water St.

Town Wharf

State Pier

Plymouth Harbor

Cape Ann
Salem
Lexington
Marblehead
Concord
★ **Boston**
0 10 mi
0 10 km
Plymouth ●

(i) Information

ACCOMMODATIONS ■
Best Western Cold Spring **1**
John Carver Inn **11**
Pilgrim Sands Motel **14**
Radisson Hotel Plymouth Harbor **2**

DINING ◆
Lobster Hut **3**
Run of the Mill Tavern **13**

ATTRACTIONS ●
Jenney Grist Mill **12**
Mayflower II **5**
Pilgrim Hall Museum **4**
Plimoth Plantation **15**
Plymouth Rock **9**

SHOPPING ●
Great Giraffe Graphic Co. **7**
Lily's Apothecary **10**
Main Street Antiques **8**
Pilgrim's Progress **6**

The round-trip fare is $12. The **Plymouth Area Link** bus (✆ **508/746-0378;** www.gatra.org/pal.htm) runs between the train station and downtown. The fare is $1, free for children under 7.

Plymouth and Brockton **buses** (✆ **508/746-4795** or 508/746-0378; www.p-b.com) take about an hour from South Station. They run more often and cost more than the train: $11 one-way, $20 round-trip.

VISITOR INFORMATION If you haven't visited the Regional Information Complex (p. 288), pick up a map at the **visitor center** (✆ **508/747-7525**), open seasonally at 130 Water St., across from the town pier. To plan ahead, contact **Destination Plymouth** (Plymouth Visitor Information), 170 Water St., Suite 10C, Plymouth, MA 02360 (✆ **800/USA-1620** or 508/747-7533; www.visit-plymouth.com), and request information. The **Plymouth County Convention & Visitors Bureau,** 32 Court St., Plymouth, MA 02360 (✆ **800/231-1620** or 508/747-0100; www.seeplymouth.com), publishes a vacation guide and several other brochures.

GETTING AROUND The downtown attractions are easily accessible on foot. A shallow hill slopes from the center of town to the waterfront.

Plymouth Rock Trolley (✆ **800/698-5636** or 508/747-4161; www.plymouthrocktrolley.com) offers a 40-minute narrated tour with unlimited reboarding, daily from Memorial Day to October and weekends through Thanksgiving. It serves marked stops downtown every 20 minutes and stops at Plimoth Plantation once an hour in the summer. Tickets are $15 for adults, $12 for children 3 to 12.

SEEING THE SIGHTS

The logical place to begin (good luck talking children out of it) is where the Pilgrims first set foot—at **Plymouth Rock** ★★. The rock, accepted as the landing place of the *Mayflower* passengers, was originally 15 feet long and 3 feet wide. It was moved on the eve of the Revolution and several times thereafter. In 1867, it assumed its present permanent position at tide level. The Colonial Dames of America commissioned the portico around the rock, designed by McKim, Mead & White and erected in 1920. The rock itself isn't much to look at, but the accompanying descriptions are interesting, and the atmosphere is curiously inspiring.

To get away from the bustle of the waterfront, head to Jenney Pond, in Town Brook Park, across Summer Street from the John Carver Inn. Ducks and geese live in the pond, and there's room to run around.

In 2005, the beloved **Plymouth National Wax Museum** closed. Plenty of other places in town can help you get your Pilgrim fix, but it's still a great loss. Check with Destination Plymouth (above) when you arrive to see whether the engaging exhibits, which illustrate scenes from the lives of the early settlers, are on display elsewhere.

GUIDED TOURS To walk in the Pilgrims' footsteps, take a **Colonial Lantern Tour** ★ (✆ **800/698-5636** or 508/747-4161; www.lanterntours.com). Participants carry pierced-tin lanterns on a 90-minute walking tour of the original settlement, conducted by a knowledgeable guide. It might seem a bit hokey at first, but it's fascinating. Tours run nightly from April to Thanksgiving. The standard history tour begins at 7:30pm; the "Ghostly Haunts & Legends" tour starts at 9pm. Tickets are $15 for adults, $12 for children 5 to 12, and free for children under 5; check the meeting place when you call for reservations. The company also offers special tours for Halloween and Thanksgiving.

Narrated cruises run from April or May to November. Call ahead for reservations. **Capt. John Boats,** 10 Town Wharf (© **800/242-2469** or 508/746-2643; www.capt john.com), offers several tours. The most eye-catching option is the *Pilgrim Belle* paddle wheeler. Its 75-minute narrated tours of the harbor ($12 adults, $10 seniors, $8 children under 12) leave from State Pier. **Whale watches** ($30 adults, $25 seniors, $18 children under 12) run from April through October. Dining and entertainment cruises and seasonal service to Provincetown are also available. **Lobster Tales** (© **508/746-5342;** www.lobstertalesinc.com) offers 1-hour cruises around Plymouth Harbor that leave from Town Wharf. The guide provides commentary as visitors observe the lobstering process, which includes hauling up traps and handling the feisty crustaceans (with rubber bands on their powerful claws). Tickets cost $13 for adults, $12 for seniors, $10 for children under 12.

Mayflower II ★ *Kids*   Berthed a few steps from Plymouth Rock, the *Mayflower II* is a full-scale reproduction of the type of ship that brought the Pilgrims from England to America in 1620. Even though it's full-scale, the 106½-foot vessel, constructed in England from 1955 to 1957, is remarkably small. Although little technical information about the original *Mayflower* survives, William A. Baker, designer of the *Mayflower II,* incorporated the few references in Governor Bradford's account of the voyage with other research to re-create the ship as authentically as possible.

Costumed guides provide interesting first-person narratives about the vessel and voyage, and other interpreters provide a contemporary perspective. Displays describe and illustrate the journey and the Pilgrims' experience, and include exhibits about 17th-century navigation techniques, stocking the ship with food and other provisions, and the history of the *Mayflower II.* Plimoth Plantation (below) owns and maintains the vessel. Alongside the ship are museum shops that replicate early Pilgrim dwellings.

State Pier. © **508/746-1622.** www.plimoth.org. Admission $8 adults, $7 seniors, $6 children 6–12. Plimoth Plantation (good for 2 consecutive days) and *Mayflower II* admission $24 adults, $21 seniors and students, $14 children 6–12, $72 families. Free for children under 6. Apr–Nov daily 9am–5pm. Closed Dec–Mar.

Pilgrim Hall Museum ★ *Kids*   This is a great place to get a sense of the day-to-day lives of Plymouth's first European residents. Many original possessions of the early Pilgrims and their descendants are on display, including one of Myles Standish's swords, Governor Bradford's Bible, and an uncomfortable chair (you can sit in a replica) that belonged to William Brewster. Regularly changing exhibits explore aspects of the settlers' lives, such as home construction or the history of prominent families. Among the permanent exhibits is the skeleton of the *Sparrow-Hawk,* a ship wrecked on Cape Cod in 1626 that lay buried in the sand until 1863. (It's even smaller than the *Mayflower II.*) Through April 2006 you can see the temporary exhibit **On the Waterfront: Plymouth's Maritime History.** Built in 1824, the Pilgrim Hall Museum is the oldest public museum in the United States.

75 Court St. © **508/746-1620.** www.pilgrimhall.org. Admission $6 adults, $5 seniors and AAA members, $3 children 5–17, $16 families. Feb–Dec daily 9:30am–4:30pm. Closed Jan, Dec 25. From Plymouth Rock, walk north on Water St. and up the hill on Chilton St.

Plimoth Plantation ★★ *Kids*   Allow at least half a day to explore this re-creation of the 1627 Pilgrim village, which children and adults find equally interesting. Enter by the hilltop fort that protected the village and walk down the hill to the farm area, visiting homes and gardens constructed with careful attention to historic detail. Once you get over the feeling that the whole operation is a bit strange (we heard someone mention Pompeii), talking to the "Pilgrims" is great fun. They're actors who, in speech, dress, and manner, assume the personalities of members of the original community. You can watch them framing a house, splitting wood, shearing sheep, preserving foodstuffs, or cooking a pot of fish stew over an open hearth, all as it was done in the 1600s and using only the tools and cookware available then. Sometimes you can join the activities—perhaps planting, harvesting, witnessing a trial, or visiting a wedding party. Wear comfortable shoes because you'll be walking a lot.

The plantation is as accurate as research can make it. The planners combined accounts of the original colony with archaeological research, old records, and the history written by the Pilgrims' leader, William Bradford (who often used the spelling "Plimoth"). There are daily militia drills with matchlock muskets that are fired to demonstrate the community's defense system. In fact, little defense was needed because the Native Americans were friendly. Local tribes included the Wampanoags, who are represented near the village at **Hobbamock's Homesite** (included in plantation admission), where staff members show off native foodstuffs, agricultural practices, and crafts.

At the main entrance are two modern buildings that house an interesting orientation show, exhibits, a gift shop, a bookstore, and a cafeteria. There's also a picnic area. Call or surf ahead for information about the numerous special events, lectures, tours, workshops, theme dinners, and children's and family programs offered throughout the season.

137 Warren Ave. (Rte. 3). ✆ 508/746-1622. www.plimoth.org. Admission (good for 2 consecutive days) $21 adults, $18 seniors, $12 children 6–12. Plimoth Plantation and *Mayflower II* admission $24 adults, $21 seniors and students, $14 children 6–12, $72 families. Free for children under 6. Apr–Nov daily 9am–5pm. Closed Dec–Mar. From Rte. 3, take Exit 4, Plimoth Plantation Hwy.

SHOPPING

Water Street, along the harbor, boasts an inexhaustible supply of souvenir shops. A less kitschy destination, just up the hill, is Route 3A, known as Court, Main, and Warren Street as it runs through town. **Lily's Apothecary,** 6 Main St. extension, in the old post office (✆ **508/747-7546;** www.lilysapothecary.com), carries a big-city-style selection of skin- and hair-care products for women and men. **Main Street Antiques,** 46 Main St. (✆ **508/747-8887**), is home to dozens of dealers; **Pilgrim's Progress,** 13 Court St. (✆ **508/746-6033**), carries women's and men's clothing and accessories; and **Great Giraffe Graphic Co.,** 11 Court St. (✆ **508/830-1990**), is an entertaining card and gift shop.

WHERE TO STAY

On busy summer weekends, it's not unusual for every room in town to be taken. Make reservations well in advance. Whenever you travel, don't book a room without checking for special packages and offers. Just about every establishment in town participates in a **Destination Plymouth** (✆ **800/USA-1620;** www.visit-plymouth.com) program that piles on deals and discounts in an effort to turn day-trippers into overnight guests.

The **Radisson Hotel Plymouth Harbor,** 180 Water St. (✆ **800/333-3333** or 508/747-4900; www.radisson.com), is the only chain hotel downtown. The 175-unit hotel, on a hill across the street from the waterfront, offers all the usual chain amenities, including a swimming pool in the atrium lobby. Doubles in high season run $180 to $225.

Best Western Cold Spring ✪   This pleasant motel and its adjacent cottages surround nicely landscaped lawns. The fastidiously maintained property has a good-sized outdoor pool. Rooms are pleasantly decorated and big enough for a family to spread out in; if adults want some privacy, book a two-bedroom cottage. The location, a bit removed from the water but convenient to downtown and the historic sights, makes the Cold Spring a good deal. The two-story complex is 1 long block inland, set back from the street in a quiet, mostly residential part of town.

188 Court St. (Rte. 3A), Plymouth, MA 02360. ℂ **800/678-8667** or 508/746-2222. Fax 508/746-2744. www.bwcold spring.com. 58 units (some with shower only), 2 2-bedroom cottages. Apr–Nov $99–$159 double; $139–$199 suite; $109–$159 cottage. Extra person $10. Rollaway $10. Crib $5. Children under 12 stay free in parent's room. Rates include continental breakfast. Packages and AAA and off-season discounts available. AE, DC, DISC, MC, V. Closed Dec–Mar. **Amenities:** Outdoor pool. Rooms for travelers with disabilities are available. *In room:* A/C, TV, high-speed Internet access, coffeemaker, hair dryer, iron.

John Carver Inn *Kids*   A three-story colonial-style building with a landmark portico, this hotel offers comfortable, modern accommodations and plenty of amenities. The indoor "theme pool," a big hit with families, has a large water slide and a Pilgrim ship model. Business features, including meeting space, make this place the Radisson's main competition for corporate travelers. The good-size guest rooms are regularly renovated and decorated in colonial style. The best units are the lavishly appointed two-room suites, with two TVs and private Jacuzzis; "four-poster" rooms contain king beds and sleeper sofas. The inn is on the edge of the downtown business district, within walking distance of the main attractions.

25 Summer St., Plymouth, MA 02360. ℂ **800/274-1620** or 508/746-7100. Fax 508/746-8299. www.johncarver inn.com. 85 units. Early Apr to mid-June and mid-Oct to Nov $119–$199 double, $229–$259 suite; mid-June to mid-Oct $159–$229 double, $269–$289 suite; Dec to early Apr $99–$179 double, $209–$239 suite. Extra person $20. Rollaway $20. Cribs free. Children under 19 stay free in parent's room. Packages and senior and AAA discounts available. AE, DC, DISC, MC, V. **Amenities:** Restaurant (American/seafood); indoor pool; fitness center; Jacuzzi; concierge; business center; room service until 10pm; laundry service; dry cleaning. Rooms for travelers with disabilities are available. *In room:* A/C, TV w/pay movies, wireless Internet access, hair dryer, iron.

Pilgrim Sands Motel ✪✪ *Kids*   This attractive motel sits on its own beach 3 miles south of town, within walking distance of Plimoth Plantation. If you want to avoid the bustle of downtown and still be near the water, it's an excellent choice. The motel has an indoor and an outdoor pool if you don't care for ocean swimming, and the helpful staff is eager to offer sightseeing and dining advice. The good-size guest rooms are tastefully furnished and well maintained. Most have two double or queen beds, and they're divided into sections (separated by doors) for smokers and nonsmokers. If you can swing it, book a beachfront room—the view is worth the money, especially when the surf is rough.

150 Warren Ave. (Rte. 3A), Plymouth, MA 02360. ℂ **800/729-7263** or 508/747-0900. Fax 508/746-8066. www.pilgrim sands.com. 64 units. Summer $145–$185 double, spring and early fall $110–$145 double, Apr and late fall $90–$110 double, Dec–Mar $80–$95 double; $150–$290 suite year-round. Extra person $6–$8 (suite $10–$15). Up to 2 children under 7 stay free in parent's room. Minimum 2-night stay holiday weekends. Rates may be higher on holiday weekends. AE, DC, DISC, MC, V. **Amenities:** Coffee shop; indoor and outdoor pools; access to nearby health club ($10); Jacuzzi; private beach. Rooms for travelers with disabilities are available. *In room:* A/C, TV, dataport, fridge, hair dryer.

WHERE TO DINE

Plimoth Plantation (p. 291) has a cafeteria and a picnic area, and occasionally schedules theme dinners.

Lobster Hut ✪ SEAFOOD   The Lobster Hut is a busy self-service restaurant with a great view. It's popular with both locals and sightseers. Order and pick up at the counter and then head to an indoor table or out onto the large deck that overlooks the action on the bay. To start, try clam chowder or lobster bisque. The seafood rolls (hot dog buns with your choice of filling) are excellent. The many fried seafood options include clams, scallops, shrimp, and haddock. There are also boiled and steamed items, burgers, chicken tenders—and lobster, of course. Beer and wine are served, but only with meals.

25 Town Wharf. ℂ **508/746-2270**. Reservations not accepted. Lunch specials $7–$9; main courses $6–$15; sandwiches $3–$7; clams and lobster priced daily. MC, V. Summer daily 11am–9pm; winter daily 11am–7pm. Closed Jan.

Run of the Mill Tavern ★ AMERICAN   This friendly restaurant sits 3 blocks inland, across from Town Brook Park. You won't mind not having a water view—the food is tasty and reasonably priced, and the comfortable post-and-beam tavern is a popular hangout. The unconventional clam chowder, made with red potatoes, is fantastic. Other appetizers include nachos, potato skins, buffalo wings, and mushrooms. Entrees are well-prepared versions of familiar meat, chicken, and fish dishes, plus sandwiches, burgers, and fresh seafood specials (fried, broiled, or baked).

6 Spring Lane, Jenney Grist Mill Village, off Summer St. ℂ **508/830-1262**. Reservations not accepted. Main courses $6–$16; children's menu $4–$5. AE, DC, DISC, MC, V. Sun–Thurs 11:30am–10pm; Fri–Sat 11:30am–11pm. Bar closes at 1am.

Index

See also Accommodations and Restaurant indexes, below.

ROMMER'S® COMPLETE TRAVEL GUIDES

aska
aska Cruises & Ports of Call
merican Southwest
msterdam
rgentina & Chile
rizona
tlanta
ustralia
ustria
ahamas
arcelona
eijing
elgium, Holland & Luxembourg
ermuda
oston
razil
ritish Columbia & the Canadian
  Rockies
russels & Bruges
udapest & the Best of Hungary
algary
alifornia
anada
ancún, Cozumel & the Yucatán
ape Cod, Nantucket & Martha's
  Vineyard
aribbean
aribbean Ports of Call
arolinas & Georgia
hicago
hina
olorado
osta Rica
ruises & Ports of Call
uba
enmark
enver, Boulder & Colorado Springs
dinburgh & Glasgow
ngland
urope
urope by Rail
uropean Cruises & Ports of Call
orence, Tuscany & Umbria

Florida
France
Germany
Great Britain
Greece
Greek Islands
Halifax
Hawaii
Hong Kong
Honolulu, Waikiki & Oahu
India
Ireland
Italy
Jamaica
Japan
Kauai
Las Vegas
London
Los Angeles
Madrid
Maine Coast
Maryland & Delaware
Maui
Mexico
Montana & Wyoming
Montréal & Québec City
Munich & the Bavarian Alps
Nashville & Memphis
New England
Newfoundland & Labrador
New Mexico
New Orleans
New York City
New York State
New Zealand
Northern Italy
Norway
Nova Scotia, New Brunswick &
  Prince Edward Island
Oregon
Ottawa
Paris
Peru

Philadelphia & the Amish Country
Portugal
Prague & the Best of the Czech
  Republic
Provence & the Riviera
Puerto Rico
Rome
San Antonio & Austin
San Diego
San Francisco
Santa Fe, Taos & Albuquerque
Scandinavia
Scotland
Seattle
Seville, Granada & the Best of
  Andalusio
Shanghai
Sicily
Singapore & Malaysia
South Africa
South America
South Florida
South Pacific
Southeast Asia
Spain
Sweden
Switzerland
Texas
Thailand
Tokyo
Toronto
Turkey
USA
Utah
Vancouver & Victoria
Vermont, New Hampshire & Maine
Vienna & the Danube Valley
Virgin Islands
Virginia
Walt Disney World® & Orlando
Washington, D.C.
Washington State

ROMMER'S® DOLLAR-A-DAY GUIDES

ustralia from $50 a Day
alifornia from $70 a Day
ngland from $75 a Day
urope from $85 a Day
orida from $70 a Day
awaii from $80 a Day

Ireland from $80 a Day
Italy from $70 a Day
London from $90 a Day
New York City from $90 a Day
Paris from $90 a Day
San Francisco from $70 a Day

Washington, D.C. from $80 a Day
Portable London from $90 a Day
Portable New York City from $90
  a Day
Portable Paris from $90 a Day

ROMMER'S® PORTABLE GUIDES

capulco, Ixtapa & Zihuatanejo
msterdam
ruba
ustralia's Great Barrier Reef
ahamas
erlin
ig Island of Hawaii
oston
alifornia Wine Country
ancún
ayman Islands
harleston
hicago
isneyland®
ominican Republic

Dublin
Florence
Frankfurt
Hong Kong
Las Vegas
Las Vegas for Non-Gamblers
London
Los Angeles
Los Cabos & Baja
Maui
Miami
Nantucket & Martha's Vineyard
New Orleans
New York City
Paris

Phoenix & Scottsdale
Portland
Puerto Rico
Puerto Vallarta, Manzanillo &
  Guadalajara
Rio de Janeiro
San Diego
San Francisco
Savannah
Vancouver Island
Venice
Virgin Islands
Washington, D.C.
Whistler

FROMMER'S® NATIONAL PARK GUIDES

Algonquin Provincial Park
Banff & Jasper
Family Vacations in the National
  Parks

Grand Canyon
National Parks of the American West
Rocky Mountain

Yellowstone & Grand Teton
Yosemite & Sequoia/Kings Canyon
Zion & Bryce Canyon

FROMMER'S® MEMORABLE WALKS

Chicago
London

New York
Paris

San Francisco

FROMMER'S® WITH KIDS GUIDES

Chicago
Hawaii
Las Vegas
New York City

Ottawa
San Francisco
Toronto

Vancouver
Walt Disney World® & Orlando
Washington, D.C.

SUZY GERSHMAN'S BORN TO SHOP GUIDES

Born to Shop: France
Born to Shop: Hong Kong, Shanghai
  & Beijing

Born to Shop: Italy
Born to Shop: London

Born to Shop: New York
Born to Shop: Paris

FROMMER'S® IRREVERENT GUIDES

Amsterdam
Boston
Chicago
Las Vegas
London

Los Angeles
Manhattan
New Orleans
Paris
Rome

San Francisco
Seattle & Portland
Vancouver
Walt Disney World®
Washington, D.C.

FROMMER'S® BEST-LOVED DRIVING TOURS

Austria
Britain
California
France

Germany
Ireland
Italy
New England

Northern Italy
Scotland
Spain
Tuscany & Umbria

THE UNOFFICIAL GUIDES®

Beyond Disney
California with Kids
Central Italy
Chicago
Cruises
Disneyland®
England
Florida
Florida with Kids
Inside Disney

Hawaii
Las Vegas
London
Maui
Mexico's Best Beach Resorts
Mini Las Vegas
Mini Mickey
New Orleans
New York City
Paris

San Francisco
Skiing & Snowboarding in the West
South Florida including Miami &
  the Keys
Walt Disney World®
Walt Disney World® for
  Grown-ups
Walt Disney World® with Kids
Washington, D.C.

SPECIAL-INTEREST TITLES

Athens Past & Present
Cities Ranked & Rated
Frommer's Best Day Trips from London
Frommer's Best RV & Tent Campgrounds
  in the U.S.A.
Frommer's Caribbean Hideaways
Frommer's China: The 50 Most Memorable Trips
Frommer's Exploring America by RV
Frommer's Gay & Lesbian Europe

Frommer's NYC Free & Dirt Cheap
Frommer's Road Atlas Europe
Frommer's Road Atlas France
Frommer's Road Atlas Ireland
Frommer's Wonderful Weekends from
  New York City
Retirement Places Rated
Rome Past & Present

THE NEW TRAVELOCITY GUARANTEE

EVERYTHING YOU BOOK WILL BE RIGHT, OR WE'LL WORK WITH OUR TRAVEL PARTNERS TO MAKE IT RIGHT, RIGHT AWAY.

To drive home the point, we're going to use the word "right" in every single sentence.

Let's get right to it. Right to the meat! Only Travelocity guarantees everything about your booking will be right, or we'll work with our travel partners to make it right, right away. Right on!

Here's a picture taken smack dab right in the middle of Antigua, where the guarantee also covers you.

The guarantee covers all but one of the items pictured to the right.

For example, what if the ocean view you booked actually looks out at a downright ugly parking lot? You'd be right to call – we're there for you. And no one in their right mind would be pleased to learn the rental car place has closed and left them stranded. Call Travelocity and we'll help get you back on the right track.

Now, you may be thinking, "Yeah, right, I'm so sure." That's OK; you have the right to remain skeptical. That is until we mention help is always right around the corner. Call us right off the bat, knowing that our customer service reps are there for you 24/7. Righting wrongs. Left and right.

Now if you're guessing there are some things we can't control, like the weather, well you're right. But we can help you with most things – to get all the details in righting,* visit **travelocity.com/guarantee**.

*Sorry, spelling things right is one of the few things not covered under the guarantee.

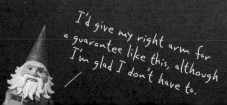

travelocity
You'll never roam alone.

IF YOU BOOK IT, IT SHOULD BE THERE.

Only Travelocity guarantees it will be, or we'll work
with our travel partners to make it right, right away.
So if you're missing a balcony or anything else you
booked, just call us 24/7 1-888-TRAVELOCITY

travelocity
You'll never roam alone

My, what an inefficient way to fish.

Ring toss, good. Horseshoes, bad.

Faster! Faster! Faster!

We take care of the fiddly bits, from providing over 43,000 customer reviews of hotels, to helping you find our best fares, to giving you 24/7 customer service. So you can focus on the only thing that matters. Goofing off.

travelocity
You'll never roam alone.™

NO NEED TO COUNT BEANS IN
BEAN TOWN

For our absolute lowest rates in Boston,
there's just one place to go.

Book Smart.℠

 Get our Lowest Rate online.
Or call **1.800.THRIFTY**® or your professional travel agent.